MULTICULTURAL EDUCATION: A SOURCEBOOK FOR TEACHERS

LOUIS COHEN
(Loughborough University of Technology)
and
ALAN COHEN
(University of Durham)

Harper & Row, Publishers
London

Cambridge
Mexico City
New York
Philadelphia

San Francisco
São Paulo
Singapore
Sydney

First published in 1986

Harper & Row Ltd
28 Tavistock Street
London WC2E 7PN

British Libraray Cataloguing in Publication Data
Multicultural education: a sourcebook for
    teachers.
    1. Minorities—Education—Great Britain
    I. Cohen, Louis   II. Cohen, Alan
    370.11'5   LC3736.G6

ISBN 0–06–318352–8

Typeset by Inforum Ltd, Portsmouth
Printed & bound in Great Britain by
Redwood Burn Limited, Trowbridge, Wiltshire.

CONTENTS

INTRODUCTION

This book is for teachers pursuing initial and inservice courses of multicultural education in universities, polytechnics and colleges of higher education in the late 1980s. Its aim is to provide an up-to-date set of readings, topics for discussion and suggestions for further research that are representative of the range of issues and emphases in current debates about multicultural education.

Multicultural education is not a unitary concept; it subsumes a variety of beliefs, policies and practices in educational provision in multiracial Britain. The choice of readings and the recommendations for further research in each section of the text are intended to reflect something of the present diversity in ideology and practice. Thus, in Section 1 'Policies and Perspectives', unequivocally anti-racist documents from the Inner London Education Authority have been included together with a spirited accusation by Robert Jeffcoate that the anti-racist stance is both obfuscatory and illiberal. In the same section, in the suggestions for study that accompany Reading 2, three contentious articles by Ray Honeyford in the right-wing journal, *The Salisbury Review* are suggested for further scrutiny and discussion.

In varying degrees throughout the six sections that constitute the *Sourcebook* one may glimpse changing perspectives that underpin thinking and practice in educational provision at both governmental and local level over the past 20 or so years. It is to a brief outline of these emphases and to discernible shifts in policies on race and on schooling that we now turn.

ASSIMILATION

Immigration to Britain has brought about fundamental changes in our society. We are now an ethnically-mixed and culturally-varied nation.

The viewpoint that dominated government policy during the early days of immigration in the late 1950s and early 1960s was that if newly-arrived immigrants could be supported during their initial period of disorientation following arrival in Britain and helped to acquire a working knowledge of the English language then they would quickly be absorbed by the host society and all would be well. In a word, *assimilation*. A major concern during the assimilation phase of educational response to immigration was to disperse pupils to different schools as a way of alleviating the impact of the language 'problem' and the 'culture shock' that the newcomers were generally believed to experience. A government paper at the time (DES Circular 7/65) discussed dispersal under the heading, *Spreading the Children*. Educational responses both nationally and locally led to an emphasis on the teaching of English as a second language, the setting up of reception centres and language centres, the institution of school-based language withdrawal groups, and to the common practice of dispersing ethnic minority children across schools. Swann (1985) points to a *problem-centred approach* to the education of ethnic minority pupils as being officially sanctioned and articulated in government policy during this period: '[. . .] the policy was a way of preventing the development of "all immigrant schools" which were *per se* undesirable [. . .] dispersal was an essential basis for cultural assimilation.'[1]

The assimilationist phase of response to the educational needs of immigrant pupils was designed to 'compensate' their linguistic difficulties and to disturb the education of the indigenous majority as little as possible.

INTEGRATION

Early in the 1960s a shift of educational emphasis could be discerned from wholly linguistic approaches such as that of the Schools Council *English For Immigrant Pupils* to a greater concern for concept formation and course content. As Bolton[2] observed, the homelands and cultures of immigrants began to feature more prominently in discussions about the choice of teaching materials and the suitability of teaching approaches. It is not difficult to see why. To teach English you have to teach *about* something, and the something that interested and engaged many teachers working with immigrant children was the culture and the lifestyles of these newcomers to British schools. The change in emphasis brought into common parlance the word, *integration*.

Basically, those who supported the idea of integration believed that factors other than initial cultural shock and the acquisition of spoken English ought to be taken into account in making educational provision for immigrant groups. They called for more detailed, planned programmes of educational and social support if immigrants were to be able to integrate with the majority society. But, as Bolton says, the emphasis was still on integrating minorities with the host society and culture in order to create a culturally homogeneous society. In principle, this meant that it was up to minority groups to adapt and change, few expectations being voiced that the host society itself should modify or alter its attitudes and practices. It was recognized, however, that if integration were to be effected, then the majority society would need to be more aware of the cultural and historical

[1] Institute of Race Relations (1969) *Colour and Citizenship – A Report on British Race Relations*, quoted in Swann (1985, p. 194)

[2] Bolton, E. (1979) Education in a multiracial society, *Trends in Education*, Vol. 4, pp 3–7

factors associated with various immigrant groups. Implicit here was the view that such knowledge would assist the host society in making allowances for differences in lifestyle, religion and culture that might hinder the integration of some immigrant groups into British society. The educational response to the integrationist view, Bolton observes, was a shift of emphasis from teaching English language to informing teachers about life in the Punjab, life in the Caribbean, and to introducing them to the basic tenets of Islam, Sikhism and Hinduism. 'Life-in-other-lands' type courses for teachers mushroomed, some teachers even going to visit India or the Caribbean on six-week tours.

The emphasis, as Swann (1985) notes, was almost exclusively upon ethnic minority pupils as immigrants from other countries rather than as an integral part of British society, despite the fact that by this time there were increasing numbers of British-born second-generation children. Many of the inaccurate and damaging stereotypes that persist today were created during this phase of educational response to the presence of ethnic minorities in our schools.

CULTURAL PLURALISM

The emergence of a second generation of ethnic minority pupils during the late 1960s and early 1970s, together with the realization that neither assimilation nor integration has worked, has led to a growing appreciation that these two forms of response are both patronizing and dismissive of other cultures and lifestyles. Not just in Britain, but all over the world, minority groups now actively assert their determination to maintain cultural continuity and to preserve their religious, linguistic and cultural differences. *Cultural pluralism* implies a system that accepts that people's lifestyles and values are different and operates so as to allow equality of opportunity for all to play a full part in society. What does this mean in terms of changes in policies and teaching practices that are actually required to make cultural pluralism a reality?

Bolton suggests that in educational terms, cultural pluralism involves broadening the content of the curriculum and teaching about race and race relations to all pupils, as well as catering for the educational needs of minority groups. Above all else, cultural pluralism involves changes on the part of the majority society in its attitudes and practices towards minority groups. Bolton's words are echoed in the concept of pluralism enunciated in the opening chapter of the Swann Report (1985):

> We consider that a multiracial society such as ours would in fact function most effectively and harmoniously on the basis of pluralism, which enables, expects and encourages members of all ethnic groups, both minority and majority, to participate fully in shaping the society as a whole within a

framework of commonly-accepted values, practices and procedures, whilst also allowing, and where necessary, assisting the ethnic minority communities in maintaining their distinct ethnic identities within this common framework.

The concept of cultural pluralism represents a decisive departure from assimilationist and integrationist viewpoints with their common focus on the perceived *problems* of ethnic minority children and their proposed *remedies* by way of *compensating* for those pupils' *disabilities*. Nevertheless cultural pluralism has come in for strong and sustained criticism.

ANTI-RACIST EDUCATION

One major objection to the cultural pluralist perspective is its almost exclusive emphasis on *'culture'*, a vague, ill-defined concept that is open to many interpretations. Preoccupation with culture, it is said, tends to obscure or to avoid the more fundamental issues to do with *race, power* and *prejudice*. That is to say, it fails to address questions [3] in connection with:

1   the economic position of black people in relation to white people;
2   differences in access to resources and in power to affect events;
3   discrimination in employment, housing and education;
4   relations with the police.

A second criticism of the cultural pluralist position is that it fails to confront what is regarded as the cardinal influence on the life situations of ethnic minority groups in Britain, that is, *racism*. In this respect, *racism* is not simply prejudiced attitudes held by unenlightened white people; more fundamentally, it refers to the structural aspects of racism as manifested both in the education system and in society at large.

The cultural pluralist response is at best regarded as tokenist, at worst as little better than a form of subtle racism, an observation expressed vehemently in the following extract:[4]

As interpreted and practised by many, multi-racial education has appeared to become an instrument of control and stability rather than one of change, of the subordination rather than the freedom of blacks in schools and or society as a whole. In the context of schools and against a wider societal background of institutionalized racism, multi-racial education programmes, from the assimi-

[3] Inner London Education Authority (1983) *Race, Sex and Class 3. A Policy For Equality: Race*, I.L.E.A, London

[4] Mullard, C. (1982) Multiracial education in Britain: From assimilation to cultural pluralism, in J. Tierney (ed.) *Race, Migration and Schooling*, Holt Education, Eastbourne

lationist's view on English teaching to the intergrationist's stance on multi-cultural and black studies, have in fact integrally contributed to the increased alienation of black youth. To be told, however politely and cleverly, that your culture and history count for nothing is to invoke responses ranging from low self esteem and lack of confidence [. . .] to political opposition and resistance. To be told that your culture and history count for something only within the pedagogic boundaries of the school curriculum and not outside the school gates in the white dominated world of work and politics is to foster the response of a 'blacks only for the black studies class'. To be goaded to integrate politically and then in practice take up your place at the bottom of society with as much of your culture intact as is permitted is, to extend Gus John's conclusion, a madness that not even a mad and subordinated black can any longer contemplate. Simply, what multiracial education, as viewed in British schools, is teaching black pupils is that they will always remain second-class citizens; and, ironically, that in order to survive or exist as blacks it is necessary to resist racist authority within and outside school.

The debate on multicultural education has shifted considerably during the last few years and is now beginning to reflect greater concern for the role that education can play in countering the pernicious effects of racism both within schools and in society at large. And yet, as the Swann Report (1985) observes: 'This concern with racism is not yet however regarded by the majority of teachers as a valid part of multicultural education as they perceive it [. . .]'. As editors (and indeed, teacher-educators) we are mindful of the complexities and the difficulties of the many social and educational issues that confront teachers in the course of their daily duties. Most face challenges that they were not prepared for either in their initial teacher education courses or in their own experiences of life. They live and work in a multiracial society. The intention of this text is to help them in their responsible task of preparing all children for life in multiracial Britain.

SECTION 1

POLICIES AND PERSPECTIVES

INTRODUCTION

This part of the *Sourcebook* consists of four readings, the first of which is a succinct yet comprehensive digest of the Swann Report, *Education For All*. In the absence of the expensive, 807-page Report, the digest is a better document for use with teacher groups than the inadequate summary sent to all schools following the publication of the Report in 1985. The suggestions for further study that accompany Reading 1 take up three important topics indirectly raised by the Swann Report: local authority policies in respect of anti-racist education (Troyna and Ball, 1985); the curriculum implications of differential educational provision for ethnic minority pupils (Partington, 1985); and the charge that teacher expectations are largely responsible for West Indian underachievement (Short, 1985).

We include I.L.E.A. documents 3 and 4, '*A Policy for Equality: Race*, and *Anti-Racist Statement and Guidelines* (Reading 2) as controversial statements of anti-racist education that merit discussion by teachers throughout the country, not least because of their implications for teacher autonomy and professional practice. In the suggestions for further study, one paper (Dorn and Troyna, 1982) speculates on the reasons for the lack of a coherent national policy on multiracial education; another, (Craft, 1984) presents the findings of a Policy Studies Institute Report on the differential levels of response of a number of L.E.As to the needs of substantial ethnic minority groups within their localities. The third suggestion for further study comprises three highly contentious articles written for the right-wing journal *The Salisbury Review* by the ex-Bradford middle-school headteacher, Mr Ray Honeyford.

In Reading 3, Jeffcoate traces the emergence of anti-racism as an educational ideology in the 1970s, and discusses the meaning of racism in the context of education. The paper is strongly critical of the I.L.E.A. *Policy for Equality* statement (Reading 2) and of the threat that such anti-racist initiatives have for the autonomy of teachers and pupils. Two booklets (*Roots of Racism; Patterns of Racism, 1982*) that, according to Jeffcoate, offer a very biased view of history are suggested for further study alongside Reading 3.

In the final Reading in the Section, 'Policies and Perspectives', Willey argues that although there has been a radical shift in theoretical objectives in multicultural education from *assimilation* to *pluralism* this has not been accompanied by concomitant changes in policy. There is, he contends, a widening gap between policy and practice. Mullard's (1982) paper in the suggestions for further study echoes Willey's concern, while Jeffcoate's (1984) discusses the principle of *positive discrimination* as a means of redistributing resources. The third suggestion for further study (Stone, 1981) is a powerful critique of multicultural approaches. Stone insists that much of what occurs in schools in the name of multiculturalism is largely irrelevant to the needs of black children.

Reading 1
THE SWANN REPORT: DIGEST OF THE REPORT OF THE SWANN COMMITTEE ON 'EDUCATION FOR ALL'

BACKGROUND

The Swann Report (likely to be so named after Lord Swann F.R.S., the Chairman of the Committee that has produced it) has as its full title *Education for All* (Cmnd 9453 HMSO). The Committee was established in March 1979 and, to meet the requirements of a specific request in its terms of reference, published an interim report (the Rampton Report) *West Indian Children in Our Schools*, in June 1981.[*]

The Committee's task was not made easier by the direction its work was given by this requirement for an interim report. The emphasis on pupils of West Indian origin was the direct consequence of the House of Commons' Select Committee's report, in 1977, *The West Indian Community*. This had drawn attention to what was seen as the poor average school performance of children from that community.

The effect of that original perspective was that many within the West Indian community itself were less than enthusiastic about the interim report. Its title summarized their concerns. *West Indian Children in Our Schools?* it was asked; are the schools not ours also? Despite its declarations to the contrary and the trouble taken with the balance of what was said, the structure of the interim report seemed to locate the educational problems within the black community itself. Either they *were* the problem or *had* the problem.

The final report seeks to redress that initial imbalance. The report deals with the way the education system, individual schools and individual teachers, should respond to a multiracial society. There are specific problems to be dealt with

[1] In *Education*, 15 March 1985

certainly, but the main thrust of the report, reflected in its title, is that any such problems should be seen in the context of a changed society to which all should now adapt themselves.

The Committee has tried to place the emphasis correctly. In so doing, if the number of resignations from its membership is any guide, it has not managed to carry all interests with it. Nevertheless, the result is the first comprehensive account of how the school system is or is not adapting itself to the presence of the, increasingly British-born, children of ethnic minority origin. If, as appears still to be the case, there remain L.E.A.s, who have not thought their way through the implications of the demographic changes that have occurred over the past 20 years, *Education for All* will prove an indispensable starting point.

The report needs to be read as a whole. Taken by themselves, its recommendations do not adequately convey its message. That is because the report, as well as recommending what to do, suggests ways of *thinking* also: it seeks to establish the role of education in a multiracial society and, in so doing, has to consider the true nature of such a society.

The report itself is in four main parts. It also incorporates a series of useful research papers which deserve specialist examination within L.E.A.s. The date of publication of the report is 14 March 1985.

ASSIMILATION AND SEPARATISM

Part 1 of the report, 'Setting the scene', deals with three main topics. The first concerns 'The nature of society'. The notion of assimilation is rejected. There is no question, even if it were thought desirable, of the ethnic minority citizens of the UK becoming indistinguishable from the majority. In varying degrees and in different respects, minorities will remain distinct.

The notion of separatism is also rejected. A society based on separatist notions is seen to be a contradiction in terms; the essence of society, as a cohesive entity, being a degree of shared experience and commitment to values, such as a belief in justice and the right of dissent itself that are held in common.

The report's view of multiracial society is that it should be pluralistic. Such a society places obligations on all its members to minorities and majorities alike. The aim of such a society is to enable all its members to join in shaping that society 'within a framework of commonly accepted values, practices and procedures'. Within that framework, ethnic minority communities would certainly be allowed, and at times assisted, to maintain their own distinctive characteristics.

The report believes failure to adopt its concept of a plural society, itself a development of the thinking which lay behind the Race Relations Act of 1976, would have serious consequences. Neither assimilation nor separatism will work but attempts at either can prove disruptive: 'unless major efforts are made to reconcile the concerns and aspirations of both the majority and minority communities along more genuinely pluralist lines, there is a genuine risk of the fragmentation of our society along ethnic lines which would seriously threaten the stability and cohension of society as a whole'. In other words, unless proper account is taken of difference, difference may prevail.

RACISM

The second topic dealt with is 'Racism: theory and practice'. Like 'democracy' and 'education', 'racism' is a difficult concept to pin down. The term can sometimes be used to describe the result of an historical process in which white people have dominated black people, at others it can be used to denote forms of racial discrimination at work in the institutions of society, at others it directs attention to prejudices against or beliefs about members, particularly black members, of ethnic minorities.

The report itself adopts a concept of racism which does not differ substantially from the one set out in its interim report. Briefly, the two components of racism are seen to be:

(1)   prejudiced attitudes by one group towards others. Such prejudices may include well-intentioned or 'humorous' stereotyping. Plainly, as education is concerned with the *affective* as well as the cognitive, this aspect of racism is very much a matter for the schools:

(2)   indirect or institutional racism. This includes the 'systems, practices and procedures', both within education and the wider society, which were originally designed for a form of society which has now changed and now have an unjustifiably adverse effect on a disproportionate number of the ethnic minority community.

The degree to which the education system can itself tackle institutional discrimination raises difficult issues. Plainly, the school, as an institution, can deal with itself. Its procedures, allocation policies, suspension record (hardly referred to in the report), staffing and promotion patterns can all be re-examined, so far as possible to remove discriminatory elements.

But as much of the institutional or indirect discrimination that affects pupils in school, such as the employment prospects of their parents, occurs outside school, there are limits to what schools can do directly to remedy matters. The point that comes through clearly, however, is that the nature and effects of racial discrimination should be considered carefully by everyone with responsibilities in the education service.

LEVEL OF ACHIEVEMENT

The third topic dealt with in Part 1 is 'Achievement and underachievement'. This goes over old ground in relation to fact and breaks new ground in relation to its interpretation. On the facts, the essential points are that the stereotype of the success of Asian pupils in the school system needs adjustment. Some elements of the Asian community, notably the children of Bangladeshi origin, are not doing at all well. Statistics of too general a nature can mislead in this respect.

Again, the latest figures confirm that, adjusted so far as the information available allows for social and economic factors associated with performance in school, children of West Indian origin are, on average, still not achieving as well as might be expected. But they are doing better than they were.

At GCE 'A' level, to take a particularly favourable example, the percentage of West Indian pupils obtaining at least one 'A' level pass has increased from 2 per cent in 1978–79 to 5 per cent in 1981–82. In this, the report sees 'scant grounds for complacency'. Even so, the implications for access to higher education and the measure of improvement that could be achieved over the next 10 years should not be missed.

On ways of interpreting performance, four important points are made. The first concerns the I.Q. argument. Briefly, the explanation put forward for differential average performance is that some ethnic groups are innately (always admitting exceptions and considerable overlaps) less intelligent than others. This, it is asserted, is confirmed by the results of I.Q. tests and performance in the school system itself. The effective rebuttal of this argument by Professor Mackintosh and Dr Massie-Taylor is set out in full in the report and is a valuable contribution to the literature.

The second point made on 'underachievement' is the need for improved statistics to reveal what is happening. Evidently, a number of individual schools know, by methods of their own devising, to what extent, so far as their performance in school is the test, they are meeting the needs of their pupils. Other schools do not know this. Nor are the facts known nationally. In an area of policy where accurate diagnosis of what is going right is as important as post-mortems on what has gone wrong, to permit ignorance of this order is verging on the irresponsible.

The third point concerns the effect on performance of racism. This is a difficult area. There is little evidence that poor performance in school is a direct result of being at the receiving end of prejudiced attitudes. There are too many examples of groups who have triumphed, educationally at least, over such attitudes for that to carry conviction. On the other hand, when racism can affect (in relation to employment, housing and other socioeconomic factors) the quality of life within which a child is brought up there is, if not a directly causal link, at least a correlation between such conditions and school performance to serve as an explanation of that performance.

The fact is, as the report notes, that little research has been done on the 'added dimension' issue. When full account has been taken of the measurable socio-economic factors, given that the answer is not simply I.Q., what is the nature of the 'added dimension which causes some minority groups systematically to underachieve in relation to others?

The final point made about 'underachievement' is contained in extracts from Professor Parekh's chapter in *Ethnic Pluralism and Public Policy* (Heinemann, 1983). He there disposes of the fallacy that there could be one single factor, 'be it class, racism, the West Indian family [. . .]' to explain the complex phenomenon of underachievement.

The annexes to the first part of the report are wide-ranging in scope. In this last section, for example, the annexes deal with five topics: the I.Q. question, the results of the school leavers survey 1981–82, a research paper into academically successful black pupils, a summary of a longitudinal study by Dr Verma and an analysis of the performance of Bangladeshi pupils in Tower Hamlets.

MULTICULTURAL ISSUES

Part II of the report, *Education for All*, deals with three related issues. The first, 'multicultural education – a historical perspective', describes the way the educational debate has been conducted over the years. The inadequacies of the still widely supported notion of 'assimilation' with the associated belief that the solution to any 'problems' that arise are to be reached by remedying defects within the minority communities themselves, are set out.

The general perspective that links the position of minority groups directly with the disadvantage of the inner cities is questioned. So too is the stance of government itself. Despite criticisms from the Select Committee and others, both the institutional structures within the D.E.S. and the thinking behind them are seen to be inadequate:

> All in all, central government appears to have lacked a coherent strategy for fostering the development of multi-cultural education and thus to have been unable to play a leading role in co-ordinating or encouraging progress in this field.

The position of L.E.A.s is not dissimilar. Only a minority are found to have clear strategies and to have devised means for ensuring these are carried out.

The first essential point to be accepted is that, in Lady Young's words (1980) [...]

it is just as important in schools where there are no ethnic minority pupils for the teaching there to refer to the different cultures now present in Britain, as it is for the teaching in the inner areas of cities like Birmingham and London.

The second essential point is that exhortation, by government and L.E.A. leaders, is not enough. Effort and resources are required to effect the necessary shifts in educational emphasis.

The second issue is 'Further research studies'. The revealing point made is how little is actually known about what is happening by way of multicultural education. In part this is due to uncertainties of definition. Of more concern, perhaps, is that such research as there has been in areas where there are few pupils from ethnic minorities in the schools indicates that very little is happening. The implication of this is that the casual stereotyping of 'immigrants' and other components of racially discriminatory attitudes is continuing unchecked.

In schools visited in one survey 'almost without exception' they saw 'the concept of multicultural education as remote or irrelevant to their own needs and responsibilities'. In other words, the view is still widely held that multicultural education is essentially to do with pupils from minority communities. As the report makes clear, in fact it describes the response of all schools to the plural society in which all pupils will be living.

The implications of the research studies are serious. They are that, in the mid-1980s, little real progress has been made in adapting our school system appropriately. Of the newly qualified teachers encountered in one survey it was said 'the whole gamut of racial misunderstandings and folk mythology was revealed, racial stereotypes were common [...].

The third issue 'Education for All: a New Approach' deals with the elements necessary to bring about change. The distinction is made between the related issues of broadening the education of *all* pupils to reflect the multiracial nature of British society and meeting the needs of ethnic minority pupils. The latter are considered [in Part 4 below]. In relation to the former, there needs to be an active challenge to discriminatory attitudes, racism in any form.

'Tokenism' is one such form, so too is separate provision of education, in separate schools or classes. The curriculum itself, from the materials used to the 'hidden' curriculum needs attention. As the then Schools Council said in evidence 'the school must be *seen* to be welcoming to other cultures and not confine itself to teaching about them in the classroom while reflecting their manifest expression'.

L.E.A.s have a major responsibility here. Coherent overall strategies are needed rather than short-term responses to particular 'problems'. H.M.I., are in a position to help the work of multicultural advisers in their inspection programmes. So too are a range of other organizations, from the School Curriculum Developmental Committee to the Examination Boards themselves. In this work they will be assisted by ethnically based statistics, without which it will remain uncertain whether policy objectives are being achieved.

TEACHING ENGLISH AND 'MOTHER TONGUES'

Part 3 of the report, 'Major Areas of Concern', deals with four important issues in three separate chapters. The first, 'Language and Language Education' begins by tackling the problem of 'linguistic prejudice'. It is a fact that a good command of English is important to anyone seeking access to employment and other opportunities in this country.

From this it does not follow that, either for English or for other European languages customarily taught in schools in the UK, claims for some absolute superiority are justified. Full acceptance of living languages, from whatever source, on equal terms should be the aim. For children for whom English is not a first language, teaching it as though it were a foreign language is inappropriate.

Teaching English as a second language (E.S.L.) to British-born children who will be continuing to live here requires a different approach. In considering what is appropriate methodologically, the Committee argue against separate language centres. They regard these as an element in an assimilationist policy (English learned so that the pupil can take his or her place in an unchanged school) and, though not initially discriminatory in *intent*, increasingly discriminatory in *effect*.

Withdrawal systems within school have similar, though less pronounced consequences. Both systems, separate language centres and withdrawal classes in school, have led to low status for E.S.L. as a subject and some lack of regard for those who teach it and those they teach. This and other disadvantages lead to the strongly urged view that language learning should take the form of 'integrated provision within the mainstream school'.

As such, to a degree, the learning of English would become, as the Bullock Report (1975) proposed, the genuine concern of all teachers. That in turn might enhance the prospect of improved second stage learning of English, during which a range of skills required in more advanced work have to be acquired. Acquiring those skills through the subject-matter on which they are to be used is the approach commended. 'We see no reason why mainstream teachers should not be expected to appreciate and indeed cater for second-stage language needs.'

Inevitably, some additional help and training for teachers will be necessary and this itself ought properly to be schoolbased.

More controversial than the teaching of English is the question of 'mother-tongues' or, perhaps more accurately, community languages. The distinction is made between bilingual education (using the mother-tongue as a medium of instruction), mother-tongue maintenance (developing a pupil's fluency in his or her own language) and mother-tongue teaching (teaching community languages as part of a modern language curriculum).

Broadly speaking, the arguments for bilingual teaching are not seen to outweigh the disadvantages; though, particularly in the primary school classroom, a 'bilingual resource' is thought to be a useful support for pupils whose first language is not English. Similarly, mother-tongue maintenance, though important, is not seen to require mainstream schools to take over the role of the different communities themselves in maintaining their traditions and the language through which they are expressed.

On the other hand, mother-tongue teaching, as part of a modern curriculum, is seen to be worth developing further. So too are the wider notions of language across the curriculum developed in depth in the Bullock Report.

RELIGIOUS EDUCATION

The second area of concern is the scope and position in the curriculum of religious education. Here a 'phenomenological' or undogmatic approach is commended. This aims at promoting understanding rather than a particular religious viewpoint. It goes beyond merely providing information about religion but stops short of the 'religious instruction' concept embodied in the 1944 Act.

The report makes it clear that there is no wish to 'reduce' Christianity to one element in a 'Cook's tour' of world religions. The aim is to 'set the consideration of Christianity, in all its spiritual depth and fullness, within a wider context of the true significance of the religious dimension to life.'

The implications for the 'daily collective act of worship' are that this should cease to be a statutory requirement. The present requirement is widely ignored. On 'religious instruction', provided this is taken to mean 'religious education' in the undogmatic form commended, the right to withdraw pupils should go. If direct inculcation of Christianity is to remain, so too should the parents' right to withdraw pupils from it.

The third area of concern is the argument for separate schools for separate communities. This is not thought to be a helpful development. There are seen to be few positive advantages either educationally or socially. The main motive for the establishment of such schools is disappointment with the performance of, or children's performance in, mainstream schools. The proper way forward is therefore to adapt mainstream systems to avoid the parental attitudes which lead to the establishment of separate schools.

The single-sex issue is particularly important here and L.E.As should recognize the combination of religious and social beliefs and values which make them of particular importance to the Muslim community.

TEACHING TEACHERS

The fourth area of concern relates to 'teacher education and the employment of ethnic minority teachers'. Here the emphasis is on ensuring that all initial training courses are based on the pluralist approach to education the report commends. The organizations which, by accreditation and in other ways, control the content of such courses are specifically asked to ensure that this pluralist approach is adopted in practice. Some institutions might, in this respect, become centres of excellence but none should opt out.

On the employment of ethnic minority teachers, the first step is to know how they are at present distributed. Such teachers are known to be under-represented in the teaching force but the degree to which the position is changing is not known. For the future, access courses with mandatory grants and encouragement to ethnic minority pupils now in school are suggested as ways of improving the supply of teachers from minority communities.

'OTHER' GROUPS

Part 4 of the report, ' "Other" Ethnic Minority Groups', contains separate chapters on the educational needs of children of Chinese, Cypriot, Italian, Ukranian and Vietnamese origin. It also deals with the long-established black population of Liverpool and with Travellers.

These specialist chapters are important in themselves. They bring together the latest research and other evidence of those working with children from these communities and add the perceptions of the communities themselves. In a separate chapter, 'Reflections and Conclusions', four matters of general interest are examined. Each is seen to reflect the degree to which the separate groups, which have few direct contacts with each other, share common experiences and concerns amounting to a defined 'ethnic minority experience'.

The first element of this experience is a strong sense of ethnic identity. This is not something presumed and half invented from the outside. It comes from within the communities themselves. It appears quite as important among the young people born in the UK as it does for their elders, born overseas and with, in many instances, a desire, however unrealizable, to return there at some point in the future.

The conclusion to be drawn from this is that where some of the majority population believe our systems should be pressing minorities to assimilate, the main minority communites believe that, if anything, the pressure to assimilate is already too strong. Schools are seen as Anglo-centric; still with too little recognition of 'the languages, cultures, histories or religions' of the minorities.

A second common feature of 'ethnic minority experience' is the influence of racial discrimination (racism) on their lives. This takes varied forms. For the Vietnamese, it may be seen predominantly as outright racial harassment. For others, where skin colour does not make for easily identifiable distinctions, it can take the form of neglect. Needs are unidentified and therefore not met. Again, in the case of the Chinese, an over-positive stereotype may have the same consequence of needs unmet. Above all there is the evidence, from the Liverpool experience, that the mere passage of time does not cause discrimination to disappear. It may, but it is unsafe to assume that it will.

The third feature, except for Travellers, was a shared concern about language learning. Procedures for teaching English 'as a second language' were seen to put the children in a remedial position and to inhibit rather than enhance their prospects of success in the mainstream of the school system. There is an apparent variance here between the approach of many specialists in this work and the members of the communities whose children they teach.

One specific complaint concerns the 'second stage' of English learning. Simple structures are well taught. The children can manage in school. But the more difficult second stage, which develops the skills necessary, for example, for examination work are, it is claimed, neglected. This lack of success is compounded by the unnecessary complex language used in some examinations where skill in English is not meant to be at issue.

As to 'mother-tongue', this was perceived as 'a key factor in maintaining their community's distinct identity'. There were generally-expressed worries conveyed to the Committee about the low status afforded to those teaching community languages and to the languages themselves.

The fourth concern, shared by the different minority groups, related to the balance of the curriculum itself. The Anglocentric nature of this is understandable on historical grounds. But the present requires new thinking. A curriculum relevant to pupils now at school needs to include elements with which those from the ethnic minorities can identify. In turn, this requires teachers who are sensitive to the point and can themselves contribute to the wider understanding of the UK and its position in the world that is now necessary.

RECOMMENDATIONS

The report ends with a summary of its recommendations. They can be grouped under seven headings:

(1) *Suggestions to those in authority.* The government, L.E.A.s, H.M.I., the School Curriculum Development Council, the Examination Boards and others are asked to study the report and act on its findings. Four particular requests are made.

First, a series of conferences should be held at which the report, which would have been made generally available would be discussed.

Second, a commitment to commissioned research in areas where information essential to sensible decision making is lacking.

Third, a decision by all concerned, including the D.E.S., to keep relevant ethnically-based statistics to enable policies to be monitored for their effectiveness or otherwise.

Fourth, an institutional commitment to bring about change. This would include thought-through policy statements by individual L.E.A.s and schools and properly located individuals and institutional structures to ensure that those policies, setting out the institution's commitment to equal opportunities for all, are put into effect.

(2) *On teaching English* to those for whom it is not a first language, the emphasis is strongly towards providing for the children in the main streams of main-stream schooling. Withdrawal from class or school for special tuition is, so far as possible, to be avoided. English is to be brought to the child rather than vice versa.

(3) *On mother-tongue and community languages*, the view is that these should be fostered but not incorporated, in any general way, into the standard school curriculum. Fostering would include arrangements for allowing the community concerned use of school premises and other facilities to enable the community language and culture to be maintained. And where speakers of any community language are in considerable numbers in any school, that language could well form part of the modern languages offer of the school concerned. There should be no different status offered to the different modern languages taught and learnt in these circumstances.

(4) *On religious education*, a multi-faith approach is suggested. The distinction is made between religious education, a matter for the schools, and religious

instruction increasingly seen as a matter for the communities adhering to particular forms of belief. Religious education is seen to be able to 'play a central role in preparing the pupils for life in today's multi-racial Britain'. In such a society, the requirement for the 'daily act of worship', required by the 1944 Education Act, is questioned.

(5) *On the creation of separate schools* by or for different minority communities, the suggestion is that these should be, so far as possible, avoided as likely to exacerbate the rejection of minorities by the majority (though some committee members disagreed). On the other hand, every reasonable effort should be made, for example by the retention of appropriately located single-sex schools, to meet the specific religious or cultural requirements of particular minority groups.

(6) *On teacher education*, the implications for education of a multiracial society should permeate all courses within teacher education. It should be the particular concern of those responsible for the accreditation of courses, for their validation and for their location and financing to ensure that this happens both in initial and in subsequent in-service training.

(7) *On the employment of ethnic minority teachers*, the suggestion that there should be a quota to be filled by teachers from any particular group is rejected. On the other hand, despite the lack of statistics, it is apparent that black teachers are under-represented in the profession and that action needs to be taken to encourage recruitment and ensure fair treatment and promotion prospects for those teachers already employed.

Finally, the Committee emphasize that the recommendations it has made need to be seen in the context of the report as a whole. The Swann Report is a comprehensive survey of the way the education service either is or should be responding to the needs of a multiracial society. It is as concerned with the way we think about that society as it is with what we do about it. Unless that thinking is right, policies are likely to be misdirected.

* SWANN'S REMIT

The terms of reference of the Swann Committee were as follows:
Recognizing the contribution of schools in preparing all pupils for life in a society which is both multiracial and culturally diverse, the Committee is required to:

(1) review in relation to schools the educational needs and attainments of children from ethnic minority groups taking account, as necessary, of factors outside the formal education system relevant to school performance, including influence in early childhood and prospects for school-leavers;

(2) consider the potential value of instituting arrangements for keeping under

review the educational performance of different ethnic minority groups, and what those arrangements might be;

(3) consider the most effective use of resources for these purposes; and to make recommendations.

REFERENCES

The Bullock Report (1975) *A Language For Life*, HMSO, London

Craft, M. (ed.) (1984) *Education and Cultural Pluralism*, Falmer Press, London

House of Commons Select Committee (1977) *The West Indian Community*, HMSO, London

Parekh, B. (1983) Educational opportunity in multi-ethnic Britain, in N. Glazer and K. Young (eds) *Ethnic Pluralism and Public Policy*, Heinemann, London

The Rampton Report (1981) *West Indian Children in our Schools. Interim Report of Inquiry into the Education of Children from Ethnic Minority Groups*, HMSO, London

The Swann Report (1985) *Education For All*, Cmnd 9453, HMSO, London

TOPICS FOR DISCUSSION

1. What does the Swann Committee recommend in respect of *teaching English and 'mother tongues'*?
2. Examine the arguments for and against '*separate schools*'.
3. Discuss the importance of the four points that Swann makes in connection with interpreting the academic performance of children of ethnic minority origin.

SUGGESTIONS FOR FURTHER READING

1. Troyna, B. and Ball, W. (1985) Styles of L.E.A. policy intervention in multicultural/antiracist education, *Educational Review*, Vol. 37, No. 2, pp 165–73. The article discusses the gradual 'racialization' of L.E.A. policy statements in Britain since the 1981 civil disturbances, and focuses on one particular style of policy intervention, namely the *monitoring procedure* initiated by a growing number of L.E.A.s.
2. Partington, G. (1985) The same or different? Curricular implications of feminism and multiculturalism, *Journal of Curriculum Studies*, Vol. 17, No. 3, pp 275–95. The author argues that the curricular implications of radical feminism towards greater curricular differentiation in schools have parallels in multiculturalism in pressures to make massive differentiation in educational provision for children of ethnic minority groups.
3. Short, G. (1985) Teacher expectations and West Indian underachievement, *Educational Research*, Vol. 27, No. 2, pp 95–101. The Interim Report of the Rampton Committee (1981) claimed that unintentional racism is widespread within the teaching profession and contributes via the self-fulfilling prophecy to the relative academic failure of children of West Indian origin.

This Reading discussed the theoretical framework and the relevant evidence on which this assertion is based. It concludes that, to be productive, future research into West Indian underachievement must relinquish the premise that teachers' expectations are chiefly responsible.

Reading 2
RACE, SEX AND CLASS.   A POLICY FOR EQUALITY: RACE; ANTI-RACIST STATEMENT AND GUIDELINES
Inner London Education Authority[1]

Document 1
A POLICY FOR EQUALITY: RACE

This Reading marks a new development in the Inner London Education Authority's commitment to achieving equality in education and employment in the Inner London education service, and in its response to the 1976 Race Relations Act. Section 71 of the Act lays on local authorities a two-fold duty in the services which they provide:
(1)   to eliminate unlawful racial discrimination;
(2)   to promote equality of opportunity and good relations between persons of different racial groups.

The Authority's acceptance of the ideas promoted in this paper is the outcome of a series of consultations with representatives of the wide range of people involved in the education services especially with members of the black and ethnic minority communities in London.*

The Reading is addressed to all those who work within the Authority and to all those for whom the Authority has a duty to provide services.

SUMMARY OF CONTENTS

This Reading briefly summarizes the main perspectives that have informed responses to education and race relations over the past three decades. These have been based on ideas of assimilation, integration and cultural diversity.

It then proposes that all future responses of the Authority should be informed

---

[1] County Hall, London I.L.E.A. (1983)

by a perspective which emphasizes equality, with central attention being given to racism, and to measures to unlearn and dismantle racism.

ADOPTING AN OVERALL PERSPECTIVE

Different people in Britain see race relations and education in different ways – they have different overall perspectives, different definitions of the problems to be solved, different understandings of the nature and role of racism, different proposals and prescriptions about what should be done in practice.

The fundamental debate is to do with three main values – assimilation, cultural diversity and equality. Most people would say they support all three of these values. However, different people understand them in different ways, and combine them together into different overall perspectives. Over the last three decades three main perspectives have evolved: a perspective emphasizing assimilation and integration; a perspective emphasizing cultural diversity and pluralism; and a perspective emphasizing equality and justice, and combating racism, which should be the basis for policies in the 1980s.

The notes which follow review briefly and critically the first two of these perspectives, concerned respectively with assimilation and cultural diversity and then commend at greater length the third, emphasizing equality.

A perspective emphasizing mainly assimilation

This perspective has four main features:

(1)   A belief that race relations in Britain are by and large good, that it is counter-productive to try to improve them too fast, and that problems are only caused by extreme right-wing groups.

(2)   A belief that curricula of educational establishments should reflect at all times British traditions, history, customs and culture.

(3)   A belief that 'children are all children', and that teachers should pay as little attention as possible to racial and cultural differences amongst their pupils/students, or to racism in education and society at large – the 'colour blind' approach.

(4)   A belief that black people, before they can possibly learn anything else or be integrated into the mainstream of the education system, need to learn to speak and write correct English.

What is wrong with this perspective is that:

(1)   It defines the black communities as 'the problem', and therefore not only fails to challenge negative views about black people but also actually

promotes and strengthens such views, both in the education service and in society.

(2) It is racist, because it is based on, and communicates, a notion of white cultural superiority. This is damaging to white people as well as to black.

(3) It discriminates against black people, since if they are to succeed in the education system they are required to ignore or disown their own cultural identity and background, and their own and their community's experiences of discrimination and prejudice.

(4) It reflects an inaccurate or inadequate view of Britain's position in world society, both historically and at the present time, and therefore miseducates everyone, white as well as black.

(5) It fails to appreciate that white people have very much to learn from the experience of black people: their struggle against oppression, their movements in daily life between two or more cultures, their achievements as individuals and communities in coping with rapid social and cultural change.

This perspective emphasizing mainly assimilation has come under increasing criticism and has been replaced in many official documents by a perspective which emphasizes cultural diversity.

A perspective emphasizing mainly cultural diversity

This second perspective has been promoted by a series of reports and papers published by the Schools Council and by numerous books and articles on multicultural education. Its main features include:

(1) A belief that British society is adequately summarized, with regard to education and race relations, as being multicultural or multi-ethnic, and that aspects of the cultures of various ethnic groups should be taught in schools.

(2) A belief that a low profile should be maintained in relation to issues of racism and that the most effective way to deal with these issues is to promote cultural diversity.

(3) A belief that such teaching about culture will promote a 'positive self-image' amongst black people, and tolerance and 'sympathetic understanding' amongst white people.

(4) A belief that educational establishments should make greater efforts to explain their policies and practices to black parents.

(5) A belief that mother tongues other than English should be valued positively by schools, and that bi-lingualism should therefore be encouraged.

This perspective represents a decisive departure from the explicit racism of the first approach. Nevertheless:

(1) Its almost exclusive emphasis on aspects of culture and cultural differences tends to obscure or ignore other issues: the economic position of black people in relation to white people; differences in access to resources and in power to affect events; discrimination in employment, housing, and education; relations with the police.

(2) It conceives of racism as merely a set of mental prejudices held by a smallish number of unenlightened white people, and hence ignores or denies the structural aspects of racism, both in the education system and in society.

(3) It reflects a white view of black cultures as homogeneous, static, conflict-free, exotic. It ignores the power relations between white and black people, both in history and in the present.

(4) It ignores the issue which black people themselves consider to be of vital importance – that is, the issue of racism and the promotion of racial equality.

(5) Although it recognizes the right of people to maintain their own cultures, in practice this is limited to support for marginal activities, which do not impinge on mainstream social policies and programmes.

(6) Responses are tokenist. In education, the changes seen to be required are in the content of certain subjects rather than in the ways in which teachers see and treat their pupils/students. Curricular changes tend to focus on what are in practice rather marginal subjects – religious education, art, topic work – as distinct from the main body of the curriculum, concerned with literacy, mathematics, science, the study of society.

For these reasons a perspective emphasizing diversity and pluralism must be included in a context which addresses issues of racism, and its effects on both white and black people. This latter perspective is not indifferent to cultural differences and diversity, nor to bilingualism. Indeed, it recognizes the positive aspects of the previous perspectives, but also recognizes the ways in which they can be distorted unless they are seen in the wider context of promoting equality and justice.

A perspective emphasizing primarily equality

This perspective will inform all the work of the Authority. It includes, as mentioned also above, some of the policies associated with the concern for diversity, particularly those which involve acknowledging and valuing black peoples' cultural identities and bilingual competence, and promoting mutual respect between cultures. However, it places them in a different context, which has as its focus:

(1) *The central and pervasive influence of racism*: There are certain routine practices, customs and procedures in our society whose consequence is that black people have poorer jobs, health, housing, education and life-chances than do the white majority, and less influence on the political and economic decisions which affect their lives. These practices and customs are maintained by relations and structures of power from which black people have been and are excluded. This web of discriminatory policies, practices, and procedures is what is meant by the term 'institutional racism',

There are also individuals in positions of power and authority who have beliefs and attitudes which hold that black people are essentially inferior to white people – biologically, or culturally, or both. Racism is a shorthand term for this combination of discriminatory practices, unequal relations and structures of power, and negative beliefs and attitudes.

Racism is morally wrong because it is contrary to basic principles of natural justice. It damages and dehumanizes white as well as black people, giving them distorted views of their identity, society and history.

As a set of routine practices and relationships racism is frequently unrecognized by white people. As a set of beliefs and attitudes it is frequently unconscious. In neither of these two aspects, therefore, is it considered by most white people to be a serious problem. On the contrary, most white people dismiss the view that Britain is a racist society with impatience and indignation.

Nevertheless, Britain is a racist society in the sense defined above. Further, racism in the wider society is reflected in and reinforced by, racism in the education system.

(2) *Black perspectives:* Opposition to racism, both in society and in the education system, should be informed by the experience of the people who bear the brunt of racism. This involves developing new kinds of consultation and liaison between white and black people, ones in which black people have considerably more power and opportunity than hitherto to express and communicate their views, and to participate in decisions which affect everyone, and in which white people listen rather than speak. This is a precondition for cooperative work in dismantling discriminatory practices, and in unlearning the effects of racism on their views of themselves and of the world.

(3) *Social, political and moral education:* All pupils/students should be learning about the theory and practice of government, rights and responsibilities, the rule of law, social justice, peaceful resolution of conflict, the role of the police, the role of the mass media, economic development, production and trade, political change. Such concepts and topics should be studied with

regard to world society as a whole as well as to Britain in particular. All pupils/students should be learning to identify, resist and combat racism in their own sphere of influence.

(4) *Removing discrimination in educational establishments:* It is necessary to remove those practices and procedures which discriminate against black pupils/students and their families. These include courses, syllabuses, schemes of work, topics, textbooks, materials and methods which ignore or deny the validity of black experience, perspectives and culture; some of the tests and other criteria, including teachers' expectations, which govern access and admission to particular schools or post-school courses, or are used to allocate pupils/students to particular sets, streams, classes or bands; some of the general priorities affecting the allocation of staffing, and other resources, within and between departments and year-groups; and some of the ways in which educational establishments communicate and consult with parents and local communities.

(5) *Training of all Education Authority staff:* Courses, workshops and conferences on the nature of racism, and on principles for combating racism in the education service, will be organized over a period not only for teachers but also for all non-teaching staff, including administrators, clerical workers, kitchen staff, lunchtime controllers, and schoolkeepers; and also for members of the Education Committee.

(6) *Code of practice:* A code of practice relating to racism and racial equality should regulate the work of all staff, both teaching and non-teaching.

(7) *Positive action on employment and appointments:* Steps will be taken, in accordance with the provisions of the 1976 Race Relations Act, to encourage the recruitment and promotion of black people at all levels of the educational system, particularly senior levels, and their appointments as school governors.

(8) *Continuous monitoring of policies and provision:* The I.L.E.A. will ensure that information is collected about its progress in promoting racial equality and that its policies are evaluated.

This perspective which emphasizes equality has not yet explicitly influenced official policies in education; neither those of the Department of Education and Science nor those of L.E.A.s, examination boards or individual schools. In view of its relative newness and unfamiliarity, there are four general points particularly worth emphasizing with regard to it:

(1) It is not linked to any one political party nor to any one part of the political spectrum. This perspective can be, and is, promoted by supporters of all the main political parties, Conservative, Labour, Liberal, Social Democratic. All the main parties support the 1976 Race Relations Act.

(2) It must be acknowledged that this perspective may seem threatening and uncomfortable to many white people. This means that measures to promote racial equality need to be fully explained and thoroughly debated. It does not, however, mean that they should be avoided or de-emphasized, for fear of a backlash.

(3) The arguments against racism, and for racial equality, need continual emphasis. There are four main sets of arguments: (a) racism is contrary to natural justice; (b) racism prevents white and black people from learning from each other's experience and culture; (c) racism gives white people a false view of their own identity and history; (d) racial discrimination is against the law.

(4) We have relevant experience in another, more familiar, field. The moral, legal and self-interest arguments about racism and racial equality are similar to those surrounding another concern in modern society, that of sexism and sexual equality. We have experience in Britain of this latter subject from which we can draw parallels, and which will guide us in the less charted work of unlearning and dismantling racism. Many of the principles underlying equality of opportunity and of treatment are present in both.

*   *Note on terminology*
The following terms are used:
AFRO-CARIBBEAN: to refer to people whose origins are in Africa or the Caribbean.
ASIAN: to refer to people whose origins are in the Indian subcontinent.
BLACK: to refer to both Afro-Caribbean and Asian people. The term black emphasizes the common experience which both Afro-Caribbean and Asian people have of being victims of racism, and their common determination to oppose racism.

Other groups who, together with the black communities, are usually referred to as 'ethnic minorities' also suffer varying degrees of prejudice and discrimination. These include Chinese, Greek Cypriots, Turkish Cypriots, Turks, Vietnamese, Moroccans. In a similar way, though not always to the same extent, some white ethnic groups, such as the Irish and Jews, experience prejudice and discrimination. In using the term 'black' in this paper, it is not the Authority's intention to exclude any minority group.

We propose that these terms should also be used in debate and consultation. We do not wish to use the terms 'immigrant' and 'coloured': 'immigrant' is now frequently inaccurate and has pejorative overtones; 'coloured' is an unacceptable euphemism to many black people.

Document 2
ANTI-RACIST STATEMENT AND GUIDELINES
I ANTI-RACIST STATEMENT

(1) The Inner London Education Authority is committed to achieving equality in education and employment in the Inner London education service. This means the development of an education service from which racism, sexism and class discrimination and prejudice have been eliminated so that the Authority can respond fully to the needs of our multi-ethnic society. This paper is concerned with one of the three major obstacles to achieving equality—racism.

Many reports, official and unofficial have indicated clearly the extent and effects of racism in education. The chief victims are black people, i.e. Afro-Caribbean and Asian communities. Other ethnic minorities are also subjected to racial prejudice and discrimination. However, it is in the interests of all our employees, students and pupils that we actively seek to eliminate racism in all our institutions and in all branches of the service.

There is, rightly, among the black communities and other ethnic minorities, an implacable opposition and resistance to racism. This is a powerful and positive factor in British society. Another force is also available to the service. This is the strong tradition in British society, of opposition to injustice in whatever shape or form. All employees of I.L.E.A. and users of the Authority's service are uniquely placed, if only they would seize their opportunity, to educate generations of young people free of racism and prejudice.

(2) It is necessary that all those who serve the Authority or benefit in any way from its services, understand what is meant by the concept of racism.

In structural terms, racism is represented mainly by the formula: racism = power + prejudice and discrimination. Accordingly, power and resources in the education service, as in other institutions of our society, are in the hands of white people. It is essential to understand that dimension of the power relations between black and white people because of the part it plays in sustaining inequality at the national as well as at the international level. Other explanations of the concept are necessary if we are to get a total picture of what the phenomenon represents.

Racist ideology, surrounding attitudes, values and beliefs, is based on the assumption that black people are inferior to white people. Embedded deeply in the procedures and practices of our institutions are many such notions. Some individuals and groups within the service may act in a prejudiced and discriminatory way, deliberately or because of such unexamined beliefs.

Given that we live and work in a society where racist practices and attitudes permeate the whole system, there are several ways in which we can be racist.

(a) We can be openly hostile to ethnic minorities on grounds of race or colour.

(b) We can claim to see no difference between white people and black people or other ethnic minorities, and thus deny the significance of racism as a factor in sustaining inequality between black and white people in our education service.

(c) Even those of us who have made every effort to rid ourselves of racism may fail to see how deep-seated racist attitudes which have been prevalent in our society for so long affect our treatment of ethnic minorities.

(d) We may fail to see how decisions we make, however fair and valid according to the traditions of our system, affect ethnic minorities adversely because of the basic inequality in our society.

The most significant manifestation of racism is the absence of black people and other ethnic minorities from positions of power and decision-making in our service. Every institution and branch of the service must take active steps to redress this imbalance and to ensure that the perspective of black people influences policy-making directly.

Racial discrimination represents the other most obvious manifestation of racism. One form of this is overt, i.e. deliberate with intent, and blatant. It includes such practices as personal abuse, graffiti, provocative behaviour and, more seriously, racist attacks by one group on members of another.

Other forms of discrimination are less easy to perceive but are by no means less important. They include procedures employed within the education service, in its administration as well as in its institutions, which however well intentioned or rooted in custom have the effect of reducing the opportunities open to members of ethnic minority groups. These procedures need to be re-examined and altered to take into account the Authority's priorities. Similarly there are deep-seated attitudes which affect adversely members of ethnic minority groups. These attitudes need to be identified, brought to the surface and openly challenged.

(3) It follows that every aspect of the Authority's work, every branch and every institution must be examined with the clear objective of eradicating racist practices and assumptions. The responsibility for developing and implementing the Authority's anti-racist policies must rest with every employee in every institution and every branch of the Authority's administration. It is for every institution and branch of the Authority therefore, to develop a coherent action programme for the elimination of racist practices.

The I.L.E.A. has a straighforward legal obligation to eliminate racial discrimination. That is to say, the Authority and everyone who works within it is obliged to comply with the provisions of Section 71 of the Race Relations Act 1976. That section places a duty on every local Authority to:

(a) eliminate racial discrimination

(b)   promote equality of opportunity, and good relations, between persons of different racial groups.

The educational duty is equally important. Following its initial Multi-Ethnic Policy Statement in November 1977, the Authority has consulted widely with community groups, teachers and heads and is currently taking new initiatives designed to eliminate racism from the education service.

(4)   In giving expression to its commitment to combat racism the Authority asks:

(a)   that all educational establishments, through their staff and governing or managing bodies and in association with the committees they serve, prepare and publicize carefully thought-out statements of their position. This must be seen as part of the Authority's legal and educational commitment.

(b)   that annual reports for governing bodies, as part of the regular process of keeping schools, colleges and other establishments under review, should incorporate information on what action has been taken on curriculum, staffing and organization to meet the needs of a multi-ethnic society.

(c)   that all administrative and other branches of the Education Service should re-examine their procedures to ensure that, however unintentionally, they do not have the effect of discriminating against members of minority ethnic groups.

The Authority itself is committed to eliminating racism and to take such action as it properly can to remedy its effects. Its success in doing so will depend upon the determination of every individual within the education service to ensure that appropriate action is taken. In issuing this statement, the Authority reaffirms its own commitment to promote equality of opportunity, and good relations, between persons of all racial groups.

II ANTI-RACIST GUIDELINES FOR I.L.E.A. ESTABLISHMENTS

Introduction

The concept of racism is a complex one and requires careful examination and analysis. Unless this is done in a consistent systematic way, a great deal of misunderstanding can arise because of the emotional responses which often underlie the positions taken up by individuals and groups whenever the issue is discussed.

   Essential to defining racism in our institutions is the perspective and under-standing of the black communities, i.e., the Afro-Caribbean and Asian com-munities who are the chief victims of racism and have developed ways of resisting it. Other forms of racism which affect such white minority groups as the Irish,

and anti-semitism, also require vigorous analysis so that they c; 34
eliminated.

The following factors are crucial to our analysis of racism:

(1) Structural factors – racism is best defined in terms of the power relations in our society. Power is in the hands of white p ~~.~.~ .~.~ ~~. institutions operate in such a way as to place ethnic minorities at a disadvantage. Any anti-racist programme needs to address itself to the issue of this unfair distribution of power.

(2) Political factors – political power and ideas have been used to divide ethnic minorities from the white communities through the operation of such measures as the Nationality Act and the Immigration Laws. In political reporting and electioneering some politicians and reporters have also used ethnic minorities as the scapegoat for political inequalities such as unemployment, housing and education.

(3) Ideological factors – much of racism is sustained by the values, attitudes and prejudices which characterize black people, their cultures, languages and lifestyles, as inferior to those of white people.

(4) Historical factors – the special character of the colonial and neo-colonial relationship between Britain and some of the third world countries of origin of the ethnic minorities, is crucial in defining racism.

(5) Cultural factors – it is also important to look at the consequences of racism at the cultural level. Therefore it is necessary to consider the all-pervasive nature of racism, how it affects all interpretations of human behaviour, literature, the arts, habits, conventions, etc.

(6) Other factors – the system of knowledge, the curriculum, media, books and learning resources that have been developed in this country present negative stereotypical and distorted images of black people and other ethnic minorities.

The existence of racial discrimination in this society is well documented as in the P.E.P. reports, acknowledged by the government in the 1976 Race Relations Act, and in a wealth of evidence from those who suffer from racial discrimination. Valuable experience from developments in schools and colleges shows that it is essential to work from the basis that we have *all* grown up in societies where racism has been a central factor in shaping the ideas and institutional practices of the societies. It has been argued that, given this, we are all in some way racist and must therefore become consciously and rigorously anti-racist, examining ourselves in our individual behaviour as well as the institutional practices we work within. This is a stance supported in these guidelines. It would obviously be ineffective to tackle avowed racists and growing children and young people without an equal concern with our own ideas and practices and the institutional practices of the education service in which we work.

ᴊtarting point

Most of the schools and colleges that have developed policies have found it essential to follow a process which includes all of the following:
(1) Placing the issue firmly on the school/college agenda and making time for discussion and development.
(2) Coming to grips with what racism is and its historical context.
(3) Considering how racism can and does operate in the school/college's particular circumstances.
(4) Analyzing both directly conscious racist behaviour and what the Rampton Interim Report terms 'unconscious racism'.
(5) Analyzing both individual behaviour and the policies and practices of the school/college.
(6) Analyzing the behaviour and practices of individuals and services that impinge on the life of the school/college.
(7) Drawing upon the advice and experience of others, including other schools/colleges and those with specialist knowledge and experience.

The policy

Each school or college will finally determine its policy in the light of its own circumstances. However, certain elements are common to all. There will be:
(1) A clear, unambiguous statement of opposition to any form of racism or racist behaviour.
(2) A firm expression of all pupils' or students' rights to the best possible education.
(3) A clear indication of what is not acceptable and the procedures, including sanctions, to deal with any transgressions.
(4) An explanation of the way in which the school or college intends to develop practices which both tackle racism and create educational opportunities which make for a cohesive society and a local school or college community in which diversity can flourish.
(5) An outline of the measures by which development will be monitored and evaluated.

External influences

Any school or college operates in, and as part of, a society. The last few years have made abundantly clear that there is a tension between traditional values of tolerance and justice and inequalities and injustices being suffered by 'minority' groups. Recent events, particularly inner city disturbances, show that this tension leads to behaviour in our society that really troubles us all. Getting the response right in the education service is no single panacea, but on the other hand no solution will prevail without the involvement of the education service. Indeed, education can give a lead in pointing to the goal of a society free from racism.

We need to be aware of the ways in which society outside the school and college adversely affects education through racism and racial discrimination. Some forms of racism we can deal with directly and must tackle firmly. These will include outsiders harming children or adults on the site, whether physically or by verbal abuse or graffiti; or using the school or college and premises to try to recruit members to racialist organizations and to be active in their own schools or colleges.

Racist attitudes may also be inculcated by the influence of the media, or through social contacts. Responses to these influences require longer-term development and will be considered later in this paper.

Most of the offences that fall in the first two categories are offences that are covered either by law or the code of practice of the school or college. It is essential that every institution is aware of the following:

(1) Breach of the Peace – Section 5 of the Public Order Act 1936.
(2) Note on incitement to racial hatred – Race Relations Act 1976.
(3) Use of school premises – Representation of the People Act 1949.

Procedures need to be laid down and effectively disseminated so that when an incident occurs, it is acted upon quickly by:

(1) Taking the appropriate immediate action.
(2) Informing the police where appropriate.
(3) Informing the divisional officer or F.H.E. or C.E.C. Branch as appropriate.
(4) Compiling a report of the incident and the action taken.
(5) Making a decision as to how the fact of the incident should be made known to the school or college population, including the governing body, and whether parents and others should be informed.
(6) Recording incidents so that monitoring of the nature and pattern of incidents can be undertaken.

When such an incident occurs, it will be difficult for a school or college to be certain as to whether it is an isolated incident or not. Also, incidents have occurred when a school or college has not been prepared. It is essential, therefore, that processes (with the assistance of Divisional Offices and F.H.E. or C.E.C. Branch) for sharing information and experience are set up. This will help to ensure that all institutions are properly prepared and warned of trends that are likely to affect them.

Experience makes it clear that the existence of a positive multi-ethnic policy and a curriculum which is multicultural is essential; this certainly helps the institution to make the right decision in dealing with hostile incidents. At the same time, a school's or college's procedures will need to take into account the age range of pupils or students, the ethnic composition of the school or college population and the climate in the local community.

Within the school or college

Obviously any anti-racist policy in a school or college must rely on the good example and active involvement of the whole staff.

The staff code is being amended to enable schools, colleges and institutes to deal with cases of racist behaviour by members of staff.

Many of the occurrences outside can be mirrored by actions of pupils and students. This is understandable since the school or college population live most of their life outside the institution.

The following list of manifestations of racialist and discriminatory behaviour or practices is given as a form of check-list. It is important that decisions made on appropriate responses are consistent with the overall position and ethos of the school. It is important too to recognise that an understanding of the cause, the reason or motive for a racialist action will have a major bearing on how that action is dealt with.

Actions by pupils or students which are clearly hurtful to others include:

(1) Physical assault against a person or group because of colour or ethnicity.
(2) Derogatory name-calling, insults and racist jokes.
(3) Racist graffiti or any other written insult.
(4) Provocative behaviour such as wearing racist badges or insignia.
(5) Bringing racist material such as leaflets, comics or magazines into the school or college.
(6) Making threats against a person or group because of colour or ethnicity.
(7) Racist comment in the course of discussion in lessons.
(8) Attempts to recruit other pupils and students to racist organizations and groups.

These actions are unacceptable anywhere. No school or college will tolerate them. Depending upon the age and experience of the pupil or student, the actions may be derived from unconscious acceptance of parent or societal attitudes or from firmly held personal attitudes. So the school or collge response needs to tackle an incident on four fronts:

(1) to deal with the perpetrator
(2) to aid and support the sufferer or sufferers
(3) to establish the line of responsibility for dealing with the incident.

(4) to deal with the impact of the incident upon the school or college population.

So, in developing procedures, each institution must question whether the prevailing ethos and climate is positively multicultural and therefore actively anti-racist and, if it is not, to set about making it so.

Procedures

The following procedures outline a full set of measures. In the case of the most serious incidents they need to be followed right the way through. It will be a matter of judgement as to how to treat each incident. This does not mean the judgement of one individual but the collective judgement of the school or college.

In dealing with the perpetrator or perpetrators, this is the range of possible actions:

(1) Firmly explaining the wrong done, with or without punishment, in line with the school or college's code and possibly informing parents.

(2) Sending the perpetrator or perpetrators to the appropriate senior member of staff either to mark the gravity of the incident or to make use of greater experience.

(3) Using the exclusion or suspension procedures, thus involving the parents and the governing bodies.

(4) Reporting the matter to the police where it is necessary to bring to bear the processes of law.

In dealing with individuals or groups who have suffered in the incident, these are the possible actions:

(1) Explaining the action taken above, and expressing the attitude of the institution towards such behaviour, allowing the pupils or students to express their own concerns and feelings.

(2) Writing to, or meeting, the parents to explain the action taken and discussing the matter with them.

In dealing with the impact of the incident upon the school or college community as a whole, it will be necessary to consider the following:

(1) Is the matter of such importance to call everybody together for an explanation and to tackle the issue by placing it in the context of the school's or college's position and policies? Will this action be helpful?

(2) Will a less direct emphasis upon the particular issue by using assemblies, other meetings, or a curriculum input be a more helpful approach?

(3) If there is a danger of distortion through rumour, or of a backlash, should tutors or class teachers explain the matter to their groups or classes?

(4) Should a letter be sent to all parents explaining the matter?

The school and college

The issues and the measures outlined to tackle them have so far tended to be focused upon the ways in which the school or college is affected by racism from the society outside. Much of it might seem a catalogue of defensive positions. It is necessary to consider now a positive and affirmative long-term development.

This development has to encompass four critical aspects:
(1) All pupils and students have a right to equality of access to what is best in the educational provision.
(2) The curriculum, for the child in preschool education through to the adult in the college or adult institute, must enable everyone to have a real understanding of the part played by racism through history to contemporary society.
(3) The educational provision must take on the work of developing inter-racial understanding and skills for inter-group and cross-cultural relationships.
(4) There must be continued vigilance and action to combat racism.
 As the school or college develops its own clear set of procedures and measures, it will be necessary to evolve ways of ensuring that the whole population is aware of the position and procedures. (It is important to remember that those at the receiving end of racism, pupils, students and their parents and teachers, will have much to offer in helping to develop good practices.) So, just as it is essential to have a written statement of the position, it is important to work through, talking with individuals and groups, to use assemblies, staff meetings and meetings with parents.
 It has been made clear, in earlier statements on racism by the Authority, that a policy on racism is not one that anybody can ignore or opt out of. We all have to be able to make the policy effective in practice. As the N.U.T. Circular 382/81 (ii) stated: 'Only by examining their own attitudes will teachers be properly equipped to combat racialism in schools'. Such an examination can be helped by attending in-service courses; a number of schools are tackling this by organizing their own seminars or discussions to increase both individual and group awareness of racism.

Elements in the work of the school or college

There are a range of elements in the life and work of the school or college which can be positively employed in order to tackle racism and so improve education.

Ethos and climate

The overall ethos and climate of the school or college can contribute to the well-being, confidence, security and identity of all pupils or students. The elements that together make up the ethos and climate can give a positive message of a multicultural position which is clearly opposed to racism and discrimination, for example:

(1) Assemblies and other group meetings should consistently emphasize the multicultural nature of society and the school or college, underline the aims of equality, and tackle issues and incidents of racialism.

(2) The displays on walls throughout the buildings should also have a similar emphasis, drawing explicitly on what is important in different cultures including languages.

(3) Meetings with parents should acknowledge the multicultural ethos and stress equality of access. Again this emphasis enables issues of racism to be raised naturally.

The content and organization of the curriculum and resources

Teachers have a great deal of control over the content of what pupils and students learn and the resources that are made available. Through their selection of content and resources they can therefore make a positive contribution.

(1) Very young children need both an affirmation of the value of people of all colours and cultures and to be helped towards avoidance of stereotypes and misrepresentations which form at a very early age.

(2) A wide range of content is important but it is essential that pupils develop analytical skills and can engage in an understanding of cross-cultural perspectives and values.

(3) Pupils and students must have opportunities to gain an historical perspective that is free from ethnocentric biases.

(4) The whole curriculum must be open to all so that no sort of restricted access is given to some pupils because of stereotyped views of ability.

Teacher knowledge and awareness: styles and methods of teaching

In order to develop the best curriculum content and approaches, teachers need to ensure that they have the knowledge of content and a real awareness of their own position in relation to race and culture. Given this, it is necessary to consider the organization of the teaching groups and the best methods of interaction. It means working out how information is best given, and when pupils or students need to work individually, to interact in small groups, or to share in a whole class group:

(1) Time is required for sorting out aims and objectives, and selection of themes and content where appropriate.

(2) Teachers' wider set of 'reference' points needs to take in both what is common to all people and what is particular to groups and individuals.

(3) It is vital to build in processes of shared learning between pupils and students.

Staff relationship with pupils and students: attitudes, expectations and treatment

The relationship between the learner and the teacher can be of very great significance. Racism can certainly affect the attitudes and expectations of both. The onus on the teacher is clear; to show equally high expectations of a pupil or student irrespective of his or her ethnic or cultural allegiance, to value cultural diversity, and to be aware of the factors which promote or undermine a pupil's or student's confidence in the school or college.

(1) Teachers will need to be well informed of the experience of young people out of school.

(2) Teachers will need to know what are the really significant cultural strengths and perspectives of the families whose children they teach.

(3) It is essential for all to become aware of the ways in which it is possible to collude with racism, without being conscious of it, in interaction with pupils and students.

Processes of selection and grouping

In the past 10 years, the education system has been criticized for discriminating against certain pupils and students by unfair processes of selection and grouping. This can occur where there are 'nurture groups', banding or streaming, or withdrawal groups, and in the selection of examination groups in secondary schools:

(1) It is essential to ensure that no selection of these kinds is affected by conscious or unconscious stereotyping of an ethnic group or black pupils.

(2) It is also important to match any special provision with a clear and accurate diagnosis of why special provision is thought to be needed.

(3) As has been stressed earlier, knowledge of pupils and students must be free of any false notions of inherent ability based on ethnic or cultural diversity.

Sharing knowledge and support

It is clear from the development work in a number of schools and colleges that it is most effective to use the resources of all the staff, pupils/students and others outside the school/college. A whole school/college policy has to be developed, using the skills, experience and expertise of the staff without regard for status in the structure.

(1) The school or college will need to analyze the contributions that different staff members (teaching and non-teaching) can make.

(2) It is important to develop means by which staff can support one another.

(3) A development that is both anti-racist and builds upon cultural diversity will need the particular involvement of those who are most aware of racism, and those who have special knowledge and experience of cultural diversity to contribute.

(4) The school or college will need to use the best support available outside.

Relationship of the school or college with parents and members of the communities with an interest in the school or college

A change in the school's or college's policy and practices of this nature would obviously require the involvement of parents and others. This involvement is particularly important since there is such a strong link between experience in society and experience in schools and colleges. More than that, the school or college can look to parents and others for guidance and support in the development.

(1) The school or college needs to acknowledge clearly and openly that it intends to tackle racism.

(2) Parents and others in the communities should be canvassed for their support in the development.

(3) The school or college will then be strengthened in its important role of tackling those who refuse to accept its firm line on racism.

Dissemination of policies and other developments

It is critical that, as policies and other developments are made, knowledge of these is shared by all who have an interest in the school or college. This will have begun by involving a great number of people in their formulation. It is necessary as well to make them public in a number of ways:

(1) Positions and policies should be made clear in school brochures and other booklets.

(2) They should be introduced to the pupils or students in assemblies and other gatherings and referred to as often as necessary.

(3) They should be discussed with parents, friends of the school and other 'interest' groups.

In-service training

There will be a number of opportunities for staff to attend courses organized by the Authority or by other organizations. It is important that those attending courses have a real opportunity of bringing back information and strategies for the whole school or college. Equally important is the training that can be set up within the school or college itself.

(1) Responsibility must be taken for finding out suitable courses and ensuring attendance.

(2) Expertise within the school or college needs to be harnessed to provide on-site seminars and workshops.

(3) London-wide and local resources, human and material, need to be used to add to the school or college expertise.

Monitoring

The developments outlined above are aimed at helping change to take place; positive change that unites people in purpose, eradicates discrimination, increases access and so provides better education. It will be necessary to monitor whether aims are realized and objectives achieved.

(1) Aims and objectives will need to be continually set out.

(2) Appropriate methods of monitoring and evaluation, recording achievement as well as registering opinion, will need to be constructed.

Conclusion

As is clear from these guidelines, there is no blueprint nor a finite set of practices or curriculum content which can be taken on by all. There is rather a set of principles, directions and methods for development. It is these that need to be addressed to all our actions, procedures and to the structures we work within. This is as important in the nursery or infant school reception class where very young children are already beginning to make sense of their world as, say, in the college or the Adult Institute.

The school or college will need to draw upon advice and support from within the Authority and from other sources. The Authority's policy is addressed to all parts of the service, so that schools and colleges can expect similar developments throughout the Authority's branches and an increased directness and volume of support.

It has been made clear that we have to harness the combined talents and resources of all our colleagues. But we must make sure that we enter into the development wholeheartedly. We are dealing with the fact of racism; for most of us this is not something of our making. Yet we are all touched by it. We must confront all the possibilities and manifestations of racism, in ourselves, in our actions and in our institutions.

TOPICS FOR DISCUSSION

1. What, essentially, are the criticisms levelled at the *assimilation* and the *cultural diversity* perspectives in Document 1 (pp 24–6)
2. Discuss the composition of the formula for racism given in Document 2 (p 30): *racism = power + prejudice and discrimination.*
3. What are the implications for teachers that, 'appropriate methods of monitoring and evaluation, recording achievement as well as registering opinion will need to be constructed.' (I.L.E.A. Document 2, p 42)
   Discuss some of the problems that might arise in implementing the policies outlined in the I.L.E.A. documents.

SUGGESTIONS FOR FURTHER READING

1. Dorn, A. and Troyna, B. (1982) Multiracial education and the politics of decision-making, *Oxford Review of Education*, Vol. 8, No. 2, pp 175–85. The article suggests that the absence of a coherent and explicit national policy on multiracial education (despite the D.E.S.s stated commitment to producing such a policy as long ago as 1971) is not simply an ideological agnosticism or failure to exercise power. Is the vacuum deliberate, the authors ask, and is it the expression of an explicit ideological position?
2. Craft, M. (1984) *Education and Cultural Pluralism*, The Falmer Press, London, pp 27–40, 'Policy responses in Education'. Contrary to Dorn and Troyna (above) it is argued that significant developments have taken place in the educational response to cultural diversity and that there is now an overall policy commitment to multicultural aims.
3. Honeyford, R. (1983) Multi-ethnic intolerance, *The Salisbury Review*, Vol. 1, No. 4, pp 12–13; Honeyford, R. Education and race – an alternative view, *The Salisbury Review*, Winter, pp 30–2; Honeyford, R. The right education? *The Salisbury Review*, Vol. 3, No. 1, pp 28–30. These three articles provide useful examples of Judaeo-Christian ethnocentrism and the use of slanted language. Multiculturalists, for example, are variously described as 'well-meaning liberals and clergymen suffering from a rapidly dating post-Imperial guilt to left-wing political extremists, often with a background of polytechnic sociology'.

Reading 3
COMBATING RACISM
R. Jeffcoate[1]

The idea that schools and local authorities should assemble a systematic

[1] In Jeffcoate R. (1984) *Ethnic Minorities and Education*, Harper & Row, London, pp. 139–63

response to the phenomenon of racism is a fairly recent one. Of more venerable lineage are narrower educational programmes designed specifically to dispel or reduce racial prejudice. These were developed principally in the USA after the Second World War as adjuncts to psychological investigations of the nature of prejudice directed against Jews and American blacks. Though open to criticism for being short-term and isolated, they were at least evaluated, which is more than can be said for most initiatives in multicultural education. The findings were, on the whole, depressing, with little impact made on deep-seated hostilities and some reports of counterproductive outcomes. However, a measure of success was claimed for strategies that went beyond the instructional or informative to involve members of different groups affectively in simulations and shared tasks (Allport, 1954). There has been one major British contribution to this tradition: the research of Lawrence Stenhouse and his colleagues into the effectiveness of different strategies for teaching race relations to adolescents.

THE STENHOUSE RESEARCH

Stenhouse's research originated in the work of the Schools Council's Humanities Curriculum Project (H.C.P.) (1967–72) of which he was director. The H.C.P. was intended for 14–16 year-olds, with the raising of the school-leaving age in 1972 in view. Its aim was to 'enhance understanding and judgement in those areas of practical living which involve complex considerations of value'. The areas initially identified were war, education, the family, poverty, relations between the sexes, living in cities, law and order, and people and work. A collection of 'value-balanced' printed and visual material attempted to represent the scale and character of the debate on each particular topic. This material was subsequently tested in a wide range of trial schools. The other distinguishing feature of H.C.P. was the pedagogic principle of 'procedural neutrality'. The role of the teachers was to chair discussions on the materials without imposing or even intruding their own opinions. The hope was that the assumption of a non-authoritarian role would render simple-minded conformity and rebellion on the part of pupils equally unlikely, thereby facilitating the search for truth and fostering their own autonomy. This did not mean that the teachers were to abrogate all their normal responsibilities. They were expected to aim for orderly and purposeful discussions, querying and challenging where necessary, restraining the voluble and encouraging the diffident, above all trying to get their pupils to submit to 'the discipline of the evidence'. Their task was summarized as 'the development of open, coherent, and rigorous enquiry'. Clearly being procedurally neutral in chairing discussions of value-balanced materials was not the same as being value-free: 'education is committed to a preference for rationality rather than irrationality, imaginativeness rather than unimaginativeness, sensitivity rather than insensitivity. It must stand for respect for persons and readiness to listen to the views of others' (Stenhouse, 1969; Parkinson and MacDonald, 1972; Ruddock, 1983). Belatedly the H.C.P. team added the topic of race to the controversial issues already identified. Recognizing that it might prove particularly difficult to handle in the classroom, they proceeded with caution, undertaking a small feasibility study in six schools before deciding to go ahead with production and dissemination. However, in January 1972 the Schools Council's programme committee rejected what came to be known as the 'race pack' (the first time any of its projects' materials had met such a fate). They did this apparently because the teachers unions' representatives on the committee found some of the ingredients extremist and doubted whether the topic of race was really amenable to the H.C.P. approach. Stenhouse and colleagues then refined and expanded their materials in a further project entitled 'The Problems and Effects of Teaching about Race Relations', funded jointly by the Gulbenkian Foundation and the Social Science Research Council between 1972 and 1975. Its aim was to explore the possibilities of three different strategies for teaching about race relations: the H.C.P. strategy of procedural neutrality; the more 'positive' strategy of the 'committed' teacher; and the use of drama.

Like their American antecedents, the two Stenhouse projects stressed the importance of evaluation. The evaluation of the 'race pack' in 1970, and of the three strategies of the later project in 1974, is about all that exists in the way of descriptions and assessments of innovations in multi-ethnic education in Britain. Rather surprisingly both projects persevered with the American practice of administering attitude scales to the students before and after the teaching and comparing the results for experimental and control groups. I say 'surprisingly' because Stenhouse was one of the foremost critics of the behaviourist school of rational curriculum planning, and because controlled experiments and attitude scales did not seem exactly in tune with the open-ended humanism of the H.C.P. philosophy. One of the five major premises of the H.C.P. was that 'the discussion should protect divergence of view among participants'. For what they are worth, the 1970 findings showed 'small but significant shifts in the direction of tolerant attitudes in the post-test situation' for the experimental but not the control groups. The 1974 findings revealed 'a high incidence of negative shifts in the control groups' for both 'committed' and H.C.P. pedagogies, 'compared with a high incidence of positive shifts in the experimental groups'. In other words, if one wishes to make students in the 14–16 age-range less racially prejudiced and more racially tolerant, it is better to teach about race relations than not to, and it does not much matter whether one adopts the strategy of 'neutral' chairman or 'committed' teacher. In the case of drama, the tentative conclusion was that, while attitudes are unlikely to deteriorate as a consequence, it is equally unlikely to be sufficient on its own.

However, the researchers were quick to qualify their general conclusions: 'these broad results mask the tendency of individual schools and individual pupils' ('a fairly substantial minority') 'to change counter to the general tendency'. It would have been surprising, they added, had this not been so, since there is a limit to what schools can realistically purport to accomplish in the fight against racism; there would also have been grounds for disquiet 'on educational grounds if the values, attitudes or outlooks of all our students moved in the direction desired by the teacher'. Nevertheless it was anxiety about counterproductive effects which lay behind some of the reservations expressed by the Schools Council's programme committee in 1972 and explains why so many secondary schools continue to give teaching about race relations a wide berth (Verma and Bagley, 1979; Stenhouse *et al.*, 1982).

Of greater interest and relevance than the experimental data, with their arid calculations of statistical significance, were the case studies of individual classrooms generated by both phases of the research. The concern displayed by Stenhouse and colleagues for the autonomy of pupils was complemented by their concern for the autonomy of teachers. They encouraged the teachers involved in the trials to tape-record their lessons, thereby involving them more actively than normal in the business of classroom research and curriculum evaluation. Self-evaluation was the ideal, and regarded as integral and essential to professional development. One of the published case studies (presented jointly by the teacher and the H.C.P. evaluator) was from the feasibility investigation of the 'race pack' carried out in 1970. The school was a boys' secondary modern in the Midlands. Over 60 per cent of its 600 pupils were 'Commonwealth immigrants' according to the official definition of the time, and most of these were South Asians. Both curriculum and discipline were 'traditional' and the 'overwhelming view' among the staff was that 'the best approach to race relations was to play it down'. The discussion group comprised half of the top form in the fourth year and included roughly equal numbers of English and South Asian pupils. The teacher, who had no experience of working within the H.C.P. philosophy, was faced with a number of problems during the six weeks of the course: what to regard as acceptable language; how to draw out reticent pupils and restrain loquacious ones; how to respond to the character assassination of the unrepresented West Indian community indulged in by English and South Asian pupils alike. But the biggest strain on his 'procedural neutrality' was imposed by a debate on a verbatim report of one of Enoch Powell's 1968 speeches on immigration. It was acrimonious, racially polarized and hard to control. Yet the pupils assured both teacher and evaluator afterwards that no harm had been done to inter-racial friendships; all had been given and taken in good part. They also claimed (and were supported by the evidence of the tests administered) that the discussions had made no impact on their attitudes though their understanding had certainly been enhanced (Parkinson and MacDonald, 1972).

The teacher in another case study, taken from the 1974 evaluation of the later Stenhouse research, encountered similar problems over language, responding to prejudiced utterances and the general control of the discussion in a more 'liberal' school with a 'prevailing ethos of reasonableness and rationality'. He differed from the first teacher in being both a 'fervent exponent of', and considerably experienced in, neutral chairmanship; and his group of fourth formers from a Yorkshire mining village were all white. He opted for permissiveness both in regard to his pupils' choice of language, since they applied labels with 'wog' and 'blackie' descriptively not derogatorily, and in regard to the direction of the discussion:

> In a sense it would be true to say that the structure and logical progression of conventional teaching was abandoned as the price to be paid for giving pupils the opportunity to follow their own, particular interests. To suggest to them that there might be a correct order and content could imply that they should also accept a 'correct' set of opinions [. . .] If pupils are to be given the opportunity to explore their attitudes in any area of controversy, they need to feel free and secure in their ability to express themselves.

'Inelegant' as certain passages of discussion may have been, he felt able to conclude:

> [. . .] this particular group came to an awareness of the limitations of their own knowledge and understanding [. . .] and indicated that they were learning to think rationally for themselves rather than to accept passively all that they were told [. . . This] strategy for teaching about race relations [. . .] cannot claim to be a way of systematically changing opinion. However, it does seem to be consistent with the concept of a society [. . .] in which the individual has, in the last resort, the freedom to choose.
> (Sikes and Sheard, 1978; Stenhouse *et al.*, 1982, pp. 234–56)

The Stenhouse research has yet to be accorded due recognition in the field of multicultural education. This is not entirely surprising for on the face of things its contribution to combating racism appears to be slight. Its strengths – the importance attached to developing rationality and autonomy in both teacher and pupil – are of a more general kind. Because they embody some of the virtues of a participatory democracy, 'of a society [. . .] in which the individual has, in the last resort, the freedom to choose', I shall be using them here as touchstones against which to judge the validity of more recent anti-racist ventures.

THE EMERGENCE OF ANTI-RACISM

Anti-racism as a self-conscious educational ideology first emerged in the 1970s. In the early years of the decade an organization called Teachers Against Racism flourished briefly; it was later followed by others such as Teachers Against the Nazis and All London Teachers Against Racism and Fascism. Anti-racism marked itself off from the liberal tradition of teaching about race relations, exemplified by the Stenhouse research, and from the publicly advocated (but little implemented) integrationist policy of infusing the curriculum with cultural diversity. These were held to be all very well in their own way but inadequate for the pressing task of eradicating racism from the education system and combating negative influences on children in the wider society. In the 1980s anti-racism has made major political advances, recently capturing I.L.E.A., other Labour-controlled local authorities and the influential National Association for Multi-racial Education, previously a bastion of multiculturalism.

A number of factors can be detected behind the origin and growth of anti-racism in the 1970s. First, there was the accumulating evidence of under-achievement among West Indians. Second, there was David Milner's replication of American research into racial identification and preference on British five to eight-year-olds in the late 1960s. Originally reported in *New Society* in 1971, his findings demonstrated the early onset of racial, and indeed racist, attitudes, with a disquietingly high proportion of West Indian and South Asian children also betraying symptoms of self-rejection (Milner, 1975). Ten years later Alfred Davey and colleagues repeated the experiment, using different tests on a slightly older age-range (seven to eleven-year-olds), and found that although self-rejection had considerably diminished, the level of stereotyping and ethnocentricism displayed by whites, West Indians and South Asians had not (Davey and Norburn, 1980; Davey and Mullin, 1982).

By this time attention had rather shifted from the embryonic racism of infant and junior schoolchildren to the virulent racialism of white, male, working-class adolescents. This provided the third main reason for the growth of the anti-racist ideology in education. White adolescent racialism was popularly associated with the recrudescence of neo-Fascist groups such as the National Front, whose ranks were swelled by dissadent Tories after the Conservative government's decision to admit the Ugandan Asians expelled by Idi Amin in 1972. No doubt the far Right, with its overtones of anti-establishment militarism, did make successful appeals to disaffected youth in the recruiting campaigns launched outside football grounds and at rock concerts. But 'Paki bashing' antedated the rise of the National Front and continued after the National Front and the other extremist parties of the far Right had reverted to their customary fissiparous insignificance, following the Conservative electoral victory in 1979 and Mrs Thatcher's promises of even tighter immigration controls.

Evidence on the prevalence of these three phenomena – black underachievement, the incipient racism of young children and the full-blown racialism of adolescents (whether associated with the fleeting resurgence of neo-Fascism or not) – has figured prominently in the anti-racist argument that what I.L.E.A. has called the 'central and pervasive influence of racism' demands a more forthright, purposeful and unremitting response than has so far been attempted.

THE MEANING OF RACISM IN THE CONTEXT OF EDUCATION

One of the problems anti-racists have in sounding convincing is that racism is used in education, as elsewhere, to cover a multitude of sins. The charge has been levelled at individual teachers and pupils, at schools as institutions and at the entire education system. These different uses need to be identified and distinguished from one another. First of all there is racism in the classical sense of a set of beliefs, largely of nineteenth-century origin, about the categorization, characterization and evaluation of human beings on the basis of their physical appearance ('scientific' racism). Second, there are the unflattering or hostile prejudices and stereotypes an individual may entertain about groups to which he or she does not belong ('popular' racism). Third, there are acts of discrimination, intimidation and violence, which some commentators prefer to describe as racialism rather than racism because they are seen as 'behaviour' rather than 'opinions' or 'attitudes'.

Finally, there is the vexed question of 'institutional' racism. I have already expressed my reservations about this addition to the vocabulary of race relations. Its shortcomings as a tool of analysis in the field of education are only too apparent. Whereas it is relatively clear how 'scientific' and 'popular' racism might manifest themselves in schools – in the attitudes and behaviour of teachers and pupils, in the curriculum and other aspects of school policy – what institutional racism refers to remains as obscure as in other spheres. I.L.E.A.'s *Policy for Equality* defines it vaguely as a 'web of discriminatory policies, practices and procedures' whose consequence is that 'black people have poorer jobs, health, housing, education and life chances than do the white majority and less influence on the political and economic decisions which affect their lives'. The trouble with this definition is that it is based on a generalized picture of black people's position in society which evidence has shown to be decidedly suspect. Matters have been further obscured in some quarters by the tendency to use 'institutional' racism to refer to patterns of inequality in outcome rather than, or in addition to, the policies, practices and procedures that are alleged to produce them. A good example would be the degree of black underachievement at 16+ revealed by the survey of school leavers in six L.E.A.s undertaken by the D.E.S. for the Rampton Committee in 1978–79. For some this underachievement is *per se* an indication of institutional racism irrespective of what might have caused it. However, it may (just possibly) be wholly unrelated to 'scientific' and 'popular' racism; or (more probably) racism in these senses may be only one factor in its complex aetiology. Institutional racism has also been applied to curriculum or organizational policy which is inappropriate to a multi-ethnic society. Again, it has to be queried whether this is a useful or valid characterization. Syllabuses in literature, geography and history which limit their choice of content to the British or European are more likely to be reflections of parochialism, teacher ignorance or sheer curriculum inertia, than of anything that could fairly be construed as racism. Similarly, failure to make concessions to ethnic minorities in such areas as school uniform or dress could be motivated as much by a wish not to be seen to favour them, as by antagonism towards them or any belief in the inferiority of their cultures.

Some discussions of institutional racism have compounded the confusion by attaching the phrase to manifestations of racism in the other senses (notably in respect of teachers' attitudes) or by using it to refer to just about anything in the education system the writer or speaker happens to dislike. The book accompanying the recent B.B.C. series on multicultural education has a section on institutional racism which defines it, rather like the I.L.E.A. policy document, in terms of 'matters of political power, hierarchy and status. It is the form in which we can be party to racism without being racially prejudiced in our personal relationships.' Thirty-three examples are then listed which emanated from the discussion of a group of Yorkshire teachers during a 'racism awareness' workshop. Most of them are instances of teacher inactivity, insensitivity or ineptitude. Whether they are hypothetical or drawn from actual experience is not made plain. Though almost all are certainly reprehensible, the link with racism (to say nothing of 'political power, hierarchy and status') is in many cases tenuous. I have pencilled 'not necessarily racist' against over half in the margin of my copy of the book. 'Describe an English village' may be an asinine essay title, and confounding 'inadequate English' with 'slow learning' may be a serious pedagogic error (examples 8 and 14 respectively), but to call them 'racist' is to devalue and trivialize the concept itself. Moreover, the second example on the Yorkshire teachers' list – treating all children the same – seems to me to be, if anything, anti-racist. It is their preferred strategy which is racist, in the classical sense:

> for black children, school should support awareness and pride that 'Black is beautiful' – or more powerfully, that they are part of the Black Consciousness – as much as it should make white children feel it's good to be white, in some of its own ways, too (Twitchin and Demuth, 1981, pp. 166–9).

School should do no such thing. 'Education', observed Stenhouse and colleagues, 'is committed to a preference for rationality rather than irrationality.' Young people who emerge from school believing it is right and proper to evaluate themselves and others on the basis of skin colour have been grievously miseducated. As to whether black children should regard themselves as 'part of the Black Consciousness' (whatever that may be), that is for them to decide individually.

ANTI-RACISM AS OBFUSCATION

Preoccupation with racism to the exclusion of all else, and with outcomes and effects rather than intentions or causation, goes some way to explaining why anti-racists have so frequently misidentified the nature of the problem to be addressed and been found fighting the wrong battle. Take, for example, one frequently cited instance of institutional racism – the congregation of black pupils in bottom streams or sets. Anti-racists are likely to argue not only that this is racist *per se*, but that it should be replaced by an arrangement which guarantees proportional representation. In fact the over-representation of black pupils in bottom streams or sets is not necessarily a manifestation of racism. No one *knows* why it occurs. The explanation is probably multifactoral and could well include factors falling outside the senses of racism defined earlier. Nor is such over-representation necessarily a manifestation of racial inequality. Working-class pupils have long been shown to 'percolate downwards' through streaming and setting systems. As most black pupils are working class, their position could simply be a more visible representation of this long-standing tendency.

The impression conveyed by the anti-racist argument is that all would be well if black pupils were distributed evenly across forms and sets. Given willingness on the part of the authorities, this outcome could no doubt be readily secured, but only at the expense of undermining the basis of streaming and setting which is supposed to be some kind of objective assessment of ability or aptitude. Moreover it would leave untouched the position of working-class pupils who were not black, and would mean that other children would have to be relegated to make room for the black pupils promoted. In other words the complexion or identity of those suffering the indignity of bottom streams or sets would be changed but the numbers would not. The problem is not that more black children are to be found there than one would expect from their proportion in the overall pupil population, but that any child of whatever colour or ethnic background should be exposed to such public humiliation and to the risk of depressed academic performance that is widely believed to be associated with it.

Similarly, anti-racists have been known to complain that voluntary schools situated in multi-ethnic neighbourhoods too often have fewer pupils from the ethnic minorities than would have been expected had a strict catchment area policy of school allocation been in operation; they have appeared to imply that under-representation is the extent of the problem to be rectified. Sometimes under-representation is certainly at least partly the result of Church complicity in the racism of white parents anxious to reduce the incidence of contacts between their children and black people. However, it could also simply be a reflection of admissions policy favouring the faithful. Increasing the proportion of ethnic minority children attending voluntary schools could only come about as a consequence of a reversal of policy (since so many of them are neither Christians nor Jews), which would no doubt somewhat affect the schools' role as institutions to preserve the faith. Yet, even were this to happen, the dual system would remain intact, arbitrarily dividing the nation's young. As in the case of streaming and setting, the problem is not so much the position occupied by pupils from the ethnic minorities, as the invidiousness of the system which their presence has served to highlight.

The superficiality of analysis that can result from a preoccupation with racism is even more evident when we consider those in the field of education who are alleged to be its perpetrators – individual teachers and pupils. Elsewhere I commented on the flimsiness of the evidence adduced to substantiate the assertion that the teaching profession is riddled with racism. Most of it is at least 10 years old, anecdotal and dependent on what teachers say in staffrooms or write in response to questionnaires. Very little derives from close observation of teachers in classroom interactions with pupils from the ethnic minorities. One piece of research undertaken in the early 1970s which does not fall into this category was Martyn Hammersley's study of a downtown secondary modern school. Hammersley, it will be remembered, queried whether it was right to interpret staffroom outbursts of hostility against West Indians simply at face value. They were, he suggested, partly expressions of resentment at the loss in prestige which these teachers saw as attendant upon the 'changing character of the pupil intake' (Hammersley, 1981).

Paul Willis's (1977) study of a counter-school culture among white working-class boys reached a similar conclusion: 'Many senior staff associate the mass immigration of the 1960s with the break up of the "order and quietness" of the 1950s and of [. . .] their peaceful, successful, schools.' He also noted a curious collusion between the staff and his group of anti-school boys. Despite the teachers' publicly stated opposition to racism, they shared with the 'lads' a sense 'of resentment for the disconcerting intruder'. These studies by Willis and Hammersley are now a decade old. They were undertaken at a time when immigration was a major political issue and Powellism a significant force. Since then both immigration and Powellism have rather receded from the national consciousness. Unfortunately there have been no recent studies to compare with those of Willis and Hammersley and which might enable us to arrive at a more up-to-date assessment of the extent and nature of racism among teachers.

The same is true of racism among pupils where even the impressionistic picture is sketchy. Once again Willis provides some useful insights, at least so far as the racism of white, working-class, male adolescents is concerned. It was one ingredient (albeit not as potent as sexism or the cult of violence) in the 'lads' ' subculture. Willis noted a clear distinction between the racism they directed against West Indians on the one hand, and against South Asians on the other. Though West Indians might be resented sexually and dismissed as 'thick', they occupied similar cultural ground and came off a good deal better in the 'lads' ' estimation than the reviled South Asians who were perceived as 'ear 'oles' (i.e. conformist and pro-school), culturally alien and overambitious. As a result it was the South Asians who became 'the target for petty intimidation, small pestering attacks, and the physical and symbolic jabbing at weak or unprotected points in which "the lads" specialize' (Willis, 1977, pp. 47–9). I think it would be generally agreed that the problem of racism (or racialism) in school is principally represented by boys like Willis's 'lads' – the disaffected unclubbables, or what the Home Office (1981) report *Racial Attacks* rather than coyly refers to as 'white youths of the skinhead fraternity'.

Yet there has been very little attempt to follow Willis in investigating the significance of such racism. The Home Office report makes the important point that it is in a sense incidental, for even if there were no ethnic minorities in Britain or racialist organizations to latch on to, these boys would still constitute a problem:

> The criminality of youthful hooliganism has worn many different fashions over the past twenty years and combating one particular fashion will not necessarily tackle the violence which uses racialism as the present means through which to express it' (Home Office, 1981, pp. 30–1).

'Paki-bashers' are very unlikely to be just 'Paki-bashers'; their addiction to violence finds its victims throughout the ranks of the weak and unwary. To the extent that they do join racialist organizations (they are notoriously fickle in their loyalties), it is not so much the racist ideology that draws them into the fold as the paraphernalia of membership, the prospect of violence and the general aura of anti-establishment disreputability and defiance. On the other hand there are pupils in school who could be described without exaggeration as budding racist psychopaths. Bob Brett, a teacher in London's East End, has characterized them as follows:

> In every school there are children for whom being racist is central to their sense of their own value. On the whole they are the most pathetic and inadequate kids, those kids that have got so little going for them that they will clutch at anything that will give them a sense of their own worth (Brett, undated).

In other words the racists themselves are as much a social and educational problem as the racialist behaviour they exhibit.

ANTI-RACISM AS ILLIBERALISM

The main reservations to be expressed about anti-racism concern recent initiatives by a few local authorities and schools which appear to threaten the autonomy of teachers and pupils and to evoke the spectres of indoctrination and totalitarianism. The most blatant example involves the London Borough of Brent. In 1983 its Labour-controlled council announced that, in the event of not enough teachers volunteering for 'racism awareness' courses, it would consider making attendance compulsory. Furthermore, willingness to attend would in future be made a condition of all new appointments to the borough's staff. This stipulation represents a gross infringement of teachers' rights. Traditionally, teachers have attended those in-service courses they thought would benefit their professional development, which is not to say that headteachers or advisers have not drawn their attention to particular courses and encouraged them to attend. But to make a course mandatory, or to make a new appointment conditional on attendance, is quite simply not compatible with education in a democracy – in a society where 'the individual has, in the last resort, the freedom to choose'. Nor for that matter, in this instance, is the course itself. Indeed it is peculiarly apt that courses in 'racism awareness training' should be made obligatory for they do not appear to attach any great importance to individuals thinking for themselves; and it is hard to imagine many self-respecting teachers attending courses bearing such a sinister title of their own accord.

The description of the racism awareness workshop attended by the Yorkshire teachers in the B.B.C. book on multicultural education suggests that the title is by no means misplaced. Conclusions were unmistakably foregone. 'To gain an understanding of the nature and effects of institutional racism' ran the second of three aims. What happened, one wonders, to those (like me) who doubted whether institutional racism was a viable concept and whether the supposed manifestations of it eventually listed were necessarily in many cases even related to racism? The overall impression conveyed is that, notwithstanding the seemingly open-ended exercises in self-exploration, the participants were expected to reach predetermined (and distinctly simple-minded) conclusions: that deep-down they and their schools were racist; that racism is something white people do to black people; that in Britain white people have power while black people do not; that racism and racial equality are endemic in Britain and inextricably bound in with the histories of slavery and empire; and that institutional racism is more important than other forms. There was no hint of recognition that racism might also be something that West Indians do to South Asians and vice versa, nor that the Irish, Jews and Gypsies might be victims too. The participants appear to have been subjected to a brand of the Marxist version of racism (admittedly somewhat diluted and vulgarized) purveyed through the unlikely methodology of encounter group behaviourism. Those running the course remain elusive. Who were they? Was this another instance (they are plentiful in the anti-racist field) of the self-appointed enlightened few presuming to 'raise the consciousness' of the unenlightened multitude? (Twitchin and Demuth, 1981, pp 161–73).

Illiberalism is also a feature of several of the recently promulgated anti-racist guidelines and policy documents. But what is more striking is that they should also have found it necessary to state that certain forms of behaviour which have always been regarded as unacceptable and intolerable should be outlawed and punished. I have not worked in a school in which personal abuse, insulting graffiti, bullying and physical assaults were held to be anything other than serious disciplinary offences. Yet the N.U.T., I.L.E.A. and a number of schools have all been moved to state publicly that racialist behaviour of these kinds should be proscribed and the perpetrators chastised. I am puzzled by their motivation, for such an unwarranted intervention could well be taken to imply that racialist bullying is more reprehensible than bullying which is not racialist – surely an untenable position.

The absurdity of this position can be readily illustrated from the chapter in the B.B.C.'s book describing a school policy on racism (*see* Reading 11). A London teacher, Shaun Doherty, emphasizing the necessity systematically to confront racist remarks, quotes the following example from his own experience:

'You fucking paki curry eater, I'll kill you.' When I heard this remark in a second year class I was doubly disturbed because it combined racist abuse [. . .] with an apparent threat of physical violence. I stopped the lesson and called the speaker out to the front, making my own sense of outrage clear to the rest of the class. This was necessary to reassure the pupil at the receiving end of such language that teachers are not neutral to it, and are ready to protect any pupil from apparent physical threats. I then publicly explained why his remarks were offensive to me; fortunately he was receptive to argument and in fact was ready subsequently to apologize. (Twitchin and Demuth, 1981, pp. 111–12)

The teacher appears to believe that other members of the profession (including me, to judge by a reference to my book *Positive Image*) would find the abuse quoted acceptable classroom behaviour. If so, I have yet to meet such teachers. More to the point is whether his own behaviour would have been different had the abuse not been racist. Let us suppose that the pupil had shouted instead 'You fucking fat bastard', or 'You fucking four-eyed git'. Would he have reacted any differently? If so, how would he have justified this to children, with their keenly developed sense of fair play? If not, why has he made such an issue out of behaviour which all teachers would find intolerable and would seek to control?

Later in the chapter the same teacher gives what he calls 'a less obvious, and more typical, example' of racism about which teacher opinion would be far from unanimous. A fourth-year boy is quoted as saying: 'Sir, I think black people should be sent back home because this country is overcrowded.' Doherty is less explicit about exactly how he responded than in the first example, but his comment conveys some impression of what ensued:

If I had failed to respond to such a view with the facts to indicate the ignorance, as well as insensitivity, it is based on, I would be guilty of fostering racist attitudes through omission. Silence may not imply agreement, but it does imply no serious disagreement, and so serves to create an atmosphere in which racist attitudes are apparently an acceptable part of classroom discourse. The intervention need not be heavy and should seek to win over the offender, but it is so important that the teacher makes his or her attitudes clear. (Twitchin and Demuth, 1981, p. 112)

Doherty fails to make the crucial point that the offending remark here belongs to a quite different category to the one in the first example. It is not racialist abuse but an expression of political opinion. As such it should certainly be expected to submit to the 'discipline of the evidence', though what the relevant facts are we are not told. I can imagine inviting the author of the remark to reconsider his opinion in the light of information about Britain's black population and the likely problems and effects of implementing his proposal. Conceivably, he might modify it as a result to the kind of voluntary repatriationism favoured by some members of the Conservative Party. But I cannot imagine impressing upon him that his view ('racist attitude' seems a bit of an overstatement) was an unacceptable part of 'classroom discourse'. As the Stenhouse research implicitly recognized, the classroom is precisely the place where adolescents should be encouraged to express and explore opinions on controversial issues such as race and immigration, for it is there that democratic procedures are more likely to be respected and tests of rationality most rigorously applied.

For some reason anti-racists appear to lose faith in normal democratic practice when it comes to engaging with racist opinions and beliefs. For example, several local authority and school anti-racist policies state that racist literature should be confiscated. One quotes the following extracts from a National Front leaflet found in school:

> Unfortunately, East End discos are very much multi-racial. White youths entering a discotheque in the East End might be approached by a gang of blacks who ask for some money, if the white refuses he would very probably be 'done over'. [. . .] We in the Young National Front think it's time that discos in East London and the whole of Great Britain were designed for us. They should not be designed especially for black invaders. [. . .] The Y.N.F. will welcome all young patriots to one of our 'ALL WHITE' discos.

> The National Front wants Britain to remain a white country and for this reason it opposes all coloured immigration to Britain. Furthermore, the National Front wants to send all coloured people back home, to their own countries, by the most humane means possible. (Quoted in N.U.T., 1983, p.17)

The justification given for confiscation in this instance is that such literature is like pornography – 'directly offensive and degrading to many of our pupils'. In fact the extracts quoted are decidedly *un*like pornography. The closest approximation to racialist abuse is the phrase 'black invaders'. Essentially they amount, like the fourth-year boy's remark quoted earlier, to an expression of opinion, here on the desirability of all-white youth clubs and an all-white Britain. In other words, they are an example of the type of 'racialist propaganda' that successive governments have consistently refused to include under the offence of incitement to racial hatred. 'False and evil publications of this kind,' argued the 1975 Home Office White Paper *Racial Discrimination*, 'may well be more effectively defeated by public education and debate [. . .] Due regard must also [. . .] be paid to allowing the free expression of opinion.'

Five years later a Green Paper amplified on the threat to democracy posed by proscription:

It would make no allowance for genuine discussion and debate or for academic consideration of such proposals. To single out political proposals for proscription by law regardless of how they are expressed, and in what circumstances, and of the possible consequences would be a new departure. In the Government's view such a departure would be totally inconsistent with a democratic society in which – provided the manner of expression, and the circumstances, do not provoke unacceptable consequences – political proposals, however odious and undesirable, can be freely advocated. (Home Office, 1980, para. 112)

The critical point is that pupils should feel free to express their opinions in the classroom, no matter what their political or ideological content may be, learning at the same time (one hopes) to test them out against publicly accredited criteria of truth and rationality and observe the rules of democratic procedure. It would, of course, be naive not to recognize that, where the content is racist, particularly fraught classroom moments may arise. Stenhouse and colleagues acknowledged that there was likely to be something especially sensitive about race as a controversial issue; and their classroom research shows their apprehension to have been well founded. But this is an argument not for proscription or evasion but for developing the skill and confidence to cope.

Another London teacher, Martin Francis (1981), has provided a good example of what can be achieved within the best traditions of child-centred primary school practice. One day a 10-year-old child walked into his class sporting a swastika armband:

I did not spot it at first. Some of his friends (who are white) came to me and complained. Because we have talked about racism before, because they have heard from black children about harassment and because we have read *The Diary of Ann Frank*, they knew what the swastika meant and felt it should not be allowed in school.

Because discussion is an accepted part of the school today, they asked for a discussion about it and we stopped the work we were doing to get round in a circle to talk. This is something that we had done before when an important issue had come up in the classroom. What followed was not a moralistic lecture from me the teacher, but the children themselves saying what they felt. White children argued that it was insulting to wear the armband and recalled some of what they had heard about the Second World War, Asian children who were friends with the boy said that people in the N.F. had threatened them or their families and challenged him to say whose side he was really on. He listened but did not reply and we went back to other work. The children continued to work with him but occasionally brought up the subject again.

At the end of the day he told me that I could keep the armband and I was quite warm towards him. He did not recant that day – it was a gradual process. Now, six months later, he has abandoned the group of older children who were in the National Front, despite them threatening to beat him up if he left. Other children in the class admire him for having left and his status has been enhanced. (Francis, 1981)

Francis concedes that such stories do not always have happy endings. I can readily understand how considerations of public order impel schools and local authorities to ban the insignia of racialist organizations, the Home Secretary or a Chief Constable to ban their marches. The need to avert threats to life and limb must obviously take precedence. But it is important to be clear that the ground for proscription in such cases is concern for public order and not the dangerous argument (often heard in anti-racist circles in the late 1970s) that racists, because they are racists, have forfeited their democratic rights. Ultimately one would hope that we might have something on the statute book resembling the First Amendment to the United States Constitution, which guarantees the right to freedom of speech and assembly of all citizens including racists. In 1977 the American Civil Liberties Union (with its many Jewish sponsors, members and officials) successfully pleaded the First Amendment, despite strong opposition, in defending the right of the American Nazi Party to hold a march through the Chicago suburb of Skokie which had the largest number of Holocaust survivors outside New York. In October 1983 the *Spectator's* correspondent in Washington described with astonishment how he had seen a 'puny' Ku Klux Klan march protected from a 'substantial crowd of counter-demonstrators' by lines of black police officers under the orders of a black police chief who also pleaded the First Amendment.

Another area of anti-racist activity where illiberalism has been prominent in recent years is the evaluation of school textbooks and children's literature. Several organizations have published criteria or guidelines for eradicating biased material and choosing new books which are not wholly consistent with cardinal educational values. Much admired in certain quarters are the guidelines for the production of anti-racist and non-racist books published by the World Council of Churches (W.C.C.) in 1980. A 'good book' is defined as one that satisfies the following 16 conditions:

(1) Strong role models with whom third world children can identify positively are presented.
(2) Third world people are shown as being able to make decisions concerning the important issues that affect their lives.
(3) The customs, life-styles, and traditions of third world people are

presented in a manner which explains the value, meaning, and role of these customs in the life of the people.

(4) Those people considered heroes by the people of the third world are presented as such and the way they influence the lives of the people are clearly defined.

(5) Family relationships are portrayed in a warm supportive manner.

(6) Efforts of third world people to secure their own liberation are acknowledged as valid rather than described as illegal activities which should be suppressed.

(7) The material is presented in such a manner as to enhance the self-image of the third world child.

(8) The material is presented in such a manner as to eliminate damaging feelings of superiority – based on race – in the European child.

(9) The illustrations provided are non-stereotypes and portray third world people in active and dominant roles.

(10) The illustrations reflect the distinctive features of third world groups rather than presenting them as 'coloured Caucasians'.

(11) The role of women in the development of third world societies and their impact on history is adequately presented.

(12) The history of third world people and their role in developing their own society and institutions are accurately presented from their own perspectives.

(13) The role of third world people in shaping historical events in their own country and in the world is accurately portrayed.

(14) The content is free of terms deemed insulting and degrading by third world people.

(15) The language of the people is treated with respect and presented in the proper rhythm and cadence.

(16) The material has been developed by an author of recognized scholarship, valid experience, skill and sensitivity. (Preiswerk, 1980, pp. 144–5)

I would have thought that the only conditions to be borne in mind when choosing (say) a new history, geography or social studies textbook for use in secondary school would be that it should be accurate and truthful, admit to the impossibility of telling the 'whole' truth, distinguish clearly between facts and its author's opinions, indicate the empirical basis for any judgements made and conclusions reached and, above all, encourage and assist pupils to think for themselves. A few of the conditions in the W.C.C. list show some regard for accurate and truthful presentation of people and events, but most seem to be preoccupied with compensating for the stereotypical and ethnocentric portraits of an earlier generation of textbooks or with the likely effects of verbal and visual content on children's attitudes. There is also a distinct strain of 'strong' relativism and 'full-blooded' pluralism running throughout, while any concern for critical inquiry or independent thought is conspicuously absent. Altogether I can well envisage the implementation of such criteria leading to the production and adoption of narrowly conformist curriculum material. Consider, for instance, the first part of condition 4 – 'Those people considered heroes by the people of the third world are presented as such'. This condition seems to make no allowance for divergence of opinion among 'people of the third world' nor for the possibility that they might be as mistaken as anyone else in the assessment of their heroes.

At a recent conference on multicultural education I came across a booklet called *They Fought for Freedom* on the bookstall of the Children's Book Trust of New Delhi. The booklet was intended, I would guess, for the middle-school age-range and consisted of brief biographies of the main leaders of India's independence movement. It appeared to me to be not so much history as hagiography. Included in the pantheon was one very controversial character indeed – Subhas Chandra Bose, a radical Bengali politician who fell out with Gandhi and Nehru in the 1930s and left India in 1942 to throw in his lot with first the Germans and then the Japanese. Bose formed and eventually became supreme commander of the Indian National Army (I.N.A.) whose troops were drawn from the ranks of Indian prisoners in Japanese hands and fought alongside their captors in the invasion of India in 1944. His ambition was to be installed as dictator of his liberated homeland. The Children's Book Trust booklet made no mention of this ambition and played down Bose's conflict with Gandhi and Nehru. No indication was given of the nature of the regimes he forged alliances with, nor was the young reader invited to consider the morality of his actions or the soundness of his judgement. He and his I.N.A. were, quite simply, 'heroic'. Such uncritical adulation is unlikely to get very far in the average British classroom. There one would hope that pupils found it possible to assess Bose's case – whether he was a hero or not – objectively, treating his posthumous deification and the contemporary British view that he was a traitor with equal scepticism.

ANTI-RACISM AND THE CURRICULUM

So far as curriculum development is concerned, there are very few examples of anti-racist teaching available that might enable one to evaluate its worth. The existing examples appear to combine multicultural content with the second of the three Stenhouse strategies for teaching about race relations – that of the committed teacher. Where the commitment is of an overtly socialist kind, the result seems to be indoctrination. This is not the place to embark on a philosophical disquisition about the necessary and sufficient conditions of indoctrination. I think I.A. Snook (1972) captured its essence when he wrote that it 'suggests that someone is taking advantage of a privileged role to influence those under his charge in a manner which is likely to distort their ability to assess the evidence on its own merits'. Stenhouse and colleagues also identified it in terms of attempts to 'evade', 'disarm' or 'subvert' the judgement of pupils.

Using Snook's definition as a yardstick one very clear case of indoctrination is the anti-racist material published in 1982 by the Institute of Race Relations (I.R.R.). This consists of two booklets for use in secondary school – *Roots of Racism* and *Patterns of Racism* – which purport to foster children's 'critical judgement' by radically re-examining 'white society and history in the light of the black experience'. What they actually do is survey 'white society and history' from a Marxist viewpoint sometimes labelled 'black vanguardism' (Institute of Race Relations, 1982). This might please the compilers of the W.C.C. checklist but is hardly compatible with recent trends in history teaching which stress the importance of nurturing children's capacities for independent historical inquiry. Another case of socialist indoctrination is the anti-racist humanities course developed by Chris Searle and colleagues in an East End secondary school whose outcome was the compilation of children's writing *The World in a Classroom* (Searle, 1977). In Searle's own version of the programme the socialist purposes are undisguised and from a rival Marxist stable to that of the Institute of Race Relations – one that aims to subordinate race consciousness to class consciousness. I have criticized Searle's intentions and the I.R.R.'s materials elsewhere (Jeffcoate, 1979; 1984). I do not propose to do so again, but to look instead at another version of the Searle course provided by one of his colleagues, Bob Brett.

Somewhat oddly Brett (undated) states no socialist objectives and carries little of the Marxist flavour of Searle's prose. Indeed in some ways his version is decidedly liberal-minded – as, paradoxically, is Searle's – combining child-centredness with integrationism ('A harmonious multi-racial classroom is a living denial of racism'). But one is left at the end with a sense of unease. Brett makes much of the need to establish 'a reasonably relaxed and non-authoritarian relationship with the kids' in order to get them to 'open up' on race and racism, not however (or so it seems) because they should feel free to speak their minds in the classroom but for strategic reasons. He recognizes that there is only a slight chance of moving the minority of die-hards (those 'for whom being racist is central to their sense of their own value', referred to earlier in this chapter), and that working-class children alienated from school values can all too easily see anti-racism as just another set of institutional rules. Brett argues for the importance of building up 'a relationship of trust' so that the teacher can strengthen 'the anti-racism of those kids who are already anti-racist' and operate in the space provided by the 'many children' who 'have contradictory attitudes to race'. His targets are the racism of white children and 'the lies, distortions and half truths of the N.F. and the electioneering of right wing politicians and media' which are at least partially responsible. His strategy is to combat the first by exposing the latter through a process of 'persuasion'.

One cannot escape the impression that non-authoritarian classroom relationships and child-centred classroom techniques are advocated not so much because they are good in themselves as because they are likely to facilitate this process. In other words their value is perceived to be instrumental rather than intrinsic. One pauses too over whether persuasion, even if confined to rational argument and the exposure of lies and myths, is compatible with child-centredness and non-authoritarian classroom relationships. Children are, of course, entitled to expect to acquire knowledge at school, and to find irrationality and untruth challenged in the classroom, but there is more to the N.F. right-wing politicians and the media than misinformation and faulty logic. What of their opinions and attitudes? If Brett was, as he seems to have been, attempting to change opinions on political issues such as immigration control and race relations policy or alter attitudes towards ethnic minorities and their cultures, then he was 'taking advantage of a privileged role' to 'infringe his pupils' autonomy'. Unfortunately it is hard to form firm conclusions about the classroom activities of either Brett or Searle. Although they are both reasonably explicit on the content of their course (the experience of the pupils and their families, East End history, slavery, migrant workers in Europe, oppression and resistance in the Third World) and although *The World in a Classroom* incorporates a generous selection of children's written work, neither of them conveys a clear or detailed picture of the *enactment* of the course. I think it can be generally said that anti-racist teaching has yet to furnish a corpus of descriptions and evaluations of curriculum in action to set beside those furnished by Stenhouse and colleagues between 1970 and 1975 and (more modestly) by myself and colleagues on the Schools Council multiracial project between 1973 and 1976.

THE TARGETS OF ANTI-RACISM

A major problem confronting anti-racists is the absence of consensus on precisely what should be fought. About controlling and disciplining racialist behaviour there has never been any disagreement; and I have already expressed my bewilderment as to why some local authorities and schools should have thought it necessary to make such an issue of proscribing actions (personal abuse, bullying, physical assault) which, in my experience, have always been disciplinary offences. The same applies to the behaviour of teachers. I am equally puzzled why the N.U.T. should have recently added to its codes of professional ethics and conduct a clause which states: 'A teacher should not behave in a racially discriminatory manner or make racist remarks directed towards or about ethnic minority groups, or members thereof.' Does this mean that there has been a time when discriminatory behaviour and insulting remarks, at whomsoever directed, have not been contrary to these codes or that they are held to be reprehensible and punishable only when the content is racist? I would be interested in hearing the N.U.T.'s justification for either position.

I would also be interested in hearing I.L.E.A.'s justification for its recent decree that staff who engage in racist activities will face disciplinary action. If this simply refers to racialist conduct at school, then I can only again wonder why such a decree should have been thought necessary. If, however, it refers, as I rather suspect it does, to members of staff joining racialist organizations and participating in their legal activities — attending meetings, distributing leaflets, going on demonstrations — then it is a breach of democratic rights and an early step on a totalitarian road. It will not be I.L.E.A.'s only one, for it has also decreed that 'all pupils should be learning to identify, resist and remove racism'. This decree is, of course, guilty of the 'essentialist' fallacy I commented on in the opening chapter — the misapprehension that there is something out there called racism waiting to be identified by those with sufficient knowledge and perspicacity. More to the point is the extraordinary presumption that an L.E.A. is entitled to prescribe what pupils should seek to 'resist and remove'.

Political action, which is what it amounts to, is pupils' own prerogative. It is for them to decide how to respond to racism, depending on which sense of the word is intended. Herein lies the nub of the matter. Everyone might agree on the need to combat racism in the sense of racialist behaviour, and on the need to expose the irrationality of racial prejudice and stereotyping (differing only over choice of strategy). However, that still leaves a vast area of opinion and belief, represented by the ideology of racism in the original sense and the politics of immigration control and race reactions, where, as often as not, it is not just a question of separating truth from falsehood, myth from reality, rationality from irrationality. If, during the course of the debate, and in possession of the relevant facts, some children argue that white people are as a group intellectually superior to black people, or come out in favour of repatriation and oppose racially mixed youth clubs or whatever, we have to accept that as their privilege. As concerned adults we may abhor these opinions. But, as teachers, our job is not to combat opinions we do not like but to uphold democratic principles and procedures.

ANTI-RACISM AND DEMOCRACY

Unfortunately, as Brett noted, although individual teachers may succeed in developing their classrooms into democratic workplaces, schools tend to be rather undemocratic institutions. The poet W.H. Auden once observed that the best reason he had for opposing Fascism was that at school he lived in a Fascist state. The same point has been made less flamboyantly by Raymond Williams:

> It is clear, on balance, that we do not get enough practice in the working of democracy, even where its forms exist. Most of us are not expected to be leaders, and are principally instructed, at school and elsewhere, in the values of discipline and loyalty, which are real values only if we share in the decisions to which they refer. (Williams, 1961, p.309)

Auden made his remark almost 50 years ago and William's analysis is now over 20 years old. Since then much has undoubtedly changed. Schools today are, in general, less authoritarian and more open, relaxed and informal. Both teachers and parents are represented on governing bodies, and many schools have parent–teacher associations, staff committees and pupil councils. There has also been an increase in consultation, and a proliferation of academic hierarchies, management structures and working parties generating piles of paper (reports, proposals, minutes, prospectuses) where previously there was none. However, it is a moot point whether these developments have been accompanied by any genuine increase in democratic participation. After a brief flirtation the teachers' unions ran away from the idea of teacher participation 10 years ago; the much heralded 'partnership' between schools and parents has yet to emerge from the realms of rhetoric; and pupils are still effectively excluded from any say in the direction of institutions ostensibly established for their benefit.

To the best of my knowledge no state school has made a serious attempt to emulate the models of pupil democracy laid down by pioneers in the independent sector like Homer Lane and A.S. Neill in the period after the First World War. Democratic participation – what Raymond Williams called 'extensive practice in democratic procedures' – is, of course, a good thing in itself, quite apart from providing the ideal training for adulthood in a democratic society. But it has a particular significance for combating racism too, as Bob Brett appeared to acknowledge. Organized racism is historically associated with totalitarianism and individual racism with the authoritarian personality. Moreover the few ethnographic studies so far undertaken rather suggest that both teacher and pupil racism may be at least to some extent expressions of powerlessness and disaffection from institutions in which their status and valuation are low. Thirty years ago the American psychologist Gordon Allport, in his classic study *The Nature of*

Prejudice, was one of the first to recognize that the school's hidden curriculum might actually be more important than the formal curriculum of syllabuses and lessons:

> [. . .] the atmosphere that surrounds the child at school is exceedingly important. If segregation of the sexes or races prevails, if authoritarianism and hierarchy dominate the system, the child cannot help but learn that power and status are the dominant factors in human relationships. If, on the other hand, the school system is democratic, if the teacher and child are each respected units, the lesson of respect for the person will easily register. As in society at large the *structure* of the pedagogical system will blanket, and may negate, the specific intercultural lessons taught. (Allport, 1954, p. 511)

More recently a British psychologist, Alfred Davey, argued along very similar lines:

> Purging the textbooks of black stereotypes, boosting the black child in our teaching materials and telling improving stories about children of other lands will not have the slightest effect on how children treat each other – if teachers make rules without explanation, if they command needlessly and assume their authority is established by convention. We learn to respect each other's individuality not by hearing about tolerance, or reading about tolerance or even discussing tolerance but by being tolerated by others and being tolerant in return. (Davey, 1977, p. 261)

I do not know why anti-racists are so distrustful of democracy. It could be the strongest weapon in our armoury.

REFERENCES

Allport, G.W. (1954) *The Nature of Prejudice*, Addison-Wesley, Reading, Mass.
Brett, R. (undated) Charcoal and talk, *Teaching London Kids*, Vol. 11
Davey, A.G. (1977) Racial awareness and social identity in young children, *Mental Health and Society*, Vol. 4
Davey, A.G. and Norburn, M.V. (1980) Ethnic awareness and ethnic differentiation amongst primary school children, *New Community*, VIII, Nos. 1/2
Davey, A.G. and Mullin, P.N. (1982) Inter-ethnic friendship in a British primary school, *Educational Research*, Vol. 24, No. 2.
Francis, M. (1981) Talking about racism, *Times Educational Supplement*, 30 October
Hammersley, M. (1981) Staffroom Racism, Unpublished manuscript
Home Office (1975) *Racial Discrimination*, Cmnd 6234, London, HMSO
Home Office (1980) *Review of the Public Order Act 1936 and Related Legislation*, Cmnd 7891, HMSO, London
Home Office (1981) *Racial Attacks*, HMSO, London

Inner London Education Authority (I.L.E.A.) (1983) *Race, Sex and Class 3. A Policy For Equality: Race*, County Hall, London

Institute of Race Relations (1982) *Roots of Racism; Patterns of Racism*, Institute of Race Relations, London

Jeffcoate, R. (1979) *Positive Image; Towards a Multicultural Curriculum*, Writers and Readers, London

Jeffcoate, R. (1984) Ideologies and multicultural education, in M. Craft (ed.) *Education and Cultural Pluralism*, Falmer Press, Brighton

Milner, D. (1975) *Children and Race*, Penguin Books, Harmondsworth

National Union of Teachers (1983) *Combating Racism in Schools*, N.U.T. London

Parkinson, J.P. and MacDonald, B. (1972) Teaching race neutrally, *Race* xiii, No. 3

Preiswerk, R. (ed.) (1980) *The Slant of the Pen: Racism in Children's Books*, World Council of Churches, Geneva

Ruddock, J. (1983) *The Humanities Curriculum Project: an Introduction* (revised edition), School of Education, University of East Anglia, Norwich

Searle, C. (1977) *The World in a Classroom*, Writers and Readers, London

Sikes, P.J. and Sheard, D.J.S. (1978) Teaching for Better Race Relations? *Cambridge Journal of Education*, Vol. 8, Nos. 2/3

Snook, I.A. (1972) *Indoctrination and Education*, Routlege and Kegan Paul, London.

Stenhouse, L. (1969) The humanities curriculum project, *Journal of Curriculum Studies*, Vol. 1, No. 1

Stenhouse, L., Verma, G.K., Wild, R.D. and Nixon, J. (1982) *Teaching About Race Relations: Problems and Effects*, Routledge and Kegan Paul, London

Twitchin, J. and Demuth, C. (1981) *Multicultural Education; Views From the Classroom*, B.B.C. Publications, London

Verma, G.K. and Bagley, C. (1979) Measured changes in racial attitudes following the use of three different teaching methods, in *Race, Education and Identity*. Macmillan, London

Williams, R. (1961) *The Long Revolution*, Chatto and Windus, London

Willis, P. (1977) *Learning to Labour: How Working Class Kids Get Working Class Jobs*, Saxon House, Farnborough

TOPICS FOR DISCUSSION

1. What is the basis of Jeffcoate's criticism of the concept of *institutional racism* defined as *patterns of inequality in outcome* (p 50)?
2. Discuss the view that compulsory attendance of 'racial awareness' courses is an infringement of teachers' autonomy (p 54).
3. What support is there for the charge that *illiberalism* is a feature of recently promulgated anti-racist guidelines and policy documents (p 55).

SUGGESTIONS FOR FURTHER READING

1. Zec, P.(1980) Multicultural education: what kind of relativism is possible? *Journal of Philosophy of Education*, Vol. 14, No. 1, pp. 77–86. Relativism insists that 'all cultures are equally valid and can only be properly understood from within their own framework of rationality'. Zec argues that relativism leads to 'ethnic segregation'.

2. National Union of Teachers (1983) *Combating Racism In Schools*, N.U.T., London.
3. Institute of Race Relations (1982) *Roots of Racism*; and *Patterns of Racism*, Institute of Race Relations, London. Two booklets for use in secondary schools which are intended to foster pupils' critical judgement by a close examination of 'white society and history in the light of black experience'. One critic (Jeffcoate, 1984) suggests that what they actually do is to survey white society and history from a Marxist viewpoint, and this, he insists, is hardly compatible with recent trends in history teaching aiming at nurturing children's capacities for independent historical inquiry (*see* page 62).

Reading 4
POLICY, PRACTICE AND NEW APPROACHES
R. Willey[1]

At the level of official policy significant changes have taken place in educational response to ethnic diversity. Initial assimilationist objectives have been replaced by pluralist aims. Early preoccupation with helping newcomers to adapt has widened into consideration of the implications for the education system as a whole of the presence of minority ethnic groups. But there has been much less progress in giving the altered objectives practical effect. Little concerted effort has been directed towards bringing about change, and a widening gap has opened up between stated policies and practice in most educational institutions.

A time lag between the development of educational theory and its implementation is to be expected. But in this case there are more complex reasons for the gulf between official rhetoric and classroom practice. Advocacy of tolerance and harmony in response to cultural difference is a relatively simple matter if confined to vague exhortation – especially when abstracted from the realities of racial discrimination and prejudice. But once attention is turned to securing equality, and to the factors which prevent equality, the task facing the education system at once assumes greater and more complex proportions. A comprehensive review of the attitudes and assumptions which underlie existing teaching is necessary; 'multicultural education' cannot simply be grafted on as an exotic addition to an established curriculum. Systematic consideration of the pervasive effects of past and present racism must, for example, be integral to the process. It is easy to incorporate pluralist aims into official rhetoric but difficult to implement them in classrooms. Teachers developing approaches in schools are finding

[1] In Willey R. (1984) *Race, Equality and Schools*, Methuen, London, pp 13–45

that what is involved is more complex than the vague and uncontentious language of official policy often suggests.

To understand the issues now being discussed in schools and the nature of the difficult decisions facing teachers, it is necessary to look at the way in which official policies have developed. These policies have established the framework within which teachers are now working. The first part of this chapter considers the nature and effects of racism and the overall context created by government race relations policies. The second section then examines the development of official educational policies. The shift from assimilationist to pluralist objectives is considered, and the way in which a widening gap between policy and practice has led to the development of new approaches which emphasize equality and the central importance of combating racism.

RACISM AND RACE RELATIONS

Early Government responses

Considerable criticism has been levelled against successive British governments of the 1950s and early 1960s on the grounds that during the early stages of immigration there was no policy on the implications for society of the presence of the newcomers. Black immigration into Britain chiefly took place at a time when the economic boom following the period of post-war austerity had created a situation in which an expanding economy was actively recruiting labour. Immigrants came initially predominantly from the West Indies and then from India, from 1955, and from Pakistan, from 1957, to fill jobs in Britain where there was a labour shortage. There were policy assumptions relating to the presence of these new immigrants, as Rose, in particular, has shown, but these led very largely to a policy of inaction (Rose *et al.*, 1969).

The distinction is important because reluctance to take positive action – particularly in the field of social policy – became a recurrent feature of much of the subsequent response. The attitude was that citizens were to be treated equally before the law; but the corollary was that equal treatment meant the same treatment and that no further action was necessary. In practice, it fell largely to voluntary unofficial agencies to fill the policy vacuum as best they could. Such early initiatives as there were were made in response to immediate welfare needs. In effect, immigrants were firmly categorized as strangers facing problems, not as citizens suffering disadvantage and exposed to racial discrimination. The principle of civil rights before the law was not considered to extend to the notion that the law might also guarantee social rights through legislation against discrimination.

The underlying assumption implicit in this early approach was that immigrants would be assimilated into existing British society – as earlier immigrants had largely been. The policy was rarely expressed in such extreme terms as those used by the Royal Commission on Population in 1949 when it declared that migrants could only be welcomed 'without reserve' if they were 'not prevented by their religion from intermarrying with the host population and becoming merged in it', but throughout this period the policy approach was that the newcomers would eventually simply be absorbed into British society (HMSO, 1949). This was the emphasis, for example, in the terms of reference of the Commonwealth Immigrants Advisory Council set up in 1962 'to assist immigrants to adapt themselves to British habits and customs'.

Immigration control

The 1960s saw a change of emphasis. Against a background of mounting evidence of racial discrimination in society, successive governments were drawn into a more interventionist role and embarked on what developed into the twin – and contradictory – major political responses to a multi-racial Britain. These policies were immigration control and anti-discrimination legislation. Under the 1948 Nationality Act immigrants from the Commonwealth were accorded full citizenship rights, but these were subsequently steadily eroded. The Immigration Acts of 1962, 1968 and 1971, based on colour consciousness, successively and disproportionately limited black immigration. In 1981 a new Nationality Act became law which created a hierarchy of citizenship which discriminated against those from the 'New Commonwealth'. The spirit and effect of these measures was in direct contradiction to the principle of 'racial equality' concurrently being propounded. The then leader of the I.L.E.A., Davis, commenting on the 1981 Nationality Act, told the Home Secretary that

> Not only will it affect the particular children involved but it will make it more difficult to develop in our education service the understanding necessary to provide an education which has the confidence of the people of Inner London. (Davis, 1981)

The context created by the Immigration and Nationality Acts inevitably weakened the positive element in the government's strategy – the Race Relations Acts of 1965, 1968 and 1976 which introduced increasingly strengthened legislation against racial discrimination. These departures from the studied inaction of the 1950s were accompanied by a redefinition of aims. In 1966 the then Home Secretary, Roy Jenkins, declared that the objective was 'integration' which he defined as 'not a flattening process of assimilation but as equal opportunity accompanied by cultural diversity in an atmosphere of mutual tolerance'. It is this broad – and vague – definition of a 'multicultural society' which has since been reiterated.

Racial discrimination

A mounting body of evidence has detailed the extent to which the 'equal opportunity' called for by the Home Secretary in 1966 – the necessary prerequisite for positive response to cultural diversity – is negated by the persistent and damaging effects of racism. The most comprehensive picture of the way this operates in Britain is contained in the findings of a research project carried out by Political and Economic Planning between 1972 and 1975 (Smith, 1977). This study demonstrated beyond argument the existence of discrimination by race in many areas of life, especially employment and housing. Blacks were found to be more vulnerable to unemployment than whites; they were concentrated within lower job levels in a way which could not be explained by lower academic or job qualifications, and within broad categories of jobs they had lower earnings than whites, particularly at the higher end of the job scale. An analysis of the patterns of employment suggested that discrimination was an important factor in the disadvantaged employment position of blacks, and case studies confirmed this. In controlled experiments of job applications for white-collar jobs, for example, Asian and West Indian applicants faced discrimination in 30 per cent of cases and in applications for unskilled jobs in 46 per cent of cases.

Comparable patterns of discrimination were shown to operate in housing. Owner occupation, while high for ethnic minorities, had none of the connotations of wealth which it had for the white population. The property involved was of low quality and unlikely to constitute a means of transferring wealth between generations. All the measures of housing quality used in the survey showed ethnic minorities to be much worse housed than whites. Black private tenants were paying much higher rents than white tenants, and ethnic minorities were found to be under-represented in council housing as a whole while startlingly over-represented in the lowest-quality housing. In another study, Rutter and Madge carried out an extensive review of the literature on deprivation generally and concluded that much of the future of ethnic minorities depended on the extent to which they were placed in a disadvantaged position through discriminatory practices; 'Although there are specific issues which arise from immigration and from differences in cultural background, to a large extent the "colour problem" is the problem of white racism' (Rutter and Madge, 1976).

Racial attacks

In an extreme form racial prejudice is also manifest in direct racial attacks. Racial violence against black people is little documented and receives little coverage in the national or local media. But it is much more extensive than is commonly realized. One official source – a 1981 Home Office Report on Racial Attacks – showed that the rate of racial victimization 'for Asians [was] 50 times that for white people and the rate for blacks [West Indians] was over 36 times that for white people' (HMSO, 1981a). Moreover, the study found that many incidents of racial attacks were not reported to the police and that 'the results presented represent only a proportion – probably a small proportion – of the number that take place'. The report acknowledged that 'the problem has deteriorated significantly within the space of the last year'. The level of attacks appeared to be on the increase. The Home Office study – hardly a document to dramatize the seriousness of the situation – reported that 'In some places there was a sense of uncomplaining acceptance among some Asians to manifestations of racial violence; the problem was thought to be so widespread that they regarded it as little more than an unwelcome feature of contemporary British life.' The report also found evidence that 'racialist activity in schools is increasing'.

Race relations legislation

When looked at in terms of the documented extent and effect of racism, government incursions into race relations legislation appear belated, hesitant and largely ineffectual. Initial approaches were marked by extreme caution. The first piece of legislation, the 1965 Race Relations Act, was limited in scope and the Race Relations Board set up under it operated conciliation procedures which were cumbersome and ineffective. In 1968 a second Act extended the grounds on which complaints of discrimination could be referred to the Race Relations Board and set up a new promotional agency, the Community Relations Commission, to encourage 'harmonious community relations'. The emphasis remained firmly on caution, conciliation and persuasion. The motivating concern of both Acts was the avoidance of racial strife rather than the provision of effective legal redress for citizens suffering from discrimination.

By the mid-1970s official policy conceded that racism was more widespread and intractable than had previously been acknowledged. A government White Paper published in 1975, after a year-long review of race relations, concluded that experience was showing that

. . . early optimism may not be justified, that the problems with which we have to deal if we are to see genuine equality of opportunity for the coloured youngsters born and educated in this country may be larger in scale and more complex than had been initially supposed. (HMSO, 1975)

The result was fresh legislation. The 1976 Race Relations Act adopted a new approach. This time an attempt was made to deal with discrimination not only in terms of intentional individual acts – direct injuries done by one person against another – but also with discriminatory effects. A widened definition of discrimination – treating another person less favourably because of colour, race, ethnic or national origins – was now allied to the concept of 'indirect' discrimination – the application of conditions that cannot be justified on non-racial grounds but which affect unequally particular groups. The new agency set up under the Act, the Commission for Racial Equality, was given new powers of investigation and was empowered to call for documents and witnesses and to issue non-discrimination notices.

But despite its new powers, the Commission for Racial Equality, like its predecessors, has made limited impact. It has found the mounting of formal investigations expensive and slow, and has tended to become bogged down in casework. The Commission's first chairman, David Lane (a former Conservative MP and Home Office Minister) argued that the law needed to be strengthened if the Commission was to be effective. But this has not happened. In 1982, Lane warned that 'all recent research has shown the persistence of racial discrimination on a serious scale' and that continuing economic recession could only make things worse (Lane, 1982). In one such piece of research Little and Robbins, in a study of transmitted deprivation, found that not only were ethnic minorities disproportionately experiencing 'the worst that our society has to offer' but that 'this is continuing through to second and subsequent generations with consequences for society as a whole which are no longer potentially serious but actually' so (Little and Robbins, 1982).

Social policy

Government has accepted – in theory – that an attack on the causes of discrimination needs to be accompanied by action to counter its deep-rooted effects. The 1975 White Paper which preceded the 1976 Race Relations Act recognized that use of the law against racial discrimination, on which government had largely relied for the previous decade, would have limited results if unaccompanied by a concerted social policy response. The White Paper argued for a 'fuller strategy'; 'a more comprehensive structure' was necessary to combat 'a cumulative cycle of disadvantage' exacerbated by racial discrimination whereby 'an entire group of people are launched on a vicious downward spiral of deprivation' (HMSO, 1975). But this theoretical analysis has not been given practical effect. When, in the summer of 1981, disturbances on the streets of Bristol, Brixton in London and Toxteth in Liverpool gave more ominous warning of the effects of continued neglect, the official inquiry conducted by Lord Scarman came to conclusions which echoed those of the Government White Paper six years earlier. 'Racial disadvantage is a fact of current British life [. . .] urgent action is needed if it is not to become an endemic, ineradicable disease threatening the very survival of our society' (Scarman, 1981). Some 30 years after the first substantial migration from the West Indies effective policies for Britain's multiracial society still remain, in the 1975 White Paper's phrase, to be 'worked out'.

EDUCATION POLICIES

The development of education policy has in many ways reflected the pattern of overall government race relations policy. The D.E.S. has consistently been reluctant to take a strong lead and has tended to react to developments, often belatedly and largely ineffectually, rather than initiate positive policies. This has led to a wide variety of uneven responses by local education authorities (L.E.A.s). The consequence of lack of central leadership and guidance has not simply been action or inaction at local level. Some of the developments which have taken place, particularly those which have been preoccupied with exotic aspects of cultural difference and have ignored the effects of racism, are now argued to have had unintended negative consequences.

Early responses: the 'problem of' immigrants

Early educational responses were dominated by a largely *ad hoc* approach to the 'problems' created by the presence of minority ethnic group pupils. The educational task was seen by the D.E.S. as the 'successful assimilation of immigrant children' (D.E.S. 1963). It was hoped that this could be accomplished with minimum disruption to the school system. By 1965 the Department was worried that 'As the proportion of immigrant children increases, the problems will become more difficult to solve, and the chances of assimilation more remote' (D.E.S., 1975). The answer was to recommend to L.E.A.s that they disperse immigrant pupils, although in the event most authorities chose to ignore this advice. At a time of increasing consciousness of negative racial attitudes among the white majority – this was the year in which the first Race Relations Act was introduced – the Department was looking over its shoulder at the response of white parents and the spectre of the 'white backlash'.

A sentence printed in italics in the 1965 D.E.S. Circular was symptomatic of early attitudes; it warned

> It will be helpful if the parents of non-immigrant children can see that practical measures have been taken to deal with the problems in the schools, and that the progress of their own children is not being restricted by the undue preoccupation of the teaching staff with the linguistic and other difficulties of the immigrant children.

Immigrants *per se* were being identified as constituting a problem. This has been a recurrent feature of much discussion of education and race; there is a common tendency to allow what Green has described as 'that critical slippage from "the problems encountered by" to the "problem of" ' (Green, 1982).

Lack of central leadership

During the 1960s, working within a broadly assimilationist policy frame, the emphasis was on helping minority ethnic group children to adapt to British schools. In practice, this was largely confined to teaching English as a second language. The D.E.S. offered spasmodic advice and, from 1965, some measure of extra funding was available for multiracial schools. But the methods adopted for administering these resources did not enable the D.E.S. either to initiate action at local level or to monitor response. Two reports in the early 1970s drew attention to the consequences. A research study showed that appropriate L.E.A. provision was patchy and uneven (Townsend, 1971; Townsend and Brittan, 1972) and a Parliamentary Select Committee Report criticized the D.E.S. for not developing a concerted strategy and providing adequate resources to fund it (HMSO, 1973). One of the Select Committee's recommendations was that a special fund should be set up and that a condition for using it should be that authorities make full reports to central government on provision and strategies in their areas. But the D.E.S. was – and has largely remained – reluctant to adopt a positive interventionist role of this kind. The proposal was rejected on the grounds that it might 'reduce the scope of local responsibility' (HMSO, 1974). When a second large-scale survey of L.E.A. provision was carried out in 1980, it found that the wide variations both in the scale and quality of services, reported 10 years earlier, still largely persisted (Little and Willey, 1981; 1983). In part, this reflects varying local situations and differing priorities within a decentralized education system. But primarily it is a result of the 'benign neglect' with which the D.E.S. has left the complexities of responding to ethnic diversity to be confronted at local level. It is partly because of this that when 'multicultural' objectives were adopted they made little impact on educational practice.

'Multicultural' objectives

During the 1970s pluralist objectives replaced policies of assimilation within a number of national education systems. In Britain the D.E.S. began referring to 'this country's multicultural society' and argued that this should be reflected in teaching in all schools. By the time the 'great debate' on the curriculum got under way at the end of the decade this view had assumed a central place in D.E.S. publications. For example, the Department's important 1981 paper on *The School Curriculum* – the result of 'several years of public discussion and Government consultation with its education partners' – was categoric about the extent to which teaching in all schools should reflect the changed ethnic composition of society:

> What is taught in schools, and the way it is taught, must appropriately reflect fundamental values in our society [. . .] the work of schools has to reflect many issues with which pupils will have to come to terms as they mature, and schools and teachers are familiar with them. First, our society has become multi-cultural; and there is now among pupils and parents a greater diversity of personal values. (D.E.S. 1981)

Closely comparable radical changes in direction at the level of theoretical policy took place in Australia and Canada. In Australia in 1966 the Minister of Immigration was explicit that the then prevailing aim was assimilation: 'We must have a single culture [. . .] we should have a mono-culture, with everyone living in the same way, uderstanding each other, and sharing the same aspirations' (Cigler, 1975). But four years later, his successor announced a change in policy. He stated that 'The earlier desire to make stereotype Australians of the newcomers has been cast aside' (Lynch, 1972). In 1975 the Australian Schools Commission was spelling out the educational implications; it urged that where groups 'have a distinctive culture of their own, as do ethnic minorities, it should be sustained and other groups encouraged to recognize its authenticity' (Australian Schools Commission, 1975). In 1981 when the Curriculum Development Centre in Canberra published its *Core Curriculum for Australian Schools*, pluralist aims had assumed a central place in directly the same way in which they had in Britain (Curriculum Development Centre, 1980). 'The multi-cultural composition and interest of our population' appeared as one of a number of changes in Australian society which, it was argued, all schools must respond to. Among the list of 'fundamental learning for all students' were included:

> Focus on general, universal elements in culture for present and future life, i.e. the common culture; acknowledge the plural, multi-cultural nature of our

society and seek a form of cultural-social integration which values interaction and free communication amongst diverse groups and subgroups, i.e. the common multi-culture.

In Canada up until the end of the 1960s 'Anglo-conformity' had been based on 'the desirability of sustaining British institutions and norms as the established basis for building Canadian society' (Palmer and Tropper, 1983). But in 1971 the Prime Minister announced a new departure into 'multicultural' policies predicated on 'assuring the cultural freedom of all Canadians'. In 1972 a Minister of State responsible for Multiculturalism was appointed, and a special Directorate was established to increase among 'society at large [. . .] awareness and appreciation of the bi-lingual and multicultural nature of our country'. By 1976 the Toronto Board of Education was declaring that 'If we are to appreciate differences and commonalities multi-cultural education must be a basis for our school system and must be directed to all students and teachers' (Toronto Board of Education, 1976).

The implications for teachers

The implications for teachers of these changes in policy assumptions are very considerable. Over a relatively short period response to ethnic diversity has ceased to be seen as the responsibility of a small number of English as a second language (E2L) specialists who would prepare children for life in mainstream schools, and has become something which – so official policy now argues – has consequences for all teachers in all schools. In 1979, Bolton, at the time a senior H.M. Inspector with responsibilities in this field, was arguing in relation to Britain that the two issues of the nature of educational provision in multiracial schools and the nature of provision for all pupils in a pluralist society were not only 'inter-related but inter-dependent' (Bolton, 1979).

If these newly promulgated objectives for all schools were to make serious impact, specific and concerted action would be necessary to bring about change – to counteract what Casso has characterized in relation to the U.S.A., for example, as 'a 200-year old history of a monolingual, monocultural and ethnocentric thrust in the public schools' (Casso, 1976). Wide consideration of the issues raised would have to be generated within schools and throughout the education service. There would need to be a significant input into in-service training programmes and into the initial training of new teachers. Detailed work on considering such things as the implications for different areas of the curriculum would have to be initiated. But in practice within the education systems of Britain, Australia, Canada and the U.S.A. such developments have either been on a limited and ineffective scale or have been non-existent. Broad policy objectives have been propounded but implementation has largely been left to vague exhortation not systematic action to secure educational change.

Neglect of racism

Above all, 'multicultural' policies have uniformly failed to address the central influence of racism. The context in which teachers are being asked to develop pluralist approaches is one in which, as has been shown earlier in this chapter, the effect of racism is well documented. The deeply damaging consequences for society have been acknowledged. The British government's 1975 White Paper, referred to earlier, accepted that 'It is the Government's duty to prevent morally unacceptable and socially divisive inequalities from hardening into entrenched patterns' and went on

> It is inconceivable that Britain in the last quarter of the Twentieth Century should confess herself unable to secure for a small minority of around a million and a half coloured citizens their full and equal rights as individual men and women (HMSO, 1975).

But the everyday experience of teachers – and of both their black and white pupils – is that the 'inconceivable' is continuing to happen. Racism is an inescapable element in the life of the societies now developing pluralist objectives. At school level, teachers are well aware of this and are increasingly arguing that response to prejudice has to be made explicit in formal school policies, in dealing with overt racialist behaviour, in the curriculum, in teaching materials, in forms of school organization, in self-examination by teachers of their own attitudes.

A gap between policy and practice

The failure of 'multicultural' objectives to combat racism and the failure to adopt serious strategies to bring about educational change have resulted in a wide gap between official theory and educational practice. This is apparent at two levels. In predominantly all-white schools, pluralist aims have made virtually no impact at all. In multiracial schools developments have often been preoccupied with cultural differences; approaches have generally remained marginal to the major concerns of the curriculum and pupils' awareness of the realities of black–white relations in society has been little affected.

In Britain a survey in 1980 of all L.E.A.s and of 300 secondary schools with few or no pupils from minority ethnic groups (under 2.5 per cent) found that official assertions about a 'multicultural' society having relevance to all schools had made minimal impact (Little and Willey, 1981). Most authorities with few minority ethnic group pupils commented that 'multicultural education' was not a matter which concerned them, and that it would in any case have very low priority as against more pressing calls on their time and energies. These authorities considered that if there was a need to take action they would hear about it from the schools, but that to take any kind of positive initiative themselves would only be divisive and would generate hostility. The great majority of head teachers expressed similar views. Typical written comments from head teachers in reply to a questionnaire were:

Presumably minority ethnic groups are here because they wish to be – why should it then be incumbent upon the indigenous population to change?

In my opinion far too much time, energy and money is devoted to a very small minority in this country [. . .] regardless of colour or creed anyone who wishes to come and settle should adapt to the British way of life and all that this implies, rather than the other way round.

I believe the emphasis should be on similarities not differences. To draw attention to racial minorities, far from being helpful, only tends to hinder assimilation and make people conscious of 'non-existent' problems.

The same survey found that although significant initiatives had been taken in some multiracial L.E.A.s, in practice overall provision continued to be over-whelmingly preoccupied with meeting the basic language needs of E2L learners. Important innovations had taken place in a minority of multiracial schools, but generally, developments had been limited in scope and remained peripheral to the main concerns of schools. Another survey, of in-service provision, concluded that there was

[. . .] no doubt about the fragmentary and incomplete provision of in-service teacher education for a multi-cultural society. Indeed, it is non-existent in many areas and in none is it wholly adequate' (Eggleston, Dunn and Purewall, 1981).

A number of other reports and surveys in the early 1980s reached similar conclusions, notably a report from the Parliamentary Home Affairs Committee on *Racial Disadvantage* (HMSO 1981b). In 1980 the D.E.S. appointed a special Committee of Inquiry into the Education of Children from Ethnic Minority Groups which published an Interim Report (the Rampton Report: Rampton, 1981). The Committee argued that urgent and wide-ranging initiatives were needed if schools were to respond effectively to West Indian pupils.

A similar situation prevails in other countries. In Canada a number of studies have documented a 'disheartening gap between the policies [. . .] and the realities' (Deosaran, 1977; Ghosh, 1978; Samuda, 1980). The Multicultural Directorate has made little impact on education; as Bhatnagar and Hamalian summarize the position 'there seems little doubt that the concept of multi-culturalism has neither affected educational policy making at the school level nor the educational practice of a very large body of teachers' (Bhatnagar and Hamalian, 1981). A survey of schools in Ontario found that 'in classroom after classroom' minority ethnic groups were 'being subjected [. . .] to continued programmes of Canadianization based on the concept of and belief in assimilation' (McLeod, 1985). In Australia, the position is much the same; for example, an Australian Department of Education report on schools of 'high migrant density' in New South Wales and Victoria found that 'most of the schools continued to function in a "narrow" assimilationist mould' (Australian Schools Commission, 1975). In the USA a branch was set up within the Federal Office of Education nominally to implement the Title IX legislation referred to in the Introduction, but its funding allocation ($2.3 million in 1978) and its effect have been minimal. When practical response was required to the 150 000 Vietnamese who entered America in 1975, Kelly has shown that a strongly assimilationist approach was adopted which made no concessions to pluralist ideology (Kelly, 1981).

Criticisms of 'multicultural' approaches

The failure of educational policy makers to address the realities of racism has led some educationalists – many of them black – to question the relevance and validity of 'multicultural' objectives altogether. These writers argue that pre-occupation with cultural difference deflects from the real issues affecting the education of black children. Official policies are seen at best as largely irrelevant and ineffectual, and at worst as positively harmful or primarily about social control.

Carby, for example, suggests that

> The paradigm of multi-culturalism actually excludes the concept of dominant and subordinate cultures – either indigenous or migrant – and fails to recognise that the existence of racism relates to the possession and exercise of politico-economic control and authority and also to forms of resistance to the power of dominant social groups. (Carby, 1980)

For Mullard multiculturalism 'is none other than a more sophisticated form of social control and it has the effect of containing black resistance' (Mullard, 1981). Dhondy argues a similar thesis: the development of 'multicultural' objectives by the educational establishment has been a conscious strategy to contain the challenge presented by disaffected black youth (Dhondy, 1978). Verma and Bagley argue that many black pupils who react against the system do so because of the effects of racism:

> The rebellion of black students in British schools is sometimes classed in pathological terms, as behaviour disorders. We believe, however, that this reaction to the alienating forces of the school may often, perhaps very often, be a form of rebellion by black students attempting to establish a meaningful form of identity based on a resistance to the alienating forces in school and society. (Verma and Bagley, 1979).

Stone has mounted a powerful critique of multicultural approaches from a somewhat different standpoint. She charges the education system with failing to educate black pupils. The introduction of 'multicultural' elements into the teaching of black children is an irrelevance based on the erroneous view that black children have a poor self image, and it deflects from the need to teach normal basic skills effectively. The prevailing reality of 'multicultural' education – based mainly on steel bands, participation in sport and Black Studies – thus adversely affects the education of black children, it is 'a misguided liberal strategy to compensate black children for not being white' (Stone, 1981).

Similar criticisms have been advanced in other countries. In America there was heated debate in the 1960s over the introduction of approaches such as Black Studies, Chicano Studies and Judaic Studies. Reaction against these developments was expressed in very similar terms to those advanced by Stone in Britain, as the title of a 1969 article in the *New York Times* by a black educator indicates: 'The Road to the Top is through Higher Education – not Black Studies' (Lewis, 1969). The argument was that good teaching of basic skills was needed, not the romanticizing of 'quaint cultural heritages with little value to the labour market' (Killian, 1983). In Canada, Davis has argued – in terms similar to those applied by Mullard to the UK – that official multicultural policies are 'a means of "containing" the demands of ethnic minorities without envisaging basic changes in the power structure of Canadian society' (Davis, 1975). As Wilson sees it:

> The Canadian multiculturalism policy seems to guarantee that we can each do our little dances and flash our pretty, lacy petticoats while we drink our ethnic drinks and admire each other's handicrafts [. . .] it does not speak to the injustice that pervades our daily lives if our hair or skin colour is unlike that of the members at the top of the column (Wilson, 1978).

Defining pluralist aims in schools

These brief extracts from some of the main contributors to the debate give an indication of the powerful critique which has been mounted against official 'multicultural' approaches. The arguments are particularly persuasive because the failure to develop strategies for applying pluralist aims to classroom practice has meant that, whatever the theoretical policies, change in schools has been minimal. But as Green has pointed out in relation to Britain, in an important rejoinder to some of the writers quoted above:

> ... multi-cultural education barely yet exists in our schools [. . .] rather than talk about multi-cultural education as an accomplished fact, we should think in terms of an agenda of reforms which have been collectively called multi-culturalism and a struggle which is being waged on the grounds marked out by this agenda. (Green, 1982)

It is in classrooms that the real issues and complexities of responding positively to ethnic diversity in society are emerging and are being confronted constructively. It is the staff of multiracial schools who – often collectively – are defining and beginning to implement pluralist developments in education. In these schools what Green calls 'an interventionist approach' is being adopted, the key to which is not simply passively reflecting diversity, but engaging positively and decisively with racism.

New approaches

In Britain the weakness of previous 'multicultural' approaches has led to the development of new policy perspectives which emphasize equality. These policies have resulted from closely related initiatives in two L.E.A.s, Berkshire and the I.L.E.A. The hitherto adopted perspective 'emphasizing mainly Cultural Diversity' is criticized on five main grounds (I.L.E.A., 1983):

(1) Its almost exclusive emphasis on aspects of culture and cultural differences tends to obscure or ignore other issues: the economic position of black people in relation to white people; differences in access to resources and in power to affect events; discrimination in employment, housing, and education; relations with the police.

(2) It conceives of racism as merely a set of mental prejudices held by a smallish number of unenlightened white people, and hence ignores or denies the structural aspects of racism, both in the education system and in society.

(3) It reflects a white view of black cultures as homogeneous, static, conflict-free, exotic. It ignores the power relations between white and black people, both in history and in the present.

(4) It ignores the issue which black people themselves consider to be of vital importance – that is, the issue of racism and the promotion of racial equality.

(5) Although it recognizes the right of people to maintain their own cultures, in practice this is limited to support for marginal activities, which do not impinge on mainstream social policies and programmes.

For these reasons it is argued that a perspective emphasizing diversity and pluralism must be included in a context which addresses issues of racism and its effects on both black and white people. This new policy approach continues to stress the importance of positive responses to cultural and linguistic diversity. But a significantly different approach is applied. The focus is on equality, and also on racism. As Sivanandan argues, the central concern must be with

. . . anti-racist education (which by its very nature would include the study of other cultures). Just to learn about other people's cultures, though, is not to learn about the racism of one's own. To learn about the racism of one's own culture on the other hand, is to approach other cultures objectively. (Sivanandan, 1982)

The policy statement adopted by Berkshire L.E.A. (1983) clearly demonstrates the important departure from the vague concerns of the official 'multicultural' objectives discussed earlier in this chapter. The authority's policy requires and supports all its educational institutions and services to create, maintain and promote racial equality and justice.

The Council is opposed to racism in all its forms. It wishes therefore:

(1) To promote understanding of the principles and practices of racial equality and justice, and commitment to them.

(2) To identify and remove all practices, procedures and customs which discriminate against ethnic minority people and to replace them with procedures which are fair to all.

(3) To encourage ethnic minority parents and communities to be fully involved in the decision-making processes which affect the education of their children.

(4) To increase the influence of ethnic minority parents, organizations and communities by supporting educational and cultural projects which they themselves initiate.

(5) To encourage the recruitment of ethnic minority teachers,

administrators and other staff at all levels, and the appointment of ethnic minority governors.

(6) To monitor and evaluate the implementation of (L.E.A.) policies, and to make changes and corrections as appropriate.

SUMMARY

This chapter has argued that the pervasive effects of racism are deeply entrenched in society. The consequences have been acknowledged in official rhetoric, but not in terms of an effective policy response. In education there has been a radical shift in theoretical objectives from assimilation to pluralism. A major consequence is that responding to ethnic diversity is a concern of all teachers, regardless of the particular ethnic composition of the school in which they work. But strategies have not been developed to implement the new objectives and a gap has opened up between policy and practice. Most importantly, the theoretical 'multicultural' objectives have failed to address the central question of racism. Schools cannot respond to ethnic and cultural diversity without confronting the realities of prejudice and discrimination. This has led to the development of new policy approaches which emphasize equality and justice.

REFERENCES

Australian Schools Commission (1975) *Report of the Inquiry into Schools of High Migrant Density*, Australian Department of Education, Canberra

Berkshire Local Education Authority (1983) 'Education for racial equality: policy paper 1', Education Department, Reading

Bhatnagar, J.K. and Hamalian, A. (1981) Minority group children in Canada, in J. Megarry (ed.) *World Yearbook of Education: Education of Minorities*, Kogan Page, London

Bolton, E. (1979) Education in a multi-racial society, *Trends in Education*, Vol. 4

Carby, H. (1980) Multiculture, *Screen Education*, Vol. 34, Spring

Casso, H.J. (1976) *Bilingual/Bicultural Education and Teacher Training*, National Educational Association, Washington, D.C.

Cigler, M. (1975) History and multicultural education, *Australian Historical Association Bulletin*, Vol. 4

Curriculum Development Centre (1980) *Core Curriculum for Australian Schools*, Canberra, C.D.C.

Davis, A.K. (1975) 'The politics of multiculturalism and Third World communities in Canada: a dialectic view'. Paper presented to the Conference on Multiculturalism and Third World Immigrants', September 1975, Edmonton

Davis, B. (1981) Letter to the Home Secretary, 31 July 1981, quoted in Nationality, children under threat, *Issues in Race and Education*, 1981

Deosaran, R.A. (1977) Educational aspirations: individual freedom or social justice, *Interchange*, Vol. 8

Department of Education and Science (1963) *English for Immigrants*, Pamphlet No. 43, HMSO, London
Department of Education and Science (1975) *The Education of Immigrants*, Circular 7/65, HMSO, London
Department of Education and Science (1981) *The School Curriculum*, HMSO, London
Dhondy, F. (1978) The black explosion in schools, *Race Today*, May
Eggleston, J., Dunn, D. and Purewall, A. (1981) *In-Service Education in a Multi-racial Society: A Report of a Research Project*, University of Keele, Keele
Ghosh, R. (1978) Ethnic minorities in the school curriculum, *Multiculturalism*, Vol. 2
Green, A. (1982) In defence of anti-racist teaching, *Mutliracial Education*, 10 (2) Spring
HMSO (1949) *Report* (Royal Commission on Population), Cmnd 7695, HMSO, London
HMSO (1973) *Education* (Parliamentary Select Committee on Race Relations and Immigration), HMSO, London
HMSO (1974) *Educational Disadvantage and the Educational Needs of Immigrants*, Cmnd 5720, HMSO, London
HMSO (1975) *Racial Discrimination* (White Paper), Cmnd 6234, HMSO, London
HMSO (1981a) *Racial Attacks* (Report of a Home Office Study), HMSO, London
HMSO (1981b) *Racial Disadvantage* (Parliamentary Home Affairs Committee), HMSO, London
I.L.E.A. (1983) *Race, Sex and Class. 2. Multi-ethnic Education in Schools*, I.L.E.A., London
Kelly, G.P. (1981) *Contemporary American policies and practices in the education of immigrant children* in J.K. Bhatnagar (ed.) Educating Immigrants, Croom Helm, London
Killian, L.M. (1983) How much can be expected of multi-cultural education? *New Community*, X (No. 3), Spring
Lane, D. (1982) Chairman's valedictory, *New Community*, X, (No. 1) Summer
Lewis, W.A. (1969) The road to the top is through higher education – not Black Studies, *New York Times Magazine*, 11 May
Little, A. and Robbins, D. (1982) *Loading The Law: A Study of Transmitted Deprivation, Ethnic Minorities and Affirmative Action*, Commission For Racial Equality, London
Little A. and Willey, R. (1981) *Multi-ethnic Education: The Way Forward*, Schools Council, London
Little A. and Willey, R. (1983) *Studies in the Multi-ethnic Curriculum*, Schools Council, London
Lynch, P. (1972) Australia's immigration policy, in H. Roberts (ed.) *Australia's Immigration Policy*, University of Western Australia Press, Perth
McLeod, K.A. (1985) A short history of the immigration student as 'new Canadian' in, A. Wolfgang (ed.) *Education of Immigrant Students: Issues and Answers*, O.I.S.E., Toronto
Mullard, C. (1981) *Racism, Society, Schools: History, Policy and Practice*, Occasional Paper No. 1, London Centre for Multicultural Education, University of London, Institute of Education, London
Palmer, H. and Tropper, H. (1983) Canadian ethnic studies: historical perspectives and contemporary implications, *Interchange*, Vol. 4
Rampton, A. (1981) *West Indian Children in Our Schools*. Interim Report of the Committee of Inquiry into the Education of Children from Ethnic Minority Groups (The Rampton Report), Cmnd 8273, HMSO, London
Rose, E.J.B. *et al.* (1969) *Colour and Citizenship*, Oxford University Press, London
Rutter, M. and Madge, N. (1976) *Cycles of Disadvantage*, Heinemann, London

Samuda, R.J. (1980) 'How are the schools of Ontario coping with a new Canadian population?' A report of recent research findings, *TESL Talk* II

Scarman, Lord (1981) *The Brixton Disorders*, 10–12 April 1981, Cmnd 8427, HMSO, London

Sivanandan, A. (1982) *Roots of Racism*, Institute of Race Relations, London

Smith, D.J. (1977) *Racial Disadvantage in Britain*, Penguin Books, Harmondsworth

Stone, M. (1981) *The Education of The Black Child in Britain: The Myth of Multiracial Education*, Fontana, London

Toronto Board of Education (1976) *The First Report of the Working Group on Multicultural Programs*, Toronto Board of Education, Toronto

Townsend, H.E.R. (1971) *Immigrant Pupils in England: The L.E.A. Response*, N.F.E.R., Windsor

Townsend, H.E.R. and Brittan, E. (1982) *Organisation in Multiracial Schools*, N.F.E.R. Windsor

Verma, G.K. and Bagley, C. (1979) *Race, Education and Identity*, Macmillan, London

Wilson, J. (1978) Come, let us reason together, in V. D'Oyley (ed.) *Black Presence in Multi-Ethnic Canada*. Vancouver Centre for the Study of Curriculum and Instruction, Faculty of Education, University of British Columbia, O.I.S.E. Toronto

TOPICS FOR DISCUSSION

1. Discuss the contention that, 'to a large extent the "colour problem" is the problem of white racism' (p 71).
2. On what evidence was Lord Scarman led to the comment in 1981 that 'racial disadvantage is a fact of current British life [. . .] urgent action is needed if it is not to become an endemic ineradicable disease threatening the very survival of our society' (p 74).
3. In what way has the development of *educational policy* mirrored the pattern of government *race relations policy* during the past 20 or so years (p 74).

SUGGESTIONS FOR FURTHER READING

1. Mullard, C. (1982) The educational management and demanagement of racism, *Education Policy Bulletin*, Vol. 10, No. 1, pp 21–40. The author argues that present policy is based on the principle of 'managing racism' which, whilst ostensibly anti-racist is, in fact, either racist in essence, racist in its consequences, or ineffective in combating racism.
2. Jeffcoate, R. (1984) *Ethnic Minorities in Education*, Harper & Row, London. Chapter 4, 'Positive Discrimination', looks at the *principle of positive discrimination* and evaluates the effectiveness of attempts that have been made so far to redistribute resources in favour of disadvantaged pupils and schools.
3. Stone, M. (1981) *The Education of the Black Child in Britain: The Myth of Multiracial Education*, Fontana, London. This is a powerful critique of multicultural approaches which are seen as irrelevant to the needs of black pupils. Multiculturalism is described as 'a misguided liberal strategy to compensate black children for not being white'.

SOCIAL CONTROL AND STEREOTYPING

INTRODUCTION

Reading 5 by Cashmore and Troyna (1983) argues that it is through the transference of ideas on race that inequalities are perpetuated. In particular, it insists that ideas flow from *underclass* groups themselves so that racial inequalities are often generated and confirmed within groups as well as imposed from the outside. The theme of the reading is supported in the suggestions for further study by a paper from the Centre For Contemporary Cultural Studies (1982) which addresses the racist structures that underpin notions of *culture, nation* and *class*; by a discussion of *racism as ideology* (Tierney, 1982) and a paper by Gabriel and Ben-Tovim (1978) on the concept of racism and its relationship to capitalism and to class.

Reading 6, Carrington's (1983) research into West Indian involvement in school sports teams, argues that pupils' over-representation in sport is, in part, a result of teachers' tendencies to see this ethnic group in stereotypical terms. His thesis is developed in terms of the reproduction of the black worker as 'wage labour at the lower end of employment and skill'. Supporting papers by Braham, Dearn and Rhodes (1982) and by Tomlinson (1981) in the suggestions for further reading explore discrimination in the labour market and in the assessment of procedures used to judge educational subnormality.

Reading 7 (Pilkingon 1984) expands the discussion of Reading 5 by exploring the responses of three key groups or agencies, the government, the mass media and the ethnic minorities themselves to race relations situations in contemporary Britain. Suggestions for further reading by Tierney (1982), Watson (1977) and the Open University E354 Unit 10 (1982) respectively, discuss D.E.S./L.E.A. responses to racism, the reactions of ethnic minorities to their experiences in Britain, and B. Parekh's account of the views of racial minorities on life and work in the UK.

Reading 5
RACE, POWER, PREJUDICE
E.E. Cashmore and B. Troyna[1]*

What is race? Something natural?
Are race and inequality inseparable?
Is race connected with power and domination?
What are the causes of racial prejudice?
How is race related to ideology?

THAT REMARKABLE URGE

A distinctive feature of human beings, as compared to animals, is the ability to act purposefully and intentionally. We behave not instinctively or as if subjected to governing forces, but with a consciousness of what we are doing. We are, for the most part, rational, often calculating and frequently goal-directed and we guide the way we act towards specific objectives. To have such objectives we need knowledge about them and how they might be achieved; we can then act on the basis of such knowledge.

A strange way to begin a study of race relations? Not really, for it is the human capacity to draw on knowledge and act out intended courses of behaviour which makes such things as race relations possible. People relate to each other in terms of the knowledge they have of each other. They are not drawn together or thrust apart by innate drives or external powers – though, in some situations, it might appear to be the case. People organize their social arrangements in terms of what they think, so there is always a very close connection between what goes on inside their heads and what they actually do in their everyday lives. The connection is an ill-defined one, but ideas and actions are inseparable.

Of course, the ideas which comprise the stock of knowledge available to use are not uninfluenced by the societies in which we live. As we will argue, no knowledge is ever neutral: it is always, in some way, affected by the social contexts. What we think has to be seen as relative to our environment. It is for this

---

[1] In Cashmore, E.E. and Troyna, B. (1983) *Introduction to Race Relations*, Routledge and Kegan Paul, London, pp 15–41
* See Note on terminology at end of reading

reason that race relations has to be seen not simply as the way in which people act towards each other. This is merely one dimension of study and, important as it is, it tells us little of the compulsions behind the actions. Race relations also involves how people think about each other, the ideas they hold about one another. It's for this reason that we accept Banton's view that to understand the nature of race relations we 'should approach it from the standpoint of the growth of knowledge' (Banton, 1977). As our knowledge of others develops, we become aware of possibilities for action. Maybe that action is to restrict contacts, maybe it is to intensify them. There is, of course, an endless array of possibilities, and race relations study is about analyzing them. But it must also find out what it is in people's heads that makes them organize social relationships in certain patterns.

There is nothing natural or inevitable about blacks in the UK and USA of the 1980s living in tight constellations in the inner cities – places commonly called ghettos. Nor is there anything natural about the high number of South Asians in manual work. For that matter, we can look at any conceivable aspect of race relations, historical or modern, whether it's slavery, rioting or underachieving at school, and argue that each deserves investigation as patterns of action – and, therefore, the results of ideas. A sociobiologist might say something like racial hostility or prejudice is 'bound to happen [. . .] human nature', But we feel that this fogs the issue. Dismissing social events as natural outcomes is ultimately obscuring and only inhibits understanding of the frequently complex processes underlying race relations.

Yet, it cannot be denied that resorting to vague theories of human nature or innate propensities to action is a beautifully convenient and, under some circumstances, plausible way of explaining what might otherwise be mysterious events. Take, the concept of race itself: it seems to contain some element of a biological reality quite separate from social relations. To talk in terms of a race implies that the world's human population is divisible into discrete portions distinguished by biological properties. We still hear, for instance, about having our race's 'blood in our veins'. Qualities like skin pigmentation are commonly thought to reflect inner characteristics. In this way, skin colour divides humanity: people fight, abuse or just despise each other simply because of skin colour. But, while the belief in the reality of race can be seen as responsible for prompting the antagonisms, it can also be invoked as an explanation of them: 'It's only natural.'

Yet, on closer examination, we can see there is far from universal agreement on exactly what race means. The concept is notoriously fragile when subjected to biological analysis, but is incredibly powerful as a force in history. Or rather, the belief in race has been – and still is – a powerful force. What we will argue is that race is real and it is part of our stock of knowledge. Our justification for this derives from Peter Berger and Thomas Luckmann (1972) who argue:

It will be enough, for our purposes, to define 'reality' as a quality appertaining to phenomena that we recoginze as having a being independent of our own volition (we cannot 'wish them away'), and to define 'knowledge' as the certainty that phenomena are real and that they possess specific characteristics.

For our purposes too, this seems to suit, for, if people recognize that race exists, undesirable as it may be, it cannot be 'wished away', it is real. The consequences it will have in their behaviour towards others will serve to reinforce its reality. If teachers believe that black students are ill-equipped intellectually compared to whites, then they will tend to have depressed expectations of their school performances and so treat them differently to whites.

Race, then, is real and, as we will see, it is real in its consequences. But it has a multifaceted reality and part of its attraction – if we can call it that – is due to its unfathomable ambiguity. Its roots are in what Jacques Barzun (1937) has called: 'that remarkable urge to lump together the attributes of large masses'. It has been defined in a bewildering variety of ways and has given rise to an equally bewildering variety of actions. In some cases, as we will document, the definition followed the action and, was invariably, manipulated to suit the action or even provide a rationalization for it.

It's possible, however, to trace a unity, for underlying all the conceptions of race there is the simple conviction that human beings are separable into types that are permanent and enduring; that there are a limited number of types and these are races fixed by biological characteristics. In itself this conviction is fairly innocuous; it constitutes an attempt to classify human populations in terms of immanent physical features.

We can imagine the classification along a horizontal parameter and think it interesting, if without immediate relevance save for aiding our comprehension of how physiological and, perhaps, psychological differences between individuals and groups occur. It is when the classification turns on its axis that its overtones become more sinister. No longer is it a simple ordering of groups on the basis of racial characteristics: now it takes on a moral complexion with some groups, or races, appearing higher than others in a ranked hierarchy. The vertical dimension introduces pernicious typologies. Races are better or worse, superior or inferior and these flow easily into ideas about dominant and dominated races. A dominating group can easily justify its position along the lines of: 'Well, we're the superior race, so we deserve to be in our dominating position. After all, it's only natural!'

In history, we find this kind of reasoning in the heart and blood of all theories about race. The concept was given life and maintained its being by this specious logic. Its vitality and power derives from inequalities and is a source of inequalities. Race and inequality are, as we shall see, intimately connected – perfect partners. The scientific bases on which the ideas of race rest may be disinterested and detached from the issues of inequality, but there again, race is not simply the preserve of academics. It is when it is in the hands, or, more accurately, heads of 'men-in-the-street' that it takes on its more powerful form. Our first approach to understanding this power, then, has to be historical. We will take Banton's advice and look at race as a growth of knowledge, a knowledge which has early origins.

SOURCES: FROM THE BIBLE TO DARWIN

The protean concept of race has as many uses as it has definitions. Barzun notes a very early interest in physical appearances of various groups taken by the ancient Greeks, including Aristotle and Hippocrates, though: 'In recent times, the first systematic division of mankind into races is that by Bernier in 1684.'

Medieval thinkers, following Aristotle's example, tried to sort out things into their essential generic properties, when stripped of their superficial features. Herbalists classified plants and herbs, mainly for medicinal purposes and one notable botanist, Linnaeus, in 1735, published a system of classifying all living phenomena. As an item of classification, the concept of race was already available; it was regarded at the time as a sort of lowest common denominator of biological forms.

The sources of the concept? Well, it's extraordinarily difficult to locate the origins of what was even then an obscure concept. The idea of separating out men on a biological basis is found in the Bible, particularly in Genesis x where the three sons of Noah are said to form three distinct lines of descent. Significantly, they all had a common ancestor in Noah, a point picked up by St Paul in Acts, xvii: 24–6: 'God [. . .] hath made of one blood all nations of men.' The New English Bible translation of this passage reads: 'He created every race of men of one stock.' The theme would seem to be that there exist several separable types of human beings, though they are ultimately unified at source through their sharing of a single ancestor. This is called monogenesis.

Whatever its origins, race was available and in use as a scientific concept by the eighteenth century when it became the basis of identifying the common descent of sets of people. Obvious physical differences were taken for granted and race was thought to account for how they came to appear so markedly different.

Up to Linnaeus, biblical stories of the earth's history were largely accepted, but the discovery of fossil remains of creatures raised severe doubts about the accuracy of Genesis and the Adam and Eve scenario. There were various attempts to reconcile the new findings with the Old Testament, most revolving around the problem of human divisions. Prior to 1800, the concept of race itself was generally taken to refer to the way physical differences between human groups were the results of the circumstances of their history. So, as the Bible alluded to it, race was more to do with lineage. But then, as Banton points out:

'In the nineteenth century race comes to signify an inherent physical quality. Other peoples are seen as biologically different. Though the definition remained uncertain, people began to assume that mankind was divided into races.' (Banton, 1977).

And it's in this sense of the word that race came to take on the significance it has in the modern world.

What followed the changed conception of race as a physical, fixed category is what Banton calls the 'racializing' process, whereby people began to organize their perceptions of each other in terms of permanent physical differences. It was a very short step from theorizing about the differentness of people to theorizing about inequalities between them: if people were of different races, those races may not all be of equal standing; some might be superior to others. Exemplifying this principle is the work of Joseph Arthur, Comte de Gobineau (1816–82), whose historical interest lay in the question of why once-great societies seemed destined to decay.

The answer, Gobineau thought, might be the fundamental inequality of races. Gobineau floated the idea of a threefold division of humans into white, yellow and black races, each of which possessed specific characteristics, such as whites with leadership, and blacks with sensuality. 'Civilizations', replete with government and art, result from the mixing of races, but this inevitably led to the dilution of the 'Great Race' and the decadence, or *dégénération*, this brought. Gobineau accepted the prevalent monogenist view that all humans descended from a single pair of ancestors but did not take this to imply that all were equal. On the contrary, some races occupied higher intellectual positions than others.

Gobineau's theories were most influential in the middle 1800s, particularly in Europe where there was widespread debate over the race issue. The counter to Gobineau's view came with Georges Pouchet who stressed the physical and mental diversities of races which he felt all had separate origins – the polygenist viewpoint. The monogenist school maintained that humans had a single origin, but since races were manifestly different, there must have been evolutionary changes. Pouchet and his school believed in prehuman ancestry giving rise independently to several species of man which were more closely related to their ancestors than to each other. In this perspective, races were fundamentally different, unrelated and irredeemably divided even at source.

The publication of Pouchet's theory in 1858 preceded by one year the release of Charles Darwin's *Origin of the Species* and of course, this work was to transform our knowledge of human evolution (though Darwin was rather guarded in his speculations in the first edition). Darwin precipitated the development of new perspectives on race as John R. Baker notes:

If man had originated not by special creation but by evolution, it was perhaps natural to suppose that the human races might represent stages in this process, or the branches of an evolutionary tree. (Baker, 1974).

This meant a complete rethinking of the concept of the finite number of permanent types, all of distinct origins (interbreeding would have no lasting impact as hybrid stocks were eventually sterile). Variations of human forms were seen as only superficial. In contrast to this and the degeneration that it implied through people like Gobineau, Darwin and his followers forwarded a process of natural selection in which the existing diversity of human forms would be reduced to a smaller number of races best suited to the prevailing environment – the survival of the fittest races. Hence, they were confident of a human progress towards an ever-improving series of races.

The principle of evolution offered an open challenge to orthodox Christianity in seeming to offer an explanation of the origins of humans in scientific terms. Adam and Eve stories were relegated to the realms of fairy tales as Darwin proposed a model of the human being as the extension of animal ancestors. In the Darwinian perspective, people were animals, albeit special ones, with a history stretching back to the Cambrian period when fossils were first preserved in rocks. All living creatures belonged to species, or distinguishable generic groups, but, crucially, they were subject to mutations; they were in a constant process of change.

Not surprisingly, after Darwin, the study of man commanded the attentions of many zoologists; humans were animals, so they were fair game for study. The German, Karl Vogt, for example, postulated a process of convergent change: he believed that, if the various races could be traced back to their origins, no single human type could be found. But, over the centuries, humans came to resemble each other in several important respects. Human races were essentially different but converging towards similarity.

Vogt's work was seen as radical in the mid-1800s and his polygenetic conclusions were tantamount to heresy. So were the theories of another German zoologist, Ernst Haeckel who, with Vogt, considered that prevailing human races were unequal in many respects. In particular, Haeckel identified the 'Indogermanic' race as intellectually superior. Small wonder then that his famous work, *The Riddle of the Universe* (1899) became a bestseller as the Nazis grew to prominence. According to Haeckel there was a scale of development with 'woolly haired Negroes' being much closer to their animal origins than the more mentally developed race.

Though it is unclear as to whether Darwin himself would have agreed with Haeckel, we can be sure that his impact in Europe was enormous, perhaps because, as Daniel Gasman argues, the Germans saw Darwin through the distorted lenses of Haeckel (1971). Nevertheless, repercussions of Darwinism were felt in the nineteenth and twentieth centuries principally in two social phenomena: imperialist slavery and Nazism. In these two, we begin to see the practical significance of the race concept. It was not only an idle idea of philosophers or speculators on the nature of humanity that helped us understand convergences and cleavages of groups. Ideas are not spontaneous; they have authors, people who try to sell their theories. And sellers need buyers who can see the practical utility and seek to use the theories as ways of augmenting actions. We do not have to question the motives of the original conceivers to recognize the significance of theories of race. Their rise to power through their adoption by others, however, often smacks less of the imperative to further understanding than the impulse to rule. As Barzun (1937) writes: 'The irony of race-theories is that they arise almost invariably from a desire to mould other's action rather than to explain facts.'

There is a popular though indefensible misconception that ideas about race grew out of the series of contacts between European explorers and the peoples whom they encountered on their voyages to the Americas, Africa and parts of Asia. We've already noted that the concept itself has much older origins than the contact period of the fifteenth and sixteenth centuries. Certainly, its meaning changed and interest in race grew rapidly after this time, but its presence lurked even before.

It is, of course, no coincidence that the growth in currency of race occurred at roughly the same time as the Europeans were widening their colonial nets and enslaving vast proportions of populations. Improvements in transport and communications meant more and more contacts with unfamiliar peoples with different physical appearances, different languages and different cultures. This inspired many to try to make sense of this new-found diversity in human beings. Race was an obvious tool of analysis; but it had other purposes.

Supposing we accept the basic principles of human inequality implicit in Darwinism. We are a country of conquerors; our conquests prove fruitful if we make full use of the materials available in the new lands. We must exploit the natural materials and make full use of the human resources. It makes sense to use our obvious military power to compel the natural populations to obey our commands. They're not compliant so we introduce a strategy: we make them our property and demand total obedience. So much so, in fact, that we lock them in irons, take them wherever we see fit, force them to do any task we desire and punish them severely if they disobey. *Ergo* slavery.

Now this poses a serious dilemma if we accept the fundamental unity and equality of all people, for it seems blatantly wrong for one group to dominate absolutely another and enforce its domination with the utmost cruelty. But a view of the world in which populations divide up naturally into distinct and unequal races is much more accommodating. The argument for slavery can be advanced much more confidently because there is nothing wrong in reducing other races to the status of chattel as long as they're seen as inferior. After all, it was obvious that the conquerors of natives must be, by the mere fact of victory, superior and therefore the better equipped to survive.

This reasoning lay at the base of a branch of Darwinism that applied itself to whole societies and this was an enormous convenience for slavers, as Barzun argues:

> It was good social Darwinism for the white man to call the amoeba, the ape, and the Tasmanian his brother; it was equally good Practical Darwinism to show that the extinction of the Tasmanian by the white colonists of Australia was simply a part of the struggle for life leading to the survival of the favoured races by natural selection. (Barzun, 1937)

The Darwinian sword could cut both ways. It could maintain that all forms of animate life were related so 'all men were brothers.' But it could also be used to support the view that races, having been established by what Darwin vaguely called 'variation,' were struggling for survival and some, the superior ones, were coping better than, and at the cost of, others.

It's easy to understand why many see the concept of racial inequality as little more than a rationalization, a means of intellectually justifying the wholesale exploitation of human beings. It was quite possible and common to entertain a Christian view, yet continue to be a slaver. Darwinism added substance to the view that blacks were not as adequately endowed as whites in the struggle for survival and would probably die out eventually. Slavery assisted a natural process.

Race had great utility in this role and served its masters well in maintaining a semblance of morality in their gross endeavours. But it is certainly not just a rationalization: although it facilitated slavery and even encouraged it in some respects, it did predate it, even if it took on very different meanings in the context of slavery and encouraged pronouncements such as the Lord Chief Justice Mansfield's when summing up the case of the slave ship *Zong* from which slaves were ejected into the sea. Mansfield informed the jury that the drowning of slaves 'was the same as if horses had been thrown overboard'.

Slaver-owners, armed with a theory of inequality and the practical experience of plantations to back it up, could quite credibly argue against those who wanted to abolish slavery that slaves were ignorant and illiterate. They were; but because of the denial of any educational facilities. Slavers ignored this and contended they were so because they belonged to an inferior race and were therefore incapable of learning. Their conduct and apparent lack of awareness was not seen as the result of the horrendous conditions they had to exist under nor the animalistic treatment they were subjected to. Race was much simpler: they had inherent natural differences and no amount of education could remove them. Philip V. Tobias (1972) sums up the slave-owner's approach: 'It is easy to deny a subservient people the benefits of civilization and then to describe them as uncivilized.'

Race as a concept, and the inequality that it entailed, was given a massive boost by slavery, which was thought to prove the existence of natural inequality. In effect, it was itself supported by the belief and, once in motion, gained impetus from the debates about the subject. The concept of race both fed a theoretical justification for slavery and was fed nourishment by the results of slavery. The ideas and the actions had a symbiotic relationship: they supported each other. But it was not only in slavery that race had application.

ALL GREAT CIVILIZATIONS . . .

Darwinism percolated across Europe, seeping through the theoretical filters of people like Haeckel and, more importantly, Houston Stewart Chamberlain, son of a British naval admiral who studied zoology under Vogt in Geneva. He later moved to Dresden where he developed a historical perspective that was to influence world history.

Published in 1899, Chamberlain's work was a gigantic exploration of what he called 'the foundations of the nineteenth century'. He traced them back to the time of the ancient Israelites, locating the critical year as 1200, the beginning of the 'middle ages' when the race of *Germanen* would emerge 'as the founders of an entirely new civilization and an entirely new culture' (quoted in Baker, 1974).

A large part of this work, which was to take on a prophetic status, was to play down the parts played by Jews, Romans and Greeks in the development of European culture. In fact, Baker notes of Chamberlain: 'He deplored the increasing influence of Jews in the government, law, science, commerce, literature, and art of Europe.'

On the unwanted effects of indiscriminate hybridization or mixing of races, he was in broad agreement with Gobineau, but without the *Leitmotiv* of gloom; Chamberlain was convinced that the strongest, best-equipped and, therefore, fittest race would be able to assume at any moment its dominance and impose itself, thus curbing the tendency to degeneration. That race was derived from the peoples of Germany who constituted a unique race. Chamberlain defined the race as created 'physiologically by characteristic mixture of blood, followed by inbreeding; psychically by the influence that long-continued historical – geographical circumstances produce on that particular, specific, physiological disposition' (quoted in Baker, 1974). The influence of Darwin in this context is very apparent.

Of course it would be misleading to cite Chamberlain as the central theoretician in what was later to become Nazism. There is a very clear complementarity between Chamberlain's version of history and National Socialist philosophy. Interestingly, however, he was rather imprecise on the exact meaning of race. The name *Germanen* refers to a mixture of northern and western European populations which are said to form a 'family', the 'essence' of which is the *Germane*. It seems that his general thrust about the inherent superiority of one group over all the rest was more important than the accuracy of his concepts in elevating him to the role of a Nazi prophet. (He died in 1927, before the Nazis came to power).

Of course, social movements such as Nazism, pay scant respect to the intricacies of theories or the complexities of concepts, when they are on a rising curve. The appeal of the movement was based on a crude and selective utilization of theoretical themes by a receptive population and a successful manipulation of them by a coherent, focused organization – the party. Chamberlain's work was selectively used, as was Gustaf Kossina's.

The idea of *Volk* came from Kossina and was meant to emphasize the essential unity of the German character with its self-assurance, reserves of strength, willingness to be led, and intractible urge towards freedom. Such attributes were thought to have enabled Germanic people to overrun large parts of Europe as Roman power declined and to establish themselves as a ruling elite.

Volk was also invoked by Otto Spengler, though with him it was less a biological or anthropological concept and more a cultural one, 'a society of men that feels itself to be a unit'. He made it clear that *Volk* was not to be equated with race in any physical sense, though he stressed the cultural superiority of the Germans and for this reason his work was enthusiastically seized upon by Nazis.

There are other less influential writers, but uniting them all is a sense of basic inequality: the race set apart and variously defined as *Germanen* or, to use the more obscure Indo-European term, Aryan, was thought to be superior and therefore destined to dominate.

Hitler's *Mein Kampf,* published in two volumes in 1925 and 1927, is a much less violent appraisal of the theories than his actions might suggest. It was a biology of animals and of human beings, noting particularly the tendency of both to draw mates from amongst their own taxa or type. On to this is built a theory of natural progress, an innate impulse to the self-improvement of species under natural conditions.

This was the theoretical foundation for a political philosophy that posited the presence of two main races: Aryans and Jews. The latter was depicted in terms of their astuteness, cunning and wile and their rise to power was seen as self-motivated and in total disregard of other groups. This power, Hitler contended, must be terminated and the purity of the Aryan, or Germanic, race be restored. 'All great civilizations of the past,' he wrote 'only perished because the original creative race died out from blood-poisoning.' His attempts to regain the racial purity of the Aryans barely need going over, though there is little indication of his future intentions in *Mein Kampf.*

In both the examples of slavery and Nazism, incomplete theories of the origins of humanity and the natural inequalities of people were used in fragmented ways. Doctrines of the racial inferiority of blacks reached their full pitch in the late eighteenth century; the Nazi ideology proliferated prior to World War II. In neither case, were there attempts to fuse elements of existing theories into logically coherent complexes. And this tells us something very important about the relationship between ideas, knowledge and action.

Ideas do not have to be clear nor knowledge sound to commission action. The action, however misguided, can then serve in such a way to enrich the original ideas. The issue of race in the slavery case was invoked to settle moral dilemmas posed by groups of people who were in the business of making capital out of exploitation. In Nazism, it was selected to support the drastic actions of a movement trying to salvage the remnants of a society in steep economic decline. Race was an expedient in both circumstances; it stood as a call to action and, as Manning Nash (1972) put it, it 'persistently crops up wherever the political and social circumstances make it functionally pertinent'.

So, we see its pertinence in the UK of the 1980s: with unemployment affecting about one in seven people, particularly the young, and prices rising at unprecedented rates, race has surfaced as a most urgent call to action. The growth of such neo-Nazi movements as the National Front and the British Movement plus the incorporation of race into mainstream political debate attests to the persistence of the concept even 30 years after Unesco had denied its validity as a scientific concept and government bodies decried its use as a political expedient. The point is that race means different things to different people and it's very hard to be even a little more precise than that, if only because even the biological, genetic evidence we have available today is perplexing and contradictory (see Banton, 1979). About this, we aren't concerned; we will not complicate our argument by entering into debates about the actual biological bases of race. As social scientists, this matters less to us than the way in which everyday people think about race. We're interested in the social reality of race rather than the search for the essential nature of the phenomenon. Race is not a problem: it's something that people create as a problem. Questions about just how fundamental are the differences between human beings are not in themselves causes for outrage, nor for abuses, less still for rioting. Yet, wherever it becomes possible to conceive and delineate those differences in terms of natural properties, there arise certain groups who seem only too eager to justify privilege or even persecution because of those properties. That's when the race question takes on social dimensions. The ideas provided by Gobineau, Darwin, Chamberlain and the others, were in themselves, harmless. But they provided, however inadvertently, criteria for exploitation, murder and genocide.

The theorists themselves were about as much to blame for these as Einstein was for the wipe-out of Hiroshima. Not a perfect parallel admittedly but one meant to convey the importance of how knowledge is used in practical circumstances. This is what we need to examine in very close detail. Some would argue that there is no complete, exhaustive set of conditions we can specify to explain and predict when and how race emerges as an instrument – something to be socially used either to instigate or justify inequalities. The range of historical circumstances in which the concept has been given purchase is very wide indeed. There are others who have tried to develop theories purporting to explain the existence of the race issue without resort to actual theories about race itself. In this type of perspective, race is seen as a distortion of reality, a way of protecting the interests of groups which hold power and intend to hang on to it with whatever means they have available.

RACE AND CAPITALISM

Oliver Cromwell Cox (1948) was interested in race relations, which he defined as 'that behaviour which develops among peoples who are aware of each other's actual or imputed physical differences'. He was not particularly interested in race itself: his focus was on contacts between groups who are conscious of each other having physical, racial differences. So, if a man looks white in the USA, but he is called black everywhere, then he is a black American; but if a man of identical physical appearance is recognized everywhere in Cuba as a white man, then he is a white Cuban – for Cox's purposes. Conversely, if two people or groups of what Cox calls 'different racial strains' come into contact with but are not conscious of each other's differences, there does not exist a situation of race relations. This may sound rather obvious to social scientists in the 1980s, but, in the 1940s, when Cox was writing, it was an important reorientation in thinking. The sociologists, Robert Park and Ernest Burgess, had, between 1930 and 1940, pushed study in a social direction, detailing the ecological influences on relationships between various groups. Park and Burgess tended to study segments of social life in isolation, looking at the ways in which race becomes an issue by examining the interactions of people living in the cities.

For Cox, this approach lacked a critical component: power. Race manifests as an issue and prompts conflict between different groups because it is a convenient device for power-holders who need any weapon they can get to prise open gaps between the working classes and thus keep them fragmented.

Cox's argument, simply stated, was that people are encouraged to think in terms of race and, therefore, inherent inequality because it benefits capitalism. This system is based on a basic split over the ownership of the means of production: the owners, capitalists, continually need to exploit the non-owners, or workers, on whom they depend for labour. Their remaining in power as owners is contingent on their ability to maintain their grip over the workers and this is best done if those workers don't perceive their common exploitation, unite and present opposition. So, it becomes necessary to keep them divided into fractions, if possible by introducing and perpetuating antagonisms between them.

The race issue performs the function perfectly: it encourages the workers to regard each other as inherently different and unequal. They arrange their relationships with each other so as to align themselves with members of their own race whom they perceive as allies. The capitalists' heaviest weapon is open racial conflict when groups organize their allegiances along perceived racial lines and clash with those of other races. But at a covert level, a simmering or latent conflict is also useful in preventing the workers from perceiving their real allegiances – with each other – and their real opposition – the capitalist class. Racial antagonism was, according to Cox, a 'fundamental trait' of capitalism. Race as a socially defined category is a product purely of the development of capitalism and Cox points to the end of the fifteenth century as the crucial date when the system began to introduce the concept as a method of dividing workers. At this stage, the Europeans were extending their links in colonizing the world and needed the racial facility to justify and promote the exploitation.

Interestingly, Cox noted that the white workers in the early stages of capitalism were as savagely exploited as blacks and capitalists invoked the race issue to justify their unequal treatment of them too, claiming that social class characteristics are transmitted through heredity. Race was an additional weapon in their arsenal.

So, the concept of race facilitated the exploitation of blacks in particular and the working class in general. It provided a justification for consigning workers to degrading employment and treatment by stating that they were innately degenerate and naturally suited to such conditions, and served the purpose of fragmenting the working class and inhibiting a united challenge against the system of domination.

In Cox's view, all the phenomena of race relations had to be seen as part of the economic system of exploitation. Race as a functional concept had clear utilities, but so had racial prejudice – the hostile or negative attitudes towards groups seen to be of a different race. There is obviously no natural reason why some groups should feel antagonistic towards another: in fact Cox reasoned that, without capitalism, the world might never have experienced racialism. Everything to do with race and race relations was, for Cox, epiphenomenal: a mere symptom of the underlying reality of capitalism, a spin-off rather than a cause of antagonism. This is, of course, in sharp contrast to the early views that race was a natural cause of antagonisms between unequal groups. In this way, Cox prompted a completely new approach: race had to be seen as a by-product, albeit a most important and functional one, of the economic system.

Cox specified 'situations of race relations' in which there was, to a greater or lesser extent, an awareness on the behalf of one or more of the groups of the different racial type of the other or others. Perceptions are organized so as to demarcate lines of alignment and cleavage and these are drawn on the basis of race. Here we return to our original theme: for all the race relations situations as depicted by Cox stress the close link between ideas about race and the social actions implied by them.

The sources of the race ideas are, from Cox's Marxian vantage point, the product of material relations, meaning that the holders of power (or of material resources) also have the power to influence the thoughts of the rest of society through ideology. Karl Marx's dictum that 'The ideas of the ruling class are in every epoch the ruling ideas' is the basis for this observation. Cox's argument here was, in a sense, a reaction to an earlier work by Gunnar Myrdal, *An American Dilemma*, published in 1944, in which it was suggested that the 'American creed' lay behind the racial conflict in the USA. Myrdal identified the problem as a 'white problem' because the system of values accepted by whites emphasized Nationalism and Christianity yet encouraged self-interests which were incompatible. Crudely put, Myrdal saw the conflicts causing race problems as arising from what whites think. Cox objected to this as superficial: for Cox, what goes on inside people's heads is a reflection of their material circumstances. Beliefs are not primary causes of action, but are part of the ruling ideas of that epoch and are, therefore, instrumental in perpetuating class inequalities and the domination of the working class.

Now, this is a critical feature of race relations studies. We will argue that it must be, for our contention is that all situations in which race is a relevant factor involve a consciousness of race; and that consciousness must be an element of study. Being conscious of race is always a condition of race relations situations. Where there is no active consciousness of race, there is no issue. Race does not become important until people start thinking about it as such.

About this point, there would be no disagreement: race is in the consciousness. There is, however, little unity in theories abouts its source. Cox would argue that it derives from unequal power relationships and the ensuing ability of dominating groups to impose their conceptions on the rest of society. Others would find this insufficiently detailed at the psychological level, finding the Cox line rather too broad, if not too crude.

That people do think in terms of race and arrange their perceptions of each other so as to accommodate the concept is beyond doubt. This is the everyday form of racism; on a national level, it can express itself in full-blown doctrines such as that of South Africa where apartheid makes sure the idea of racial inequality pervades the whole of society. Actions based on such ideas, we call racialism. Racism is a kind of theoretical basis of or justification for racialist behaviour.

But, some would argue, racism and racialism are expressions not so much of the forces of capitalism, but manifestations of more fundamental human prejudices, reducible to what psychologists call inter-group tensions. In contrast to Cox's approach, theorists of this persuasion try to examine race at the level of the individual or group personality. Let's see what light these throw on our subject area.

PREJUDICE

'Do all whites suffer from unpleasant body odour?' A ridiculous question, maybe, but in it are hidden the elements of racial prejudice. Let's look at it more closely: the two give-away words are 'all' and 'whites', the former generalizes, the latter specifies. Implicit in the question is the assumption that a segment of society can be distinguished by an observable characteristic – skin colour, in this case, white – and that we can impute properties to all those sharing that characteristic. As soon as we do this, we establish a basis for prejudice.

Prejudices are usually based on faulty or incomplete information. For instance, if a person is prejudiced against blacks, we mean that they are orientated towards behaving with hostility to blacks: they think that, with the odd exception, all blacks are very much the same. But, the characteristics they assign to blacks are probably inaccurate or, at best, based on a grain of information that the person can apply to blacks as a whole. This generalization is called stereotyping and it involves attributing identical properties to any person in a group regardless of the actual variation among members of the group. Like all blacks are gifted in sport, but are limited intellectually; this is based on the evidence that some black sportsmen are very competent and some black schoolchildren do not achieve good examination results. But not all. The stereotype is a way of simplifying our view of the world. Yet it can get insidious.

Examination results might make it easy to think of blacks as stupid and this can lead to a justification for depriving them of an education (in the same way as the early race theorists used incomplete biological knowledge to construct a stereotype that justified slavery). In a similar way, feminists argue that the stereotype of women as biologically equipped only for domestic or menial jobs has been serviceable for justifying sexual inequality in employment. We don't necessarily have to be aware of working with stereotypes; often we are brought up to accept them and cannot entertain alternative images. But, crucially, the stereotype images function in such a way as to prejudice us against another group.

In all race relations situations, there are prejudices based on stereotypes. Historically, the more politically and economically powerful groups cultivate the images and act towards disadvantaged groups using them as gauges for their behaviour. As we have seen, race and the stereotype of distinct racial groups served their masters adequately and so were useful for justifying action. They helped to keep the slavers from feeling immoral and un-Christian.

This makes prejudice seem merely an afterthought, whereas there may be many other factors lying behind it. Competition over scarce resources is an obvious one: as we will see, prejudice against blacks and South Asians in the UK seemed to rise in proportion to fluctuating demands of the labour market in the 1950s; as the number of jobs being sought after diminished, West Indians and Asians became more threatening competitors in the job market and hostility against them increased. This type of situation is almost exactly paralleled in John Dollard's (1938) study of a small American industrial town in which there was initially no apparent prejudice against local Germans. The jobs got scarcer and 'scornful and derogatory opinions were expressed about these Germans' and these tended to give the whites some self-satisfaction. This goes to show that prejudice is by no means limited to visibly different groups.

Related to this is the scapegoat production: deteriorating prospects on the job front might lead to worsening material conditions, like deteriorating standards of living, poor housing, limited diets and so on; so people look for possible causes. Of course, the deep-rooted social and economic causes of the decay are usually complex and obscure, so something more comprehensible is looked for. A quite logical move is to turn attention to visible and powerless groups, like immigrants.

People transfer the causes of their own problems to what they deem racial groups. A famous American study by Carl Hovland and Robert Sears related precisely the number of lynchings of blacks between 1882 and 1930 with the changing price of cotton (1940). Similarly, the rising importance of racist movements like the National Front and the British Movement in the UK of the 1970s and early 1980s was largely a response to unemployment figures exceeding three million. The activities of these organizations prompt comparisons with Hitler's scapegoating of Jews in Nazi Germany.

In fact, it was mounting anti-Semitism which gave rise to one of the most famous studies into prejudice conducted by Theodor Adorno and his associates. Unlike the two previous explanations of prejudice as grounded in social processes, the study identified what was called *The Authoritarian Personality* (1950). People possessing this showed certain tendencies such as being anti-Semitic, anti-black, intolerant to weakness, rigid in beliefs and extremely suspicious of minority groups. The values and attitudes associated with these people were thought to stem from childhood experiences rather than social circumstances. People learn prejudices and develop them in later life.

Thomas Pettigrew used the Adorno study's scale for measuring prejudice for a separate research project that came to the conclusion that prejudice is very simply a matter of conforming to norms (Pettigrew, 1958; 1959). In other words, if everybody you associate with resents Asians, then you tend to as well. Prejudice is not seen as an inbuilt component of the personality, but as a fluid processual thing, coming and going, depending on where a person lives and whom he uses as reference groups. It is a socially transmitted phenomenon.

Racial prejudice, then, can be viewed as a result of self-justification, competition, personality or conformity; we can approach it as a social phenomenon or an individual one. What is certain is that prejudice against racial groups is a factor in all situations of race relations. Being conscious of other groups as sharing properties that are undesirable is a necessary condition. And this observation reinforces our statement that race relations studies must take account of what goes on inside people's heads as much as how people actually behave towards each other.

These studies of racial prejudice seem to be light years away from the early investigations of people like Linnaeus and Gobineau, yet they are linked, however tenuously, by the concern with race. No matter how much we object to its presence or how vile we find its intrusion into our lives, it is there and it has consequences. We accept that race was in use scientifically and that its history predates colonialism, yet we also believe that no satisfactory account of race relations in contemporary society can proceed without reference to colonialism and the 'racializing' process accompanying it. As we pointed out, the concept of race prior to the nineteenth century was markedly different to the one that both facilitated and justified the colonial exploitation of peoples of a different colour. Race was anchored to a basic premise of human inequality and it has remained in that sea-bed ever since. Where people have perceived others as racial groups, they usually grade them higher or, importantly, lower on some scale of status or prestige. It is as well to remind ourselves at this stage that being conscious of race, though it may work as a tool of ruling groups, can also pervade the consciousness of ruled groups, the exploited.

This we take to be of the utmost significance, for an argument [in this Reading] is that it is through the transference of ideas on race that the inequalities are perpetuated. But, whereas such ideas are explained by some as the result of ideological domination, 'the ideas of the ruling class' theme, we prefer to see ideas also as flowing from the underclass groups themselves. Groups designated racially inferior contribute to the maintenance of inequalities by believing in them or even not rejecting them. So racial inequalities are often generated and confirmed within groups as well as imposed from the outside.

None of this is meant to indicate that we intend to ignore the vital parts played by state agencies and institutions in creating and maintaining ideas about fundamental divisions and stratifications. These do arise historically from material dominance and exploitation. By including the ways in which the ideas are embodied in the culture of disadvantaged groups, we do not intend to reverse the flow of ideology.

Note on terminology

ENVIRONMENT   Very basically, this refers to everything external to the individual: a social environment may be composed of other people; a physical environment of actual material products. In both instances, the individual is susceptible to outside influences. The importance of the idea of environment is in the observation that 'no man is an island': he always responds to and is shaped by the influences of other people and things. So, he may be influenced by prejudiced friends and become prejudiced in his own ideas.

MONOGENESIS   The view that all humans are descended from one essential source; it derives from the Bible but was given credibility by Linnaeus who advocated 'The great chain of being' concept, meaning that all creation is arranged in strict hierarchical sequence with creatures distinguished from each other in a series of linked gradations. This contrasts with POLYGENESIS, the thesis that argues that the differences existing between living creatures was due to their being separately created, i.e. from distinct, unrelated sources; thus there is separate development.

SOCIAL DARWINISM   An approach to the study of society. It emerged in the late nineteenth and early twentieth century and gained impetus with the acceptance of Darwin's doctrines of evolution. Basically, the idea was to transfer Darwin's principles on natural selection to the social world. Societies were said to evolve in patterns whereby some institutions and 'races' of people survived because they were better suited to the environment. Thus there was a gradual evolution towards perfectability.

EXPLOITATION   The act of bringing people into service and using their labour to gain profits or advantages.

ARYANS   Originally, the Aryans were thought to be wandering tribes from Northern India. But the infamy of the concept of the Aryan grew with Hitler's Nazism, which was based on the myth of a supreme race called the Aryan. Influenced by Nietzsche's predictions on the future race of supermen, Hitler experimented with eugenics to further his aim of creating what he thought would be a pure, unpolluted race of people which would lead all others.

RACIALISM   The action of discriminating against particular others by using the belief that they are racially different, and usually inferior. It is the practical element of the race concept.

IDEOLOGY   In one sense, this describes a general apprehension of the world, a way of interpreting and explaining things that go on about us. But a Marxian view would be that ideology is a false way of interpreting the world – a way that is disseminated by the ruling classes and accepted by those who are ruled. In this way, domination is facilitated by the ruled group's lack of questioning. In both senses, an ideology is a picture of the world, an attempt at comprehending its complexities and an effort to situate oneself in the world.

APARTHEID   The political system which strictly enforces total separation of groups designated as different races. Different races have different legal and moral rights and are prevented from mixing with each other. In South Africa, for example, whites are given privileges in all areas of society. Non-whites are given separate facilities and barred from using the same living areas, recreational areas, etc. In effect, it constitutes a rigid political caste system with whites enjoying innumerable advantages.

RACISM   The doctrine that the world's population is divisible into categories based on physical differences which can be transmitted genetically. Invariably, this leads to the conception that the categories are ordered hierarchically so that some elements of the world's population are superior to others.

PREJUDICE   An inflexible mental attitude towards specific groups of others based on unreliable, possibly distorted, stereotyped images of them.

STEREOTYPE   A mental image held about particular groups of people constructed on the basis of simplified, distorted or incomplete knowledge of them.

An example would be a stereotype of Jews: all of them are mean. This isn't accurate, but is a widely held stereotypical image of them.

SCAPEGOAT   Term taken from the ancient Hebrews who used to transfer symbolically their sinful deeds to a goat which they let loose in the wilderness; the scapegoat is an object or group of people which others blame for their problems, when in fact those problems are caused by other factors.

REFERENCES

Adorno, T.S., Frenkel-Brunswik, E., Levinson, D.J. and Sandford, R. (1950) *The Authoritarian Personality*, Harper & Row, New York
Baker, J.R. (1974) *Race*, Oxford University Press, London
Banton, M. (1977) *The Idea of Race*, Tavistock, London
Banton, M. (1979) Analytical and folk concepts of race and ethnicity, *Ethnic and Racial Studies*, Vol. 2, No. 2, pp 127–38
Barzun, J. (1937) *Race: A Study in Superstition*, Harcourt Brace & Co., New York
Berger, P.L. and Luckmann, T. (1972) *The Social Construction of Reality*, Penguin, Harmondsworth
Cox, O.C. (1948) *Caste, Class and Race: A Study of Social Dynamics*, Doubleday, New York
Dollard, J. (1938) Hostility and fear in social life, *Social Forces*, Vol. 17, pp 15–26
Hovland, C. and Sears, R. (1940) Minor studies of aggression, *Journal of Psychology*, Vol. 9, pp 301–10
Myrdal, G. (1944) *The American Dilemma*, McGraw-Hill, New York
Nash, M. (1972) Race and the ideology of race, in P. Baxter and B. Sansom (eds.), *Race and Social Difference*, Harmondsworth, Penguin, pp 111–22
Pettigrew, T. (1958) Personality and sociocultural factors and intergroup attitudes, *Journal of Conflict Resolution*, Vol. 2, pp 29–42
Pettigrew, T. (1959) Regional differences in anti-negro prejudice, *Journal of Abnormal and Social Psychology*, Vol. 59, pp 28–36
Tobias, P.V. (1972) The meaning of race, in P. Baxter and B. Sansom (eds.), *Race and Social Difference*, Penguin, Harmondsworth, pp 19–43

TOPICS FOR DISCUSSION

1. Discuss the view that the concept of *race* as used by biologists has little or no relevance to our understanding of the social, economic and political differences among men.
2. What support is there for Oliver Cromwell Cox's assertion that the phenomena of race relations must be seen as part of the economic system of exploitation, that is to say, they are merely a symptom of the underlying reality of capitalism (p 102)
3. Psychological explanations of *racism* and *racialism* focus on inter-group tensions. On what evidence do they draw to support such an assertion?

SUGGESTIONS FOR FURTHER READING

1. Centre for Contemporary Cultural Studies (1982) *The Empire Strikes Back: Race and*

Racism in 70s Britain, Hutchinson and Co., London. A volume of essays exploring the place of race and racism in the political transformation of Britain in the late 1970s. Britain, it is argued, is very different from its popular image as a liberal democracy; our notions of *culture, nation* and *class* rest on deeply racist structures.

2. Tierney, T. (1982) *Race, Immigration and Schooling*, Holt, Rinehart and Winston, Eastbourne. Chapter 1 'Racism, colonialism and migration' discusses *racism as ideology* and examines the ways in which this relates to aspects of a capitalist system.

3. Gabriel, J. and Ben-Tovim, G. (1978) 'Marxism and the concept of racism', *Economy and Society*, Vol. 7, No. 2-10. A discussion of the relationship of racism to capitalism, of race to class, and of anti-racist policies and strategies.

Reading 6
SPORT AS A SIDE-TRACK: AN ANALYSIS OF WEST INDIAN INVOLVEMENT IN EXTRA-CURRICULAR SPORT
B. Carrington[1]

Some years ago Harry Edwards (1973) made the poignant reference to black athletes as 'the twentieth century gladiators for white America', in a critical commentary upon the over-representation of blacks in American sport. There are signs of a similar development occurring in contemporary Britain where, during the past decade, there has been an upsurge of black involvement in sport at every level. Much prominence has been given by the mass media to the achievements of athletes of Caribbean descent – such as Daley Thompson, Sonia Lannaman, Justin Fashanu, Garth Crooks, Viv Richards, Maurice Hope and many others – who have made considerable inroads into several amateur and professional sports, in particular, track and field events, soccer, boxing and cricket.

It is not surprising, therefore, that a number of studies undertaken in British secondary schools, have revealed that West Indians are more likely to participate in extra-curricular sport and to play in school sports teams than pupils of other ethnic groups. From the evidence available, it would seem that West Indians are set to become 'the twentieth-century gladiators' for white Britain!

This paper is primarily concerned to analyze West Indian involvement in school sports teams. From the standpoint that this phenomenon cannot be 'read'

[1] In Barton, L. and Walker, S. (1983) Race Class and Education, Croom Helm, London, pp 40–65

simply in biologistic or naturalistic terms. Section I of the paper attempts to explore the inter-relationships between West Indian school failure, the apparent success of this group in school sport and their structural position in the social formation. In Section II, the preliminary findings of an ethnographic study undertaken in a multiracial, urban comprehensive school, are presented. The paper concludes by addressing some of the policy implications raised by the research.

I RACE, SCHOOLING AND SOCIAL REPRODUCTION

Despite various state interventions to curb racism and offset racial disadvantage, the structural position of West Indians in Britain has barely altered since the initial phases of immigration. If anything, it has deteriorated. The bulk of the West Indian population – along with a substantial part of the Asian population – entered this country during the 1950s and early 1960s as a 'reserve army of labour' to fill the low status, often menial occupations, formerly spurned by the indigenous workforce during a period of full employment and economic expansion. The subsequent recession and crisis of capital accumulation in the 1970s and 1980s have served to consolidate their largely secondary position within a segmented labour market. Black workers, especially the young, have continued to face higher levels of unemployment than their white counterparts. Furthermore, widespread discrimination in the labour market has also ensured that those West Indians who are 'waged' have remained concentrated in the unskilled and semi-skilled strata of the working class. In Britain, as in the USA, sport would appear to be *one* of the few spheres where blacks (albeit a tiny minority) have been able to gain legitimate success.

The education system has played a major part in maintaining the apparently immutable position of black workers in the class structure and labour market. Whilst it is acknowledged that credentials *per se* neither guarantee entry to the labour market nor access to positions within the occupational structure, they nevertheless function as a 'screening device' and as such may be regarded as an essential precondition of entry to certain forms of work. In view of this, therefore, it can be argued that the education system, by facilitating West Indian academic failure, has not only legitimated the exclusion of this ethnic group from all but the more menial forms of wage labour, but during a period of mass unemployment, has legitimated their exclusion from the labour market altogether.

The massive underachievement of West Indian pupils, from primary through to tertiary stage, has been well documented and needs little elaboration here. West Indians tend to be overrepresented among the poorer readers in primary schools, fare much less well than their Asian and white peers in C.S.E., 'O' and 'A' level examinations, and are markedly under-represented on full-time degree courses. Several policies and practices within education have been identified as variously contributing to the educational disadvantage of this ethnic group. These include: the reluctance of the D.E.S. (until recently) to acknowledge fully 'racially specific' forms of educational disadvantage or to pursue 'racially explicit' policies; the non-representation, misrepresentation or devaluation of black culture, history and language through ethnocentric and/or racist curricula, school tests and pedagogy; the use of culturally biased and inaccurate assessment and selection procedures resulting in the placement (and misplacement) of West Indian pupils in non-academic streams and Special Schools; racism within the teaching force itself. It is proposed to focus upon this latter 'determinant' of West Indian academic failure, because it is hoped to show it is also a critical causal factor in the apparent success of this ethnic group in extra-curricular school sport.

It is not surprising, given the history and structure of British society that many teachers should operate with – either wittingly or unwittingly – racist frames of reference, or act and behave in a manner which could be judged as racist in terms of its consequences and effects. In this paper, racism is viewed as a body of ideas rationalizing and legitimating social practices which reinforce an unequal distribution of power between groups usually (but not always) distinguished in terms of physical criteria. Notwithstanding this, however, it should be noted that it is not strictly possible to talk of racism in the singular, or to abstract it from its social and material context. The forms taken by racism vary considerably. Whereas, on most occasions, it surfaces at the level of commonsense, on others, it surfaces in the form of a 'worked-out' ideology, such as biologism. Racism is variously premissed upon beliefs, presuppositions, preconceptions and misconceptions, forms of augmentation and 'theories' about the biological and/or cultural superiority of one racial group and the concomitant inferiority of others. In general terms, I endorse the characterization of racism outlined by David Wellman in *Portraits of White Racism* (1977). Emphasizing racism's materiality, that is its social dimension, he states:

Racism has various faces; it manifests itself to the world in different guises. Sometimes it appears as 'personal prejudice' which, it is argued here, is really a disguised way to defend privilege. Other times racism is manifested ideologically. Cultural and biological reasons are used as rationalizations and justifications for the superior position of whites. Racism is also expressed institutionally in the form of systematic practices that deny and exclude blacks from access to social resources.

Later in the same account Wellman stresses that racism is expressed in both subtle and crude terms, and that racism may be regarded as having both intentional and unintentional forms. He notes:

> The essential feature of racism is not hostility or misperception, but rather the defence of a system from which advantage is derived on the basis of race. The manner in which the defence is articulated – either with hostility or subtlety – is not nearly as important as the fact that it insures the continuation of a privileged relationship. Thus it is necessary to broaden the definition of racism beyond prejudice to include sentiments that in their consequence, if not their intent, support the racial *status quo*.

As Rampton and others have indicated, whilst few teachers are consciously or deliberately racists, there are many who are subconsciously or unintentionally racist in outlook and behaviour. It is well known that teachers generally operate with preconceived notions about the patterns of behaviour and levels of ability of different categories of pupil, and these stereotypes (which may relate to race, class or sex) not only influence teachers' attitudes and behaviour towards the category in question, but also the curriculum content and teaching style selected. In the case of racial stereotyping, there are indications that teachers are more likely to view West Indian pupils in prejorative terms and compare them unfavourably with their Asian or white peers. Teachers, it would seem, tend to regard West Indians as a problematic group – disruptive, aggressive, unable to concentrate, poorly motivated and with low academic potential. Moreover, whilst teachers often underrate West Indian academic potential, they are more likely to stereotype this group as having superior physical and practical capabilities and have higher expectations of their potential in areas such as sport, drama, dance and art. The submission of the National Association of Headteachers to the Rampton Committee gave explicit articulation to the stereotype, sparking off a furore among sections of the West Indian Community, who were reported as being 'horrified' and 'appalled' by the nature of Heads' evidence. The Association claimed:

> If there is a difficulty of cultural identity among second generation West Indians, there is also much to counterbalance that deficiency including their natural sense of rhythm, colour and athletic prowess.

What effect do such stereotypes have upon pedagogical practice? As Maureen Stone (1981) has argued in *The Education of the Black Child in Britain*, they not only prompt teachers 'to cool out' black pupils and divert them away from the pursuit of credentials but may also provide a rationalization for West Indian pupils in the non-academic bands receiving 'a watered down curriculum'. Her research suggests that in some schools black pupils are being encouraged to devote time and energy to ethnically specific cultural pursuits, such as steel bands, during the normal timetable, when they already have very heavy commitments in extra-curricular sport. She notes, referring to the Head and many of the white teachers in a London comprehensive school:

> They were, as far as they were concerned, doing their best to encourage West Indian cultural forms in school; since West Indians performed best in sport it made sense to encourage them to succeed in an area where they were competent. To the black teachers it was simply the school confirming the old racial stereotype: 'Music and Sports that's all we're good at' was the way one of them put it to me. They saw black children being seduced into activities which were immediately rewarding but carried no prospect of future advancement, and to them it was ironic that this was done in order to give the black children identity and improve their self esteem through their own cultural forms.

The growing involvement and apparent over-representation of West Indian pupils in school sports teams, as indicated by the research of Sargeant (1972), Wood (1973), Beswick (1976) and Jones (1977), not only lend support to Stone's argument, but also, appear to confirm the anxieties of many West Indian parents and community leaders that schools are sponsoring black academic failure by channelling black pupils away from the academic mainstream and into sport.

Whilst stereotypes held by teachers of West Indian pupils undoubtedly perform a critical function in facilitating this channelling, account must also be taken of other related factors when analyzing black involvement in school sport.

In common with certain other curricular and extra-curricular activities (e.g. Steel Bands, Black Studies, drama, etc.) sport may provide the school with a convenient and legitimate side-track for its disillusioned black low achievers, for whom schooling may have little or no relevance. In this sense, the school may utilize black sports involvement as a social control mechanism; a means of 'gentling the masses' and curbing, containing or neutralizing pupil disaffection and resistance to schooling. Black pupils, therefore, may be encouraged by teachers to promote their sporting abilities in the earnest hope that success in one sphere of school activity will compensate for failure in most others. Hal Lawson's (1979) observations about the role of physical activities in American ghetto schools would appear apposite to the situation in Britain. He notes:

> Commonly, they are employed as devices to compensate for academic tasks and as an arena in which 'motor minded' students may enjoy some success. In either instance, social control, not education, appears to be the concern.

Whilst there is probably a growing number of disaffected black youth in British schools who recognize that they are being processed for marginal positions in society and the labour market and who reject all aspects of schooling, including extra-curricular sport, there are, nevertheless, many others who are prepared to cooperate with channelling. Their reasons for doing so will vary. Some, like the 'Mainstreamers' studied by Barry Troyna (1979), may underplay their ethnicity, reject the oppositional features of black culture, and seek to gain social acceptability by promoting their academic or athletic abilities at school. In contrast, it is likely that other West Indian pupils will look upon sport as providing an opportunity to 'colonize' one major area of school activity and make it their own. Undoubtedly, there will be some who will have internalized the stereotype of black physical prowess and athletic superiority, or who identify with (and in certain cases seek to emulate) the achievements of prominent black sports personalities such as Fashanu, Hope *et al*. As Kew (1979) has argued, these athletes, as symbols of black success, now constitute 'significant others' for many black youth in Britain. Furthermore, with conventional routes to status blocked, some young blacks (in common with some of their white working-class peers) may hold unrealistic aspirations of a career in professional sport and look upon it as providing an alternative to menial wage-labour or the dole queue, and a means of escape from the 'ghetto'. Insofar as opportunities for social mobility via sport are extremely limited and, as Cashmore (1981), Gallop and Dolan (1981) and others have argued, only a tiny minority of the most able and talented youngsters ever gain a place in the sporting elite, sport can be regarded as providing this section of youth with little more than an 'imaginary solution' to problems which at the concrete level remain unresolved.

II HILLSVIEW COMPREHENSIVE SCHOOL – A CASE STUDY

Edward Wood and I have explored these and related issues for a period of 16 months at Hillsview, an 11–16, mixed comprehensive school, located in a declining inner urban area in Yorkshire.

Hillsview was selected for investigation primarily because of its ethnic composition. We felt that since the Asian population of the school was relatively small, it would be easier to make direct comparisons between West Indian and white pupils. There are nearly 1 000 pupils at Hillsview (4 per cent Asian, 32 per cent West Indian, 64 per cent white). The school has a teaching staff of 55. Of these there is one Asian teacher; the remainder are white.

Formerly a secondary modern, built in the 1950s, Hillsview has an S.P.S. designation and many of the characteristics associated with that status. The school serves a 'rough' working-class neighbourhood. Its catchment area comprises of a run-down interwar council estate and several streets of decaying 'two up, two down' Victorian terraces. Most of the men in the locality are employed as manual workers in the textile, chemical and engineering industries. With opportunities for female employment in the area restricted, few of the women, with children at the school, are waged. In April 1981, it was estimated that about 22 per cent of the white pupils and 35 per cent of the black had fathers who were out of work. Hillsview's pupils have a grim present and face the prospect of an even grimmer future as youth unemployment mounts, and as opportunities for apprenticeships and unskilled work in the locality steadily diminish. The school has a reputation for being 'rough' and 'tough' which extends far beyond its immediate catchment area. Teachers in adjacent schools appeared to view their Hillsview colleagues with disdain. Many parents too – even those with modest aspirations for their children – were highly critical of the school. As Donalyn, an Easter leaver remarked:

> My mum thinks this school is rubbish. She wanted me to go to Brampton 'cos it's not so rough and has a better reputation for work and behaviour.

Hillsview School does not have a distinguished academic record and, as a whole, could be considered to be underachieving for West Indian and white pupils alike. The overall attainment levels for West Indian pupils were nevertheless found to be depressed in relation to those of their white peers. Of the 1980 school leavers, for example, only 2 per cent of West Indians and 4 per cent of whites obtained five or more 'O' level passes or their C.S.E. equivalent. Moreover, the proportion of each ethnic group achieving less than five but more than one 'O' level pass (or C.S.E. grade one) was 21 per cent in the case of West Indian pupils and 35 per cent in that of whites. These ethnic differences in attainment were especially pronounced amongst male pupils.

The aim of the research was to capture something of the 'lived experiences' of pupils and teachers in an institutional setting and to describe, analyze and assess the responses of each to channelling. To this end, a variety of research techniques were employed. We began by conducting informal group discussions with the pupils. Initially, these took place during school time but on fairly neutral territory – a local sports centre used by the school for some of its P.E. lessons. Later in the research, having established a rapport with a large cross-section of pupils, further discussions were arranged on the school premises with various groups.

Similar discussions were conducted with groups of teachers. Questionnaires were administered to the entire teaching staff and to each pupil in the fourth and fifth years. In-depth, semi-structured, follow-up interviews were undertaken with 46 teacher respondents and a heterogeneous sample of 50 pupils. The latter group comprised boys and girls, blacks and whties, drawn from both the upper and lower bands. These pupils showed some variation in their respective commitments to the school, the pursuit of credentials and sport. Data were also gathered from other sources, namely: lesson observation and consultations with local authority advisory staff, careers officers, and teachers in adjacent schools.

Indications of channelling

Although there is a tendency for pupils of West Indian origins to be clustered in the lower bands or streams in schools, there was little evidence of this at Hillsview. Whilst West Indian and white pupils were found to be proportionally represented in both the upper and lower bands, the relatively small Asian population was concentrated in the upper band.

An analysis of the ethnic composition of the school sports teams, however, revealed an altogether different picture. Leaving aside the question of Asian participation (only two or three Asian pupils played regularly in school teams) it was found that whereas West Indian pupils accounted for 32 per cent of the school population, they nevertheless occupied 63 per cent of the team places. (Note, the analysis covered all of the teams *regularly* fielded by the school, from first to fifth years, viz. soccer, rugby, basketball, netball, hockey and athletics. Despite the strong tradition and passion for cricket in Yorkshire, the school no longer has a cricket team!)

Most of the white male team members (67 per cent) and almost all of the female team members (93 per cent white and 92 per cent West Indian) came from the upper band. This finding is not unusual for, as the work of Hendry and Thorpe (1977), Hargreaves, (1967), Corrigan (1979) and others has suggested, extra-curricular activities, including physical activities, tend to attract more conformist pupils; viz. pupils, often with academic inclinations, who are more readily able to identify with the school as an institution. Many of the West Indian male team members, however, did not fulfil these criteria, for 68 per cent came from the lower band and, of these, there was a substantial proportion of disaffected pupils who appeared to reject most aspects of schooling except for sport, or in some cases, other practical curricular and extra-curricular activities such as metal work, woodwork, drama etc. The following question immediately arises – why were these black boys willing to take part in school teams when most of their disaffected white peers simply rejected extra-curricular sport as 'just another school subject outside school hours'?

Very few teachers at Hillsview appeared to be overtly hostile to ethnic minorities or gave the impression of being 'consciously racist' in outlook. Many, in fact came across as 'liberal minded' and genuinely concerned with the well-being of pupils, irrespective of their colour or ethnic background. Notwith-standing this, however, often there appeared to be a disjunction between the attitudes and values held by some teachers and their behaviour and practices in the classroom. Some, including those who regarded themselves as non-racist or even anti-racist, behaved in manner which, in Wellman's (1977) terms, could be described as 'racist in consequence, rather than intent'. Several indicated that they held lower expectations of West Indian pupils and were prepared to tolerate poorer standards of academic work and behaviour from this group. One, concerned to make education a less alienating experience for his black pupils and anxious to establish a good relationship with them, when asked if he varied his approach in the classroom to suit pupils of different ethnic backgrounds, replied:

> I'm reluctant to push black kids too hard . . . I frequently indulge them – and myself – in informal conversations relating to music, home life, etc.

Others, who regarded West Indian pupils as posing a particular control problem, recounted the strategies they employed in the classroom to assuage this group, e.g.

> I tend to give West Indians as much oral work as possible because even the bright ones become agitated when not writing well.

> Inevitably, I'm more lenient towards blacks. I try to avoid confrontation. I tend to ask them to do something, rather than telling them to do it.

> I recognize that West Indians have a lower flash point. Whereas I might bark at a white kid, I'm more patient with the more volatile West Indians.

Undoubtedly, there were some teachers at Hillsview School who operated with pejorative stereotypes of West Indian pupils and viewed their behaviour, academic abilities and parent culture in a negative manner. There were several occasions in interview when teachers referred to this group as 'lacking in ability', 'unable to concentrate', 'indolent', 'insolent', 'disruptive', 'aggressive' and 'disre-spectful of authority'. Frequently, our respondents alluded to a cultural-deficit model when accounting for West Indian academic failure. Some alleged that 'West Indian parents do not value education as much as other groups' or said that 'West Indian parents do not support their children emotionally or educationally'. Furthermore, black resistance to schooling was often viewed by teachers as a form of deviance emanating from an authoritarian family upbringing. The following teacher's comments are typical of this genre:

> They [West Indian pupils] are more resentful of authority because they come

from a stricter background. Their parents treat them very badly. They're only supposed to speak when spoken to and if they do anything wrong they're likely to get belted . . . We're not in a position to exercise that sort of authority. They just don't see us as any sort of threat.

However, it should be stressed that there were teachers at Hillsview – albeit a minority – who rejected their colleagues' stereotypical rationalizations of West Indian academic failure and resistance to schooling. Instead they offered accounts which took cognizance of the position of this ethnic group in a racially structured society and labour market. A science teacher remarked:

We are trying to ask West Indians and Asians and anyone else who's not English to adhere to our society, our methods of teaching, the way we live, the way we do everything.

Referring to the invidious position of West Indians in the labour market, a languages teacher recounted a conversation with some of her older black pupils, noting:

There's little hope for them – In my class, West Indian kids say to me – 'Miss you're wasting your time. School work doesn't matter. I shan't get a job – I don't want to know.'

Whereas the teachers tended to underrate the academic potential of black pupils, their comments about the abilities of this group in low-status, practical activities were often laudatory. West Indians were variously described as having 'a well-developed artistic ability or sense of colour' or 'greater athletic prowess then white pupils', and as being, 'ideal for dance and drama' or 'capable of achieving better results physically then academically'.

Teachers' explanations of West Indian involvement in school sport

During interview, teachers were shown tables detailing the ethnic composition of school sports teams and invited to comment upon the high level of West Indian involvement.

Although there is a substantial body of research suggesting that no credence can be· given to naturalistic interpretations of black sports involvement (viz. accounts based upon speculative assumptions about innate racial differences in physique or motor skills), many teachers, nevertheless, explained the over-representation of West Indians in school teams in these terms. Often explicit references were made to what Gallop and Dolan (1981) characterize as 'the physiological myths surrounding black athletic success'. For example, one of the science staff who also assisted with coaching contended:

> West Indians are superior in the power that they can generate compared to white kids. They seem to possess better musculature and don't have the fat you often find on a British kid.

Similarly, a humanities teacher believes that:

> The physique of West Indian children generally, would appear to be in line with getting better results at sport.

Invariably, there were some teachers, who not only perceived West Indians as having superior physical endowments and skills, but who looked upon sport as providing an appropriate channel for compensating these supposedly 'motor minded' pupils for their academic failure. As one of the P.E. staff remarked:

> West Indian pupils seem to be more muscular, more physically developed and have better physical skills than white children of the same age. Only rarely does one see a weak, flabby or poorly coordinated West Indian child. They have a raw talent and are immediately attracted to an area where they can excel.

Similarly, a humanities teacher claimed:

> Sport gives them [West Indian pupils] a chance of success. Whereas they're not successful in the classroom they can show their abilities on the sports field.

Some teachers, often those eschewing stereotypical rationalizations of black academic failure, offered alternative accounts of West Indian sports involvement to those discussed above. A few recognized that prominent black athletes often constitute significant others for West Indian youth, for example:

> There are few black heroes – especially around here. West Indian pupils identify with black sportsmen. Maybe it's the influence of television. They have suddenly realized they're good at something. In school sport West Indians are the only ones who'll volunteer; you have to dragoon the others into taking part.

On the other hand, the accounts provided by some respondents revealed an awareness of the symbolic significance of the territory of the school for West Indian youth. A drama teacher, alluding to this, stated:

> The school provides West Indian pupils with something they really need. [. . .] When something is going on after school (a dramatic production or sports fixture), there are far more West Indian kids hanging around or riding bikes.

Other teachers were more explicit than this particular respondent. Several felt that West Indian pupils had sought to 'colonize' the school sports field and interpreted the growing involvement of this group in sport as an expression of their ethnicity. According to one member of staff.

West Indians live in a tightly knit community. It could be that one or two are good at sport and others practise a bit harder and go along to be with their friends . . . Indigenous children no longer want to participate because they feel outnumbered. When there were only two or three West Indians in each team they were accepted by other team members. But as the numbers became five, six or seven this began to affect the thinking of some of the white pupils.

The question of 'colonization' will be considered later in this account when the reasons given by pupils for taking part in (or opting out of) extra-curricular sport are examined.

Sport as a side-track

There were strong indications from both pupils' and teachers' remarks during individual interviews and group discussions that sport provided the school with a convenient side-track for many of its disaffected West Indian pupils. Although the teachers did not seek to secure a truce with disaffected pupils by openly trading additional *curricular* sport and a reduced academic workload for more conformist behaviour on the part of the pupils, it was found that sports involvement was utilized by teachers as a control mechanism – but in a more subtle and convert manner. Whereas one of the school rules stated quite unequivocally that non-attenders and disruptive pupils would be barred from taking part in school teams, it was apparent that this rule was interpreted with a good deal of flexibility! For example, one teacher, when asked 'Are badly behaved pupils or truants allowed to play in a school team?' replied:

Yes – I've let such pupils off detention to play in a team, even though there's a formal school rule which says they should not play.

Other teachers also indicated that they felt that the sanctions normally taken out against the non-conformist pupil might be waived in the case of a team member, and seemed to advocate an 'unspoken truce' with disaffected pupils, whom they believed ought to be encouraged to play in school teams. Whilst some justified this practice in the belief that success in sport would serve to compensate low-achievers for academic failure, others sponsored the involvement of such pupils in school teams in the hope that it would enable them to identify more closely with the school as an institution, for example:

Lessons and playing football are part and parcel of the same thing. Sport is the only thing that some children are good at. I think a case can be made for badly behaved pupils or truants playing in a team. If a child is badly behaved in school but is good at football – this is a positive thing to build on.

Once you reject them it's difficult to get them back. Kids are kept in the mainstream through sport at school because, at least for the short period of time, they're accepting the rules which the school has laid down.

Many pupils appeared to be aware of this 'unspoken truce'. As Alex, a West Indian rugby player intimated:

Sometimes you're stopped from playing for legging it – but if you come late or muck around in the corridors, you're still allowed to play.

Similarly, a member of the soccer team contended:

Most of the teachers and the headteacher are not bothered about truanting – but you've got to be in school on Friday if there's a game on Saturday.

In addition to the indirect forms of sponsorship referred to above, some direct pressure was placed upon pupils to participate in school teams. This usually came from the P.E. staff themselves, or from other teachers who assisted with coaching. On most occasions, teachers appeared to rely on their powers of persuasion when recruiting players for teams. However, on others more coercive means were employed!

Female staff, cognizant of the disdain shown by many adolescent girls for team sports – though not necessarily aware of the reasons for this – said that they had made certain concessions to team members to ensure their continued support. Girls, it appeared, were no longer compelled to participate in the time-honoured ritual of communal bathing after a match!

Several pupils, mostly West Indians, reported that P.E. staff had pressurized them to take part in school teams. One West Indian girl said a games teacher 'nagged' her incessantly until she finally agreed to play hockey. Another black pupil recounted the following:

The P.E. teachers kept on telling me how good I was at running. They worked on me [persuaded] to go along to athletics practice even though I didn't like the idea.

Sometimes consensual methods were abandoned in favour of force. As Ronald, a West Indian pupil, with commitments in several sports teams explained: 'Teachers kept pushin' me around (when I was) in the first year. They threatened to lower my report if I didn't play.'

Some pupils, however, told how they resisted such force. Garry, a white school rejector, recalled an incident where a teacher had 'asked' him to play in the rugby team. 'He used to threaten me by saying he'd give me a bad report and by thumping me and twisting my arms . . .', but added defiantly, 'I only turned up for one game.'

Let us now consider in more detail the reasons given by pupils for their involvement in (or rejection) of extra-curricular sport.

As we have already seen almost all of the female team members and about two-thirds of the white male team members were drawn from the upper band in the school. In general terms, the explanations which these pupils offered for participating in sports teams reflected their more favourable position in the school hierarchy.

Both black and white female participants tended to stress the social dimension of sport and said that playing in a school team gave them an opportunity to be with their friends. A few found the competitive aspects stimulating or indicated that they 'played for fun' or 'to keep fit'. Many said that they participated because they were 'proud to represent the school' or 'wanted to do something to help the school'. The impression gained of the majority of female participants, in contrast to the findings of Fuller (1980), was of conformist pupils firmly ensconced within the consensual fold of the school.

It came as no surprise that boys (from each ethnic group) tended to look upon sport as an appropriate channel through which to express their masculinity, enhance their male identities and maintain contacts with their peers. As one boy responded when asked why he played soccer for the school: 'It's a real man's game, that's all.' Many boys stressed the cathartic value of sport claiming that it 'helped them to wind down', 'relax' or 'relieve tensions'. Predictably the boys gave greater emphasis than the girls to the competitive aspects of sport, saying they 'enjoyed the challenge', 'liked the spirit of competition' or found it 'fun to meet and beat other schools'. Unlike the girls, few boys expressed mainstream conformist sentiments when accounting for their involvement in sports teams. According to David, a West Indian rugby and soccer player: 'There's little winning for the school at heart. You're winning for the team – the school has very little part.'

Disaffected white pupils at Hillsview tended to spurn extra-curricular sport, even though many of the boys spent much of their spare time playing soccer or Rugby League. Their rejection of school sport was allied to their rejection of school *per se*. Thus, Paul summed up the feelings of this group, when he said: 'I'm good enough to play in the football team – but I just don't bother to . . . Sport is just another subject after school.'

Unlike Paul and many of his white peers in the lower band, a substantial caucus of disaffected black youth played regularly in school teams, even though their responses to other facets of school and schooling appeared ambivalent or negative. In contrast to their white counterparts, these pupils appeared to regard sport as qualitatively different from other school activities. As Roy, a West Indian rugby player with an undistinguished academic record who, it seemed, was at war with the school, explained:

> I take part because I'm not forced to do so. Rugby isn't like lessons. If you're sitting in the back of the class you're picked on . . . but if you're playing rugby it's of your own free will.

How is this differential response to be interpreted? Could it be that disaffected black pupils tended to cooperate with this form of channelling because their rejection of school was not as complete as that of their white working class peers? As the authors of the report *Disaffected Pupils* have observed:

> For the white boys and girls disaffection meant a *severing of contact with the school* and *all that it stood for*, whereas for the black boys – even the most difficult in the teachers' eyes – their approach to school was riven with contradictions. They were both for it and against it and their hostility was always tempered by a recognition that it was essential in achieving the type of career to which they aspired. (Bird *et al.*, 1981)

It would seem likely, therefore, that ethnic specific sub-cultural factors play some part in the high level of West Indian involvement in school sport. Could it be, with the apparent lack of competition from white working class pupils, West Indians have easy access to an almost 'deserted field'?

In addition, the apparent readiness of black youth in Hillsview, to cooperate with channelling appeared to be related to the growth of ethnic consciousness among this group. As I have already suggested, there were signs that black pupils looked upon sport as an opportunity to 'colonize' one major area of school activity and to make it their own. Indeed, there were indications, not only from the school staff but from pupils (black and white alike) that West Indians had 'colonized' school sport and regarded the sports field as their territory. A variety of strategies were deployed to control this territory. According to one West Indian team member, Joanne:

> In some teams the coloured girls are right nasty. They shout at the white girls, who then drop out because they're frightened that we will make life uncomfortable for them.

Other black pupils, like Alex, informed us that pupils often played a part in team selection and that 'white lads were frequently overlooked unless they were friendly with coloured lads in the team.'

There could be little doubt that racial boundaries at the school had become more sharply delineated as a result of the sponsorship of West Indian involvement in sport. Whilst the boycotting of extra-curricular sport by some white pupils could be read as a manifestation of working class resistance to schooling, with others it was more directly related to racial considerations. Indeed, it could be argued that racism within this sector of the school population played an important part in determining the ethnic composition of the sports teams. As one white pupil conceded: 'There's a lot of prejudice at this school . . . Some kids won't play for the school because they just don't like West Indians.'

'Sport – That's all we're good at' (or the Self-fulfilling Prophecy at work)

The question of whether pupils at Hillsview School shared their teachers' preconceptions of their abilities was approached indirectly: pupils were asked (both individually and in groups) to account for their school's distinguished record in sport. From their responses, it was apparent that some pupils – both black and white – had internalized low expectations of their academic abilities, or racial stereotypes of black athletic prowess and physical superiority. Several pupils saw athletic success as compensating for academic failure, e.g.

Hillsview's pupils are not very clever academically so they concentrate on sport where only physical fitness is essential and excel. (Andrew; white)

Pupils don't seem to do all that well in academic subjects so they push all the more harder in sport. (Beverley; black)

There were some who utilized racial stereotypes in their accounts, as the following extracts indicate:

It's because of the coloureds. They're better at sport than white people. Most of them are big, fast and aggressive. (Michelle; white)

In Hillsview most coloured people believe they're better at sport than white people. (Hilson; black)

It's because of the coloured blood. If it wasn't for the coloured blood our school wouldn't be as good as it is. (David; black)

In contrast to the above, other pupils variously explained the frequent successes of the school teams in terms of: the rough and tough nature of the school catchment area; the quality of its training and coaching facilities; or the pre-occupation of many of the staff with sport; e.g.

We're surrounded by a rough area. People round here tend to be strong and hard. There are very few middle-class kids in the school. (David; black)

We've got very good sports facilities; teachers are very involved with sport. (Mandy; white)

The other teams are scared of us 'cos we're bigger and rougher. Sport's the best thing that goes on at this school. More goes into sport than other lessons. (Malcolm; white)

Aspirations: imaginary and real

Despite their heavy commitments in school teams and although some had internalized the stereotype of black physical superiority, none of the West Indian pupils approached during the course of the research seemed to endorse the chimerical notion of sport as a viable channel for social advancement. Whereas a few male pupils (i.e. 7 black, 11 white), when asked 'If you could have any job in the world what would it be?', indicated that they held fantasies of a career in professional sport (usually soccer), only one (a white youth) appeared to perceive this as a *real* option. If West Indians did not hold unrealistic aspirations of a career in sport, what were their aspirations? Along with Bird *et al.* (1981), Fuller (1980) and Sharpe (1976) it was found that the aspirations of these pupils, despite their low attainment levels, tended to be higher than those of their white peers. West Indian boys, for example, were more likely to eschew lower status manual jobs than white boys. Many aspired to skilled manual work, and indicated that they hoped a declining job market would not prevent them from becoming engineering apprentices, mechanics, electricians etc. Similarly, West Indian girls gave the impression of being more ambitious than white girls. Unlike the latter, they seemed to be less attracted to factory work or routinized 'white-blouse' work, and more likely to aspire to 'careers' in such fields as nursing, teaching or social work. Many expressed similar views to those of Melanie, who informed us: 'I want a good education and then to get a good job . . . Perhaps a games teacher or a nurse if I'm good enough.'

Often aspirations of ambitious black pupils were tempered by a sense of realism. As Donna replied, when asked if anything worried her about finding a job: 'Employers might not like your colour even if you have the necessary qualifications.'

SUMMARY AND CONCLUSIONS

In conclusion, an attempt has been made to show that the over-representation of

West Indian pupils in school sports teams is in part the outcome of channelling by teachers who have a tendency to view this ethnic group in stereotypical terms, as having skills of the body rather than skills of the mind. By encouraging these allegedly 'motor minded' pupils to concentrate on sport in school perhaps at some expense to their academic studies and by utilizing (particularly in the case of disaffected, non-academic black males) extra-curricular sports involvement, as a mechanism of social control, teachers have inadvertently reinforced West Indian academic failure and, concomitantly, have thereby facilitated the reproduction of the black worker as 'wage labour at the lower end of employment, production and skill'. What, if anything, can be done to interrupt this cycle?

In general terms, I accept the thesis that schooling in capitalist formations is a 'conservative force' and that the school system: (1) transmits a culture supportive of the established social order and the class interests which dominate it; (2) implicitly favours those with access to power and resources; and (3) by teaching different skills, values and dispositions to different sectors of the school population, schools latently recreate the class structure with its attendant racial and sexual divisions. However, like Giddens (1979) and others who seek to distance themselves from the excessive determinism of certain Marxist and sociological accounts of cultural and social reproduction, I would stress that reproduction neither occurs automatically nor takes place 'behind the backs of social actors'. Schools are no more cogs in a capitalist machine, than teachers the unreflexive purveyors of ruling ideology, or pupils, the passive recipients of know-how, values and dispositions appropriate to their future positions in the socio-technical division of labour.

The school system – along with other cultural and political institutions – is a site of struggle. The conservative face of schooling, therefore, must be regarded as contingent rather than pre-given. To accept the need for a politics of education and policy initiatives within education, whether to tackle race-, class- or gender-based forms of educational disadvantage, is to accept the *specificity* of institutions such as the school and to recognize that teachers (along with other social actors), whilst not wholly free, are not 'automatons', 'passive objects', 'cultural dupes' or 'the mere bearers of the mode of production'.

Whilst I recognize that racist attitudes, values and practices are deeply entrenched within the fabric of British society, history and culture, and acknowledge the limitations of educational reform *per se*, I do not accept that teachers (or other agents of cultural and social reproduction) are incapable of appraising, evaluating and – over time – changing their attitudes and practices in relation to particular social categories and groups. 'Racially explicit' policies, therefore, such as those advocated in the Rampton Report (1981) and by Kirp (1979), Little and Willey (1981), must now be pursued. From this and other ethnographic research, it is evident that *one* starting point for such a policy would be to address the issue of racism within the teaching force itself. Without such initiatives in the field of education and further interventions, for example, to curb discriminatory practices in the labour market, West Indians will continue to function as a repository of menial wage-labour and as 'gladiators' for white British society.

REFERENCES

Beswick, W.A. (1976) The relationship of the ethnic background of secondary school boys to their participation in and attitudes towards physical activity, *Research Papers in Physical Education*, Vol. 3, No. 2

Bird, C. *et al.* (1981) *Disaffected Pupils*, Brunel University, Uxbridge

Cashmore, E. (1981) The black British sporting life, *New Society*, 6 August

Corrigan, P. (1979) *Schooling the Smash Street Kids*, Macmillan, London

Edwards, H. (1973) The black athlete: twentieth century gladiators for white America, *Psychology Today*, November

Fuller, M. (1980) Black girls in a London comprehensive school. In R. Deem, (ed.) *Schooling For Women's Work*, Routledge and Kegan Paul, London

Gallop, P. and Dolan, J. (1981) Perspectives on the participation in sporting recreation among minority group youngsters, *Physical Education Review*, Vol. 4, No. 1

Giddens, A. (1979) *Central Problems in Social Theory*, Methuen, London

Hargreaves, D. (1967) *Social Relations in a Secondary School*, Routledge and Kegan Paul, London

Hendry, L. and Thorpe, E. (1977) Pupils' choice, extra curricular activities: a critique of hierarchical authority?, *International Review of Sport Sociology*, Vol. 4, No. 12

Jones, P. (1977) An evaluation of the effect of sport on the integration of West Indian schoolchildren. Unpublished Ph.D. Thesis, University of Surrey

Kew, S. (1979) *Ethnic Groups and Leisure*, S.S.R.C./Sports Council, London

Kirp, D. (1979) *Doing Good by Doing Little*, University of California Press, Berkeley

Lawson, H. (1979) Physical education and sport in the black community, *Journal of Negro Education*, Vol. 48, No. 2

Little, A. and Willey, R. (1981) *Multi-ethnic Education: the way forward*, Schools Council, London

Rampton Report (1981) *West Indian Children in our Schools. Interim Report of Inquiry into the Education of Children from Ethnic Minority Groups*, HMSO, London

Sargeant, A.J. (1972) Participation of West Indian boys in English school sports teams, *Educational Research*, Vol. 14, pp 225–30

Sharpe, S. (1976) *Just Like a Girl*, Penguin, Harmondsworth

Stone, M. (1981) *The Education of the Black Child in Britain*, Fontana, London

Troyna, B. (1979) Differential commitment to ethnic identity, *New Community*, Vol. 7, No. 30

Wellman, D. (1977) *Portraits of White Racism*, Cambridge University Press, New York

Wood, E.R. (1973) An investigation of some aspects of social class and ethnic group differentiation in a school-based Junior Activities centre. Unpublished M.Ed. Thesis, University of Newcastle-upon-Tyne

TOPICS FOR DISCUSSION

1. What evidence does Carrington adduce to support his assertion that 'The education system has played a major part in maintaining the apparently immutable position of black workers in the class structure and labour market'? (p 111)

2. 'If there is a difficulty of cultural identity among second generation West Indians, there is also much to conterbalance that deficiency including their natural sense of rhythm, colour and athletic prowess.'
   (National Association of Headteachers' evidence to the Rampton Committee, April 1980)
   What are the origins of stereotypes? How are they maintained? What are their effects upon educational practice?

3. How is extra-curricular sport at Hillsview Comprehensive School used as a mechanism of social control?

SUGGESTIONS FOR FURTHER READING

1. Braham, P., Pearn, M. and Rhodes, E. (1982) *Discrimination and Disadvantage in Employment: The Experience of Black Workers*, Harper & Row, London. An account of the widespread discrimination in the labour market, despite state legislation intended to curb racism in employment practices.

2. Tomlinson, S. (1981) *Educational Subnormality: A Study in Decision-Making*, Routledge and Kegan Paul, London. The issue of educational subnormality in respect of non-white pupils is *solely* concerned with children of West Indian origin. Tomlinson argues that 'professionals' (headteachers, doctors, educational psychologists) employ assessment procedures in judging educational subnormality that are unformulated, unclarified and largely non-educational. She goes on to ask the more fundamental question as to the purpose that a subnormality categorization serves in complex, industrialized societies such as Britain (*see* Reading 12, pp 250–254).

3. Cashmore, E.E. and Troyna, B. (1983) *Introduction to Race Relations*, Routledge and Kegan Paul, London. Chapter 9, 'Media, racism, reality', discusses the ways in which the media both reflect and shape racialist attitudes.

Reading 7
RESPONSES – THE STATE, THE MASS MEDIA AND RACIAL MINORITIES
A. Pilkington [1]

A race relations situation was defined in the first chapter as one in which two features are present: racialism and racism. Racialism refers to practices which disadvantaged people on the basis of their supposed membership of a particular race; racism refers to beliefs which consider that the disadvantaged group in question is inherently inferior. In the course of this book, we have amassed a great deal of evidence to show that racial minorities in Britain have met extensive racialism and racism with the result that their life chances have been impaired. To the question posed earlier, as to whether the entry of West Indians and Asians has given rise to a race relations situation in Britain, our answer must therefore be an emphatic yes.

Once it is recognized that Britain has a race relations situation, the question arises as to how people have responded to this situation. In this chapter, attention will be focused on the responses of three key agencies/groups: the state, the mass media and the minorities themselves.

THE ROLE OF THE STATE

In beginning our examination with the state, we are turning to a sector which is generally recognized to be an important determinant of people's life chances. Needless to say there are different conceptions of the state. But whether we go along with the claim of some Marxists, that the state primarily serves the long term interests of capital, or with the claim of some conflict theorists, that the state responds to the demands of a plurality of groups, we need to acknowledge the 'autonomy' of the state. Its actions are not at the beck and call of any one social group and make a significant contribution to the pattern of race relations.

The state did not anticipate the scale of immigration from the New Commonwealth and Pakistan and made no plans to help the newcomers settle in Britain.

[1] In Pilkington, A. (1984) *Race Relations in Britain*, University Tutorial Press, Slough, pp 145–82

The measures taken by governments have therefore tended to be reponses to immediate problems. In the process, however, a policy accepted by both the main political parties emerged. This policy has two aspects: controls over immigration on the one hand and measures designed to combat racial disadvantage on the other hand. While the Conservative party was the first to advocate immigration control which the Labour party later came to support, the latter was the first to put forward measures to redress racial disadvantage which the Conservatives then came to accept. Let us deal with each aspect in turn.

The opportunity, which the British Nationality Act of 1948 offered citizens of the British Commonwealth to enter Britain, seek work and settle here with their families, lasted throughout the 1950s. The right of West Indians and Asians to migrate to Britain was indeed defended by politicians in both the main political parties. While Conservative spokesmen pointed out that citizens of the Commonwealth were 'British subjects', Labour spokesmen emphasized that they were 'our comrades' (Rex and Tomlinson, 1979). It is true that a vociferous minority on the back-benches objected to the arrival of black immigrants but such views did not gain much support in Parliament. The anti-immigration lobby gained a more responsive audience at the local level, however, where the white residents often felt resentment towards their new neighbours. Such feelings came to a head in the race riots in Nottingham and Notting Hill in 1958 when some white youths openly attacked blacks.

The riots shook many politicians out of their complacency and prompted them to take one of two positions. According to the first view, the riots exemplified racism. Disadvantaged whites had vented their frustrations on a group of people whom they considered inferior. For there to be racial harmony, governments needed to devise policies to combat racism and to eradicate the disadvantages faced by both whites and blacks. According to the second view, the riots indicated that traditional British tolerance towards immigrants had been stretched beyond reasonable limits. The presence of a large number of black and culturally distinct immigrants had provoked resentment. To allay people's anxieties and thus promote racial harmony, governments needed to restrict the number of black immigrants and encourage those already here to assimilate.

Although the subject of race relations rarely arose during the 1959 election, the re-elected Conservative government faced mounting demands for immigration control as immigration rose. Eventually the government succumbed to the pressure and passed the Commonwealth Immigrants Act of 1962. Under the Act, citizens of the British Commonwealth had to acquire an employment voucher to come to Britain unless they held passports issued in Britain or through a British High Commission abroad. Although the Act was vigorously opposed by the Labour party, the election of the Conservative candidate Peter Griffiths at

Smethwick in the 1964 general election, prompted the party to change its mind. The Conservative candidate's victory on what most commentators consider to have been an extremely racist platform had been gained against the national trend. The lessons were not lost on the Labour government. Far from repealing the 1962 Act, it tightened it up and reduced the number of work vouchers for Commonwealth immigrants in 1965.

Two events in 1968 confirmed that the second view depicted above had won the day. They were the passing of legislation apparently designed to reduce the number of East African Asians entering Britain and what one writer has called 'the rise of Enoch Powell' (Foot, 1969). Let us take each in turn.

The 1962 Act did not cover East African Asians who had opted, on the independence of Kenya and other African countries, to hold British passports. When, however, many of them took up their right to migrate to Britain during 1967, as a result of the Kenyan government's 'Africanization' policy, panic set in. The Commonwealth Immigrants Act of 1968 was rushed through Parliament and became law within a week. Under the Act, people who held British passports did not have the right to enter and settle in Britain unless they had a 'close connection' with the country, for example a parent or grandparent born here. The Act proved to be racially discriminatory in nature. For its effects were to allow Kenyan whites to enter Britain but to prevent Kenyan Asians from doing so until they were lucky enough to be granted one of the limited number of vouchers issued each year.

If 1968 witnessed a piece of legislation which was effectively racialist, it also saw a leading politician apparently lend respectability to racism. In graphic language, Powell advocated halting black immigration and indeed exploring ways of repatriating black people already here. Unless such measures were taken, he argued, the future was fearful. In his most famous speech, he concluded: 'As I look ahead I am filled with foreboding. Like the Roman I seem to see "the River Tiber foaming with much blood".' Although this speech was denounced by many politicians and caused him to be sacked from the Shadow Cabinet, Powell received phenomenal support from the public. In the light of this, few politicians were tempted any longer to take a more liberal line on immigration. Indeed, with the election of a Conservative government in 1970, a new Immigration Act was passed, which codified the previous legislation and tightened the controls on black immigration even further.

Under the 1971 Immigration Act, Commonwealth citizens needed permission to enter Britain unless they fell into one of three categories: they were 'patrials' and thus had a 'close connection' with the country; they were close relations of those who had emigrated to Britain under previous legislation; or they were part of the quota of East African Asians accepted each year. If they did not fit into one of these categories, they needed to be in possession of a work permit which henceforth had to be renewed annually. In effect the Act reinforced the racially discriminatory nature of the previous immigration legislation. In view of the paucity of 'patrials' in the New as opposed to the Old and predominantly white Commonwealth, virtually the only black immigrants allowed in since the Act have been close dependents of those already here and East African Asians who had ' been granted British passports.

The only occasion in which a significant liberal gesture has been made since then was in 1972 when President Amin expelled all British Asians from Uganda. Aware that these British passport holders would otherwise be stateless the British government reluctantly admitted 27 000 refugees. This manifestation of liberalism did not last long, however. Indeed the emergence of a 'new political phenomenon' in the shape of a political movement, for whom racism was a central plank, probably helped to persuade most politicians against any further liberalization (Taylor, 1979).

The new political phenomenon was the growth in support for an extreme right-wing movement, the National Front. The movement had been formed in 1967 from other extreme right-wing movements and inherited from its predecessors both its personnel and ideology (Taylor, 1978). Indeed continuities have been detected between the National Front and two previous fascist movements, Mosley's British Union of Fascists and Leese's Imperial Fascist League. Not only were leading members of the National Front connected with these movements, but they also retained, as a central element in their ideology, the belief that Jews were conspiring to overthrow the natural order, in which the white race was dominant, so that they could rule the world themselves (Billig, 1978). In seeking popular support, leaders of the National Front played down this ideological strand and emphasized instead the need for black immigrants to be repatriated. Such scapegoating of blacks (Nugent and King, 1979) brought the party little success until the government decided to admit the Ugandan Asians in 1972. Capitalizing on the issue, National Front candidates in the local elections in 1973 gained some electoral support with over 10 per cent of the vote in a number of cities. More important, however, than its electoral support – which only remained at this kind of level in 1976–77, when a panic had arisen about the numbers of East African Asians being admitted to the country – was the publicity which the party received through its demonstrations and election campaigns.

The visibility and apparent popularity of a party, which openly expressed racist views, may have encouraged the main political parties to maintain a very restrictive immigration policy. In this context, it is interesting to note that in an interview in 1978 before she became Prime Minister, Mrs Thatcher made reference to the National Front. After pointing out that some white people felt 'swamped by people with a different culture', she spoke of the fears 'driving some people to the National Front', a party considered to be at least 'talking about some of the problems'. In the light of this the decision of the Conservative party to advocate further immigration restriction becomes understandable and may have contributed to the debacle of the National Front in the general election in 1979. Certainly there have been few signs of any relaxation in the way immigration legislation has been administered since then. Indeed the passing of a new Nationality Act in 1981, to bring citizenship law in line with the changes effected by the immigration legislation of 1962, 1968 and 1971, has been seen by some commentators as yet further evidence of racial discrimination.

Two kinds of Commonwealth citizens had been created under the 1948 Act, citizens of the Independent Commonwealth countries on the one hand, and citizens of the UK and the Colonies on the other hand. The 1981 Act replaced the latter form of citizenship with three new ones: British citizenship, British Dependent Territories citizenship and British Overseas citizenship. Only those who are British citizens, mainly 'patrials' have the right to settle in this country. Those who hold British Dependent Territories citizenship, mainly people in Britain's remaining colonies, have the right to settle in the dependency in question while those who hold British Overseas citizenship, the remainder, do not have the right to settle in any country at all. Much of the criticism of the Act has centred on the last form of citizenship. For some of the people in this category – mainly Asians – do not have any other nationality. The unwillingness of the government to give British citizenship to those without any other 'contrasts markedly with the solicitude shown to certain people – mainly white' (Bonner, 1983) and suggests racial discrimination.

What conclusions can we draw then from our review of the measures adopted by governments in the field of immigration? The evidence indicates that the controls have not only got tighter but have also in their operation proved more racially discriminatory. The success of the anti-immigration lobby in winning local support for its measures before 1962, Griffiths' victory at Smethwick in 1964, the popularity of Powell's speeches from 1968 and the visibility of the National Front during the 1970s meant that politicians were frequently re-minded of the existence of strong opposition to black immigration and were therefore persuaded to adopt increasingly restrictive controls. Fearful of the electoral consequences of appearing too liberal, a leading member of the Labour cabinet, Richard Crossman, explained that after Smethwick the party 'felt [it] had to out-trump the Tories by doing what they would have done and so transforming their policy into a bipartisan policy' (Crossman, 1975). Euphemistically, the cry was for 'immigration control, but it became increasingly clear that the parties' main concern was to 'out-trump' each other in their control of *black* immigration.

In view of the importance attached to this, it is perhaps not surprising to learn of the extraordinary and sometimes inhuman lengths government officials concerned with immigration have gone to in order to ensure that only those who are entitled to come enter the country.

If immigration legislation and administration have tended to be racialist, being apparently presaged on the assumption that an increase in the number of black immigrants is inherently undesirable, the same is not true of the other aspect of government policy in the field of race relations. Measures designed to combat racial disadvantage reflect the adherence of governments to liberal principles. Such measures have taken two forms, being concerned either with disadvantage which stems from racial discrimination, or with disadvantage which has other sources. Let us deal with each form in turn.

The government has attempted to combat racial discrimination through a series of Race Relations Acts. The first in 1965 outlawed racial discrimination in certain places of public resort and set up a Race Relations Board to receive complaints of discrimination and, if necessary, act as a conciliator. In view, however, of evidence of substantial racial discrimination in other fields, a second Act was passed in 1968 outlawing racial discrimination in employment, housing and commercial services. If the Race Relations Board was unable to conciliate the two sides in a dispute, it was empowered to take the case to court. The Act also set up a new body, the Community Relations Commission, to promote 'harmonious community relations'. Although overt racial discrimination declined considerably following the Act, evidence that considerable covert discrimination still persisted prompted the Government to pass the third Act in 1976.

The most recent Race Relations Act was strongly influenced by antidiscrimination law in the USA. As such, it diverges from the previous Acts in three main ways. Firstly, the definition of racial discrimination is extended to include indirect forms, where practices have a disproportionately adverse effect on a particular racial group, even when there is no intention to discriminate. Secondly, the Commission for Racial Equality (C.R.E.), which replaces both the Race Relations Board and the Community Relations Commission, is empowered to carry out its own investigations of organizations to find out whether they are discriminating. If discrimination is discovered it can require the organization to change its practices and check that this has been done. Thirdly, individuals who believe that they have been discriminated against can take their complaints directly to the courts or industrial tribunals.

Although writers from different theoretical positions believed that the Act might significantly reduce the level of racial discrimination (for example, Sivanandan, 1982 on the one hand, and Smith 1977 on the other hand), the signs so far are not promising. Take the case of employment, where, following the

American experience, the C.R.E. has urged employers to adopt formal equal opportunity policies in the hope that they will check their existing practices for possible discrimination and take appropriate action. Initial evidence suggests that this policy is proving less effective than in the USA in providing 'a steady improvement in the opportunities for some blacks' (Braham *et al.*, 1981). Three broad reasons have been put forward for this.

The first concerns the law itself. 'The prospect of successful litigation against those who discriminate is much greater and the economic consequences for those successfully sued are vastly greater' in the USA (Bindman, 1981). While the courts in the USA have tended to be sympathetic towards legislation where the objective is to end the 'social wrong' of racial discrimination, British courts have often been keener to protect 'the private right of the individual, including the right to discriminate on the grounds of the colour of a man's skin' (Griffith, 1977). As a result the latter have been 'much less willing to accept that discrimination has been proved' (Bindman, 1981) so that in the period 1978–80, only 97 complaints of discrimination in employment (18 per cent of those taken to tribunals) were upheld and in the majority of these cases no compensation was given. The derisory amounts of compensation which have tended to be awarded in Britain again provides a contrast with the situation in the USA. In Britain, damages cannot be awarded where indirect discrimination which is unintentional occurs, and there is no possibility of a 'class action', where claims can be put forward in court simultaneously on behalf of a large number of complainants, each of whom may receive damages. The consequence is that, by comparison with the USA, employers do not face the possibility of huge fines.

The second reason for the relative ineffectiveness of anti-discrimination legislation concerns the state. The state is in a powerful position, both as an employer and through its contracts with firms in the private sector, to promote an effective equal opportunities policy. In contrast to the USA, a low priority, however, has tended to be given to this.

The third reason why the Race Relations Act has not been as successful as had been hoped concerns the C.R.E. The body has been severely criticized by the Home Affairs Select Committee for overstretching itself and thus failing to fulfil its law enforcement duties satisfactorily (Home Affairs Committee, 1981). Certainly the results of its investigations into organizations suspected of discrimination have so far proved disappointing, with too many being directed at small organizations and with only one having been translated into a published report by 1982. The problem does not, however, lie purely with the C.R.E. It has not been given the resources and the government support necessary for it both to enforce the law and undertake promotional work.

Racial disadvantage does not stem purely from racial discrimination but arises also, for example, from the fact that black people tend to live in inner cities. Aware of this, governments have devised a number of 'colour blind' measures which it is hoped will prove beneficial to the disadvantaged generally. In view of the fact that black people tend to be disproportionately disadvantaged, it is expected that they will particularly benefit from these measures. As yet, however, there are few signs that these attempts to deal with the problems of racial minorities by stealth have proved any more successful than the anti-discrimination legislation (Runnymede Trust, 1980). Commenting on government policy in the field of housing, Rex has argued that there has not been 'any clear policy towards immigrant minorities. At best the policies which have been evolved have been piecemeal compromises to deal with contingencies as they arise' (Rex, 1981). And in similar fashion, with reference to government policy in the field of education, Little has concluded that 'no national policy on ethnic minority education has emerged' (Little, 1978).

To conclude that the measures governments have devised to combat racial disadvantage have so far proved relatively ineffective is not to claim that they were 'conceived in terms of giving the impression [of] something [. . .] being done' (Ben-Tovim and Gabriel, 1982). The organizations, such as the Campaign Against Racial Discrimination, which first put forward these proposals, genuinely wished to end racial discrimination and the government, in making a positive response to this demand, acted in line with liberal principles.

Having examined both aspects of government policy in the field of race relations, what conclusions can we come to? Government policy has exhibited the influence of two contradictory traditions, racism and liberalism. While immigration policy and administration have tended to exemplify the first tradition, the measures designed to combat racial disadvantage have tended to exemplify the second tradition. In view, however, of the fact that both main political parties reached a consensus during the 1960s that tight control on *black* immigration was a necessary prerequisite for racial harmony, it is the first tradition which has been the more dominant one (Parekh, 1978). In seeking to appease public opinion, by imposing steadily tighter controls on black immigration, governments appear to have not only acted in a racially discriminatory way but also to have reinforced racist attitudes in the electorate (Dummett and Dummett, 1982). Although it is true 'that neither party has sought to exploit the race issue to anything like its full extent' (Lawrence, 1978), it is also that neither party has stood steadfastly by liberal principles and thus opened up the possibility of liberal attitudes in the electorate being reinforced.

Government policy in this field does not have to take the form which it has done. It is not determined in some mechanistic way by public opinion any more than it is by the needs of capital. Rather it is the product of human decisions. If racial disadvantage is to be combatted and race relations to be improved, the major political parties must stop trying to out-trump each other in seeking to appease 'racist sections of public opinion' and instead take decisive action to fight racism and eradicate the deprivations faced by both whites and blacks.

THE MASS MEDIA

While the state is in probably the most powerful institutional position to influence race relations, it is the mass media which constitute for most people the major source for their picture of what is going on. Indeed it is primarily through the mass media that the messages of the politicians are transmitted and the latter learn about the state of public opinion. Before, however, we examine the news media, reference needs to be made to the entertainment media.

Although we do not turn to the entertainment media to find out what is going on in the field of race relations, such media do nevertheless provide us with images of people and countries and in this way lead us to hold certain expectations about relations between people with different skin colours. In view of the evidence which indicates that racial attitudes are picked up at an early age, much of the research here has been conducted on the media aimed primarily at children. The conclusions of the research are uniformly bleak, as three reviews have pointed out.

> In their comics children are provided with a world in which blacks hardly figure; but where they are present in the action it is as superstitious natives, docile, humble servants, or brute savages. (Husband, 1974)

An image of the world is conveyed which derives from colonialism and visualizes both black people and the countries they come from as 'primitive'. Such assumptions are also apparent in children's popular fiction. Again, if blacks do figure, they are allotted limited roles, tending to oscillate between 'naughty, evil and menacing roles', such as the golliwogs in the Noddy stories, on the one hand, and being 'merry, simple, childlike people', such as Little Black Sambo, on the other hand (Dixon, 1977). A similarly one-sided treatment is even apparent in school textbooks where 'one finds again the same unfavourable images of black people and the same pictures of white-dominated black countries' (Laishley, 1975). What tends to be true of the media aimed primarily at children seems to apply generally to the entertainment media. These 'reflect on the whole a white man's world in which coloured people, if they are visible at all, tend to have a marginal or subordinate position or to strike a discordant note in an otherwise harmonious world.' (Hartmann and Husband, 1974).

In moving from the entertainment media to the news media, the question arises as to whether the latter also present a picture of the world in which black people only tend to figure as problems. The most systematic evidence pertinent to this question comes from a study which analyzed the treatment of race in the British national press between 1963 and 1970 (Hartmann, Husband and Clark, 1974) Every thirteenth issue of the *Times, Guardian, Daily Express* and *Daily Mirror* was examined over the seven-year period to discover what the race related material was about. The content analysis revealed that

> Race in Britain was portrayed as being concerned mainly with immigration and the control of entry of coloured people to the country, with relations between white and coloured groups, discrimination and hostility between groups, and legislation, and with the politician, Enoch Powell. (Hartmann and Husband, 1974)

The fact that these increasingly became the main terms in which race was presented suggests that a framework for the presentation of race news developed over this period, whereby black immigration was seen as a threat and black people as a problem. Thus despite the fact that the newspapers held different attitudes towards Enoch Powell and the accuracy of his statistics on immigrant numbers, there was agreement on the fact that immigration was a critical issue because of the undisputed assertion that a large black population needed to be avoided. Items which did not fit this framework tended to be seen as increasingly peripheral so that the positive contribution of black people to our society was discounted and the underlying sources of racial tension in the unequal way resources are distributed in our society was ignored.

Confirmation of the existence of a framework, which depicted black immigration as a threat and black people as a problem, across the news media can be found in two further studies of race relations reporting, the first a study of the coverage of the local press between 1963 and 1970 (Critcher *et al.*, 1977) and the second of television in 1970. On the basis of a content analysis of five West Midland newspapers, Critcher *et al.*, noted that immigration constituted a significant element in race reporting and that the issue was 'defined almost exclusively as a problem of control'. A similar conclusion was reached by Downing, who pointed out that the media

> [. . .] have used whites in overwhelming preference to blacks to define the issues; and the whites they have used have often been those determined to expel the black minority from Britain. (Downing, 1980)

In view of this, it is not surprising to learn that a content analysis of three-quarters of news bulletins, current affairs programmes and documentaries during 1970 revealed that the vast bulk of time devoted to race in Britain concerned black immigration, or Enoch Powell and that 'the taken-for-granted framework' of the coverage rested on 'the fundamentally racist view that "immigration *creates* problems" ' (Downing, 1975).

Although the news media's coverage of race related material since 1970 has not received the same systematic analysis, the studies which have been done agree that the media continue to present black people in a negative light. In 1976, for example, over a period of six weeks a 'combination of stories' appeared which

> [. . .] left the strong impression that Britain was being taken over by swarms of Asians, who were not only 'conning' their way into Britain illegally, but once they got here were 'conning' a 'lush living off the state'. (Evans, 1976)

As time has passed, however, the notion of swarms of black people entering the country has become less central and the issue of immigration has been replaced by others. One such issue is 'mugging'.

'Mugging' was first used by the press to describe a specific crime in England in 1972. According to Hall *et al.*, the term had served to symbolize the crisis of law and order in American cities so that when it was transferred to Britain it meant much more than a particular kind of street robbery. It evoked images of black youth mindlessly creating havoc in the inner city. Since 1972 such images have solidified so that mugging has now become unambiguously associated with West Indian youth in certain areas such as Brixton (Hall *et al.*, 1978). The prominence given to such a crime is illuminating when put alongside the media's neglect of racial attacks.

In November 1981, a Home Office study revealed that Asians were 50 times and West Indians 36 times more likely to be victims of racially motivated attacks than whites. The survey was in Smith's words 'curiously underplayed by the mass media' (Smith, 1982). Four months later, the Metropolitan police issued its annual crime figures which purportedly showed that blacks were more likely that whites to be involved in 'robbery and other violent theft', i.e. the category of crime which incorporates mugging. Despite the fact that 'robbery and other violent theft' comprised the smallest category of crime in London, involving only 3 per cent of recorded offences, the media latched on to the figures and in the process conveyed the totally unwarranted impression that black people were disproportionately criminal (Pierce, 1982).

The relative weight given to the Home Office study on racial attacks and the Metropolitan police's racial breakdown of one category of crime, is not so curious when it is recognized that the news media tend to adopt a framework for race related news which assumes that black people constitute a problem. As one assistant editor of a major national newspaper has put it, 'everything to do with coloured people takes place against an underlying premise, that they are the symbols or the embodiments of a problem' (Young, 1971). Items which fit this framework are given prominence, while contrary items are played down.

To argue that the news media tend to present black people in a negative light does not imply that there is some kind of media conspiracy against black people. In many newspapers, there is a marked contrast between the news headlines and the editorials, with the latter qualifying the sensationalism of the former and emphasizing the need for racial tolerance. This indicates that the news media do not consciously set out to convey a negative image of black people. That such a picture is unwittingly conveyed is a result of newsmen following their normal practices.

To illustrate what these practices involve – and therefore why some items become news rather than others and why they are presented in one way rather than another – let us take the case of a daily newspaper. The latter faces at least three demands: a need to ensure that news is regularly produced every 24 hours, a need to ensure that the news is interesting and a need to ensure that the news is intelligible. Let us take each demand in turn.

To enable it to produce news regularly, a newspaper relies on certain routines. One routine is to allocate specific proportions of a paper to different types of news (e.g. home, foreign, sport, etc.). In the process of maintaining a particular balance between these different types of news, irrespective of what happens in the real world, the organization of the newspaper clearly affects what items become defined as news. Of more importance, however, to race news is the routine whereby preference is given to events which occur within a period of a day. Such a routine tends to mean that the media focus on the manifestations of racial conflict and not their underlying causes. A demonstration, especially when accompanied by violence, therefore becomes news while the factors which lead up to it and make it explicable are ignored.

Although the adoption of various routines enables newspapers to produce news regularly, it does not ensure that the news is interesting. This is where 'news values' comes in. These comprise a set of assumptions, generally shared by journalists across the news media, about the kinds of events which are newsworthy and how they should be presented. The employment of such values involves a stress on the unusual, on the dramatic, on conflicts and on personalities, especially well known personalities. 'Two things follow from this: the first is that journalists will tend to play up the extraordinary, dramatic, tragic etc. elements in a story in order to enhance its newsworthiness; the second is that events which score high on a number of these news values will have greater news potential than ones that do not' (Hall *et al.*, 1978).

In the light of our discussion of news values, the form which race relations reporting has taken becomes more explicable. While the positive contribution of black people to our society scores low on all news values, Enoch Powell's famous speech in 1968 almost perfectly meets the requirements of a good news story. After all, the speech – expressed in dramatic language and rife with personal anecdotes – was by a leading politician apparently in conflict with his party on a matter of public concern (Seymour-Ure, 1974).

In addition to the need to produce news regularly and in an interesting way, newspapers must also ensure that the news is intelligible. To this end, journalists tend to present news within frameworks which are already familiar to the audience. Earlier, we argued that 'our whole way of thinking about coloured people, constitutes a built-in predisposition to accept unfavourable beliefs about them' (Hartmann and Husband, 1971). In view of this, it is perhaps not surprising that the media imported from America a framework for race reporting which visualizes black people as a problem.

This framework depends upon a particular image of society – a consensus image – according to which people in Britain are assumed to share the same fundamental values. One such value which the British are deemed to hold is that of tolerance. In view of this, responsibility for any problems which arise between white and black people is laid at the door of those who are not 'truly' British – perhaps a few 'sick' or 'corrupt' whites, but more often blacks. In scapegoating black people in this way, the media not only confirm Britain's image of itself as an essentially tolerant society, but also convey a sense of its people as united against an alien threat. Such a picture inevitably gives the impression that Britain is fundamentally a white society. Take, for example, the media's coverage of the National Front. Despite the fact that the N.F.'s explicit racism was condemned, their right to propagate such a belief system was defended. In the process, 'the "freedom" of black people to be protected from the N.F.'s racial insults [was] constantly overlooked' and the impression underlined 'that blacks exist outside the mainstream of British society' (Troyna, 1982).

Even if it is granted that frameworks, which presume that people in Britain share fundamental values in common, are frequently used by the news media to interpret events (Cohen and Young, 1981), the question still arises as to the origins of such frameworks. Of crucial importance here are those in powerful institutional positions. They are frequently consulted by the mass media and given preferential access to it, for two main reasons. The first stems from the fact that the media need to ensure that news is produced regularly. Faced with the problem of constantly working against the clock, journalists find it helpful to turn to institutional spokesmen who can be relied upon to provide a story. The second stems from the professional values of journalists. Obliged to be as objective as possible, journalists constantly turn to 'accredited sources', notably representatives of the major institutions. The result of giving such preferential access to those in powerful positions is that these ' "spokesmen" become [. . .] the primary definers of topics' (Hall *et al.*, 1978). As such, they provide the initial framework for understanding these topics and are the first to outline what the main issues are. Alternative frameworks and alternative interpretations of the main issues do of course get a hearing, but once a topic has been defined in a particular way, it is extremely difficult to change the terms of the debate.

'Once race relations in Britain [had] been defined as a "problem of numbers", for example, most of the discussions of the issue centred on the question of numbers. Those who suggested that the primary problem should instead be British racism were seen as "not addressing the problem" '. (Hall *et al.*, 1978)

In the light of our discussion of the significance of those in powerful institutional positions for the production of news, the congruence between the issues defined by both the state and the media as central becomes more explicable. Given the institutional links between the Metropolitan police and crime correspondents, it is understandable that the media have given more prominence to 'mugging' than racial attacks.

To argue that the news media tend to present black people in a negative light, through following their normal practices, is not to claim that the coverage inevitably has to take a particular form. Newspapers do differ in the topics they highlight, in the tone they adopt and in the depth of their coverage (Braham, 1982). Take, for example, the coverage given to the Metropolitan police's disclosure in 1983 that blacks were still more likely than whites to be involved in 'robbery and other violent theft'. For the *Sun*, this was a major story. Blazoned over its front page were the headlines *BLACK CRIME SHOCK* and two subsidiary headlines *Twice as many muggings as by white thugs* and *82% of all attacks in one London area*. So important was the story considered to be that it continued on page two (although not on page three) with a new headline. *BLACK MUGGINGS SHOCKER* and warranted a leader the following day. For the *Guardian*, by contrast, this was not a major story. It made no references to the topic on the day it broke in the *Sun* and even on the following day did not consider it worthy of front page coverage. The topic appeared on the back page under the headline *Garbage crime figures come under attack* and was taken up in a leader, in which the statistics were criticized for being misleading. If the priority given to the topic was different, so was the tone adopted. While the *Sun* conveyed the impression that black people were disproportionately involved in crime, the *Guardian* was at great pains to avoid giving this impression. As to the depth of coverage, while the *Sun* took the figures at face value, the *Guardian* critically examined them and presented them in context.

Even if the news media do not necessarily present black people in a negative light, there is nonetheless a tendency for them to do so. In view of this, the question arises as to the effects of such a presentation on people's attitudes and perceptions.

Research on the effects of the mass media on people's attitudes has tended to show that the media reinforce already existing attitudes rather than bring about significant changes. To give one example, a study of viewers' responses to the television series, '*The nature of prejudice*' indicated that on the whole the programmes served to confirm previous views (Elliott, 1972). Such a conclusion is not surprising in view of what we know about selective perception. People do not passively respond to media material but actively use it. Content which contradicts existing attitudes tends therefore to be ignored or forgotten, while content which backs them up is more likely to be sought out and remembered. The result of this is that the media are normally unable to override the effects of other socializing agencies such as the family and the influence of the groups to which individuals belong.

To argue that short term exposure to media material does not have a marked impact on people's attitudes is not to suggest that the media have no important effects. In particular there is some evidence that 'the media provide people with a picture of the world which makes the development of one kind of attitude more likely than another' (Hartmann and Husband, 1974).

The most systematic attempt to show that the mass media's race relations coverage influences people's perceptions of what is going on comes from a survey by Hartmann and Husband. In this study, white schoolchildren, aged from 11 to 15, and their parents were interviewed and asked a series of questions about race. Despite the fact that the respondents came from different parts of Britain and lived in areas with different levels of black settlement, there was a remarkably similar perception of the major issue in race relations. Too many black immigrants were thought to be entering the country.

Although it is likely that some of the respondents came to the belief that 'immigrant numbers are too great' through first-hand contact with black people, it is difficult to see how those living in areas with few black people could have acquired their belief other than through the mass media. Confirmation that the media were indeed a crucial source for this belief emerged from the content analysis of the press and during the survey itself. The content analysis of the press revealed, as we have already seen, the same preoccupation with the question of numbers and in the course of the survey many of the respondents indicated that they had derived their information about race relations from the mass media (Hartmann and Husband, 1974).

Further evidence of the media's influence on people's perceptions of race relations come from a study by Little and Kohler. According to their survey,

58 per cent of the respondents felt that race relations had deteriorated nationally between 1970 and 1976, while only 17 per cent of them felt that they had deteriorated locally. As the authors point out,

> [. . .] views about change in one's locality are largely based upon direct experience of relations and feelings in that locality. A national or general view, however, can be based only upon secondary sources, in particular, the media. (Little and Kohler, 1977).

All in all, there do seem good grounds for believing that the news media do play a major part in defining for people what the major issues are in race relations. In focusing on issues like immigration and crime among black people, however, the media may well have amplified white people's anxieties about black people – anxieties which the government then feel they need to respond to. This is not inevitable, however, and, as we saw earlier in our discussion of press coverage of the 'mugging' statistics, newspapers can – if they are extremely careful (Critcher, 1979) – avoid presenting black people in a negative light.

THE REACTION OF RACIAL MINORITIES

Finally, we come to the racial minorities themselves, and to the question of how they have reacted to a race relations situation in Britain. According to Phizacklea and Miles, there are three possible strategies open to them. They can organize around colour, class or ethnicity (Phizacklea and Miles, 1980). Let us examine each strategy in turn and see what has so far been the most common basis for organization.

In view of the fact that the racial minorities have been subject both to racialism and racism, one might have expected a consciousness of colour to emerge and become a significant basis for organization. In practice, however, the minorities have tended to be more aware of their cultural differences so that it has been rare for them to organize together on the basis of colour. Occasionally they have come together for a specific campaign, but such 'black unity' has so far proved extremely fragile. As Moore has pointed out, we still 'seem to be a long way from the day when all non-white immigrants and their descendants in the UK refer to themselves as "blacks" ' (Moore, 1982).

If 'black unity' has not constituted a very feasible strategy for the minorities, what of 'class unity'? In view of the fact that black people are predominantly working class, one might have anticipated that their response to disadvantage would take a similar form to that of their white comrades. And there indeed do seem to be signs of similarities. Thus evidence indicates that 'black workers are just as likely as white workers, or more so, to vote Labour and join a trade union'

(Phizacklea and Miles, 1980). Electoral support for Labour and union membership do not of course necessarily indicate class consciousness. The former may exhibit a preference for a party which is rather more liberal than its main rival on race relations, while the latter may merely be convenient. Nevertheless, evidence of a willingness on the part of black workers to participate in industrial action, such as strikes, alongside white workers does point to a degree of class unity.

Despite the fact that industrial disputes have often brought black and white workers together in opposition to management, there has been a tendency on the part of some writers to think that disputes which primarily involve black people are 'complicated by a racial element'. We must be wary of making such an assumption (Bentley, 1981). Take, for example, the dispute which arose at Grunwick in 1976. Here the basic demand of the strikers was to gain union recognition from an employer who had refused to accept one. The fact that the strikers were primarily Asian women was irrelevant. Indeed, in this particular case, the 'solidarity' which was shown towards those fighting for union recognition by other (often white) workers was 'considerable' (Phizacklea and Miles, 1981).

If there have been signs of class unity during industrial disputes, there have also been some indications of it during local campaigns. Thus – to give one example – the decision of the local authority to slum clear Moss Side, Manchester, gave rise to a number of housing protest movements, each 'characterised by a multi-racial membership' (Ward, 1979).

To point to examples of black and white people acting together should not blind us, however, to the occasions when racial divisions have inhibited collective action. Although both the Labour Party and the Trades Union Congress have campaigned against racism, there have been instances in which the Labour movement has failed to support black workers and has indeed been involved in discriminatory practices. The disputes at Mansfield Hosiery Ltd and Imperial Typewriters, for example, stemmed from the fact that the white-dominated unions were more anxious to restrict access to promotion opportunities to whites than represent the interests of Asian workers. The latter were therefore 'forced to organise as an Asian workforce, relying on the resources of the Asian community rather than their unions' (Moore, 1982). In other words, they turned to 'ethnic organization'.

In view of the fact that the racial minorities belong to different groups, with their own distinct cultures, it is not surprising that organizations have frequently formed around ethnicity. Keen to maintain their cultural distinctiveness, the minorities have not only created a plethora of neighbourhood-based organizations to enable their community life to function, but have also used these organizations to further their interests in the wider society. Sometimes this has involved waging campaigns to change prevailing practices. Thus – to give one example – the Sikhs have fought to be allowed to wear turbans rather than crash helmets on motorcycles.

To point to the existence of distinct ethnic groups among the racial minorities is not to suggest that the boundaries between such groups are rigid or that the beliefs and values which they espouse are static. While the experience of being rebuffed by British society has tended to encourage the minorities to maintain a separate ethnic identity, 'the ethnicity of the second generation is rather different from that of their parents' (Ballard and Ballard, 1977). In particular there is evidence that a wider ethnic identity is developing, with the children becoming aware of themselves as Asians or West Indians and not just Mirpuris or Trinidadians.

Of the three possible bases for organization we distinguished earlier – colour, class and ethnicity – the latter has proved the most common. The cultural distinctiveness of the minorities has allowed ethnic organizations to emerge and the racism of the wider society has ensured that they maintain their importance. We must be careful, however, not to think that such an ethnic response precludes a class response. The minorities are not, as we have seen, totally reliant on separate organizations and especially at work are represented by the same organizations as their white colleagues. Whether the reaction of the second generation continues to be mainly on ethnic lines or not will depend to a large extent on the actions of the wider society and not least the Labour movement. If 'class unity' is to develop then the recognition which the unions now have of racism in their midst will need to be translated into decisive action to combat it Phizacklea and Miles, 1981).

In the course of examining whether the minorities have been more likely to organize around colour, class or ethnicity, reference has been made not only to the responses of those who migrated but also to those of their descendants. Given the importance of the latter for the future of race relations, let us explore further the reactions of the second generation. We shall begin by looking at Asian youth and then go on to West Indian youth.

ASIAN AND WEST INDIAN YOUTH

According the many commentators, young Asians face a range of distinctive problems. As one writer puts it, 'Asian youth suffer very distinctly from inhabiting a different world at home from that at school'. The culture which is imbibed at home clashes with that picked up at school so that the children invariably experience some stress. Attracted by Western values, they subsequently often come into conflict with their parents during adolescence. There is obviously some truth in this picture. Thus there are indeed significant differences between British and Asian cultures. Particularly important are their respective conceptions of the relationship of the individual to the community. While the British tend to place paramount importance on the freedom of the individual, Asians tend to believe that 'the interests of the group as a whole always take precedence over those of the individual members' (Ballard, 1979). The British consequently tend to view marriage as a contract between two individuals and Asians to picture it as an arrangement between families. In view of these contrasts between British and Asian cultures, it is not surprising to learn of Asian adolescents expressing a preference for the 'western model of marriage based on individual choice' (Brah, 1978) and of conflicts between them and their parents (Ballard, 1979).

We must be careful, however, not to caricature the situation. Although Brah discovered that his sample of 15 to 16 year-olds in Southall tended to express a preference for own-choice marriages, he also noted that there was 'an acceptance on the part of these teenagers of the prospect of arranged marriages'. Similarly, after acknowledging that many young Asians in Leeds did 'rebel against their parents' social and cultural values during their teens', Ballard pointed out that 'by their late teens and early twenties the majority of them do largely conform to Asian behavioural norms within the sphere of family and community life'. There are a number of reasons for such conformity, of which two in particular stand out: the process of socialization in the home and the experience of racial discrimination outside. Growing up in an Asian family encourages individuals to feel loyalty to their community and being rejected by British society helps to reinforce this feeling.

To acknowledge the deep loyalty of young Asians to their community does not mean that they completely adhere to their parents' values. They 'are not faced with an either/or situation', whereby they have to choose between two completely distinct cultures but instead 'work towards their own synthesis of Asian and British values' (Ballard, 1979). In the light of this, it is noteworthy that young Asians do tend to be more individualistic and militant than their parents (Brah, 1978). While a growing individualism indicates some acceptance of British values, an emerging militancy points to a fierce rejection of these values and vehement pride in their separate cultural identity.

If there is some evidence that young Asians are adopting a more militant response to racism that their parents, there are also indications that young West Indians are exhibiting a greater willingness to reject their stigmatized position in society than their parents. Indeed, according to many commentators, what distinguishes the responses of young West Indians to their disadvantaged position is their resistance to white society or, as one writer puts it, their 'rebellion' (Brake, 1980). Three accounts in particular come to this judgement: those by Pryce (in Roberts, 1982), Hall *et al.* (1978) and Cashmore and Troyna (1982).

On the basis of fieldwork conducted between 1969 and 1974 in Bristol, Pryce discovered a variety of 'life styles' within the West Indian community. Although he acknowledged that the majority of West Indians were 'ordinary, steady [. . .] law abiding' people, he paid particular attention to those who rejected 'slave labour' and 'shit work' – the 'hustlers', the 'first generation refusers' and the 'teenyboppers', the 'second generation refusers'. While both the hustlers and the teenyboppers had chosen 'the criminal path of survival as an expression of their contempt for the system that "puts them down" ', the latter had in addition developed a consciousness of themselves as black. In view of the attractions of a life style which positively values black people to those subject to 'endless pressure', Pryce anticipated that West Indian youth would increasingly adopt a teenybopper life style and reject white society (Pryce, 1979).

This expectation is echoed by Hall and his colleagues. In their view, the rejection which the first generation of West Indians met ruled out for most of them the possibility of assimilation into British society. They therefore turned to each other and created a space for themselves in particular areas where they could feel at home. In other words, they created a 'colony' within white soceity. The birth of this colony not only made possible 'an alternative black social life' but also enabled a 'new range of survival strategies' to emerge. While 'the majority survived by going out from the colony every day to work [. . .] others survived by taking up permanent residence inside the ghetto and in some cases taking up 'that range of informal dealing, semi-legal practices, rackets and small-time crime known [. . .] as hustling'. Brought up in this colony 'the second generation simply *is* a black generation, knows it is black and is not going to be anything else but black.' Aware of the racism of British society, it is less willing than the first generation to put up with a stigmatized position. This 'refusal' sometimes gives rise to conflict between the generations with the result that the youth leave home, take to the streets and drift into petty crime (Hall *et al.*, 1978).

A similar emphasis on the centrality of blackness for West Indian youth can be found in the account provided by Cashmore and Troyna. According to these writers, young West Indians 'perceive clearly that blackness is a potential obstacle to advancement in society and [. . .] have now resigned themselves to this perception' (Cashmore and Troyna, 1982). Despite the fact that they do not 'adopt one cultural life style, but mix many', there is nonetheless a recognition among them that 'they are black and share the expreriences of all other blacks in some way'. This realization emerges during the later stages of their secondary school education and the encounter with the wider society reinforces its salience. Aware that British society is racist and yet believing 'they cannot change things', such youngsters are inclined to give vent to their frustrations through violence. Sometimes this takes a collective form and communities are disrupted for short periods of time. These occasions reveal in an extreme form the 'antagonistic values, and frequently oppositional attitudes' of many young West Indians (Cashmore and Troyna, 1982).

For all three accounts of West Indian youth which we have been examining, the major source of the purportedly growing black consciousness and resistance to British society lies in Rastafarianism, a movement which emerged during the 1930s among the black poor in Jamaica. 'The inspirational springboard for Rastafarianism' was provided by Marcus Garvey who, in addition to his advocacy of repatriation to Africa, was credited with having made the following prophecy: 'Look to Africa when a black King shall be crowned for the day of deliverance is near' (Troyna, 1978). When Ras Tafari was subsequently crowned Emperor of Ethiopia and assumed the title of Haile Selassie I, many of Garvey's supporters believed the day of deliverance had arrived. A Black Messiah had emerged to lead his people from Babylon to the promised land of Africa. At last the social order, which had resulted from white imperialism and had belittled black people for so long, was to be toppled and replaced by a new one.

The Rastafarian movement has survived in Jamaica but more importantly, for our purposes, began to take root during the 1970s among West Indian youth in Britain. Its adherents are clearly visible – they wear their hair in locks, put on woolly hats decorated in Ethiopian colours and adopt a distinctive style of speech which expresses the sense of unity ('I and I') felt by brothers and sisters who have been touched by God. The distinctive appearance of Rastafarians symbolizes their disengagement from Babylon, a society which devalues black people. While most West Indian youngsters are not Rastafarians, the latter are seen as having had a pervasive influence through the medium of Reggae music on the consciousness of West Indian youth (Hebdige, 1979). In particular they have encouraged West Indians to recognize blackness as a central aspect of their identity, take pride in their colour and feel opposition towards a society which they recognize can meaningfully be described as Babylon.

What are we to make then of the picture of West Indian youth depicted in the three accounts above? There is clearly some truth in it. The Rastafarian movement has gained more support over time and has helped to generate among West Indian youth a positive attitude towards blackness and a critical attitude towards a society which disparages black people. Nevertheless, we must be extremely careful not to assume that what is true of the most visible West Indians is generally true of young West Indians. In focusing on Rastafarianism and in highlighting the likelihood of West Indian youngsters becoming 'teenyboppers' or turning to street crime/violence, these accounts have concentrated on the 'exotic' and 'deviant' and have ignored the activities of the less newsworthy but more numerous ordinary West Indians (Allen, 1982). In the process they may well have exaggerated the extent of 'alienation' felt by most young West Indians and have unintentionally given the impression that the majority of young West Indians are not law abiding. Such an impression is totally unwarranted (Gaskell and Smith, 1981).

Although the responses of young West Indians and Asians to their situation have generally been as unnewsworthy as those of their parents, there have been occasions when their actions have taken a more dramatic form and have brought them to public attention. The most notable occasion was in 1981, when their involvement in the riots which disturbed a number of British cities was frequently commented upon.

The 1981 riots were not unprecedented in British history. People who have felt that they couldn't gain redress for their grievances from the authorities have often got together in crowds, employed violence and created temporary disruption. Nor were the 1981 riots particularly severe by comparison with others. There was only one death, for example, which resulted from the troubles and that an innocent bystander struck by a police van. Nonetheless, the sight of nightly confrontations during April and July between youth and the police, accompanied by extensive property destruction and some looting, was rare in postwar Britain and was generally recognized to be serious.

Although the 1981 riots took most people by surprise, a forerunner of what was to come took place in Bristol in 1980. Here, following a raid on a cafe suspected of selling illegal drugs, clashes took place between the mainly West Indian youngsters who tended to use the cafe as a major meeting place and the police. Others, including some white youngsters joined in and before the police were able to restore control, significant property destruction and looting had taken place. While these events inevitably provoked a great deal of comment, they did not have the impact of the 1981 riots, which began in an area more closely associated in people's minds with West Indians and continued later in cities throughout Britain.

The 1981 riots did not of course take the same form. While the April confrontations between youth and the police involved mainly West Indians, the disturbances in Southall and in Toxteth, which initiated the wave of rioting in July, involved in the one case mainly Asians and in the other case whites as well as blacks. Despite these differences, the major disturbances did tend to share certain common features. They took place in deprived multiracial areas in which unemployment was high and police/community relations were poor. Matters were often sparked off by an apparent instance of 'police injustice' and, with the exception of the incidents at Southall, West Indian youngsters were usually at the forefront (Kettle and Hodges, 1982).

There are many explanations of the riots on offer, with each one tending to pick out different features to focus on (Taylor, 1981). Thus some emphasize the youth of the participants, others their disadvantage and yet others their race. Although we clearly do not have time to look at each one, reference does need to be made to the explanation offered by the 'official' report on the Brixton disorders (HMSO, 1981, The Scarman Report).

For Scarman, the riots 'cannot be fully understood' unless attention is paid to the situation confronting young West Indians. The latter are extremely vulnerable to disadvantage, mainly because they live in declining inner city areas but also partly because of racial discrimination. As a result, they 'feel neither socially nor economically secure'. Such a sense of insecurity is compounded by the fact that they are not well represented in the political system and because organizations hostile to them are free to demonstrate against them. Feeling politically as well as socially and economically insecure, they 'protest on the streets' where some of them 'live off street crime'. This brings them into regular contact with the police, whom they distrust, so that the possibilities of a serious clash are heightened. Such an eventuality is not inevitable, however. What precipitated it, in the case of the Brixton disorders, was the police decision to persist with a stop and search operation, known as 'Operation Swamp', whereby the area was saturated with officers in plain clothes looking out for street criminals. Although there had been previous operations of this kind – which had left behind an increasing distrust of the police and had only reduced the level of street crime temporarily – this time the tension was so high that an apparent instance of police harassment was able to spark off serious disorders. As Scarman puts it, 'the violence erupted from the spontaneous reaction of the crowds to what they believed to be police harassment'. While the publicity given to the disorder on the Friday meant that whites did participate in the rioting on the Saturday and Sunday, 'the riots were essentially an outburst of anger and resentment by young black people against the police'.

The Scarman Report was generally well received by people of different political persuasions, with most accepting Scarman's contention that poor police/community relations underpinned the riots. What this apparent unanimity masked, however, were disagreements over the question of who was primarily responsible for the breakdown of police/community relations.

For some commentators, major responsibility lay with the police, whose 'policies' and 'attitudes' exhibited 'racism' (Scraton, 1982). Although systematic evidence is hard to come by in this area, examples of police practices, which have had a racially discriminatory impact, are now well documented. A useful summary of the kinds of practices which have had this impact is provided by Kettle and Hodges. They point to instances where racial attacks have not been given systematic police attention and yet the rights of racist organizations, like the National Front, to march through multiracial areas under police protection have been rigorously upheld. They delineate occasions when black community events, such as the Notting Hill Carnival, have been subject to a particularly massive and visible police presence; when black meeting places, such as the Mangrove Restaurant, have been subject to reported police raids which have failed to result in convictions; and when black people have been subject to identity checks and 'passport raids' because of their colour. Above all else, however, they list examples of where 'the everyday use of police powers of stop, search, arrest and questioning on the street and in the police station' has led to discriminatory treatment. In this context, it is interesting to note that a Home Office study found that in the Metropolitan police district, 'blacks were [. . .] most heavily arrested in offences where there was particular scope for suspicion to be aroused from preconceived views'. One of these offences was that of being a suspected person. Under the provision of the Vagrancy Act of 1824, police were entitled to arrest someone 'on suspicion of loitering with intent to commit an arrestable offence'. Since blacks were over ten times more likely to be arrested in the Metropolitan police district for 'sus', it is not surprising that the issue became 'a symbolic precis' of the criticisms levelled 'against the police by the black community' (Roberts, 1982). Although 'sus' was abolished in 1981, the police have stop and search powers which have had 'effects similar to the use of "sus" ' (Harman, 1982). This has been especially true when the police have attempted to combat street crime by saturating an area like Brixton with extra police, such as the Special Patrol Group. On these occasions, Kettle and Hodges point out it is black people who have been most likely to be stopped (Kettle and Hodges, 1982).

While this catalogue of examples of police practices which have had a racially discriminatory impact has convinced some commentators that it is the police who were overwhelmingly responsible for the breakdown in police/community relations, other commentators have been less impressed by the evidence. They admit that there are instances of police injustice but claim that these are rare and that generally blacks and whites are treated equally. The fact that blacks have been more likely to receive police surveillance and to be stopped and arrested for certain offences stems from the fact that they are more likely to be involved in street crime. According to this view, it is not then the police but the black community which was mainly responsible for the breakdown of police/community relations in the main riot areas.

The defenders of the police have a case. While the evidence indicates that examples of disciminatory treatment are far from rare, it is true that no systematic study has been done to gauge just how common police discrimination is. What is more, there are grounds for believing that young West Indians are disproportionately involved in street crime. Thus the Home Office study in the Metropolitan police district, which we mentioned earlier, came to the conclusion that 'victims' reports and arrest rates point to '[. . .] blacks [being] excessively involved in recorded street crime' (Stevens and Willis, quoted in Roberts, 1982). While such figures need to be interpreted with care since they may reflect a racial bias on the part of the police, it seems unlikely that the over-representation of young West Indians to this kind of crime can be accounted for wholly in this way (Smith, 1982). As Lea and Young argue,

> [. . .] it would be implausible to believe that a high recorded rate of street crime for black youths is *merely* a function of police prejudice, although the latter undoubtedly results in an exaggeration of the contribution of black persons to the actual crime rate. (Lea and Young, 1982)

To recognize the limited nature of our evidence on police discrimination and to accept that young West Indians are over-represented in one kind of crime does not of course mean that we are bound to agree that it is the black community which was mainly responsible for the breakdown of police/community relations. Far from it. The police are in a much more powerful position than the minorities and therefore must take primary responsibility for the breakdown in relations.

While the police must be held primarily responsible for 'the catastrophically bad relationship between the police and young black people' (Kettle and Hodges, 1982), we must remember that the police do operate under certain constraints and in particular have to cope with the problem of an increasing crime rate in the inner city consequent upon the rise in unemployment. The latter sets 'the scene', as Lea and Young point out, 'for the development of a vicious circle whereby relations between police and community deteriorate in such a way that each step in deterioration creates pressure for further deterioration'.

For there to be 'consensus policing', a community must act as a source of information to the police so that the latter can 'catch and/or deter individual law-breakers'. As unemployment generates more crime, however, the police begin to adopt a more aggressive policing policy and turn to operations which involve the 'random stopping of "suspicious" youth'. This inevitably results in large numbers of innocent people being stopped and searched. Once this happens the community 'begins to become alienated from the police'. It 'comes to see any attempt at an arrest by officers as a symbolic attack on the community' and ceases to provide the police with any information which can help them identify individual offenders. Faced with this situation, the police adopt an even more aggressive policing policy and so the vicious circle continues. In this context, 'whatever racist sentiments exist within the police force are reinforced'. If the drift towards 'military', policing is to be counteracted, the authors argue that the conditions which generate crime need to be attacked and that the police need to be made more accountable to the community (Lea and Young, 1982). As yet neither of these policies has been seriously pursued.

SUMMARY

In the course of this [Reading], we have examined the responses of the government, the mass media and the minorities, themselves, to a race relations situation. What has been emphasized throughout is that the responses did not have to take the form they did. The same point applies to the future. Whether race relations in Britain improve or deteriorate will depend on what actions people take and in particular what the dominant institutions in our society choose to do.

REFERENCES

Allen, S. (1982) Perhaps a seventh person?, in C. Husband (ed.) (1982) *Race in Britain: Continuity and Change*, Hutchinson, London
Ballard, C. (1979) Conflict, continuity and change, in S. Khan (ed.) (1979) *Minority Families in Britain*, Macmillan, London
Ballard, R. and Ballard, C. (1977) The Sikhs: the development of South Asian settlements in Britain, in J. Watson (ed.) (1977) *Between Two Cultures*, Blackwell, Oxford
Ballard, R. (1979) Ethnic minorities and the Social Services, in S. Khan (ed.) (1979) *Minority Families in Britain*, Macmillan, London
Ben-Tovim, G. and Gabriel, J. (1982) The politics of race in Britain, 1962–1979: a review of the major trends and of recent debates, in C. Husband (ed.) (1982) *Race in Britain: Continuity and Change*, Hutchinson, London
Bentley, S. (1981) Industrial conflict, strikes and black workers: problems of research methodology, in P. Braham, E. Rhodes and M. Pearn (eds) (1981) *Discrimination and Disadvantage in Employment*, Harper & Row, London
Billig, M. (1978) *Fascists: A Social Psychological View of the National Front*, Harcourt Brace Jovanovich, New York
Bindman, G. (1981) Positive action, in P. Braham, E. Rhodes and M. Pearn (eds) (1981) *Discrimination and Disadvantage in Employment*, Harper & Row, London
Bonner, D. (1983) Out of the labyrinth – a clear and enduring scheme of citizenship, *Journal of Social Welfare Law*, Vol. 23, pp 247–286
Brah, A. (1978) South Asian teenagers in Southall: their perceptions of marriage, family and ethnic identity, *New Community*, Vol. 6, No. 3, Summer
Braham, P., Rhodes, E. and Pearn, M. (eds) (1981) *Discrimination and Disadvantage in Employment*, Harper & Row, London
Braham, P. (1982) How the media report race, in M. Gurevitch, T. Bennett, J. Curran, and J. Woollacott (eds) (1982) *Culture, Society and the Media*, Methuen, London
Brake, M. (1980) *The Sociology of Youth Culture and Youth Subcultures*, Routledge and Kegan Paul, London

Cashmore, E. and Troyna, B. (eds) (1982) *Black Youth in Crisis*, Allen and Unwin, London

Cohen, S. and Young, J. (1981) *The Manufacture of News: Deviance, Social Problems and the Mass Media*, Constable, London

Critcher, C. (1979) Black and white rag, *The Social Science Teacher*, Vol. 8, No. 4, April

Critcher, C., Parker, M. and Sondhi, R. (1977) Race in the provincial press: a case study of five West Midlands newspapers, in (1977) *Ethnicity and the Media*, U.N.E.S.C.O., London

Crossman, R. (1975) *The Diaries of a Cabinet Minister*, Vol. 1, Hamish Hamilton and Jonathan Cape, London

Dixon, B. (1977) *Catching Them Young: Sex, Race and Class in Children's Literature*, Pluto Press, London

Downing, J. (1975) The (balanced) white view, in C. Husband (ed.) (1975) *White Media and Black Britain*, Arrow, London

Dummett, M. and Dummett, A. (1982) The role of government in Britain's racial crisis, in C. Husband (ed.) (1982) *Race in Britain: Continuity and Change*, Hutchinson, London

Elliott, P. (1972) *The Making of a Television Series*, Constable, London

Evans, P. (1976) *Publish and Be Damned*, Runnymede Trust and Radical Statistics Group, London

Foot, P. (1969) *The Rise of Enoch Powell*, Penguin, Harmondsworth

Gaskell, G. and Smith, P. (1981) Are young blacks really alienated? *New Society*, 14 May

Griffith, J. (1977) *The Politics of the Judiciary*, Fontana, London

Hall, S., Critcher, C., Jefferson, T., Clarke, J. and Roberts, B. (1978) *Policing the Crisis*, Macmillan, London

Harman, H. (1982) Civil liberties and civil disorder, in D. Cowell, T. Jones and J. Young (eds) (1982) *Policing the Riots*, Junction Books, London

Hartmann, P. and Husband, C. (1971) The mass media and racial conflict, *Race*, *XII* (January)

Hartmann, P. and Husband C. (1974) *Racism and the Mass Media*, Davis Poynter, London

Hartmann, P., Husband, C. and Clark, J. (1974) Race as news: a study in the handling of race in the British national press from 1963 to 1970, in (1974) *Race as News*, U.N.E.S.C.O., London

Hebdige, D. (1979) *Subculture: The Meaning of Style*, Methuen, London

HMSO (1981) (The Scarman Report) *The Brixton Disorders 10–12 April, 1981*, HMSO, London

Home Affairs Committee (1981) *Racial Disadvantage 1980–81*, HMSO, London

Husband, C. (1974) Education, race and society, in D. Holly (ed.) (1974) *Education or Domination*, Arrow, London

Kettle, M. and Hodges, L. (1982) *Uprising! The Police, the People and the Riots in Britain's Cities*, Pan Books, London

Laishley, J. (1975) The images of blacks and whites in the children's media, in C. Husband (ed.) (1975) *White Media and Black Britain*, Arrow, London

Lawrence, D. (1978) Prejudice, politics and race, *New Community*, Vol. 7, No. 1, Winter

Lea, J. and Young, J. (1982) The riots in Britain 1981: urban violence and political marginalization, in D. Cowell, T. Jones and J. Young (eds) (1982) *Policing the Riots*, Junction Books, London

Little, A. and Kohler, D. (1977) Do we hate blacks? *New Society*, 27 January

Little, A. (1978) *Educational Policies for Multiracial Areas*. University of London: Goldsmiths' College, London

Moore, R. (1982) Immigration and racism, in R. Burgess (ed.) (1982) *Exploring Society*, British Sociological Association, London

Nugent, N. and King, R. (1979) Ethnic minorities and the extreme right, in, R. Miles and A. Phizacklea (eds) (1979) *Racism and Political Action in Britain*, Routledge and Kegan Paul, London

Parekh, B. (1978) Asians in Britain: problem or opportunity, in, Commission For Racial Equality (1978) *Five Views of Multiracial Britain*, CRE, London

Phizacklea, A. and Miles, R. (1980) *Labour and Racism*, Routledge and Kegan Paul, London

Phizacklea, A. and Miles, R. (1981) The strike at Grunwick, in, P. Braham, E. Rhodes and M. Pearn (eds) (1981) *Discrimination and Disadvantage in Employment*, Harper & Row, London

Pierce, G. (1982) Unleashing an uncritical press, *The Guardian*, 15th March

Pryce, K. (1979) *Endless Pressure*, Penguin, Harmondsworth

Rex, J. (1981) *Social Conflict*, Longman, London

Rex, J. and Tomlinson, S. (1979) *Colonial Immigrants in a British City*, Routledge and Kegan Paul, London

Roberts, B. (1982) The debate on 'Sus', in E. Cashmore and B. Troyna (eds) (1982) *Black Youth in Crisis*, Allen and Unwin, London

Runnymede Trust and Radical Statistics Group (1980) *Britain's Black Population*, Heinemann, London

Scraton, P. (1982) Policing and institutionalized racism on Merseyside, in, D. Cowell, T. Jones and J. Young (eds) (1982) *Policing the Riots*, Junction Books, London

Seymour-Ure, C. (1974) *The Political Impact of Mass Media*, Constable, London

Sivanandan, A (1982) *A Different Hunger*, Pluto Press, London

Smith, D. (1977) *Racial Disadvantage in Britain*, Penguin, Harmondsworth

Smith, S. (1982) Race and crime statistics, *Race Relations Fieldwork*, Background Paper No. 4, August

Taylor, S. (1978) Race, extremism and violence in contemporary British politics, *New Community*, Vol. 8, No. 1, Winter

Taylor, S. (1979) The National Front, in, R. Miles and A. Phizacklea (eds) (1979) *Racism and Political Action in Britain*, Routledge and Kegan Paul, London

Taylor, S. (1981) Riots: some explanations, *New Community*, Vol. 9, No. 2, Autumn

Troyna, B. (1978) *Rastafarianism, Reggae and Racism*, National Association For Multiracial Education, London

Troyna, B. (1982) Reporting the National Front: British values observed, in C. Husband (ed.) (1982) *Race in Britain: Continuity and Change*, Hutchinson, London

Ward, R. (1979) Where race didn't divide: some reflections on slum clearance in Moss Side, in R. Miles and A. Phizacklea (eds) (1979) *Racism and Political Action in Britain*, Routledge and Kegan Paul, London

Young, H. (1971) The Treatment of Race in the British Press, *Race and the Press*, Runnymede Trust

TOPICS FOR DISCUSSION

1. How coherent do you consider government policy on race and immigration to have been?

2. To what extent do the media continue to depict non-white ethnic minority groups in a limited range of roles?

3. How significant are police/community relations for the future of race relations in Britain? How can they be improved?

SUGGESTIONS FOR FURTHER READING

1. Tierney, J. (1982) *Race, Immigration and Schooling*, Holt, Rinehart and Winston, Eastbourne, Chapter 7, 'Educational responses to racism', describes the responses of the D.E.S., the L.E.A.s, the Schools Council and the teachers' unions to racism.
2. Watson, J (1977) *Between Two Cultures*, Blackwell, London. The first five chapters of this edited book are concerned with the responses of ethnic minority members to their experiences in Britain.
3. Open University (1982) *Ethnic Minorities and Community Relations*, Unit 10, E354, Open University Press, Milton Keynes. This book contains an account by B. Parekh of British responses to black immigration and the responses of the racial minorities themselves to their experiences of living and working in the United Kingdom. This may be usefully updated by reference to a short account of how young Asians see the English by M. Stopes-Roe and R. Cochrane (1985) As others see us, *New Society*, 1 November, pp 187–189. This study was conducted with 40 Sikh, 40 Hindu and 40 Muslim families and shows that young Asians hold decidedly different views from those of their parents of many matters of contemporary life in Britain.

LANGUAGE ISSUES

INTRODUCTION

In Reading 8, Edwards (1983) argues that it is vital for those involved in the education of black children to understand the patterns of language-use in the black British community and the symbolic role which Creole continues to play. Creole is a rule-governed, linguistic system; it is not simply 'bad' or 'broken' English. In the suggestions for further reading, an extract from Hall and Jefferson (1976) further elaborates the discussion by Edwards on the symbolic role of Creole in its suggestion that West Indian youths have developed Creole as a symbol of group identity and as a way of resisting assimilation and preventing infiltration by dominant groups. Honey's (1983) paper is in spirited opposition to language theorists who insist that 'any variety of English is just as good as another'.

Reading 9 by Rees (1983) is a timely reminder of the over-simplification of concepts such as *ethnic group* and *educational attainment*. Rarely has the educational position of children of Asian and of European origin been conceived as involving many more than two culturally and linguistically distinct ethnic groups. Nor, according to Rees, has it been the practice to recognize, in the curriculum provided, that the majority of these children are bilingual or multilingual. Ming Tsow's (1983) paper in the suggestions for further reading looks at linguistic and educational needs in contemporary Britain. Brook (1980) points to the inadequacy of current provision for mother-tongue reading in Britain despite our subscription to an E.E.C. directive to make mother-tongue teaching available to children of migrant workers within the European Community.

Reading 8
LANGUAGE IN THE BRITISH BLACK COMMUNITY
V. Edwards[1]

LANGUAGE IN A CARIBBEAN CONTEXT

The mid-1960s saw the influx of large numbers of Caribbean settlers into the UK. They spoke a variety of English, completely unfamiliar to the majority of indigenous British people, which is known as 'Creole' by linguists but generally called 'patois' by West Indians themselves. When people from many parts of West Africa, speaking a wide range of different languages, were transported as slaves to the Caribbean, there was an urgent need to develop some common mode of communication. The simple pidgin evolved in the early years of slavery was developed into a full-blown language – or Creole – by subsequent generations, and whereas the pidgin had served only rudimentary communication needs, the Creole was expanded into a full and very adequate linguistic system. There are various differences from one West Indian territory to another, particularly in some aspects of vocabulary and intonation. There remains, however, a core of common grammatical features found in the speech of all or most of the islands.

French Creoles, spoken by Saint Lucian and Dominican settlers in Britain, bear the same relationship to French as English Creoles do to English and, although the vocabulary base is different, they have much in common with the Caribbean English Creoles.

A recurring question in discussions of West Indian language is whether Caribbean varieties should be classed as dialects of English or as a separate language. They are arguably further removed from standard English than any British dialect and writers like Sutcliffe (1982) make a strong case for treating them separately. The distinction between 'language' and 'dialect' is, however, extremely hazy. The linguistic situation in Scandinavia, for instance, can most usefully be described as a continuum of dialects from Norway in the north to Denmark in the south. Yet Danes, Swedes and Norwegians form three distinct

---

[1] In Edwards, V. (1983) *Language in Multicultural Classrooms*, Batsford Educational, London, pp 46–59

political units and are adamant that they speak three distinct languages. Relatively small linguistic differences assume considerable importance and help to define three separate national identities. The various dialects of the Arab world, on the other hand, are characterized by differences far greater than those held to delimit separate languages in Scandinavia. Strong ideals of religious and cultural unity, however, lead Arabs to minimize these differences. There are thus no clear or well-defined criteria for establishing whether we are dealing with a language or a dialect and ultimately the politician is in a better position to make such a decision than the linguist. Those wishing to promote a separate Jamaican identity, for example, might find it helpful to treat Jamaican Creole as a language quite distinct from the English associated with a colonial past.

STRUCTURE OF WEST INDIAN CREOLES

West Indian Creoles are perfectly regular, rule-governed linguistic systems which should properly be described in their own terms rather than by comparison with other systems such as standard English. Examples of such descriptions can be found in works like Bailey's (1966) *Jamaican Creole Syntax* and Sutcliffe's (1982) *British Black English*. For present purposes, however, I have chosen to outline the main contrasts between West Indian Creoles and English, emphasizing throughout that we are dealing with grammatical differences rather than deficiencies. This is not because I wish to fit West Indian language into an English mould, or to minimize the ways in which it functions quite autonomously, but simply because I recognize that English speakers will inevitably make comparisons between the two systems. There is a tendency to label any departures from the standard as 'inadequate' or 'incorrect' and so I feel that it is important to squarely challenge such assumptions.

FEATURES OF WEST INDIAN CREOLES

(1)   Creole does not usually mark plural nouns as English does:
      Me have three brother and two sister
      Here the number makes it obvious that we are dealing with plural nouns. But when Creole needs to show that it is referring to more than one person or thing and there are no plural words in the sentence, it uses 'de . . . -dem':
      De girl-dem come here all the time
(2)   There is often no agreement between subject and verb:
      The boy come in the morning
      My brother go to work
      The English 's' for the third person singular is, in fact, a relic of an older

system (e.g. thou givest) and is largely redundant.

(3) The Creole verb does not inflect for tense:

My mother come here yesterday

I see John last week

Creole does, however, have another way of showing time relations. In Jamaican Creole we find:

Mary a go home = Mary is going home

('a' shows that an action is in progress)

John en go home = John went home

('en' shows that an action took place in the past)

(4) Creole shows possession not with the genitive marker, 's' of British English, but by the relative positions of possessor and possessed:

British English	Creole
John's hat	John hat
The teacher's book	The teacher book

(5) Pronouns only show person and number. They don't usually show case or gender. In Broad Jamaican Creole you find:

(a) me   we

(b) you   unu

(c) him, it   dem

Thus, you might have:

me see him brother yesterday = I saw his/her brother yesterday

unu make we go back = you let us go back

(6) The verb 'to be' in Creole is largely redundant (compare also Russian). Both adjectives and verbs and, in some situations, nouns and locatives can follow the subject:

Winston coming

Winston good

Winston the father

(7) There is no separate passive form in Creole:

The food eat quick = the food was eaten quickly

The property sell = the property was sold

(8) Some words and constructions common to Creole and British English have different meanings:

Anne is easy to annoy = Anne annoys people easily

Mind you don't go home = Be sure you go home

(9) Some words and constructions are completely different:

A walk me walk make me come so late = It's because I walked that I'm so late

Me nyam all the food = I ate all the food

BRITISH BLACK LANGUAGE

'West Indian' is a misleading and inaccurate label for the British-born children and grandchildren of the original settlers in this country, many of whom have never set foot in the Caribbean. A distinctive British black community is emerging which has retained many elements of West Indian language and culture, but which is also showing a high degree of innovation and adaptation.

WHO SPEAKS CREOLE?

Many teachers and other observers feel that most British Black children conform to local linguistic norms and sound like their white peers. Rosen and Burgess (1980), for instance, included questions in their survey of the *Languages and Dialects of London School Children* which assessed the strength of dialect features in children's speech, and concluded on the basis of teacher estimates that between 80 and 90 per cent of children of West Indian origin are 'basically London (or standard) speakers who occasionally deepen overseas dialectal features'. As few as 10 to 20 per cent of these children regularly used Creole in certain contexts and less than 4 per cent used a 'full Caribbean creole'.

There is, however, a certain subjectivity in estimates of this kind which is highlighted by the very different results achieved by other researchers. Sutcliffe (1978), for instance, in a study of the language attitudes and use of some 47 first and second generation West Indians in Bedfordshire found that almost 95 per cent of subjects admitted using some Creole, and 78 per cent thought that they at least occasionally used Creole of a broadness equivalent to, '*mi aks di man fi put im money iina mi pockit*'. Hadi (1976) replicated this experiment in a West Midlands secondary school and found that over 70 per cent of her sample of 22 West Indian pupils admitted to using sentences like '*mi aks di man . . .*'. In both cases, these researchers drew on children's own self-estimates in structured group interviews, having established their own positive attitudes towards Creole before beginning the interview by, for example, playing and discussing tapes of West Indian and other speech.

Palmer (1981) approached this question in two quite different ways. First she gave a well-motivated class teacher copies of the Rosen and Burgess questionnaire and discussed with him how it should be completed. When the questionnaires were returned, she visited the class herself and, after playing and discussing tapes of various languages and dialects, she withdrew small groups and administered the Sutcliffe questionnaire. She found that children's self-estimates of Creole usage were consistently higher than those of the teacher, although he had consulted the children before completing the questionnaire. Tomlin's (1981) study of a random sample of West Indian subjects in Dudley might also be mentioned at this point. One hundred per cent of the people who took part in street interviews admitted to Tomlin, a black student teacher, that they regularly used Creole in some situations.

The discrepancy between the findings of Rosen and Burgess and the other researchers can undoubtedly be attributed to different methodologies. The low status of Creole is such that a certain degree of under-reporting is inevitable and it is interesting that a higher proportion of children admitted using Creole to researchers who presented themselves as friendly and interested adults than to teachers. This is not to suggest, of course, that teachers are either unfriendly or uninterested. However, their role as authority figures may well have affected children's responses. The actual questions which were asked may also go some way to explaining observed differences. The fact, for instance, that children were offered a specific example ('mi aks di man . . . ') against which they could measure their own usage may well have given them more confidence to reply positively.

It is ironical that the use of teachers as researchers simultaneously represents the greatest strength and the greatest weakness of the Rosen and Burgess survey. They formed a tremendous pool of on-the-spot, interested and well-motivated researchers; their participation in the survey stimulated discussion and led ultimately to a realization of the exciting potential of linguistic diversity as a classroom resource. The use of teacher researchers, however, also led to what Rosen and Burgess (1980, pp 2–3) describe as

[. . .] a compromise between the delicacy of information we would have liked to obtain and what it would be reasonable to expect to collect with the assistance of teachers who made no special claim to expert knowledge.

The Rosen and Burgess survey was made under difficult circumstances with limited funding and, without the use of teacher researchers, would have been a totally impractical exercise. A number of important questions, however, are raised by both results and methodology – how legitimate is it, for instance, to make use of labels as imprecise as 'occasionally deepens dialect features' or 'basically a London speaker'? None the less, the study is an important one in that it has started to document the nature and extent of diversity. Rosen and Burgess openly acknowledge its weaknesses and make no extravagant claims for its findings. Most important, they show something of the complexity of diversity and its centrality for education.

WHEN IS CREOLE USED?

An adequate description of British black language use requires more precision than the rather vague observation that most black Britons can approximate to both the local white norm and more 'focused' Creole speech. Some investigation has been done on this subject but it relies heavily on either researcher speculation or British black subjective judgements. It does appear, however, that British black children are particularly sensitive to situation. Hadi (1976) asked first-year children in a Walsall secondary school if they would change from the way they spoke to their friends when speaking to certain adults. The results show some very interesting tendencies:

Table 8.1 Self-estimates of language use in English and British black children

		British black %	English %
Head teacher	No change	6	25
	Change	94	75
Doctor	No change	12	31
	Change	88	69
Milkman	No change	17	77
	Change	83	23
School dinner lady	No change	13	55
	Change	87	45

Source: extrapolated from Hadi (1976)

In all four cases a higher proportion of British black than English children say they would change their speech. And, whereas the English children tend to discriminate between low and high status adults, the proportion of black children who say they would change the way they speak remains uniformly high across all four groups. Hadi speculates as to whether this sensitivity to situation is an indication of insecurity on the part of black children. It seems more probable, however, that since the British black community has a wider range of language at its disposal, black children are able to make an additional distinction which is not available to their English peers.

Hadi (1976) and Sutcliffe (1978; 1982) also challenge the long-held assumptions about the simple split in West Indian language use whereby 'Creole' is spoken at home and 'English' at school. It emerged in the Sutcliffe study that subjects' own rate of use was highest in the peer group situation when talking to black friends in the playground. Parents' use of Creole to children, however, is correspondingly high, though subjects' own use to parents is low. Scores for use to brothers and sisters tended to be intermediate to low. Hadi's findings were not as conclusive as those of Sutcliffe, but there was certainly general agreement that Creole was used widely to their friends at school and was often triggered by stress – anger, excitement, joy, playing cards, 'when there is a fight' or 'someone shout at me'.

The asymmetrical use of Creole reported in Sutcliffe (1978; 1982) is something which has not previously attracted comment in a British setting. Sutcliffe (1982), however, draws parallels with research on this phenomenon in both black American and Caribbean communities. He suggests that the use of Creole is akin to the *tu* form in French, whereas more English usage is associated with the *vous* form. He points to a pattern in which younger people are expected to use 'English' to their parents and even older brothers and sisters, but parents and elders are allowed to use Creole to their juniors. A very similar situation prevailed with the use of *tu* and *vous* in France a generation or so ago. Interestingly, drama and literature emerging from the British black community – in particular, *Jennifer and Brixton Blues* (Richmond, 1978) and *Ballad for You* (Johnson, 1978) – contain family dialogues which confirm Sutcliffe's observations.

Valuable information on the use of Creole outside the family is contained in Crump's (1979) study of the language of black children in a Haringey mixed comprehensive school. She considers the importance of language as an integral part of a person's identity and relates the language varieties of black adolescents to their involvement in partiuclar youth cultures. Children's comments, together with observations of the classroom and the playground, suggest that it is only when pupils develop an orientation towards one or another of the major youth cultural groupings that differences in language become apparent. Those pupils who by the third and fourth years use patois and take pride in 'talking black' are those who turn to the all-black world of reggae and sound systems. The strength of Crump's study lies in its sensitive and sympathetic handling of the situation of black children in Britain. She does not, however, undertake any kind of linguistic analysis and children's speech appears only in quotations which illustrate the various points she makes in her sociological analysis.

Crump's observations are confirmed by various writers concerned with the sociological phenomenon presented by black people in Britain rather than more directly linguistic considerations. Hebdige (1976), for instance, comments on the ways in which West Indian youths have developed Creole as a symbol of group identity:

Language is used [by members of certain West Indian sub-cultures] as a particularly effective way of resisting assimilation and preventing infiltration by members of the dominant groups. As a screening device it has proved to be invaluable, and the "Bongo talk" and patois of the Rude Boy deliberately emphasize its subversive rhythms so that it becomes an aggressive assertion of racial and class identities. As a living index of the extent of the Black's alienation from the cultural norms and goals of those who occupy high positions in the social structure the Creole language is unique.

Leitch (1979), from her position as an insider in the British black community, argues that the language used by children of Caribbean origin in Britain varies very considerably depending on where in the Caribbean their family comes from; the social background of the family, how long they or their family have lived here, and, most important, the proportion of the people they associate with who are of Caribbean origin and speak a Creole, and the extent to which they identify with Caribbean or British culture. She suggests that the language of many of these children is influenced by the Creole or other language of the parents; peer group language; language of the school and media which may be the standard; London Jamaican; and Rastafarian terminology and structure.

Thomas (1979), like Leitch and Crump, does not undertake a linguistic analysis of children's speech, but offers nonetheless some interesting insights in an ethnographic report based on participant observational study in a multi-ethnic primary school. She develops the metaphorical construct of 'personal space' which she conceives in terms of 'territory' that can be infringed or vindicated by the interactional processes to which we are exposed. Thomas reports a wide range of Creole usage in the children in her school, from a few stock phrases copied from their mothers' rebukes or from pop songs to the ability to hold long conversations in patois. She examines the social significance of this Creole usage in the classroom, suggesting that black pupils use Creole to reinforce group communication, to threaten an outsider to the group who violates their personal space, or to signify inclusion if they wish to vindicate an outsider.

CODE SWITCHING

The linguistic situation of the British black community would appear to differ from that of West Indians in the Caribbean in two main respects. First, it is frequently claimed that the vast majority of West Indians both understand and use Creole, whereas in Britain it is confined to a very small segment of the population. Second, most members of the British black community are capable of producing a variety of English close to the local British norm and, in some cases, indistinguishable from it, whereas very few West Indians have a good command of the local standard English. The polar varieties which can be achieved by many black Britons are thus, not surprisingly, much further apart from those of most West Indians in the Caribbean. The range of linguistic variation in the West Indies is usually described in terms of a dialect continuum (Edwards, 1979), but it seems possible that the British black situation can be better described in terms of a bilingual continuum.

One of the characteristics of British black language use which is consistent with the notion that we are dealing with a bilingual community is the high degree of code-switching between Creole and English. This can take place from sentence to sentence:

> I hate coffee. *mi laik tii.*
> The duppy came and saw Brother Brown. *An di dopi snach di kaan.*
> *Yu gat rak stik iina yu hiez.* You're got rocks sticking in your ears.

from clause to clause:

> When me sister loses her temper *mi gaan so.*

and even from phrase to phrase:

> and he did see . . . he did see the um.. . . *di dopi*
> and so the donkey *lif op* his leg
> Why don't you come with me to the . . . *tu di griev.*

Code-switching of this kind is an extremely widespread phenomenon which has been documented for bilingual communities as far apart as Ghana (Ure, 1974), India (Kachru, 1978) and America (Hernandez-Chavez *et al.*, 1975). It has been demonstrated that this switching is not random but subject to grammatical constraints and is triggered by a range of psychological variables, such as hesitation, and sociological variables, such as topic and audience. The discovery of such constraints is of considerable importance because it indicates that switching is not simply an inability to keep two languages apart but an extremely complex ability found in some bilinguals.

The recognition of this code-switching behaviour in the British black community is extremely recent (Edwards, 1982) and a great deal of work remains to be done before we can say with any degree of confidence what precisely is taking place. It would seem to indicate, however, that we have greatly underestimated the complexity of the linguistic situation of black people in Britain. Educators have tended to view black pupils either as linguistically assimilated or as linguistically lacking, in the case of those who continue to show Creole influence in their speech. It is very important, therefore, that we should understand the rule-governed nature of language behaviour and the symbolic role which Creole continues to play in the lives of many black Britons, as well as the social mechanisms underlying the long-term survival of Creole.

THE SCHOOL RESPONSE TO THE LANGUAGE OF BLACK CHILDREN

West Indian Creole speaking children arriving from the Caribbean posed a number of important questions which schools identified only slowly and on which central government provided little or no guidance for a disturbing period of time. Ignorance about the rule-governed nature of West Indian speech was widespread. A report by the National Association of Schoolmasters (N.A.S., 1969), for instance, considered that: 'The West Indian child usually arrives speaking a kind of 'plantation English' which is socially unacceptable and inadequate for communication' (p. 5). An A.T.E.P.O. (Association of Teachers of English to Pupils from Overseas) (1970) report describes West Indian language as 'babyish', 'careless and slovenly' and 'very relaxed like the way they walk'. Even Townsend (1971), who acknowledges the validity of West Indian children's language, talks of their 'abbreviated sentence structure, different pronoun values and restricted vocabulary'.

West Indians, for their part, had grown up in a society where the institutions, including education, were closely modelled on the British system. They had been indoctrinated into believing that West Indian Creoles were 'bad talk' and 'broken'. When they came to what many people regarded as 'the mother country', it was therefore understandable that they should insist that they spoke English, since to have admitted otherwise would have been tantamount to an acceptance of the low status attached to Creole speech. Problems concerning mutual intelligibility between West Indian parents and children on the one side and teachers on the other were common throughout the early years of settlement (cf. Rose et al., 1969; Edwards, 1979).

Any official recognition of the language needs of West Indian children was extremely slow, and D.E.S. statistics served to conceal rather than to draw attention to the true situation. Section two of Form 7i, a supplement to the annual statistical return made by schools which was introduced in 1966, required teachers to classify 'immigrant' children according to their knowledge of English as follows:

(1) No problem
(2) Reasonably good spoken English but weak in written English
(3) Some English, but needing further intensive teaching
(4) No English

It seems reasonable to assume that if teachers were required to choose between either group (2) or group (3) when classifying West Indian children, they would come out in favour of group (2) (cf. Power, 1967). Yet the following year the D.E.S. amalgamated groups (1) and (2) and groups (3) and (4) on the assumption that only those children in groups (3) and (4) would require specialized language teaching. Such a move effectively excluded the possibility that West Indian children might need specialist help, albeit of a different nature from second language learners.

The actual arrangements for teaching West Indians reflect the unfortunate consequences of a lack of policy on either a national or a local level. Comments reported by Townsend and Brittan (1972), for instance, reveal the bewilderment and confusion which must have been experienced by teachers and pupils alike:

> We once arranged special coaching for West Indians whose English was very poor, but they tended to resent this, not accepting that there was anything wrong with their English, so little progress was made and the project abandoned.

All too often the solution adopted with West Indian pupils (as with non-English speaking children) was to place them in classes with remedial indigenous children:

> Boys of West Indian origin: in each year we have a class for retarded pupils. Although not designed as such, all of these classes have about 90 per cent West Indians or pupils of West Indian origin.

Only in a very few cases did schools or L.E.A.s make any serious attempt to meet the language teaching needs of West Indian pupils (cf. Rose *et al.*, 1969).

Large-scale West Indian immigration predated migration from South Asia by several years. Yet it was not until 1967 that the Schools Council commissioned a project with aims similar to the Leeds project but whose brief was to develop teaching materials specifically for West Indian pupils. Although the number of children who might benefit from such materials was probably no smaller than the number of non-English speaking children, the budget for this project was less than a third of that made available to the Leeds team. The *Concept 7–9* materials produced by the 'Teaching English to children of West Indian origin' research team (cf. Wight and Norris, 1970; Wight, 1969, 1970) were originally envisaged as a language course for West Indian children, but later the emphasis was changed and it was decided that many of the language skills that could be usefully developed with West Indian children would also be beneficial to a good number of native British children. The authors of the material maintained that the language of West Indian children (and, presumably, working-class white children) was perfectly logical and regular and that attempts to teach the standard should be reserved for children's writing and not their speech. However, they did feel that non-standard speakers needed to develop a whole range of verbal strategies which would enable them to take part more successfully in the education process. This stance has since been criticized (Sutcliffe, 1978; Edwards, 1979) on the grounds that the strategies which the materials were designed to remedy can in fact be found in the language which children use in non-school settings, and that the most plausible explanation for children's avoidance of particular verbal strategies in the classroom – if indeed this is the case – would seem to be in terms of situational constraints rather than an inability to do so.

The underachievement of West Indian children, first officially recognized with the publication of the D.E.S. *Statistics of Education* for 1970, was a major concern throughout the decade (Townsend, 1971; HMSO, 1977; C.R.C. 1976; Rampton, 1981). A particular bone of contention in the early 1970s was the question of the assessment of the ability of West Indian pupils. Although intelligence tests were waived in the case of non-English speaking pupils, they were a normal part of the evaluation of West Indian children until 1974, despite strong evidence that intelligence tests have little validity because of their cultural and linguistic bias (Haynes, 1971). The possibility that language played a part in the underperformance of West Indian children was finally acknowledged in 1973 with the publication of the Select Committee on Race Relations and Immigration report on Education:

> More familiarity with the problems of West Indian children has shown that many of them also need special attention in the teaching of English [. . .]. There is little doubt that neglect of special attention in the past has handicapped many children. It may partly account for the disproportionately large numbers of West Indian children in E.S.N. schools in London [. . .] and for the generally lower standards of achievement of West Indian pupils in some schools. It is not, of course, the only reason, but it is one which is now recognized and can be dealt with. (HMSO, 1973, p. 13).

Following the report, a D.E.S. memorandum to Chief Education Officers on 1 November 1973 drew attention to the fact that West Indian children as well as non-English speakers may have language difficulties. The only recommendation made by the Select Committee as to how the problem could be 'dealt with', however, was that L.E.A.s should consider how best 'with tact and discretion' they could convince West Indian parents that some of their children might need special English teaching. The Bullock Report (1975) offers only slightly more guidance. It stresses the need for a positive attitude towards the language and culture of West Indian children, which should be encouraged by initial and in-service training. It also suggests that work relating both to dialect and to improving the ability to use standard English should be encouraged on a much larger scale. Yet it gives no indication of the most suitable materials and approach for this task. Nor does it set out criteria for selecting those children in need of special teaching and it ignores the possible resistance which British-born children and their parents might offer.

Many of the difficulties in formulating a coherent policy on the language needs of children of West Indian origin can be traced to the extensive delays in recognizing their special situation within the British education system. Although some West Indian children continue even today to show the influence of Creole in their most formal speech, reading and writing (cf. Edwards, 1981), by the mid-1970s the majority had been born in Britain and could produce speech indistinguishable or at least close to the local white norm. The C.R.C. (1976, p. 5) sums up the situation thus:

> It is ironical that at a time when Creole dialect did cause problems of communication and comprehension in schools, the question was ignored. However, by the time Creole had been identified as an educational issue, the majority of West Indian children were no longer speaking it in schools. It is often pointed out to us that some time during the early years at secondary school many West Indian pupils who up till then have used the language of the neighbourhood, begin to use Creole dialect. But its use is a deliberately social and psychological protest, an assertion of identity, not a language teaching problem.

Current practice would still seem to be little influenced by a coherent language policy. Little and Willey's (1981) survey of 70 L.E.A.s shows that no more than a handful have made serious attempts to evaluate the needs of West Indian pupils. They point to the importance of clarifying the extent to which and the ways in which these children have 'special' language needs, and of providing guidance and support to teachers. The Rampton Report (1981) on *West Indian Children in Our Schools* goes at least some of the way towards clarifying these needs. It stresses the importance of promoting positive teacher attitudes towards the language of West Indian children through initial and in-service training. It also follows the I.L.E.A. policy statement of 1977 in encouraging schools to give West Indian pupils every opportunity to make full use of their linguistic repertoire through creative work in English, drama and discussion. It recognizes the possible ambivalence of West Indian parents to the use of an essentially low-status language variety in the classroom, but argues that imaginative and creative use of a child's home language assists in developing awareness of different forms of language – including standard English – and their appropriateness for different situations.

Such an approach is radical and represents a significant departure from the practices of the 1960s and the greater part of the 1970s. Inevitably, it has attracted vituperative comment. The I.L.E.A. statment encouraging the use of Creole in poetry and drama drove one head teacher to announce that he would allow Creole in his school only 'over his dead body' (*Sunday Times*, 16 October 1977). It remains to be seen whether this head teacher and many of his conservative colleagues in the teaching profession will be persuaded of the wisdom of this current policy lead, or resist it to the end.

SUMMARY

The language of West Indian migrants differed in many important respects from both standard and British dialects of English. Yet for many years the rule-governed and systematic nature of these differences was overlooked by many schools and teachers, who seemed to think that West Indians simply spoke 'bad' or 'broken' English. Reports as to the continuing influence of 'patois' or 'Creole' on the children and grandchildren of the original settlers are conflicting, but there are strong indications that it remains an important social and linguistic force for many British black people. Adaptations and developments of Creole in Britain remain to be studied in depth. It is essential, however, that those involved in the education of black children should understand the patterns of language use in the British black community and the symbolic role which Creole continues to play.

REFERENCES

Association of Teachers of English to Pupils From Overseas (A.T.E.P.O.) (Birmingham Branch) (1970) Work Group of West Indian Pupils Report
Bailey, B.L. (1966) *A Transformational Grammar of Jamaican Creole*, Cambridge University Press, London
The Bullock Report (1975) *A Language For Life*, HMSO, London
Community Relations Commission (1976) *The Select Committee on Race Relations and Immigration Enquiry on the West Indian Community. Evidence on Education from the Community Relations Commission*, C.R.C., London
Crump, S. (1979) The language of West Indian children and its relevance for schools. Unpublished M.A. dissertation, University of London Institute of Education
Edwards, V. (1979) *The West Indian Language Issue in British Schools: Challenges and Responses*. Routledge and Kegan Paul, London
Edwards, V. (1981) Black British English. A bibliographical essay on the language of children of West Indian origin, *Sage Race Relations Abstracts*, Vol. 5, Nos. 3 and 4, pp. 1–26
Edwards, V. (1982) Research priorities in the study of British Black English. Paper given at the British Association of Applied Linguistics conference on Language and Ethnicity, January
Hadi, S. (1976) Some Language Issues. Unpublished paper based on a survey undertaken

as part of the Schools Council/N.F.E.R. Education For a Multiracial Society Project

Haynes, J. (1971) *Educational Assessment of Immigrant Pupils*, National Foundation For Educational Research, Windsor

Hebdige, D. (1976) Reggae, Rastas and Rudies, in S. Hall and T. Jefferson (eds) (1976) *Resistance Through Ritual: Youth sub-cultures in post-war Britain*, Hutchinson, London

Hernandez-Chavez, E., Cohen, A. and Beltrarno, A. (1975) *El lenguaje de los Chicanos*, Center for Applied Linguistics, Arlington, Virginia

HMSO (1973) *Select Committee on Race Relations and Immigration, Session 1972–1973, Education*, Volume 1, Report, HMSO, London

HMSO (1977) *Select Committee on Race Relations and Immigration, Session 1976–1977. The West Indian Community*, Vol. 1: *Report*, HMSO, London

Johnson, J. (1978) Ballad for you, *Race Today*, January/February

Kachru, B. (1978) Towards structuring code-mixing: an Indian perspective, *International Journal of the Sociology of Language*, Vol. 16, pp 27–46

Leitch, J. (1979) West Indian language: the state of play, *The Caribbean Teachers Asscociation Quarterly Newsletter*, Vol. 12

Little, A. and Willey, R. (1981) *Multi-ethnic Education: The Way Forward*, Schools Council Pamphlet No. 18, London

National Association of Schoolmasters (1968) *Education and the Immigrants*, Educare, Hemel Hempstead, Herts

Palmer, P. (1981) An investigation into the language of children of Jamaican origin in Manchester. M.A.A.L. project. Department of Linguistic Science, University of Reading

Power, J. (1967) *Immigrants in School. A Survey of Administrative Policies*, Councils and Education Press

Rampton, A. (1981) *West Indian Children In Our Schools, Interim Report of the Committee of Inquiry into the Education of Children from Ethnic Minority Groups*, HMSO, London

Richmond, J. (1978) Jennifer and Brixton Blues, *New Approaches to Multiracial Education*, Vol. 6, No. 3

Rose, E. *et al.* (1969) *Colour and Citizenship. A Report on British Race Relations*, Oxford University Press, Oxford (Published for the Institute of Race Relations)

Rosen, C. and Rosen, H. (1973) *The Language of Primary School Children*, Penguin, Harmondsworth

Rosen, H. and Burgess, T. (1980) *Language and Dialects of London School Children*, Ward Lock Educational, London

Sutcliffe, D. (1978) The language of first and second generation West Indian children in Bedfordshire. Unpublished M.Ed. Thesis, University of Leicester

Sutcliffe, D. (1982) *British Black English*, Blackwell, Oxford

Thomas, R. (1979) Vindication and infringement: towards an ethnographic analysis of classroom interaction. Unpublished M.A. dissertation, University of London Institute of Education

Tomlin, C. (1981) The extent to which West Indian linguistic differences hinder or enhance learning. Unpublished dissertation, Dudley College of Education

Townsend, H. (1971) *Immigrants in England: the L.E.A. Response*, National Foundation For Educational Research, Windsor

Townsend, H. and Brittan, E. (1972) *Organization in Multi-racial Schools*, National Foundation For Educational Research, Windsor

Ure, J. (1974) Code-switching and 'mixed speech' in the register systems of developing languages, in A. Verdoot (ed.) (1974) *Proceedings of the 3rd International Congress of Applied Linguistics*, Vol. II, Applied Linguistics, Julius Groos, Heidelberg

Wight, J. (1969) Teaching English to West Indian children, *English For Immigrants*, Vol. 2, No. 2

Wight, J. (1970) Language, deprivation and remedial teaching techniques, A.T.E.P.O. (1970)

Wight, J. and Norris, R. (1970) *Teaching English to West Indian Children: the research stage of the project.* Schools Council Working Paper No. 29, Evans/Methuen, London

TOPICS FOR DISCUSSION

1. Interpret the changes that 'English' and 'Black British' children say they would make in speaking to the people listed in Tables. 1 (p 167).
2. Discuss 'code-switching' in terms of the symbolic role that Creole has for many black Britons.
3. What, in your view, should be the objectives of an educational policy on the language needs of children of West Indian origin?

SUGGESTIONS FOR FURTHER READING

1. Clark, M.M., Barr, J.E. and Dewhirst, W. (1985) Early Education of children with communication problems. Particularly those from ethnic minorities. *Educational Review*, Offset Publication No. 3, University of Birmingham. This is a report of the findings of research funded by the D.E.S. 1982–84. See especially Part II 'The language abilities of children in a variety of settings'.
2. Honey, J. (1983) *The Language Trap: Race, Class and the Standard English Issue in British Schools*, National Council for Educational Standards, Kenton, Middlesex. The purpose of this pamphlet is to take to task those language theorists who insist that 'any variety of English is just as good as another'. In questioning the proposition, Honey discusses Black English Vernacular and the work of the American sociolinguist William Labov.
3. Hall, S. and Jefferson, T. (1976) *Resistance Through Ritual: Youth Sub-Culture in Post-War Britain*, Hutchinson, London, pp 135–55. D. Hebdige, *Reggae, Rastas and Rudies*, shows how West Indian youths have developed Creole as a symbol of group identity, as means of resisting assimilation and preventing infiltration by members of dominant groups.

Reading 9
ETHNIC GROUP, BILINGUALISM AND ATTAINMENT
O. Rees[1]

INTRODUCTION

The attainment of children from 'ethnic minority groups' within English society has attracted a great deal of interest over the last two decades. In considering their performance as a group in relation to the indigenous population two major tendencies are apparent.

In the first place a broad conception of 'ethnic group' has prevailed. The pedagogic and research focus has been on two groups, by implication assumed to be rather homogeneous, of West Indian and Asian children. The characteristics which thus appear to differentiate them from the indigenous population are colour, cultural pattern and region of origin. In so far as questions of language have entered into educational thinking, interest has been directed towards the different problems that the two broad groups pose as learners of standard English.

Children of Asian origin have generally been considered as 'non-English speakers' who as a result of schooling become 'second-language learners'. Children of West Indian origin are considered in more enlightened circles as 'second dialect learners'. And where there are groups of children of European origin, Italian or Greek-Cypriot for example, these may be regarded as being in the same general position as children of Asian origin. But the educational situation of both children of Asian and of European origin, on which this paper concentrates, has rarely been conceived as one involving many more than two culturally and linguistically distinct ethnic groups. Nor has it been the practice to recognize in the curriculum provided that the majority of these children are in practice bilingual or multilingual.

It is interesting to note that precisely this point was made in the Bullock Report in 1975. This stated that:

> [. . .] when bilingualism in Britain is discussed it is seldom if ever with

[1] In Bagley, C. and Verma, G.K. (eds) (1983) *Multicultural Childhood*, Gower Publishing, Aldershot.

reference to the inner city immigrant population, yet over half the immigrant pupils in our schools have a mother tongue which is not English, and in some schools this means over 75 per cent of the total number on roll. The language of the home and of a great deal of central experience in their life is one of the Indian languages, or Greek, Turkish, Italian or Spanish. These children are genuine bilinguals, but this fact is often ignored or unrecognised by the schools.

But it is not simply recognition by schools which matters but the nature of that recognition.

The second major tendency has been to limit the conception of 'attainment' which informs discussion of the position of ethnic groups in specific ways. Thus Phillips (1979), for example, in a study of underachievement in different ethnic groups (he means West Indian and Asian groups) makes use of tests of English listening vocabulary and of English word recognition. Another important and possibly more useful indication has been public examination success (Driver, 1977). Thus attainment is involved in both in terms of a limited range of performance criteria and in terms of a monolingual and mainly monocultural English-orientated domain. For bilingual children with a distinctive cultural identity and cultural knowledge this may represent a serious difficulty.

In this paper the nature of educational provision in England for children of Asian and European ethnic groups is considered in the light of their widespread bilingualism or multilingualism. And our conception of attainment for such groups is examined and related to the kind of curriculum adopted. In doing this the implication of two principles is also considered. The first of these is the principle embodied in the 1944 Education Act that a child should have an education which is appropriate to his 'age, aptitude and ability'. The second is contained in the directive adopted by the Council of the E.E.C. on 25 July 1977 that ethnic minorities have a right to the maintenance of their home language and culture through the school system of a member state.

ETHNIC GROUP AND LANGUAGE

Within England the term 'ethnic group' has come to be used to indicate groups of recent settlers. Their children are usually considered to have special educational needs, though this need is most often seen in terms of their difficulty 'fitting in' to existing social, linguistic and cultural patterns. Thus the two ethnic groups most often discussed – West Indian and Asian – are widely regarded as educationally disadvantaged and underachieving. Their difficulty is often construed as being fundamentally a matter of learning and using standard English. Recent research in the UK, with a limited conception of the notion of ethnic group, of attainment and of the role of bilingualism (Phillips, 1979; Driver, 1977) has challenged the basic contention that they are underachieving.

Discussion of the issue on these lines is not however likely to be very useful, since a number of over-simplifications, assumptions and omissions tend to colour and direct the way in which the ethnic group – attainment relationship is conceived.

(1)   The homogeneity of broad ethnic groups, defined by the host society and by the perceived saliency of certain criteria (colour, for example), is a gross over-simplification. Where language is considered and the perceptions of ethnic group members are a relevant focus, a very much more differentiated view of relevant groupings is necessary. It is in fact significant that we tend to differentiate European ethnic groups by language while avoiding this in the case of Asian groups.

(2)   Attainment, as a general assessment of developmental progress in children from ethnic minority groups, is unlikely to be fully characterized in terms of judgements and measurements conceived within a monolingual framework and derived from a monolingual and essentially monocultural school system. The range of criteria need to be quantitatively wider and qualitatively appropriate to bilingual children.

(3)   For bilingual children the assumption that they are inadequate monolinguals (implied by the exclusive 'second language learning' focus) and their cultural rejection by the school must be taken as an important element in their school performance.

As a move towards a more satisfactory characterization of 'ethnic group' the definition given in Sills (1968) may be considered. This suggests that an 'ethnic group' is a 'distinct category of the population in a larger society where culture is usually different from its own'. In addition he goes on to clarify this by stating: 'the members of such a group are or feel themselves or are thought to be, bound together by common ties of race or nationality or culture'. It would be appropriate to emphasize the linguistic content of the notion of culture by adding 'common ties of language'.

Clearly where 'ethnic group' is defined in this way we are not dealing with a unitary concept in the sense that an individual's ethnic group membership is unique or independent of the observer or of the immediate context. The salient criteria, especially those of culture, kinship, religion and language will be more finely differentiated where the 'ethnic group member' is arbiter, than where outside observers are involved. For the school any general conception of 'ethnic group' membership in their children is not, in a sense, relevant. What matters in providing for children in a way that is appropriate to their aptitudes and abilities is the conception of 'ethnic group' implicit in the attitudes of the local community. And even more important is that conception of 'ethnic group' which takes into account linguistic and cultural distinctiveness as it is salient to curricular patterns. These two considerations will not necessarily be compatible.

BILINGUAL CHILDREN

At the simplest level a bilingual child is one who 'has two languages' (O.E.D.). But a more traditional view of bilingualism, in keeping with much everyday usage, is Bloomfield's:

> In the extreme case of foreign language-learning the speaker becomes so proficient as to be indistinguishable from the native speakers around him [. . .] In the cases where this perfect foreign language-learning is not accompanied by loss of the native language, it results in bilingualism, native-like control of two languages. (Bloomfield, 1935)

This kind of definition, however, is rather unhelpful. The distinction between 'bilingual' and 'monolingual' is arbitrary and conceptually difficult to sustain; it is too closely tied to considerations of some ideal competence and not to the practicability of using each language as a medium of communication, and almost by definition no child is bilingual since adult competence in neither language will be present.

For reasons of this kind it is more helpful to consider a bilingual child as one who is able to *use* two languages at any level whatsoever and to focus attention for educational purposes on describing the nature and extent of the use of both languages. Depending also on the theoretical and practical criteria we use to distinguish what are two 'languages', we are concerned among 'ethnic groups' with a pretty wide range of situations for which no clearly worked out research, let alone educational taxonomy, exists (Rees, 1976).

Such a description would certainly refer to the context and domain where each language or both were used to the control of syntactic, semantic and phonological features in deploying different language functions, to the differences in performance between modalities and for input/output, and to the nature of the relationship in an individual bilingual between the two languages. A bilingual speaker may not be regarded either as two monolingual speakers in a single person! The relationship between the two languages represents an additional, qualitatively distinct, dimension of functioning. From this the possibility of language switching, translation, inter-language comparison, metalinguistic awareness and a set of symbolic flexibility arise. Conceptualizing 'attainment' in the bilingual child must involve considerations of this kind.

The extent of the presence of bilingual children from ethnic minority groups in England and the characteristics of the speech communities to which they belong is not well documented. The national Census does not directly seek such information and while the Department of Education and Science has recently funded a 'Linguistic Minorities Project' to document patterns of bilingualism, this will not report for a number of years. Recent discussions or surveys (for example, Khan, 1980; I.L.E.A., 1979; Rosen, 1978; Campbell-Platt, 1978) point to the relative size and enormous complexity of the matter. In the I.L.E.A. survey, for example, over 100 individual 'languages' spoken as a first language in their schools by about 10 per cent of pupils are mentioned. While the language classification adopted by respondents is approximate it is instructive to note that five European and four Asian language groups are mentioned as being spoken by more than 1000 pupils.

Given the traditional attitudes of this country towards languages other than English it may well be difficult to move towards a situation where such children are catered for in a manner which is appropriate to their bilingualism and where the curriculum is conceived in terms of the use of two languages. Practical problems and the absence of appropriate teacher training and inadequate staffing resources seem insuperable at this stage. Nevertheless it should be argued that in principle such a change of perspective is necessary. In addition, it is misleading to consider bilingualism as a 'problem' in educational terms. This is an inappropriate attitude; the problem lies in existing curricular patterns, in the social and economic conditions of ethnic minority groups, and in educational assumptions within a monolingual and monocultural tradition.

In the rest of this discussion, to simplify matters, attention will be concentrated on a particular but prominent group of bilingual children within the schools. These are Punjabi-speakers; by which is meant speakers of a related set of language variants described as Punjabi, and of English. Following a discussion of the general relationship of ethnic group and attainment research on educational provision through two languages for this group will be considered.

BILINGUALISM AND ATTAINMENT

Firstly, it would be useful to say something about the development of our present conception of the relationship between bilingualism and attainment. In doing this those intelligence test scores which have been the focus of research during this century are taken to be a general measure of attainment. These are still culturally loaded but may be relatively unaffected by factors directly related to the forms and conditions of schooling for bilingual children within 'monolingual' societies. The performance of bilingual children on intelligence tests is not here considered as having any theoretical implication, but simply as a particular kind of performance measure, albeit with a specific range of tasks and contents. But this specific range may have relative advantages here in tending to be less school-dependent than traditional measures of attainment, and thus indicate more clearly whether bilingualism in itself is an educational disadvantage.

The literature in this area is large and has been reviewed from time to time (Arsenian, 1937; Darcy, 1953; Peal and Lambert, 1962; Anisfield, 1964; Ben-Zeev, 1977). The earliest judgement of the influence of bilingualism on performance in intelligence tests was that it resulted in a decrement in performance by comparison with monolinguals (Arsenian, 1937; Darcy, 1953). But early studies were methodologically unsound and had ignored the social correlates of bilingualism; in many of the situations where research had taken place bilinguals occupied a relatively inferior social, educational and economic position as minority groups within a dominant monolingual society.

Later studies, adjusting for such socio-economic factors, tended to show that, at least on non-verbal tasks, differences between monolinguals and bilinguals were not present. On verbally orientated tasks small differences still remained (Darcy, 1953) though the cultural and linguistic bias involved in tasks applied to both monolingual and bilingual speakers might invalidate this comparison.

More recent developments have arisen from the work of Peal and Lambert (1962) and Anisfeld (1964) to suggest that certain kinds of feature in performance may be more readily available to bilinguals than to monolinguals (Ben-Zeev, 1972; Cummins and Gulutson, 1974; Segalowitz, 1977). This work suggested that bilingualism *per se* is not detrimental to performance but may confer certain advantages in terms of cognitive development, cognitive flexibility and set to symbolic flexibility.

At this stage it would be premature to make a definite judgement on the probable nature of the bilingualism-attainment relationship where other factors are equal; but there is no justification for the view that bilingualism is detrimental to a child's intellectual development. And given that other research (Segalowitz, 1977) and the principles embodied in the 1944 Education Act and the directive of the E.E.C. point to education through both a child's languages as a necessary condition of effective and equitable educational provision, it is reasonable to argue that a fundamental reappraisal needs to take place.

THE BILINGUAL CHILD AND THE CURRICULUM

We come now to consider how existing primary school curriculum patterns suit children who are bilingual in a dialect of Punjabi and in English. In effect one asks how far existing educational provision is appropriate for the aptitudes and ability of a bilingual child. In making generalizations it is recognized that there are variations in curricular patterns and that certain schools have been able to make limited use of two languages within the classroom.

There seem to be a number of prevailing assumptions which underlie the kinds of curricular experience which are provided for bilingual children in English primary schools. The first of these consists in treating children of Asian origin as a broad but rather homogeneous group. The effect of this is to minimize cultural and religious variation and to ignore the potential relevance of different languages, dialect and patterns of bilingualism. It is likely that Punjabi is an important element in the social and cultural identities of the Sikh and Muslim speakers of the language. Its use distinguishes them from other Asian groups and their two dialects, with regional and religious associations, contribute to the sharp distinction between them. The characteristic pattern of the bilingualism of these two Punjabi-speaking ethnic groups is also different, reflected in their written forms and in the relationship of Punjabi with Urdu for the Muslim speaker.

A second assumption seems to be that it is educationally appropriate to regard Punjabi-English bilinguals as monolingual 'second language learners' for pedagogic purposes. While it is perfectly true that this is convenient on the grounds of cost, staffing and resources, and that it reflects an early pattern of response to rapid immigration in an earlier period, it is unreasonable to argue that this takes account of the existing aptitudes and abilities of young children or that it can be unequivocally defended as a long-term basis for curricular planning for bilingual children.

The third assumption is the belief, widely held, that effective control of English as a means of access to educational opportunity depends on spending the whole or even the bulk of each school day learning through the medium of English. It is not necessary to dispute the usefulness of English within the larger society while still questioning the curricular strategy which convention assumes is needed. International experience and research does not support this assumption (Spolsky, 1977; Rees and Fitzpatrick, 1980).

Finally it is often said that Asian parents have no wish to see their home language introduced into the school and that they want the child to use only English there. While this may have been true at one time (Khan, 1980) recent research in this country (Bedfordshire Education Service, 1980; Rees and Fitzpatrick, 1980) suggests that this is no longer true in a simple fashion. There is clearly room for parent and teacher understanding of the issues involved in the use of more than one language within the school.

While it would be fair to say that not all schools or all teachers can be regarded as making all these assumptions, or of making them as points of principle rather than of practicality, it seems that in practice this is broadly the case. Recently, at school level and in terms of general educational policy, there has been a willingness to recognize cultural distinctions between indigenous children and those from minority groups. These distinctions are however cultural rather than linguistic and selected for their compatibility with the idea that multicultural education involves a curriculum which is experienced equally by children of all backgrounds. While this may be desirable in itself, the logical extension of this process to linguistic aspects of a child's cultural identity and to his bilingualism is not compatible with the widely held axiom – that equality of opportunity consists in providing for all children within the same basic curriculum. This apparently desirable principle leads to a curriculum compatible with the aptitudes and abilities of the majority of children and a curriculum which is monolingual and mainly monocultural (with ethnic overtones).

RECENT RESEARCH ON THE EDUCATION OF BILINGUAL CHILDREN

Two recent attempts have been made to initiate research into the possibility of using two languages within the primary school curriculum, in Bedford (with Sikh speakers of Punjabi) (Bedfordshire Education Service, 1980) and in Bradford (with Muslim speakers of Punjabi) (Rees and Fitzpatrick, 1980). Other ventures involving the use of children's mother tongue in the classroom have also been initiated on a small scale within various L.E.A.s.

At the time that the project in Bradford was initiated (1978), in common with most primary schools in Britain, the use of Asian languages was limited to those schools where a teacher or a nursery nurse was able to speak a particular language. In general, this use appears to have been limited to dealing with specific difficulties, especially when children were starting school, and for contacts with parents (as with the liaison teacher service which Bradford operates).

During the same period the Council of the E.E.C. adopted a directive (25 July 1977) relating to the provision of education for the children of migrant workers which articulated, as had the U.N.E.S.C.O. Convention against Discrimination in Education (1960), the rights of ethnic minorities to the maintenance of home culture through schooling (Claydon, Knight and Rado, 1977). There had also been a considerable development of practical and research interest in bilingual education for linguistic minorities in countries which had traditionally adopted monolingual patterns of education (for example the USA, Australia and Canada). In fact, as long ago as 1953 a U.N.E.S.C.O. conference published a monograph on 'The Use of Vernacular Languages in Education' where it was considered axiomatic that the best medium for teaching was the pupil's mother tongue. Similar points have been made more recently by other writers (Savile and Troike, 1971).

In the USA, where the position of minority ethnic and linguistic groups can be considered in some ways like that of Asian groups in Britain, the growth of interest and of practical action on bilingual education has been marked. Under political and educational pressure there has been some change from a mono-lingual and assimilationist [2] approach towards a pluralist [3] policy involving bilingual education programmes where these are appropriate. Much attention has been devoted there to the meaning of the principle of 'equality of provision' in a multilingual and multicultural society and the problem has been the subject of legal debate (Teitelbaum and Hiller, 1977). As a result of social and political pressures there have been two Bilingual Education Acts and a variety of related legal decisions. Many school boards have evolved programmes of bilingual education and policy guidelines which define what is called 'Bilingual-bicultural' education. Similar changes have also taken place in, for example, Sweden (Lasonen and Toukomaa, 1978), Australia (Claydon *et al.*, 1977) and Canada (Lambert and Tucker, 1972).

All this can be taken as an indication of the developing awareness of the new migrants and settlers in many Western European and North American countries. One of the earliest indications of British interest in bilingualism and its educa-tional significance in English schools was the conference in 1975 on 'Bilingual-ism in British Education' convened by the Centre for Information on Language Teaching and Research in collaboration with Leicestershire Education Auth-ority and other Midlands Education Authorities (C.I.L.T., 1976). Given the lack of experience with bilingualism in the English context, discussion focused on other (indigenous) models for bilingual education. In retrospect, these seem not to be wholly appropriate bases for considering the bilingual education of, for example, Asian children in English inner city areas.

The Department of Education and Science also became interested in formu-lating a policy on the education of the child whose home language was not English. What this means in practice is a policy that can apply to children from a wide variety of linguistic backgrounds and with a wide variety of different skill levels in English as they enter school. The 'Mother Tongue and English Teaching Project' was part of their response to this problem and it sought to mount a bilingual education programme and evaluate the progress of Punjabi/ English speakers within it during their first year at school.

There is a fundamental distinction to be made in considering both these

[2] Assimilationist – refers to educational programmes where members of a minority language group are intended to become indistinguishably full members of the majority culture and where there is no institutional support for their culture.
[3] Pluralist – in educational terms refers to a system where a minority language community can count on institutional support for the maintenance of their culture (including language).

programmes and the supplementary 'schools' and classes held by communities for their children and about which there is presently little systematic information. The distinction to be made is between what may be called a 'language teaching programme' whose primary function is the maintenance of some specific mother tongue and its associated cultural patterns and what may be called a 'bilingual education programme' where the school curriculum as a whole (together with therefore the associated cultural elements) is developed in a fully coordinated way through two languages and by the bilingual child. Which kind of focus is appropriate in particular contexts is a central issue in the development of the education of bilingual children in the UK (Fitzpatrick and Rees, 1980).

The Bradford Mother Tongue and English Teaching Project originated from the interest of the Bradford Education Authority in providing for the educational needs of young children of Asian ethnic origin. Many of these speak an Asian language at home and come to school with little or no knowledge of English. Existing practice in the district follows one or two major patterns. In the city area many non-English speakers initially attend Infant Centres where they can acquire sufficient command of English and preliminary educational skills to be able to cope, with assistance, in an ordinary First School. They tend to be transferred to a First School, as soon as they acquire this basis, after between one and six terms from entry to the Infant Centre. In the rest of the district children go immediately to First Schools where provision is made for special help in second language learning.

As a result of discussion with the research directors and with other interested parties, the project was planned so as to mount a one-year bilingual education programme, [4] to describe the context in which it took place and to provide information about its progress and outcome. The programme was intended for rising five year-olds whose parents were of Asian origin and who attended school in the Bradford area. The children involved were speakers of Punjabi (Mirapuri variants) who entered school in September 1978. At that point they were judged to have little or no knowledge of English. Some 70 children were involved in both the bilingual education programme and in the control groups.

One Infant Centre in the Bradford City area and one First School outside the city were identified as having a sufficiently large intake of Punjabi speakers for the research design. They also met other criteria (Rees and Fitzpatrick, 1980). Through Punjabi-speaking liaison teachers, evidence of the general acceptability

---

[4] A 'bilingual education programme' is taken to be a complete programme of work during the school week through the medium of two languages and which is planned as a whole. Work in both languages is not simply directed at learning the language but a general educational function. Note here that a 'bilingual' child is taken to mean one who has any discernible level of communicative performance available in two languages.

of a bilingual education programme was obtained; virtually all parents of entrants to the schools were willing to allow their children to participate. This may, however, reflect their sense of trust in the schools rather than a clear conception by parents of the implications of such a programme. Subsequent interviews with parents have revealed support for a bilingual education programme on cultural and instrumental grounds, but there has been little evidence, as one might expect, of an understanding of the educational or developmental justification for such a programme.

The intention behind the project was to provide information on teaching through both mother tongue and English in a bilingual programme. Substantial use of a child's mother tongue (i.e. home language) in the classroom, as well as English, was planned. The curriculum was to consist of a programme of general education in the first year of school which could facilitate the child's adaptation to school, promote linguistic and cognitive development and facilitate the acquisition of English. The children entered the two schools in September 1978 and the bilingual programme ran until July 1979. During the course of the year a comparison was made between children who worked according to existing practices (i.e. almost wholly through the medium of English) and children taking part in the bilingual education programme. The attainment of the children, their cognitive and linguistic development and their use of Punjabi and English in the classroom were monitored using a variety of relatively unobtrusive techniques.

At the same time the research team collected information about the context in which the programmes took place. This included a study of teachers' attitudes to the use of Asian mother tongues in school, an intensive investigation of the background of the children, and research into parents' attitudes to bilingual education, to education and schooling generally, and into their aspirations for their children. The results from this field study will be linked with the classroom data in the interpretation of the study.

RELATIVE PERFORMANCE IN EXPERIMENTAL AND CONTROL CURRICULA

At the present time it is possible to give a preliminary report on the relative progress of children who were randomly allocated to the two conditions. The first condition was a curriculum involving the use of two languages as educational media (experimental condition) and the second a curriculum on existing (monolingual English) lines (control condition). Here the performance of the children on a limited number of tasks at the end of their school year is outlined. Methodological questions underlie the selection and interpretation of these tasks and the design of the whole research programme but they cannot be considered here (but see Rees and Fitzpatrick, 1980 and Fitzpatrick and Rees, 1980 for example).

Three kinds of performance measures are considered below and these were obtained through individual testing of each child by a familiar person.

Non-verbal tasks

These are nominally 'non-verbal' tasks which can be considered to be relatively independent of linguistic skill for their performance. Where a language needed to be used to give the task instructions this was English, but every effort was made to select tasks where what was required could be inferred by the child from the materials and from the examples provided by the tester. Four performance measures were obtained:

(1) A raw score for the Weschler Pre-School and Primary Intelligence Scale on the Block Design sub-test.
(2) A score for copying simple shapes adapted from the Graphic sub-test of the Porch Index of Communicative Ability in Children (P.I.C.A.C.).
(3) A score for copying complex shapes adapted from the Graphic sub-test of the P.I.C.A.C.
(4) A score for copying letter shapes adapted from the Graphic sub-test of the P.I.C.A.C.

Measures of communicative performance using English

These tasks were developed through earlier work with modifications of the sub-tests of the Porch Index of Communicative Ability in Children. Each task makes use of a series of common objects which are present throughout a session for the child to handle or to refer to (pencil, spoon, crayon, key, penny, fork, and a practice item). Scoring involves a complex multi-dimensional system to assign a response to an ordered series of categories. The tasks involved the following kinds of activity:

(1) Verbal – object function
(2) Auditory – object function
(3) Verbal – sentence completion
(4) Auditory – following instructions
(5) Verbal – describing an object

The split-half reliability of these sub-tests is reported in Table 9.1.

Measures of communicative performance using Punjabi

These tasks were derived from the English-medium measures described above through translation into the vernacular Punjabi used by the children. Even so the

Table 9.1   Split-half equal length Spearman–Brown reliability coefficients for odd–even items (N = 6) ordered by difficulty level

Task	English medium	Punjab medium
Verbal: object function	0.91	0.94
Auditory: object function	0.78	0.65
Verbal: sentence completion	0.62	0.86
Auditory: following instructions	0.87	0.85
Verbal: describing an object	0.91	0.99

Note: These and other tables are based on an N of 69 subjects.

Table 9.2   Mean age, W.P.P.S.I.[1] Block Design Score and Graphic Task Scores for treatment groups after 10 months at school

	Bilingual education groups	Control groups
Age on entry to school	58.8 months	59.3 months
W.P.P.S.I. block design raw scores	8.0	9.2
Graphic task		
simple shapes	5.4	5.1
complex shapes	4.0	3.8
Letter shapes	5.8	5.5

[1] Weschler Pre School and Primary Intelligence Scale.

tasks should not be regarded as directly comparable to the corresponding English-medium task. They do however map the same kinds of linguistic and communicative performance in the two languages.

In Table 9.2 the mean value of the 'non verbal' measures for the experimental groups and the control groups are shown. Examination of the difference between the distributions on each measure for the two groups and for a specific difference in the measures with the Kolmogorov – Smirnov two-sample test gave a result in each case which was not statistically significant. There was therefore no evidence in this area that the groups differed as a result of the different curricula they had received.

Where tasks involving communicative performance are considered, for the experimental and control groups, it appears that preliminary results suggest a complex pattern. Data showing the probability of a child giving a response which

Table 9.3   Mean response probabilities for treatment groups on communicative ability tasks

Bilingual Education Group		Mid category responses	Upper category responses
English medium	Verbal tasks	0.26	0.30
	Auditory tasks	0.30	0.43
Punjabi medium	Verbal tasks	0.38	0.27
	Auditory tasks	0.50	0.31
Control Group			
English medium	Verbal tasks	0.26	0.36
	Auditory tasks	0.18	0.43
Punjabi medium	Verbal tasks	0.25	0.24
	Auditory tasks	0.53	0.14

can be scored as in an upper category (i.e. a response which is accurate but possibly incomplete, delayed or distorted) or in a mid category (i.e. responses which are accurate but self-corrected or corrected after repetition or which are almost accurate) is given in Table 9.3.

The remaining responses fell into the lower categories (i.e. inaccurate responses or responses which were incomprehensible or absent).

In commenting on the pattern shown it is important to recognize from the outset that comparisons between Punjabi-medium and English-medium tasks are to be avoided on methodological grounds. Translation and a need to interpret the category system in terms of syntactically distinct language make the pairs of tests non-equivalent, in principle. In the experimental group the total number of responses observed in verbal tasks was 540 for each language medium and 486 for the control group. The equivalent figures for auditory tasks are 360 and 324 respectively.

The only area where the experimental group may show a tendency to score lower than the control group is on English-medium verbal tasks. Further examination of the data indicated that the difference derives primarily from the Verbal: object function tasks. Here the experimental group gave response probabilities of 0.43 and 0.38 for mid and upper category responses while those for the control group were 0.32 and 0.51 respectively. The scoring criteria for the upper categories did however involve a strong dependence on syntactic accuracy and rather little on lexical productivity. When this latter criteria was examined in terms of the number of words produced for response to each item, the

Table 9.4   Mean number of words used in response to items in the Verbal: Object
Function task

Item	Bilingual education group	Control group*
Pencil	1.6	1.2
Spoon	1.9	1.4
Crayon	1.8	0.9
Key	2.0	1.0
Penny	2.4	2.2
Fork	1.7	1.3
ALL	1.9	1.3

* The difference between treatment groups is statistically significant (Mann–Whitney U test:
2 tail; p = .002).

experimental group then show a tendency to obtain higher mean scores. This is
shown in Table 9.4.

A number of relevant conclusions may be drawn in relation to this preliminary
consideration of results. Provision of a bilingual education programme in the first
year at school does not in practice necessarily constitute a danger to a child's
progress. In the areas examined here progress is as good as that in monolingual
conditions on balance. Given that there are institutional and personal benefits
and a positive effect on the mother tongue, the provision of a bilingual education
programme might be beneficial for some young Asian children. Indeed the
pattern of performance at the end of the first year at school may be one which, in
the longer term and cumulatively, works in favour of the experimental groups. A
follow-up study will try to examine this possibility. The results in an English
school setting tend to challenge the usefulness of those assumptions discussed
earlier in this paper and suggest that the time has come for a radical reappraisal of
educational provision for bilingual children from minority ethnic groups.

REFERENCES

Anisfeld, M.E. (1964) A comparison of the cognitive functioning of monolinguals and
    bilinguals. Unpublished Doctoral dissertation, McGill University
Arsenian, S. (1937) *Bilingualism and Mental Development*, Teachers College, Columbia
    University, New York
Bedfordshire Education Service (1980) E.C. Mother Tongue and Culture Pilot Project
    1976–80. Report for the Colloquium at Cranfield Institute of Technology
Ben-Zeev, S. (1977) Mechanisms by which childhood bilingualism affects understanding
    of language and cognitive structures, in P.A. Hornby (ed.) *Bilingualism*, Academic
    Press, New York

Ben-Zeev, S. (1972) The influence of bilingualism on cognitive development and cognitive strategy. Unpublished Ph.D. dissertation, University of Chicago

Bloomfield, L. (1935) *Language*, Allen and Unwin, London

The Bullock Report (1975) A Language for Life, H.M.S.O., London

Campbell-Platt, K. (1978) *Linguistic Minorities in Britain*, Runnymede Trust, Briefing Paper

C.I.L.T. (1976) *Bilingualism and British Education: The Dimensions of Diversity*

Claydon, L., Knight, T. and Rado, M. (1977) *Curriculum and Culture*, Allen and Unwin, Australia

Cummins, J. and Gulutson, M. (1974) Some Effects of Bilingualism on Cognitive Functioning. Unpublished research paper, University of Alberta, Canada

Darcy, N.T. (1953) A review of the literature on the effects of bilingualism on the measurement of intelligence, *Journal of Genetic Psychology*, Vol. 82, pp 21–58

Driver, G. (1977) Cultural competence, social power and school achievement, *New Community*, Vol. 5, pp 355–61

Fitzpatrick, F. and Rees, O.A. (1980) *The Education of Bilingual Children: A Framework for Discussion*, Mother Tongue and English Teaching Project, Working Paper No. 3

I.L.E.A. (1979) *Report on the 1978 Census of Those I.L.E.A. Pupils for Whom English Was Not a First Language*, I.L.E.A., London

Khan, V.S. (1980) The 'mother tongue' of linguistic minorities in multi-cultural England, *Journal of Multilingual and Multicultural Development*, Vol.1

Lambert, W.E. and Tucker, G.R. (1972) *Bilingual Education of Children*, Newbury House, Rowley, Mass.

Lasonen, K. and Toukomaa, P. (1978) Linguistic development and school achievement among Finnish immigrant children in mother-tongue medium classes in Sweden. Research Report No. 70, Department of Education, University of Jyvaskyla

Peal, E. and Lambert, W.E. (1962) The relation of bilingualism to intelligence, *Psychological Monographs*, No. 76

Phillips, C.J. (1979) Educational under-achievement in different ethnic groups, *Educational Research*, Vol. 21, pp 116–30

Rees, O.A. (1976) Language organization and language change in bilinguals. Unpublished Ph.D. Thesis, University of London

Rees, O.A. and Fitzpatrick, F. (1980) The origin and development of the Mother Tongue and English Teaching Project. M.O.T.E.T. Working Paper No. 1

Rosen, H. (1978) *Interim Report on the Survey of Linguistic Diversity in London Schools*, Institute of Education, University of London

Savile, M.R. and Troike, R.C. (1971) *A Handbook of Bilingual Education*, T.E.S.O.L., Washington, D.C.

Segalowitz, N. (1977) Psychological perspectives on bilingual education, in B. Spolsky (ed.) (1977) *Functions of Bilingual Education*, Newbury House, Rowley, Mass

Sills, D.L. (ed.) (1968) *International Encyclopaedia of the Social Sciences*, Macmillan, London

Spolsky, B. (ed) (1977) *Frontiers of Bilingual Education*, Newbury House, Rowley, Mass

Teitelbaum, H. and Hiller, R.J. (1977) Bilingual education: the legal mandate, *Harvard Educational Review*, Vol. 47, pp 138–70

TOPICS FOR DISCUSSION

1. In what ways have the linguistic needs of ethnic minority groups been over-simplified, and, indeed, misunderstood?
2. What do we know of the relationship between bilingualism and pupil attainment?
3. What are the institutional and personal benefits deriving from the provision of bilingual educational programmes?

SUGGESTIONS FOR FURTHER READING

1. Tansley, P. and Craft, A. (1984) Mother tongue teaching and support: a Schools Council enquiry, *Journal of Multilingual and Multicultural Development*, Vol. 5, No. 5, pp 367–384. A report of the Schools Council's *Mother Tongue Project* for primary school pupils in England and Wales. The survey identifies the support given by L.E.A.s to mother tongue teaching and to L.E.A. mother-tongue policies.
2. Brook, M.R.M. (1980) The 'mother-tongue' issue in Britain: cultural diversity or control?, *British Journal of Sociology of Education*, Vol. 1, No. 3, pp 237–56. An E.E.C. directive requires member states to make available to the children of migrant workers within the Community teaching of the mother-tongues of their families' countries of origin. Reservations are expressed about the way in which the directive has so far been interpreted in Britain. An alternative policy emphasis is outlined.
3. Tsow Ming (1983) Ethnic minority community languages: a statement, *Journal of Multilingual and Multicultural Development*, Vol. 4, No. 5, pp 361–84. A paper from the Commission For Racial Equality concerning the linguistic and educational needs of contemporary Britain. It summarizes bilingual issues posed by self-help education in mother-tongue teaching and itemizes the major conclusions of research on bilingual learning.

THE MULTICULTURAL CURRICULUM

INTRODUCTION

Reading 10 (Lynch, 1983) is a succinct examination of the tasks involved in developing a multicultural curriculum at three levels: at national or local authority level; at the level of the school; and at the individual teacher level. The paper raises a series of questions in respect of each level of conceptualization. Lynch's theoretical contribution is complemented in the suggestions for further reading by Craft and Bardell's (1984) account of multicultural curriculum development in a variety of subject areas. The paper by James and Jeffcoate (1981) provides another view of the tasks involved in developing a set of objectives as a guide to the construction of a multicultural curriculum. Tomlinson and Tomes (1983) contains detailed information on curriculum issues in respect of ethnic minorities in British schools.

Reading 11 is a summary of three practical accounts of the development of anti-racist policies in an infant, a primary and a comprehensive school. It might usefully be examined in conjunction with the I.L.E.A. *Policy For Equality* documents contained in Reading 2. The accompanying suggestions for further study by Brown (1984), Saunders (1982), and Twitchin and Demuth (1981) all address practical ways in which teachers can combat the effects of institutional and individual racism.

Reading 10
THE MULTICULTURAL CURRICULUM: SOME GUIDELINES FOR ACTION
J. Lynch[1]

To implement the convenant inherent within the kind of multicultural curriculum suggested in this book will be no easy matter. For one thing it would be naive to assume that a majority of the population of this country, let alone its governmental circles and administration, is convinced that Britain in the 1980s is, or should be, a multicultural society. For another, it is unlikely that substantial additional resources will be immediately available for the re-jigging of the

[1] In Lynch, J. (1983) *The Multicultural Curriculum*, Batsford Academic, London, pp 119–29

professional and cultural capital of the teaching force, which is by and large a necessary accompaniment.

On the other hand, teachers in many different parts of the country have demonstrated already that they are the ones who are capable of designing and introducing multicultural curricula and materials. In this respect, it is the grassroots development towards multicultural education which has been most impressive in this country. For this reason, without assuming that all teachers are at the same stage of 'multicultural competence' or that all schools have the same need, this [Reading] seeks to indicate some initial guidelines for action. I am conscious in doing this that for some teachers a number of the guidelines may already have been implemented, but for others I hope that they may be novel in large part.

This [Reading] takes a look at what needs to be done to strive towards the ideal of a multicultural curriculum at three different levels: the systemic, by which I mean national or local authority level; the institutional, that is the school level; and the individual teacher level.

SOME TASKS FOR SYSTEMIC ACTION: NATIONAL

Firstly, it is important at the national level that an unequivocal and explicit commitment is made by the government of the day to multiculturalism as one of the basic values of our society. That means not only that there would be legislation, as there is, which outlaws racial discrimination, but that it would cover the whole range of cultural criteria seen as legitimate dimensions of the cultural diversity of our society. Any remaining discriminatory legislation against particular groups for historical or other reasons should be rescinded. Any loopholes to prejudice or discrimination must be closed so that it is not possible for a particular institution to hide behind charitable status, for instance to discriminate against women, as certain prestigious educational foundations appear to be doing. Nor would it be possible for particular occupational groupings to achieve discrimination *de facto*, whilst of course abhorring it *de lege*, as is alleged to be happening in certain sections of the armed forces.

Additionally, and in the education sector, each of the government departments with responsibility should issue a 'consultative document' on multicultural education which would eventually, after considerable discussion, result in an amended 'School Curriculum' document. This document must acknowledge multiculturalism as something more than an issue, namely, a central and pivotal value domain of our society. As has happened with Circular 6/81 this would need to be followed up by a system of monitoring and evaluation. A revised circular would be necessary and a unit specifically devoted to the appraisal on a national basis of local authorities' and schools' progress towards multicultural education and a multicultural curriculum. The unit would have no inspectorial or enforcement power, but would have the task of providing the information, on the basis of which the normal channels of inspection and enforcement could be set in motion if necessary.

It is important here to note that any talk of coercion is entirely out of place. The process has to be seen as part of a wider process of discourse and dialogue. As part of its function, however, it is to be hoped that the unit could stimulate professional performance; identify more closely areas of special need; indicate 'good practice' such as collaborative and other learning/teaching strategies, which takes advantage of the cultural diversity of society and the school system; indicate to authorities and schools how they may design and implement their own ongoing review procedures; and assist in the generation of a climate of discussion and dialogue, both lay and professional, which will assist in the involvement of diverse cultural groups in education, its process, organization and control, and the improvement of provision.

SOME LOCAL PRIORITIES FOR ACTION

Within the context of an overall government policy for multicultural education, the partnership between central and local government, by now a traditional strength of education in this country, must continue and be strengthened. Because of the aimlessness of much that passes for multicultural education at the moment, however, all L.E.A.s will need to formulate, through an exhaustive process of consultation, an approved, explicit and readily understandable policy statement on multicultural education. This might include references to the nature of multiculturalism both nationally and locally, indicating both areas of special need and special provision and those areas which are common to the support of cultural diversity. It will need to include reference to support and resource issues; to be convincing to local minority committees, it is essential that it should include reference to the even-handedness of the systems of education and their examination and pupil appraisal procedures. Such documents will need to be both persuasive and sensitive statements of reason and policy; brief and concise yet comprehensive, societal yet adaptive and expressive of local circumstances, working papers yet firm enough to be susceptible to implementation.

Such an overall policy statement would no doubt include items such as the following. It is the policy of the L.E.A.:

(1)   not to discriminate on the basis of race, ethnicity, sex, marital status, disability, etc.;

(2) that the curriculum, teaching methods, material and texts will reflect the cultural diversity of British society, nationally and locally;

(3) that one major aim of education and the curriculum will be a reduction in stereotyping and the elimination of prejudice, discrimination and bias;

(4) that education will foster appreciation of the unity of human kind and respect for its diversity;

(5) that examinations will be 'culture-fair' and even-handed;

(6) that teachers will be supported in the achievement of a multicultural education provision appropriate to both local and national needs;

(7) to support the maintenance and enhancement of bilingualism in general and mother tongue competence, both oral and written, in particular;

(8) to explicitly support equal job opportunities linked with an appreciation of the importance of the recruitment of ethnic minority staff.

Local provision will of course be organized around the focus of local needs, with the need for frequent local 'need-assessment' surveys as a baseline to the response to the differing district, age and cultural profiles. Regular and thorough research and evaluation is an inevitable part of such a policy as are also intensive contacts with the local community and particularly parents. Moreover, if scarce resources are going to be maximally exploited this will call for a networking of resources and the encouragement of a policy of staff exchanges between schools and between education and teacher education.

Within the context of the overall policy statement, distributed to all within the locality, there will need to be operational guidelines which can be drawn up by working parties including officers, advisers, teachers, elected members, community members, parents and, as appropriate, pupils, whose task would be to set out the main parameters for the achievement of the policy statement. It will be necessary, but not sufficient alone, that elected members should participate. Nor is it prudent to envisage the process as a once-and-for-all mechanism but rather part of the continuing discourse, which includes the identification and ordering of priorities for a given financial period and the establishment of an outline schedule of consultation and implementation.

Further, the working parties will need to continually address new areas of knowledge, as the educational implications of adapting policies of multiculturalism deepen and the requirement arises for new policy statements for newly or differently perceived areas of need. The working parties will need, for example, to give attention to the improvement of communications between local authorities, teachers, parents, pupils, minority groups and the community in general, which by dint of its very success may generate new needs and approaches as the intercommunicative competence and intercultural understanding and skills of the parties improve.

But the support for teachers and their profession is in many cases totally lacking at the moment, as two recent surveys indicate. At local level a means of stimulating the development of multicultural curricula has to be found through support and in-service provision for teachers. We already know, for instance, that in 1981 at least 18 of the 97 L.E.A.s surveyed by Matthews (1981) were providing special funding for multicultural curriculum development, and this seems a practice which has also proved effective in the USA and Australia. But we also know from the same survey that only 14 of the 67 local authorities from whom information was collected referred to links with ethnic minority groups in the community, and that 16 authorities made no provision for in-service education in the field. So there is considerable scope for expansion there.

Equally, the survey by Eggleston and his colleagues (1981) indicated the fragmentary and incomplete nature of current I.N.S.E.T. provision. There were no methods to ensure help for teachers facing acute difficulty in multicultural classrooms and what help was available was spasmodic and frequently unknown to teachers. Moreover, it was often not related to the needs of schools and minority groups.

Thus, once again, the crucial importance of a coherent and well-supported district-wide policy for the design and implementation of support and in-service provision for teachers is one of the tasks which local authorities will need to attend to urgently, in so far as they have not done so already, and if they wish to develop multicultural provision and multiculturalism. Such support is an essential stepping-stone to the multicultural curriculum and as such it needs to be included in the overall implementation strategy and guidelines. Thus a rolling programme of policy guideline development, implementation, appraisal and improvement will be necessary. From learning to learn and to share will come learning to improve which, in turn, will generate new needs to learn to learn.

I suppose what I am proposing is similar to the process of delivering people from intellectual, moral and spiritual bondage which education represents for many at the moment, and of recognizing education, as Stenhouse (1978) argues, as the potential instrument of a redistribution of the means of autonomy and judgement. The right to judgement is redistributed as is the autonomy to feel in a position to formulate tentative judgements subject to critical public appraisal.

THE INSTITUTIONAL LEVEL: SOME SUGGESTIONS FOR BEGINNING

The first task for any school in attempting to plan the introduction of a multicultural curriculum is inevitably a reappraisal of where it has got to, what it offers, with what kind of success and how this reflects and relates to its immediate communities. This is inevitably going to involve a lot of work and for this reason, and for others equally, the task will need to be tackled on a basis of team work. The school is not alone however, and can, if it wishes, have access to pupil and community resources which can greatly share and therefore lighten the burden.

One approach which has been suggested by Reynolds and Skilbeck (1976) is that of what they term 'situational analysis'. This involves a review of broader contextual issues (external factors) and the immediate school environment (internal factors). In this first case, this involves such items as community assumptions and values, expectations and requirements of parents and employers and shifts in general ideological movements in society. Amongst the internal factors would be included such factors as teachers, their values, skills, knowledge and experience, and perceived and felt problems and shortcomings of the existing curriculum.

Alternatively, and focusing on the curriculum in particular, a school could use Scrimshaw *et al.*'s (1976) matching pairs of descriptive and narrative questions. These cover the range of objectives and how they are characterized, the values and beliefs underlying that selection of objectives, whether all objectives are for all pupils or only some, and if the latter, how the selection for the individual is made, what 'knowledge-imprints' the components of the curriculum represent and how groupings are related to it and, finally, the methods which are used to evaluate the school's success and how these methods are related to the school's objectives.

One school set about the task pragmatically, looking at the work of the school under four headings: curriculum, including content and resources; pastoral; school culture; teacher attitudes. A small working party was established which looked at these areas in detail with the assistance of other staff more specifically concerned with them. An analysis was made in each area, recommendations were worked out and a report drawn up. The recommendation list from the Schools Council Report *Multiethnic Education: The Way Forward* (1981) was then quoted and the school report presented to a staff assembly.

It would also be possible for a largely intuitive or impressionistic approach to be adopted and certainly the importance of 'rampant reflection' in the appraisal of education should not be underestimated – or overestimated. But most schools will probably prefer a more systematic analysis, such as or similar to the ones quoted above, which is consistent with their skills and resources, to a rather more subjective approach. Whatever balance they decide on they, that is the school staff, will need to attempt an initial formulation of the kinds of questions they wish to pose and the areas they wish to address. This will certainly include some of the following and no doubt others besides:

(1) What are the national and local goals inherent within multicultural education that we should be addressing?

(2) What information/evidence do we have of the performance of particular kinds of pupils and how can we take account of it in our planning?

(3) What should our policy on multicultural education as a whole, and particular aspects of it such as mother-tongue teaching and English as a second language, be?

(4) What is the 'cultural identikit' of our pupils and the community from which they come? What languages and religions are represented? What cultural values and customs are manifest? What occupations and styles of life?

(5) In what ways can the cultural diversity of our pupils and community be meaningfully represented in our school, its organization, curriculum, teaching/learning strategies and examinations? Are our policies for withdrawal groups and referral fair and balanced? Or do they implicitly discriminate against certain cultural groups?

(6) What should be the major components of our curriculum and how should these reflect the community of which we are a part? How can they be involved in it?

(7) What scope should there be for meaningful representation of pupils, parents and the wider community in the life and decision-making of the school? How can dialogue and discourse be encouraged?

(8) Which means should we adopt to evaluate the work of the school and how can we develop culture-fair means of assessing and examining our pupils?

(9) How can resources and resource work be maximized and equalized for all pupils?

(10) Are our books and teaching materials multicultural value for money? Do they contain inaccurate, racist or discriminatory stereotypes? Are they ethno- or eurocentric or do they seek to offer a wider world view?

(11) What policy of staff development do we need in order to support our aspiration to introduce multicultural education and to design and implement a multicultural curriculum and appropriate examinations?

To tackle such questions, one school might establish an initial joint working party to outline and draw up 'the shopping list', and perhaps sketch out an outline policy. Another larger one might envisage a series of working parties to agree particular aspects of the policy and its implementation: mother tongue, the whole curriculum, home–school relations, teaching methods, internal organization and grouping, materials and resources, English as a second language, religious and moral education, mother tongue issues, examinations.

Certainly, what evidence we have would seem to suggest that where such groups are established, they increase corporate awareness and thus provide an essential platform for multicultural education. The idea of sharing explicit within a working party, its collaborative and teamwork approach, probably approximates more closely to the needs of most teachers than does that which is available in more formal course provision. Moreover, the needs of individual schools are so different that such appraisal as we are suggesting is probably best carried out at school level, although, of course, not without outside assistance and participation. That does not, however, rule out joint enterprise with other institutions and individuals perhaps sometimes in the role of honest broker; nor should it exclude the opportunity for an individual member of staff to do an intensive study of relevance and value to the school, perhaps as part of an advanced study opportunity.

SOME SUGGESTIONS FOR THE INDIVIDUAL TEACHER

The Keele Report on in-service provision for individual teachers (Eggleston, 1981) speaks of

> [. . .] the experiences of many of the teachers we have interviewed, faced with the day to day and minute by minute problems of working in classrooms with children whose cultural, community, intellectual and linguistic situations are diverse and which they only incompletely understand.

and further:

> [. . .] many teachers have keenly felt professional needs to identify and develop new styles of teaching that are more appropriate for a multicultural society; these include considerable numbers of teachers who are not themselves teaching many pupils from ethnic minority groups.

However good the policy statements and guidelines, it is, in the last resort, on the individual teacher that the full responsibility for the implementation of multicultural education falls. Something of what this involves may be gauged from a recent report. The interim Rampton Report (1981) for instance, says that teachers should

> be prepared to examine and reappraise their attitudes and behaviour, to challenge all manifestations of racism and to play a learning role in seeking to change the attitudes of society as a whole [. . .].

This is a tall order for anyone but particularly for a busy teacher involved in a rapidly changing world, who may be worrying about whether there will be a job at all in the near future and is subject to often conflicting demands and expectations from sometimes strident groups in society. With so many demands and such diverse needs what should be the teacher's priorities in the shorter and longer terms?

To some extent, the answer to this question is what it has always been. The teacher needs to know his/her pupils, know his/her material and resources for teaching and to know his/her job, that is, how to teach.

Under the heading of knowing his/her pupils', he or she will need to take account of sociocultural background factors such as the home and community, as well as such factors as the values and learning styles of the pupils. Under 'material and resources for teaching' comes both curriculum content and examinations as well as the texts and aids which he or she uses.

'Knowing his/her job' means that teachers will have to understand how to motivate and teach in a pluralist classroom where often attitudes to rewards, achievement and life in general are very different from their own. In each of these cases they will need continually to update their knowledge and understanding, acquire new values, develop new skills and be able to demonstrate to themselves, their pupils and their wider professional and lay community that they have climbed this ladder of experience. In other words the reflexivity of their ascent is not only with regard to themselves but also to their pupils and peers. (See Figure 10.1)

	Knowledge and understanding of new content	Acquisition of new and changed attitudes	Development of new skills and techniques	Demonstration of new personal and social behaviours
Self				
Pupil/ Community				
Curriculum/ Resources				
Job/ Teaching– Learning Strategies				

Figure 10.1   A planning matrix for individual teacher development in multicultural education

As an initial step the teacher might like to pose the following questions:

(1) How far does what I teach reflect the diversity of the British multiculture of the 1980s?

(2) Is the content free from bias, stereotyping and racism? Is it as fair as I can make it to all cultural groups? Does it eschew ethnocentrism and Eurocentrism and aspire to achieve a world view?

(3) Does my teaching deliberately invite the participation of all cultural groups? Do I take the opportunity to show individuals from different cultural groups in different occupational and social roles?

(4) Do my teaching strategies enhance the individual pupil's self-worth and respect of others? Both those who are similar to and those who are different from him or her? Do they seek to recognize and comprehend different kinds of motivation and life-views?

(5) How do I need to change the content of my teaching to improve the pupils' understanding of their own culture and the heritage of other pupils?

(6) Do I draw widely enough on the resource potential of all pupils, staff, parents and the wider community?

(7) Do I have equally high academic expectations of pupils from all cultural groups?

(8) Do I tend to minimize controversial issues or do I try to tackle them in an open, frank and mature way which invites the contributions of the pupil and plays down my own opinions?

(9) Are the materials, texts and displays which I use as free as possible from racism, stereotyping, distortions, patronization, omissions and derogatory language? Do they acknowledge and express the worthy contributions of all cultural groups to national and local life?

(10) Are the examinations and assessment methods which I use as culture-fair as possible?

(11) Finally, the teacher may wish to ask about ways in which he can help himself. What are my more immediate need in terms of staff development and where can I obtain assistance?

In terms of this last question, teachers may like to reflect on the grid represented by Figure 10.1. They may wish to consider whether their most immediate need is for information concerning their own pupils, the composition of the school's community, or content for their curricula – for example, concepts, statistics, descriptive information tasks for analysis, materials from the Commission for Racial Equality and details of sources of information. They may feel they need a more formal course and wish to investigate where this is available and on what terms. If very little has been done they may wish to suggest to the head and staff the need for a working party to begin to draw up a plan – or even just to begin to 'talk the thing through'.

It is no exaggeration to say that much of the weight of introducing multicultural education falls on the teachers. It will test their skill, expertise and professional commitment to the utmost. Many have already shown that they are fully able to cope with the new perceptions of them and their functions implicit in a multicultural curriculum. But they are only human and sometimes inflated expectations of what they may be able to achieve have been expressed and efforts made to press sectional views as universally acceptable and accepted. Teachers, individually and as a body, can be a very potent influence on the development of a harmonious multicultural society, through a flexible and vital multicultural education. But if much of the rest of society is pulling in the opposite direction, their task is made more difficult, if not impossible.

In the decades since the passage of the 1944 Education Act, teachers have shown themselves well able to change in innumerable different directions: new examinations, new kinds of schools, new curricula, new methods of teaching, new salary structures, new ranges of pupils, both in terms of ability and age, and now, with regard to cultural background, new legislation affecting relations and communications with parents and the community. There is no evidence that they will be unequal to the challenge of the multicultural curriculum, provided other educational and social sectors also play their part in the shared enterprise which is multicultural education.

SUMMARY

This [Reading] has
(1) identified some of the more immediate tasks in 'getting started' with multicultural education;
(2) suggested that it is possible to consider these tasks at system, school and individual levels;
(3) proposed items for inclusion in local authority policy statements;
(4) referred to three ways of beginning needs-assessment at school level;
(5) offered a checklist of items which would be amongst those to be considered by the individual teacher.

REFERENCES

Eggleston, S.J. *et al.* (1981) *In-Service Education in a Multiracial Society*, University of Keele, Keele, Staffs
I.L.E.A. (1983) *Anti-Racist Guidelines for Schools and Colleges*, County Hall, London
Matthews, A. (1981) *Advisory Approaches to Multicultural Education*, Runnymede Trust, London
The Rampton Committee Report (1981) *West Indian Children In our Schools: Interim Report*, HMSO London

Reynolds, J. and Skilbeck, M. (1976) *Culture and the Classroom*, Open Books, London
Schools Council Report (Little, A. and Willey, R. 1981) *Multiethnic Education: the Way Forward*, Schools Council Pamphlet, No.18, London
Scrimshaw, P. *et al.* (1976) *Towards the Whole Curriculum*, The Open University Press pp 10–13 (OU Course E 203: Curriculum Design and Development, Unit 9)
Stenhouse, L. (1978) 'Towards a vernacular humanism', Dartington Hall Conference Papers

TOPICS FOR DISCUSSION

1. What *national* and *local* tasks are suggested as prerequisites of multicultural curriculum development?
2. Compare the L.E.A. policy suggestions (p 199) with those contained in the I.L.E.A. document in Reading 2. In what ways do they differ?
3. Use the list of questions on p 203 to assess your own level of *multicultural competence*. Where do you suspect your immediate needs lie?

SUGGESTIONS FOR FURTHER READING

1. Craft, A. and Bardell, G. (1984) *Curriculum Opportunities in a Multicultural Society*, Harper & Row, London. An account of multicultural education in a variety of subject areas including Mathematics, Chemistry, Biology, Home Economics, English, Modern Languages, History, Geography, Social Sciences, Religious Education, Music, Art and Design, Physical Education, Dance and Outdoor Pursuits.
2. Tomlinson, S. and Tomes, H. (1983) *Ethnic Minorities in British Schools: A Review of the Literature 1960-1982*, Heinemann Educational Books Ltd, London. A review of the literature on multicultural education in Britain which contains detailed information on curriculum issues. See especially Chapter 7.
3. James, A. and Jeffcoate, R. (1981) *The School in The Multicultural Society*, Harper & Row, London. Chapter 1, 'Curriculum planning in multicultural education', develops a set of objectives as a guide to the construction of a multicultural curriculum and discusses factors governing the selection of those objectives.

Reading 11
THE IMPACT OF AN ANTI-RACIST POLICY IN THE SCHOOL COMMUNITY
Mike Mulvaney
CHILDERIC SCHOOL: DEVELOPING A MULTICULTURAL POLICY
David Milman
DEVELOPING A WHOLE SCHOOL RACIST POLICY[1]
Peter Mitchell, Liz Lindsay and Maura Healey

THE IMPACT OF AN ANTI-RACIST POLICY IN THE SCHOOL COMMUNITY

Gayhurst Infants School has a roll of about 200. It is in Hackney and its intake reflects the multicultural character of the area.

Mike Mulvaney, formerly Head Teacher at Gayhurst School, is now Head Teacher at Laburnum Infants and Junior Mixed School.

I was once told, by someone who should know better, that schools in poor areas should provide a haven for children to escape the poverty of their environment.

That environment for many children is the inner city, and, for the majority in my present school, includes either: unemployment or a 12-hour working day in sweat shops; overcrowded, cold, damp housing with many of the surrounding flats boarded up; a denial of basic rights through D.H.S.S. benefits; inadequate health care resulting from lack of interest and random cuts in the health service. For black people (I use the word in its widest possible sense) this common experience is compounded by overt and institutional racism.

It is tempting, and easy, to withdraw into the school and use it as a fortress against a hostile environment. It is possible to make the school comfortable,

[1] In Straker-Welds, M. (1984) *Education For a Multicultural Society*, Bell and Hyman, London, pp 27–33; pp 34–42; pp 46–57

warm, and beautiful. We can use textiles and teasels, stuffed owls and soft lighting, double mounting to really magnificent effect. We can isolate our schools completely until they look as though they had been lifted directly from rural Lincolnshire, Berkshire, or Oxfordshire. We can even have an anti-racist policy that operates fairly effectively in the school. However, we only have the children for six to seven hours a day. The rest of the time they must function within the environment that we successfully shut out or disregard.

Educational isolation is not a new phenomenon but an ongoing experience that only changes in the way in which it is achieved. Between the wars, in the East End of London, it was the Jews and working-class activists that suffered the worst persecution. They experienced fire bombing, children were beaten up on the way to school, they were denied job prospects, and were the objects of hostility of the establishment. The majority of the Jews handled such racism by moving out of the area and losing their language and cultural identity – otherwise known as integration. The discrimination against activists resulted from their conscious political choice, a declaration, and despite the injustices committed against them, their political awareness led them to expect it and to cope with it.

The response of schools to this, and the general appalling poverty of the area, was to home in on the 3Rs and to impose a rigid discipline and authoritarianism similar to that which imposed the conditions that children were suffering in their homes.

The modern black experience has been, and is, that despite political inactivism they have still been bombed, murdered, discriminated against, and harassed because, whatever their attitudes, political philosophy, income or adherence to culture, they are a recognizable minority.

Over the past 10 years, the education service has been involved in a game of liberal educational semantics. In multiculturalism we (teachers) have passed through a number of stages from viewing cultural pluralism as a problem, through celebration, to affirmation, which is where most of us have rested. Many of us have briefly turned our schools into Hindu temples or Gurdwaras. We have, every other year, celebrated Id or Diwali, or laid on the odd carnival with colourful costumes and a steel band borrowed from another school.

There are enormous spin-offs from this hierarchical form of culturalism. The 'minority' parents turn out to provide food, costumes, artefacts, etc., and appear to be eternally grateful. At the end of all such events staff and parents say 'namaste' to each other, and the school reverts to its celebration of white, male, middle-class experience. The parents return to their own experience.

MULTICULTURAL POLICY AT GAYHURST INFANT SCHOOL

At Gayhurst Infants School the staff group developed a policy on racism and cultural pluralism that was based upon experience and practice. It reads:

The school is multicultural, and all that goes on within it must strive to reflect and build upon this basis.

Culture is central to a child's identity, and the learning environment must reflect the cultures of those learning within it and within society at large.

Teachers must become aware of the cultures from which children come, and the customs and attitudes within them.

Teachers can encourage positive ethnic/cultural self identity by initiating activites which reflect a multicultural society. They should aim to give broad-based information and images about each cultural group, drawing as much as possible from the children's experience in a way that avoids the risk of stereotypes.

Questions about racism, name-calling incidents, etc., should never be side-stepped or over-responded to. Children should be given appropriate information when and where situations arise. Teachers must avoid the denial of differences that do exist between groups and cultures because these act as a cover for racism.

It is important for teachers to be sensitive to the feelings of parents and children where these relate to cultural conflict.

Teachers must be aware of the racist connotations in language, and avoid such language personally and discourage its use at all times.

Recognition must be given to the positive value of mother tongue and dialect. Different languages should be shared and given positive images in the classroom. Labelling, letters home, etc., need to be comprehensible to all children and families.

The school as a body should form the closest possible links with organizations and groups representing minorities, and bodies which seek to further the aims of multicultural education. In the same way the school should dissociate itself from, and condemn, any group that is overtly racist or indulging in racist practice without self-examination.

The school as a body will condemn and oppose racism in all its manifestations wherever it occurs, and particularly in the school community and the community it serves.

At best, such a policy can only be a compromise between existing staff views and attitudes. There is much that could be added, and words that should be omitted. The policy is only valid at the time it was written (1980) and for a short time afterwards. Given changes in staff, children and parents, levels of awareness, and the community it should be reviewed and modified annually. Most importantly, a policy should be an affirmation of practice and not an unrealistic list that can never be achieved.

When the draft statement was completed by the staff, it was taken to the parents for any discussion and amendment they thought was necessary. Generally they were supportive when each point of the policy was discussed. At the end one parent said, 'It's just as well it was explained to me because I couldn't understand a bloody word of it'. This made us realize that the policy is very jargonistic, and a group of parents and teachers offered to rewrite it in a more understandable form. It read:

> This school is multicultural. Religion, language, and custom make children what they are, and the children know about themselves and each other. Therefore, we as teachers must know about, and understand, the children's backgrounds to help them feel good about themselves, and to make them sensitive to how others feel and live.
>
> Questions about racism, name calling, etc., should never be side-stepped or over-responded to. Children should be given appropriate information about racism when and where situations arise. Teachers should avoid denying differences that do exist between people because this acts as a cover for racism. Teachers must be aware of the racist meanings that can be in language, and avoid its use at all times.
>
> Sometimes parents and children grow apart because parents expect the children to keep their religion, language, and customs when the children feel under pressure not to. We must be sympathetic and sensitive to both parties. The school must help children to keep their mother tongue which should be seen in notices around the school and in letters home.
>
> The school must work closely with organizations and groups that represent people of different religions, language and customs.

This now appears in the school booklet, but the original remains the school policy.

SCHOOL AND COMMUNITY

At Gayhurst, there were some good examples of anti-racist teaching, teaching of mother tongue, books and materials that reflected the ethnic mix of the school, E.S.L. teaching integrated into the day-to-day curriculum. Racist and imperialist books were removed from the library, the developing racist attitudes of children were generally, but not always, challenged, and important letters home were translated. The practice and policy were, to some extent, effective within the school, but in the normal course of events would have had little impact upon the immediate or wider community.

It is only possible to bring community issues into the school, and vice versa, if time and space have been created for parents to feel comfortable there. They need to feel that their doubts and worries will be heard sympathetically, and that there are structures through which they can make an impact upon the curriculum and organization. For a number of years, the school has systematically worked at methods of building a partnership between home and school which included casework on welfare rights and housing.

The Nationality Bill is a piece of racist legislation that, for the first time, provides a tiered structure of British citizenship. It discriminates against black people living here and abroad. It made many, who have lived here virtually all their lives, feel anxious about their future. It was obvious that a large number of children and parents would be affected by the Bill. Several parents approached the school seeking assistance in understanding the implications for them and their families. We were not able to offer a great deal of help because the Bill is a complex piece of legislation. The problem was taken to the Parent Teacher Association which organized a meeting with representatives of the Hackney Council for Racial Equality and the local law centre. At the meeting it was impossible to understand all of the implications of the Bill and to answer, in detail, the concern that many parents had. The law centre offered to organize a series of evening courses for six parents who could act as counsellors to other parents and members of the community. After training, the counsellors offered a series of day and evening clinics to advise parents and families on how the Nationality Bill would affect them. They had the continuing support of the law centre for any inquiries they had difficulty answering.

This was a good example of how a school can be a catalyst to effective community action. It achieved the twin objectives of organizing opposition to the Bill, and enabling local people to cope with its effects. An additional spin-off was that prompt action allowed parents to register before the government increased the registration fee.

In 1980 two Sikh children transferred into Gayhurst from a local school. Their father explained that the move was necessary because the children had suffered racial harassment on the way to school, and the mother had twice been assaulted whilst accompanying the children. The journey to Gayhurst was shorter, and the children could be watched from the house all the way to school across a public open space. The father apologized that the mother had not come to school with him. She had stayed at home because the parents could not leave the house unoccupied since the property had been damaged by attacks in the past. That evening two teachers visited the family and found them living, eating, and sleeping in one room. The rest of the house had been gutted by a fire that was caused by petrol poured through the letter box. Hackney Council Housing Department had refused to rehouse the family because they claimed, without a scrap of evidence, that the damage had been self-inflicted. They had repaired the front door and put corrugated iron over the smashed windows, but had refused any other repair to the fire and smoke damaged interior.

The children were cowed and looked constantly terrified, and the parents were out of their mind with worry. Sympathetic noises between 9 a.m. and 4 p.m. would have done little to help the family or relieve their suffering. We had no option but to become involved in a campaign which was then being mounted by various anti-racist community groups.

A public meeting was organized at the Hackney Family Centre and was attended by the family, representatives of the groups, and parents and teachers from the school. At the meeting the parents and teachers, with others, organized to escort the children to and from school, to have at least two people in the house every night to allow the family to get some rest, to call the police whenever harassment occurred, and to put pressure upon the Council to rehouse the family in a less exposed position.

These objectives were achieved, but the Council consistently refused to rehouse the family. At a full Council meeting, attended by members of the campaign, a teacher from the school sat on the floor of the chamber and refused to move until the Council made a commitment to rehouse the Singh family. At first the Council members refused to acknowledge her presence and then they adjourned for an hour. At the end of the adjournment, it was announced that the question of rehousing would be reconsidered. The family were rehoused as a result of community, parental, and school action. As a result of these measures the local community was left in no doubt about the position of the school in opposing racism, particularly as we had responsibility for coordinating coverage in local and national press, and on television and radio.

Unfortunately, this is not a fairy story with a happy ending. Shortly after moving into new accommodation in Clapton, Mr Singh responded to some youths offering racial abuse outside his house. He was hit across the head with a cricket bat, and the resulting fractured skull and brain damage will be a constant reminder to him, and his family, of the racism in our society.

In 1982, the teaching staff voted that the police should not enter the building except in an emergency. The decision supported a Hackney Teachers' Association policy that members should not invite the police into their schools until the Hackney police had seriously examined their racist practice and established a dialogue with the local community. It was a particularly difficult and controversial decision because the local beat constable was well liked and respected in the local community. The children related to him largely because of the accoutrements of his office – the uniform, radio, etc. However, in discussions with the children a very different perspective emerged, particularly from the black children.many could give examples of parents, friends, and sisters and brothers who had been mistreated at the hands of the police. At five, six, and seven years of age, the children understood that a black person was more likely to be stopped on the streets, or to be pulled over when driving. Hackney Council for Racial Equality have an alarmingly thick dossier on racial harassment by the police in Hackney – a notorious example is the mishandling of the Colin Roach affair. There must be many children, who given their knowledge of family and community resentment against the police, feel threatened by their coming into school. It could also be a barrier to establishng good relationships between children and teachers.

The parents were anxious to discuss the staff decision, and a well attended meeting was organized by the P.T.A. Representatives of the police, the black community, the union, and an I.L.E.A. member were invited to speak – only the police declined. After a full, and sometimes heated, debate where the I.L.E.A. member was the main speaker against the decision, the parents voted to support the school policy.

The P.T.A. was at one time organized by a large committee elected at the annual general meeting. Some time back, a parent was elected who was known to have extreme right-wing views and was suspected of being a racist. Shortly after he was elected, I was informed that he was to stand as a candidate for the National Front in the local council elections which were due soon. The teaching staff met to discuss the situation, and the majority felt that we should ask the committee to vote him off. There were three main reasons for this decision. The first was the constitution of the P.T.A. which was quite clear that its aim was to support the educational advancement of all the children in the school. An avowed racist would find that impossible to comply with. The second was that the teacher members felt that sitting on a school committee with a member of the National Front might destroy their relationship with black parents, and would certainly raise serious doubts about their anti-racism. Lastly, we were seriously concerned that he might use his membership of the committee to advance his cause at the election hustings.

The proposal in favour of his expulsion was put to the committee and was passed by a narrow majority with most members abstaining. The decision caused a serious split in the P.T.A. from which it took a long time to recover, and the school was accused of having a political bias. Such a stance is political. We could also have been accused of being humanitarian and just. Schools presumably would not back away from a principled position on being accused of the latter two, nor should they on the first.

There is little doubt that schools do not have a high standing amongst the black community, despite the thirst that it has for education. There are a number of reasons for this, but one of the most important is the overt and institutional racism that black parents and children have suffered in schools over the past 20 years. Naturally they now regard schools as racist and with great suspicion.

I suspect that all the anti-racist policies that schools are preparing will have very little effect upon the alienation that the community feels. The possession of a policy and its operation within the school will not have a great impact upon the community at large. Unless the school is overtly anti-racist, and taking a principled position on these issues in the community, it will, despite the best intentions, be regarded as racist. Eventually, we must recognize that racism is a black issue that the black community must struggle against and find solutions for. As white middle-class teachers, the best that we can do is to examine ourselves, our practice, and support them in that struggle.

CHILDERIC SCHOOL: DEVELOPING A MULTICULTURAL POLICY

Childeric School is a primary school in Deptford with about 200 on the roll. A wide range of different cultures is represented in its pupils, including large groups of Afro-Caribbean, Turkish and other nationalities, and pupils from Chile, Sri Lanka, Bangladesh and West Germany. Over 30 have English as their second language.

David Milman is Head Teacher at Childeric School. He is author, with Tina Milman, of a series of topic project books called *Take a Look* and a book on moral education called *What do you think*, both published by Blackies. He is a member of the National Association for Multicultural Education (N.A.M.E.)

For generations Childeric School has struggled to provide an education for local children. After a recent Harvest Festival assembly one of our guests, a senior citizen, wrung my hand, 'Do you know', she said, 'I was here in 1913; it's changed so much. I've been sitting looking at all the little black and white faces.' She had pinpointed the latest and perhaps most dramatic change in the neighbourhood and therefore in the school, the change in the ethnic composition of the local population.

Childeric is a special priority area school. As such we receive extra allocations of staffing and money to help us try to meet the needs of children from a wide variety of ethnic origins and social backgrounds. There is massive unemployment in the area. About half our children come from one parent families and well over half qualify for free school meals. About a third of our children are either on the child abuse register or have social workers attached to their families.

The staff is, on the whole, a young one but the majority of the teachers have taught in the school for over 10 years. When I was appointed to the school in January 1981 the previous head had been there for many years. His deputy and another male teacher had served the school since the war. In September of 1981 I was lucky enough to be able to appoint my own deputy.

I found Childeric was a school organized on traditional, formal lines. Discipline was highly structured and authoritarian, as was the organization of the school. I felt that parents were treated in a reasonably friendly way but somehow kept at a distance. In terms of multi-ethnic education it was clear that the leadership in the school favoured an assimilation approach. There were however among the teaching staff notable individual exceptions to this attitude. There was also quite clearly a level of concern to meet the individual needs of children and an awareness of the sorts of problems which mitigated against success in the school context. However in my opinion the approach was not uniform across the whole school. The school roll was falling and this created problems and challenges of using space in an interesting and creative way.

The tragedy of the New Cross fire happened during my first term at the school. While we collected money for the uncle of one of our pupils killed in the fire, and as the marchers set out from the park opposite the school we could hardly help but reflect again on the nature of our job serving a multi-ethnic community.

DEVELOPING A MULTICULTURAL CURRICULUM

As a new head I had my own list of priorities for the school. At the top of this list was the need to develop the curriculum and this of course included the development of multi-ethnic education. I was clear that I wanted this to be a whole school development. It has always seemed to me that any development has greatest value for those who are actually involved in initiating and planning the change and that working parties had great value for those members of staff involved and far less for those who received documents from afar. It also seemed to me that the development of a multicultural curriculum could only proceed in an atmosphere of frank discussion, of honesty and commitment to change. As a teacher aware of the seeds of racism in myself and of the conditioning I had received from my own upbringing and culture I knew how difficult it could be when one's own, often unrealized, prejudices are exposed. I also felt that the only climate which would properly nurture such joint development was one of democracy. Imposition from above and authoritarian directives seem to me to be both anti-educational and antithetical to the development of multi-ethnic curriculum.

The first task then, for myself and my deputy Brenda Taggart, was to signal to the staff that the approach of the new leadership team in the school was going to be different. As a staff we started to take joint decisions about almost everything from discipline to how we should allocate our resources. We viewed curriculum development as a whole school concern and were involved in a continuous process of evaluating where we were and which major initiatives we wished to tackle next. None of this was as easy or painless as it sounds but it was generally welcomed. As we moved forward it became plain that people were relaxing and gaining confidence in the new atmosphere. Brenda and I made sure that our doors were always open and that we were around after and before school. Gradually, on an individual basis or in staff meetings, people began to come forward with their concerns. Clearly there was a range of these about multi-ethnic education, including the lack of it. Clearly there was no school policy on racism and there was a growing demand from the staff that we should do something about it.

I signalled my commitment by redesignating the home–school liaison post-holder, Nina Hurst, as a teacher with special responsibility for multicultural education. We initiated a course of staff meetings and started by examining our attitudes. We used the services of outside speakers, notably Ruth Ballin of the B.B.C. and Iris Morrison of Lewisham Teachers' Centre. Nina herself, and for much of the first two years, Juliet Bartlett, who took over Nina's post while the latter was on confinement leave, took a prominent part in discussions.

Our growing awareness led us to examine our curriculum provision. It was becoming obvious that what we were engaged upon was an enterprise that affected the whole life of the school as well as the curriculum. We realized that multi-ethnic education was not a new subject on the curriculum to be timetabled among the humanities – rather there was a need for us to examine all of our practices with the multicultural dimension in mind.

We grew to feel the need for some sort of statement of our aims and beliefs. Our discussions had also led us to become more aware of racism – both the institutional racism inherent in any Eurocentric primary school and racism in our pupils and the wider community. It was clear that we would also need some sort of policy and a sensitive uniformity of approach in combating this racism.

The examination of our curriculum practices can best be illustrated perhaps by looking in more detail at the library development. I had widened the scope of Enid Pheasey's post to embrace both the Junior and Infant libraries. The Infant library had been newly created as a large room became vacant. Another large classroom was turned into a maths and science room with a staff workshop and school artefacts collection attached. We had also developed a school dark room and a parents' room. One of Enid's first jobs was to draw up a school policy document on sexism and racism in books and to examine and revitalize the library stock. In this we were much helped by one of I.L.E.A.'s advisors, Janet Holman. Enid, helped by the staff, drew up a policy document. We weeded out the library books which we felt were sexist, racist or misleadingly Eurocentric, as well as many that were just old and tatty. At the same time we committed ourselves to an expenditure of many hundreds of pounds on replacing books. Staff were fully involved both in the process of weeding and reselecting. We spent time and effort trying to find books which presented positive black images that reflected the nature of a multi-ethnic society and which accurately portrayed the contributions of all societies to our world. Anybody who has undertaken this sort of exercise will know how difficult it can be to find the right kind of materials. We found ourselves writing off for catalogues, trying to locate minority bookshops and contacting embassies and multi-ethnic centres round the country.

Staff discussion as we weeded out the books and selected new ones was at times intense and heated. For example did we approve of *Robinson Crusoe* or *Epaminandas?* Did the bland illustration and story line of the *Seven Chinese Brothers* convey an unfortunate stereotype? What was wrong with Kipling's poems of the British Raj? Should we have a reserve shelf of books which were racist and sexist but which raised interesting points for debate? At one point in a session with Ruth Ballin, a teacher threw up her hands in despair – 'Honestly I sometimes feel frightened to open my mouth'. We were beginning to come to terms with our own social conditionings and educations.

Of one thing we were sure – that however difficult the task may be, we were not going to accept unthinkingly outside, expert prescription but choose and decide for ourselves. Advice and sympathetic help was welcomed but we were the ones who knew our own children best and who ultimately had to live with the consequences of our choices and take responsibility for them.

I proposed to Enid that she might present a report on her work to the governors and that part of this report should include the book policy document. By now we had all become so absorbed in our activities that we were a little taken aback by the reaction of some governors. However I had taken the precaution of inviting Mike Hussey of the Multi-ethnic Inspectorate and Janet Holman to the meeting and we survived some quite strong negative reaction.

The next step in our development was to prepare a further document for ourselves and then for the governors. This comprised an aims statement, 'Aims for Education in a multi-ethnic society', a job description for the multi-ethnic post holder, a policy statement on racism and a headteacher's statement and introduction. We felt this would begin to signal to all those working in the school, to the governors and through the parent governors to the parents exactly what our attitudes and beliefs were.

At this point it may be helpful to quote from a discussion document which we presented to staff and subsequently to the governors.

(1) The pupils at Childeric School come from a variety of cultures, all that goes on should reflect and build on this. Recognition of the cultural diversity should also go hand-in-hand with the recognition of cultures not represented by the school population, including Vietnamese, Greeks, Bengalis and children from travelling families. This should not only take the form of having brown faces on the wall, but there should be recognition of the positive value of mother tongues and dialects. Different languages should be shared and given positive images in the classroom and school generally. Labelling and letters home need to be comprehensible to all children and their families. Differing life styles should be understood and brought out.

(2) We must all look at our own prejudices and realize that we see things from a point of view influenced by our own culture, by the media, by what we were taught. We must question the assumptions we make about the children, their families, their environments – are we influenced in our approach by what we think, not what really exists? Class, sex, age, as well as race, come into the sort of judgements we make.

(3) We must be aware of the racist connotations in language and avoid such language personally and discourage its use at all times, e.g. talking about black looks, black marks.

(4) We should be aware of stereotyping, whether of class, sex, age or race, and challenge it.

(5) We should be aware of the ease with which prejudice can be taught and reinforced.

(6) We must encourage positive racial/cultural identity by initiating activities which reflect a multicultural society. We should aim to give information and images about each cultural group, drawing as much as possible from the children's experiences keeping in mind point 4.

(7) To extend point 6, the school should make as much contact as possible with parents, community groups and organizations and bodies seeking to encourage and foster aims of multicultural education.

(8) Any form of racism should be tackled, never ignored. It should be dealt with by giving the children any appropriate information necessary, but care should be taken never to over-respond. There are ethnic differences which cannot be ignored but from children of the age we teach much of the racism is regurgitated from the parents and the children are

often ignorant of the significance of what they are saying. This ignorance should not be left uncorrected. Racist remarks from parents should not be ignored either, since inaction can be taken as a sign of agreement. Hopefully once the stance of the school is recognized, then parents will realize it would be inappropriate to voice them. Ancillary staff should be made aware of the non-racist stand the school is making.

(9) We must be sensitive to the cultural conflict some parents and children have. We should recognize that to encourage all our children to reach their full potential, they should be helped to fully develop their social growth. All our children should have this opportunity, equally, to be equipped to live harmoniously in our multi-ethnic society. *Nina Hurst 1982*

We presented our policies to the school governors with a certain amount of trepidation and were delighted to find that they were accepted with enthusiasm. About this time we had a reconstitution of the governing body of the school. A black parent governor and a black non-teaching staff representative were appointed. I also suggested the cooption of Sandra Fuertado, who runs the young mothers' project at the Pagnell Street Centre.

Parents

We also addressed ourselves to the parents. A room with attached toilet became available on the ground floor of the school. Maureen Harniman, teacher in charge, lower school, and Anne Arnott, the reception teacher, were very keen to have a parents' room. We furnished and carpeted the room and moved in a kettle, toys and books. Maureen and Anne instituted a series of Wednesday morning meetings and a mothers' club was born. A substantial number of mothers began to turn up on a fairly regular basis. We were delighted that these represented an ethnic mix and that the mothers all seemed to get on extremely well. We ensured that there was always at least one teacher present.

There was an obvious demand for some specific event each time. Besides teachers talking about various areas of the curriculum we have invited in outside speakers. We have had nursery and school nurses, welfare rights workers and others. Maureen made films about reading and play activities throughout the school. The reading film was used to launch our own version of 'pact'. The play film gave rise to much interest. It was our experience that many parents were puzzled that what they saw as nursery play activities continued in the Infants department. We were concerned to try to explain what we thought was the central importance of educational play in the primary curriculum. Anne was completing a diploma in Early Childhood Education at Goldsmiths' College. As part of her special study she interviewed a cross-section of parents about their attitudes and expectations with regard to play in school.

On the surface much of our work with parents is not specifically concerned with multi-ethnic education. However there are obviously as many views of education as there are parents and cultures. We feel that it is our job to find out what these expectations are and to explain what we are trying to do. We see education as a partnership between home and school. All this is essential if we are to provide a climate of frankness and cooperation in which barriers can be broken down and multi-ethnic education can flourish.

Ancillary staff

The other group whom we wished to reach and with whom there can be problems of resistance to change was the ancillary workers in the school. Lunchtimes and playtimes are parts of the day when young children are at their most relaxed and most vulnerable. They are also outside the protective umbrella of the teaching staff. Ancillary staff often know the children well and live in the neighbourhood of the school. We needed to open up channels of communication with our ancillaries; we needed to cash in on their knowledge and experience and to get our messages over to them. We also felt that, traditionally, their status was low in the school. They had to feel that their opinions and feelings were valued. We placed a notice board in the ancillary staff room on which the day's events were written, just as they are in the teaching staff room. The deputy meets them daily. Maureen arranged to have some meetings with them. I now meet them regularly for half an hour a week. At the moment we are working our way, child by child, through the class lists. Within this somewhat informal context I have ample opportunities to reiterate the messages we want them to consider. We seem to have moved on from the 'you'd understand if you had to live with them' syndrome and to have begun to notice an increase in the sensitivity with which they handle children. We have managed to recruit one Turkish helper – little enough, but every little bit counts.

It ought to be obvious that intentions need to be translated into actions. It would be quite wrong to assume that the staff of the school were not already aware of many of the issues which we had raised. I was lucky in serving with a staff of dedicated and extremely hardworking professionals. Management teams cannot change schools single-handed. They can, at best, inspire, encourage and support. What we had talked about as a staff, indeed still do, was the need to be sensitive to the needs of individual children. There has always been value in starting our work from the rich variety of experience, cultural and otherwise, which children bring to school with them. Respect for persons – all persons – has always underpinned good work in the primary school. If we observe our children carefully and try to respond to their varied and changing needs, then we are halfway to providing a broad and stimulating curriculum. If we teach children to observe closely, to question, challenge and hypothesize then they will reject stereotypes and dead received knowledge. In some ways good primary practice and good multi-ethnic education can be seen as synonymous. We feel as a staff that what really matters is the curriculum offer we make the children and our own attitudes and beliefs as they are manifested in our everyday encounters with them.

Resources

As a staff our preliminary work led to the feeling that we needed many more resources, as well as a deepening of our own understanding of the complexity of issues involved. Nina, Juliet and the rest of the staff have worked on building up a bank of resources. These range from puzzles, toys and books that reflect the multicultural nature of our world, through films, slides and posters to other learning resources such as those produced by A.C.E.R. (Afro-Caribbean Resource Project).

We decided to try to build a collection of artefacts, including multicultural artefacts. We begged, borrowed, scrounged and bought. Parents and teachers brought us things from their holiday visits. We bought materials from Ujamaa in Brixton. We commissioned a doll-maker to make us dolls that were sensitively ethnic. There is a range of resources in the community as well as in the school. Our celebration of the festival of India illustrates our use of these. We decided that our contribution to the 1982 National Festival would take the form of a school week in May. For a fortnight before, classes undertook preparatory lessons and went on a series of visits. The theme for the festival carried right across the curriculum, including not only geography, religious studies and history, but also claywork, fabric printing, painting, drama, creative writing and mathematics.

One group of children studied the ritual of a Hindu wedding, and performed the ceremony at one of our special assemblies. Another group worked on a class drama and produced the story of the Elephant and the Seven Blind Men from the Pali Canon, another item shown in an assembly. Yet another group of top juniors and first-year infants made puppets and gave an enchanting rendering of the old woman and the rice thief – a nice example of cooperative teaching.

Most of the children produced some written work, many classes produced books looking at different aspects of life in India. Some of the children had an opportunity to wear Indian clothing. Everyone sampled Indian food one lunch-time, when our cook produced a chicken curry and Indian sweet.

Classes visited the Vasna exhibition at the Museum of Mankind and the Commonwealth Institute festivities. We also turned over one of our school halls to our own exhibition. The exhibition included a display of costumed dolls, on loan from the Ujamaa centre, and books borrowed from our own library, local libraries and from I.L.E.A. There was a display of Indian clothing and ornaments (borrowed from children, parents and other sources) creative writing, painting, fabrics, a history of numbers and many photographs. The exhibition provided a platform for displaying the children's work and a means of sharing information and gaining a wider experience of the many facets of India. Care was taken throughout not to show an Oxfam or deficit model of the Indian sub-continent.

FUTURE DEVELOPMENTS

Our work on enriching the curriculum is ongoing. We have a teacher, Beti Camp, working on E.S.L. work across the school. Much of her work is done in the classroom alongside the class teacher. Madeleine Clark, our Maths post-holder, is looking at ways of increasing the multicultural component in our maths teaching. Where we have not been able to find appropriate materials we have tried to create them. Maureen was helped by parents to make a set of bilingual language master cards, each card has posted on to it a photograph, many of them of our parents and their homes.

We have looked hard at the images around the school, the notices we put up and the types of letters we send home. We have regular festivals and events. Our Christmas festivities, for example, have become much more international. Some of this could be dismissed as 'tokenism'. Bilingual posters, celebrations of Diwali and the Chinese New Year do not necessarily imply fundamental change. I take 'tokenism' to imply an outward gloss without any real inner meaning. However, we felt that we should take every opportunity to 'signal' to children and parents what we were about. I feel that this 'signalling' goes well beyond tokenism if it is seen by staff for what it is – not an end in itself but a public commitment to a set of shared ideals and purposes which need to be underpinned by real and sustained curriculum work and commitment to the life of the community.

The future seems to be full of promise and challenge. The staff has been joined by a full-time teacher of Afro-Caribbean origin and we have a Common-wealth Exchange teacher from Jamaica for the year. We have also been joined by Basil Morgan of I.L.E.A.'s Primary Curriculum Development Project (for pupils of Caribbean origin). He will be helping us to look not only at our curriculum offer but at the hidden curriculum. This is exactly what we need to be doing at this particular stage of our development.

I am aware that this account has been very much from the personal perspective of a headteacher. Perhaps this is as it should be. Changing is a very personal matter. A head is after all in the position to have an overview of the life of a school. Perhaps change is most fruitfully initiated from above. However, change only happens if everybody wants it, or comes to see the need for it. In the last analysis everybody concerned with the school is equally important to the process.

There are still so many things to be achieved at Childeric. However, we have made our own small beginnings. We have moved forward cautiously, questioning and arguing as we go. This cautious approach is not born of indecision or educational doubt, but rather of our determination to get things right. Above all we have tried to take as many people with us as possible. Development has to be by the whole school and not just by parts of it. This is the importance of having a whole-school policy which is a living reality and not just an empty phrase. Our next step will be a greater movement out to support the community.

DEVELOPING A WHOLE SCHOOL ANTI-RACIST POLICY

Quintin Kynaston is a mixed comprehensive school with 1050 on the roll. It is situated near Swiss Cottage in North London. Its intake is drawn from a wide area, from all social classes and many different cultures. Its teaching is organized on a mixed ability basis.

Peter Mitchell, formerly Head Teacher at Quintin Kynaston is now Visiting Professor of Education at the University of London Institute of Education. He has lectured at several N.A.M.E. conferences.

Maura Healey is Deputy Head at Quintin Kynaston. She is author of *Your Language*, (Macmillan) and coeditor of *Pastoral Care in Education*, the journal of the National Association for Pastoral Care in Education.

Liz Lindsay is Head of Biology at Quintin Kynaston, and convenor of the multicultural and anti-racist working party. She is convenor of the A.L.T.A.R.F. (All London Teachers Against Racism and Fascism) secondary workshop, a member of Camden C.C.R. Education Committee and of the G.L.C. Ethnic Minorities Unit educational working party and Education Committees.

AN OVERVIEW: ARTICULATING A POLICY
(Peter Mitchell)

Developing a school policy on racism in a secondary school

The cultural mix in Quintin Kynaston is not exceptional for a London school but nevertheless there are over 40 first languages spoken in addition to English. Over the last four years we have become more acutely aware of the need for a school consensus, amongst staff and students, on matter relating to racism. Pressures on pupils from political groups outside school have attempted to exploit the uncertain economic future faced by many adolescents. Racism as represented in the political ideas of these groups strikes at the fundamental aims of comprehensive education. It is because of this that we believed we should develop a coherent policy on racism which made our position explicit to everybody connected with the school.

To be effective any school policy has to be thought through in relationship to the school as a whole, and teachers and students have to become personally committed to the policy. This is particularly the case where a policy is giving expression to moral values held by the school.

The aims of the school

Thinking about aims is often caricatured as a self-indulgent exercise which bears little relationship to the practical issues involved in making schools work. At Quintin Kynaston we have tried to use aims to give direction to our work and to guide actively curriculum and pastoral policy decisions. They are certainly not enshrined in the staff handbook and kept separate from actual policy-making.

The four most important aims are:
(1) to demonstrate that all students are of equal value;
(2) to give all students access to the main areas of knowledge;
(3) to value the students' own knowledge gained through their common sense learning;
(4) to see learning in school as essentially a preparation for continuous learning in the years beyond school.

Racism impinges directly on the first and third aims. It seeks to promote the idea that children from certain races and cultures should be provided with an inferior education because they are of less value to the community than other pupils. It denigrates the culture and perspectives of these groups so that a feeling of inferiority is generated amongst them.

Giving all students the confidence to learn is central to the purpose of comprehensive schools. The multicultural aspect of schooling is another dimension to being comprehensive which begins with embracing pupils who have different achievements and social backgrounds.

Whole school policies

The idea that the school should have a policy on racism is in keeping with the school's general emphasis on whole-school policies. We attempt to bring coherence to students' learning by focusing on the learning process in all our courses. Learning is thus reinforced from course to course as we attempt to meet our aim of preparing pupils to continue learning beyond school. A process curriculum also forms a basis for school policies on language and numeracy development.

All courses in the first three years are taught to mixed ability groups. This type of grouping supports the idea that students are equally valued. It also draws staff together in the joint planning of courses.

The school's commitment to mixed ability teaching and cross curriculum learning provided a sympathetic context for the discussions we held on the school's attitude towards racism. Where the curriculum is organized as a collection of disciplines it is probably more difficult to promote dialogue across the school. If this is the case then there is a possibility that a school policy will make no significant difference to the life of the school.

The procedure for school policy-making

For a number of years we have made decisions on all major school policies at full staff meetings. Establishing the school's policy on racism has thus followed the same procedure as that used for all other policies. The setting up of the multicultural and anti-racist working party resulted in part from the Authority's initiative in putting forward it own thought on the importance of multicultural education to schools.

Each year we decide on major areas of concern which need to be reviewed. The subjects chosen are then posted in the staff common room so that any member of staff may join the working party. The groups then meet on average five times per term.

Before making recommendations on school policy, they will normally report to staff meetings so that staff are kept in touch with how their findings are developing. This was a particularly important part of the development of the school's policy on racism. The multicultural and anti-racist working party drew together a group of staff with a particular interest in the subject of multicultural education of which the issue of racism is only a part. Through their reports to staff meetings they were able to make the whole staff aware of the issues involved in such a sensitive part of school life.

We ensure that all staff attend staff meetings which are chaired by a rotating chairperson selected by departments. The agenda for staff meetings is organized by the agenda sub-committee which is made up of representatives of teaching and non-teaching staff. Each time the working party wished to report back to staff they had to put their request for time to the agenda subcommittee, who would allocate them a place on the agenda and a time to make their presentation and, if necessary, to answer questions.

This pattern of work gave an immediate legitimacy to the working party's deliberations and helped reinforce the idea that the commitment of all staff is needed if a policy on racism is to have any significant influence on school life. The working party was convened by Liz Lindsay, who has taken an active part in the work of A.L.T.A.R.F. It is inevitable that some staff will be quicker to sense the urgency of an issue like racism than others. The subject matter of some disciplines is a constant reminder of how easy it is to slip into the stereotyping of groups. Particular tutor groups may manifest prejudices which alert a teacher to the extremes of thinking which may be commonplace in the everyday experience of some adolescents. The working party drew together staff who were prepared to give their own time to making the school as a whole more aware of how racism could undermine the very principles with which we worked as a comprehensive school.

Setting out to raise the consciousness of one's colleagues is no easy task. Nobody wants to be told that they are insensitive to such issues as racial prejudice whether directly or by implication. It has been important for the working party to make full use of the opportunities to keep staff informed of how their findings, and possible recommendations, were developing. Report-back sessions were an important way of preparing the school for the publication of a policy on racism. A policy statement cannot be an effective influence on school life unless the time is taken to patiently build the context which will support it.

An important contribution to the continuity of the working party's efforts was the detailed minuting of their meetings by Liz Lindsay.

The policy

The policy statement agreed by staff falls broadly into three parts.
Part 1 deals with comprehensive school aims and racism and attempts to make

explicit the way racism is antithetical to the aims which guide our work as a school.

Part 2 covers the curriculum content and processes which relate to learning about race, culture and racism. The content areas include the characteristics of race and culture, the historical study of migration and the political and economic sources of racism. (In support of this work the working party has undertaken a survey of curriculum content across the school.)

All the studies recommended for inclusion in the curriculum are to involve active research and participation in discussion by pupils. The teacher's role in these discussions is to facilitate a climate in which reasonable discussion can take place. Expanded guidelines on the ground rules for discussion have been prepared for staff by the working party.

Part 3 of the policy concerns the needs of staff to be vigilant over matters relating to racism. Any racist behaviour must be reported immediately to the head or deputy head and it will be dealt with as a matter of priority. The policy makes it clear that all staff are responsible for transmitting school policy and there must be no ambiguity in the way the school reacts to racist behaviour.

Assemblies are used for explaining school policy. They are also used to introduce studies which may be controversially included in the curriculum. In the past 18 months two such topics have been covered. A march through Paddington by an extreme political group led to a letter going to all parents which expressed the school's opposition to the march. The reason for our attitude was explained in assembly and the whole matter was discussed in social education period. We recently made a study of the Nationality Bill which followed the same pattern. We also invited the local law centre into school to advise anybody who felt they might be affected by the Bill.

The fact that social education is a 70-minute period each week, taken by the form tutor, has supported the work of the multicultural working party. The social education programme includes political, moral and religious education amongst its concerns. Both the content and discussion techniques involved in studying race, culture and racism are in harmony with social education. Form tutors remain with their forms from years 1 to 5 and have a responsibility for every part of the social education programme. Again, therefore, the majority of staff are involved in thinking out how to approach important issues raised by the working party and the social education course development team. The work I've been describing has been supported through I.N.S.E.T. funds (see Liz Lindsay).

Conclusion

I am often asked if the policy makes any difference to the school. Having a clear position certainly helps minority groups to feel supported. It also helps those young people who may feel prejudiced to know where they stand in relationship to the school. If they have been disciplined for racist behaviour they are welcomed back to return to their studies. We have to assert that every student must be free to learn, irrespective of their social or cultural background, if we are to function as a comprehensive school.

CURRICULUM INNOVATION: PUTTING IT INTO PRACTICE
(Maura Healey)

If you are starting from scratch in designing a course then it ought to be possible to get it right in principle and to 'design in' the flexibility to allow it to change in response to evaluation or to changed circumstances. At any rate there are precious few excuses for going badly wrong.

The social education (S.E.) course we run at Quintin Kynaston took a year of basic planning and is subject to regular review. For all its strengths and weaknesses it provides:

(1)   a vehicle for transmitting the 'values held by the school which are moral in character';

(2)   a vehicle whereby the 'common sense learning of students' can be enhanced;

(3)   a vehicle which allows the school to acknowledge and learn from the range of cultures and life experiences of its students.

Our brief was to develop a programme around the areas traditionally covered by titles such as religious, moral, health, political and sex education and to integrate it with careers, study skills and library-user education. The course was to be taught by over 40 tutors to all students from first to sixth year.

We teach a 20-period week. One period a week is allocated to social education. The timetable is blocked so that a whole year group is taught S.E. at the same time. Each form is taught by its tutor. The head, all three deputies, the head of year and the deputy head of year are timetabled to be available for each year group's social education lesson. This facilitates team teaching and micro-teaching.

The course development team consists of the six deputy heads of year, the head of careers and myself. Right from the start, we have been given ample financing and a great deal of support and advice from inside and outside the school. That support has continued and several items of our programme have been developed by the school's mixed-ability working party and our multi-cultural and anti-racist working party.

The process of planning and writing the course began in earnest in 1979, although an embryonic course had been developed over the several previous years. Social education was already timetabled before the course development team was appointed, so our first year of operation was pressured. Fortunately we did not allow ourselves to rush into a premature use of commercial material or other easy ways of packaging S.E. Rather we used the first year to pilot one or two ideas and, most importantly, to thrash out what kind of course we ultimately wanted. This lengthy process of discussion has stood us in good stead in that it allowed us to achieve a degree of understanding, consensus and commitment which has enriched the course and allowed us to make significant progress in the area of anti-racist teaching. Moreover it has given us some stable criteria for evaluating our work and helped us to define priorities for further development.

We were able to work effectively because the school's objectives in valuing all students and helping them develop autonomy had been fleshed out in its organization. The mixed ability of years 1–3 continue in many subjects in the fourth and fifth year. The mixed-ability tutor groups are very stable. They have the same tutor, head and deputy head of year right through to fifth year. They spend two weeks with their tutor in our residential centre – one in their first year and one in their third year.

All the teachers in the school had had experience of cooperative course planning and development, and there was commitment to the principle of social education and preparedness to work together through a process of innovation in materials and methodology.

The course development team's work involved making decisions, choosing this approach rather than that, this topic rather than another. We worked on the fundamental assumption that the 'socially educated people' can think for themselves, decide what value to give to the different kinds of evidence about the world that come their way, make decisions about their responses to that evidence which give proper weight to the consequences of those decisions on themselves and others, and finally accept responsibility for those consequences.

We never saw ourselves as being in the business of simply telling students what the 'socially educated' person ought to do in any given situation. That would be no way to develop autonomy. Rather we would focus on the process of making decisions – journeys not destinations.

This is not to imply that the school as an institution has no opinion as to what the socially educated person would do, should do, in certain specific situations. Indeed the ways in which the school operates and the position it takes on various moral/social/political issues are part of the evidence s/he encounters about how people manage the world. Our stance against physical violence for example is clear and unswerving but it only makes sense if, in our dealings with the issue, we share with students the 'journey' of thought and experience we travel on the way to a destination.

We came later to plan content. We needed to define a series of 'arenas for debate' of value and relevance to our students. The task was to attempt to find ways within these arenas for the 'learning to be independent' to take place. We wanted to value, and exploit as a learning resource, that experience and knowledge of the world which students brought with them to school. We needed too, to anticipate their needs. We ended up with a spiral curriculum in which the topics and concepts are 'revisited' over five years and re-examined in the light of students' increased experience.

The 'arenas for debate' which emerged, and the emphasis on journeys rather than destinations, have implications for the role of the tutor in social education.

It means that tutors had to be explicit about the aims of the programme in helping students reach their own decisions. They had to become the enablers of reasoned discussion rather than moral/political arbiters. We have had to work hard to develop these kinds of skills in ourselves. It is not an easy role. It makes demands of tutors in terms of management of groups, materials and ideas.

We have attempted to build on, reflect and articulate a multicultural society in a variety of ways:

(1) Our material is designed to promote talking and listening – and sharing of ideas.

(2) A major study for all students is a lengthy unit developed jointly by the S.E. team and the multicultural and anti-racist working party with the help of John Wright. Its topic is bias and it aims to involve students in active research and analysis of bias in the media – particularly books and newspapers. One successful resource is a tape of three students describing different encounters with biased material and their response to it. One wrote to a publisher, one invited a journalist to school.

(3) We have taken a stance on events which affect our students' lives. When the British Movement marched through Paddington, we redesigned the term's programme so that each tutor group discussed the implications of the march and the origins of racism. It was vital that everyone understood the school's sense of outrage and its values.

(4) Similarly assemblies and lessons were designed to focus on the Nationality Bill. Work was done on immigration in order to dispel myths and to aid understanding of the politics involved. A surgery was held at the school over a period of time by West Hampstead Law Centre so that students or their families could seek advice.

These specific topics are examples of units in which anti-racist teaching is prominent among the learning objectives we would identify. However they can only work in a context in which they are supported by the rest of the course and by the whole school policies.

As far as the rest of the S.E. course is concerned, we were paradoxically blessed by the poor quality of much of the commercial materials available. We had to write our own. We had to look beyond the basic schools TV programmes for our films and videos. Necessity was the mother of invention. We often make mistakes but our errors are quickly spotted and a thoroughgoing annual evaluation of the course identifies areas for rewriting and rethinking. We have not been lumbered with course books and expensive resources which can easily blunt criticism simply because it is so difficult to throw them out.

So throughout the course we have attempted to challenge stereotypes and prejudice and to develop in our students the skills of critical independent thinking. For example, much of our work on study skills taught as part of the social education programme focuses on the skills of gathering and using information, and emphasizes the importance of active interrogation of texts. This reinforces work done elsewhere on bias.

The social education course is supported by whole school policies on racism and by the clarity of the school's aims. Because all tutors teach S.E. the planning of the course, the writing of materials, the in-service training we undertake to support it and the involvement of tutors in its evaluation offer a useful basis for discussion and development of those policies. It also offers tutors from all disciplines the opportunity to move from awareness of school policy to action.

Outward and blatant manifestations of racism have virtually vanished within school but there is much still to be done. We need to help *all* students develop the skills and strengths to fight stereotyping and discrimination. We continue to face the problems of the differing status accorded to different cultures. We need more and better resources. We will always need in-service training and support. We need to constantly evaluate this and other courses. Students participate in this process – but not enough.

CHANGING THE CLIMATE – THE PROCESS
(*Liz Lindsay*)

Formation of the working party 1978

As early as 1977, Peter Newsam issued to all schools a document on multi-ethnic education. The year 1978 saw the growth of organized overt racist activities in the community with the government immigration laws giving a certain respectability to racist prejudices, which were also becoming more evident within the school.

Protest movements such as A.L.T.A.R.F. which in March 1978 organized a rally attended by 2000 people, were formed to counteract racism, and in 1978 a small multicultural anti-racist working part (M.C.A.R.W.P.) was set up at Quintin Kynaston and was invited to present to the staff a paper summarizing the Newsam document and attempting to make them more aware of the presence of and the reasons for racist attitudes. The small working party has continued to report the results of their research to staff meetings, has produced documents and initiated discussions on its numerous recommendations and has attempted to increase staff awareness with respect to issues such as:

(1)   political, economic origins of racist attitudes which result from ignorance and prejudice;
(2)   evidence of and methods of dealing with racist behaviour within the school;
(3)   liaison with parent and community groups;
(4)   the continued development of an anti-racist curriculum;
(5)   surveys to establish the linguistic diversity of the students at Quintin Kynaston and their needs as E.S.L. students.

Recommendations of the working party accepted by the staff have been gradually incorporated into school policy so that decisions are seen as the responsibility of *all* staff and not a few individuals.

By 1980 with greatly increasing unemployment figures and economic gloom, fascist groups, especially the British Movement, gained greater support from students and there was an increase in grafitti and racial abuse in the school.

Adoption of Quintin Kynaston policy on racist behaviour 1980

In September 1980 the working party presented to a staff meeting an outline of a suggested school policy on racist behaviour, stressing that any successful policy required strong support from the hierarchy and a consistent approach by *all* staff to specific racist incidents. Appropriate school responses were outlined clearly to a checklist of racist offences. The working party recommendations were accepted by the staff and incorporated into the school handbook.

The effectiveness of the school policy on racist behaviour has been monitored by the working party. There appears to be a greater confidence in teachers and students in tackling any racist incidents and the number of these inside the school has decreased. However attitudes of the 'hard core racist' have probably changed little and their activities may now be confined to activities outside the school. This seemed to be confirmed by the number of Quintin Kynaston students who took part in a B.M. March through the Paddington area in late 1980. On this occasion the school made its opposition to the B.M. very clear in social education and assemblies and by letters to parents and the local press.

Programme to change attitudes

The working party has always stressed that the most important need is to change racist attitudes held not only by the extreme neo-fascist groups but unconsciously by the vast majority, who fail to recognize examples of racism and who may behave unintentionally in a racist manner.

Programmes which assist students to explore the full social and economic (as well as moral) implications of racist issues are urgently required. Any general programme must do more than 'teach respect' for other groups by moralizing or by examining their cultures and must involve research and participation by students themselves so that students can understand the political and economic basis of racist ideas as well as of the more blatant neo-fascist activities.

E.S.L. provision at Quintin Kynaston

The Quintin Kynaston intake began to change by 1979 as a result of the primary school link scheme, resulting in an increase in the number of E.S.L. students with a mother tongue other than English and a decrease in the number of Afro-Caribbean students.

A survey carried out by the working party in 1981 established that 100 students must be classified as E.S.L. students with 43 different mother tongue languages. With the help of the Netley Language Centre, a document was prepared by the working party on the implications of the presence of E.S.L. students.

The working party stressed the need for at least one full-time E.S.L. teacher on site to support students in the mainstream classroom and to advise teachers. Since then, our needs have increased and we now need two full-time E.S.L. groups. The arrangement of E.S.L. students travelling to a language centre was considered unsatisfactory socially as there was little interaction with English-speaking students. It was also considered unproductive not to learn English language in a context where learners are required to use the English language for a particular purpose.

Early in 1981, Quintin Kynaston was extremely fortunate to have John Wright appointed as 0.5 teacher funded by I.N.S.E.T. to research the school's needs to develop some appropriate material for incorporation into school policy programmes. With cooperation from the working party, he produced some excellent documents containing a great amount of not readily available information and gave guidelines for teachers and tutors for class discussions. He also initiated work on E.S.L. classes by setting up a Cantonese class. John assisted the working party unit's strong recommendations for an E.S.L. teacher. In September 1981, Quintin Kynaston obtained its first full-time E.S.L. teacher on-site.

Last year, an E.S.L. teacher was appointed and, despite very poor accommodation, he has greatly assisted the introduction and integration of the new E.S.L. students into school life and has greatly increased their confidence and their ability to learn. At the same time, we feel the school should review and ask for more resources for extra E.S.L. teachers and for some mainstream teachers to be timetabled to prepare materials.

Liaison with parents and community

Parents are made fully aware that Quintin Kynaston, a comprehensive school respecting all students of equal value and importance, is intolerant of racist behaviour and aims to provide a secure environment where all students are free to learn. Leaflets are distributed at stalls at annual school fairs, and surgeries are set up at some parent–teacher nights, where specialists from West Hampstead Law Centre are present to provide on request information and advice to families regarding, for example the recently introduced Nationality Act.

The working party considers that the school should gain sufficient credibility with the community on its anti-racist stance, so that families gain enough confidence to report to the school any harassment suffered from racist groups.

Links have been established with the Camden C.C.R. Racial Harassment Monitoring Group because one of the Quintin Kynaston students was identified as being a member of a gang harassing a Bengali family. Some members of the working party also serve on the Camden C.C.R. Education subcommittee.

In-service conferences

In order to increase staff awareness and understanding of the racism experienced by students in the community, the working party organized a conference for Division 2 teachers. Workshops were led by members of the Law Centre, Camden C.C.R. and the C.R.E. This was later followed by a conference on anti-racist strategies in the classroom. The response to both conferences was positive and we have since organized further conferences as requested by the participants using I.N.S.E.T. funds.

Student involvement

During the past 12 months Quintin Kynaston students and the students' council have become increasingly involved in monitoring the effectiveness and helping to implement the anti-racist policy. Their interest was stimulated by their active participation at the end of 1982 in the production of A.L.T.A.R.F.'s

B.B.C. Open Door Programme 'Racism . . . the 4th R'. Students wrote scripts and interviewed the Quintin Kynaston head, Peter Mitchell, regarding the school policy and also Azim Haajee, from the West Hampstead Law Centre, regarding the work of the centre within the school. Some students were involved in a discussion about the way racist ideas are reinforced by some curricula which they considered should be revised. A poem and artwork by students were also part of the programme.

A video made at the school by a group of upper-school students records a discussion by students of their experiences at the school. The working party intends to use this video to increase staff awareness of students' experience.

A number of sixth formers and a fifth-year student who, as part of her English coursework, researched the effectiveness of the school anti-racist policy, concluded that the existence of the school policy was not made explicit enough, especially to incoming students. After a discussion with the school council, the students and the Council have together produced a leaflet to be issued to all incoming students in the new school year. The leaflet very briefly explains that the school has both an anti-racist and anti-sexist policy and that all students are equally valued.

The leaflet assures new students that the school will support them if any other student attempts to discriminate against them on the grounds of sex or ethnic origin.

Recently, some sixth-form students addressed a staff meeting and were critical of the exclusion from the school policy of any mention of possible racist behaviour amongst teachers. The students wanted assurance that if necessary, action would be taken against members of staff who behave in a racist manner. They also considered that the school should be explicit on its anti-racist standard not only during interviews with incoming students but also in the recruitment of teachers.

Urgent provision for 1983–84

While Quintin Kynaston's anti-racist policy (September 1980) has proved reasonably effective with respect to overt and intentional racism, there is an urgent need for further development of resources to attack 'prejudice and ignorance' among both staff and students in which unconscious, unintentional racism thrives. Many original programmes still need to be designed in all subject areas by people who have an awareness, understanding of, and insight into, not only racism, but also of the school and classes for whom they are developed. Members of the working party have not had the considerable amount of time for research discussion and production required to develop many of the ideas for appropriate resource material. All teachers are subject to tremendous pressure with their heavy teaching loads, meeting and extra-curricular activities.

The I.L.E.A. in its publication, *Anti-Racist Guidelines for Schools and Colleges* (April 1983) stresses the urgent need to encourage students to make an analysis of racism which must take into account economic and power relations, political, historical and cultural factors. Hopefully, the I.L.E.A. multi-ethnic staff will soon have prepared for issue to schools original material for all subject areas which will motivate and stimulate students' own research, discovery and discussion in the classroom. Such material can supplement but not replace the type of material best prepared by school working parties, appropriate for the classes for whom they are designed.

TOPICS FOR DISCUSSION

1. Examine the charge (p 213) that 'the Nationality Bill is a piece of racist legislation'.
2. Compare the statements of school policy from Gayhurst (p 211) and Childeric (p 220). How are they alike? Where do they appear to differ in their emphases?
3. In what ways might the development of the Quintin Kynaston anti-racist policy have drawn upon a wider group of participants in its formulation and construction?

SUGGESTIONS FOR FURTHER READING

1. Brown, M. (1984) The child's eye view, *Multicultural Teaching*, Vol. 2, No. 2, pp 10–16. A review of the *World Studies 8–13 Project* which attempts to bring multicultural issues into the primary school curriculum. The report gives details of successful classroom practices and contains descriptions of pupils' responses to the materials and methods.
2. Saunders, M. (1982) *Multicultural Teaching: A Guide For the Classroom*, McGraw-Hill, London. Chapter 7, 'Curriculum strategies to combat negative stereotyping' describes quantitative and qualitative techniques for identifying negative racial stereotypes in children's literature.
3. Twitchin, J. and Demuth, C. (1981) *Multicultural Education: Views From the Classroom*, B.B.C., London. Chapter 15 'Racism awareness in the school system' discusses *individual, cultural* and *institutional racism* and suggests practical ways in which teachers can combat their effects.

SECTION 5

PUPILS AND TEACHERS

INTRODUCTION

The focus of Section 5 of the Sourcebook is on the underachievement of certain ethnic minority groups, in particular, children of West Indian origin. Reading 12 (Cohen and Manion, 1983) presents a broad overview of the literature on underachievement that includes a critique of the alleged association between 'race' and 'intelligence', a review of research on teacher attitudes and behaviour in relation to ethnic minority group achievement, and a brief account of the socioeconomic circumstances of non-white ethnic minority groups. The suggestions for further study focus entirely upon the contradictory findings of the relationship between ethnic minority status and educational attainment. Driver's (1980) research reporting the *superior* performance of children of West Indian in comparison with their 'English' peers is accompanied by a detailed critique of Driver's methodology by Taylor (1981). The third of the suggestions for further study is Figueroa's (1984) critical commentary on the methodology of studies to do with ethnic minority underachievement.

Reading 13 is a short extract on teacher expectations from Twitchin and Demuth (1981). The classic research of Rosenthal and Jacobson (1981) provides the starting point for discussion of the pervasiveness of so-called *teacher expectancy effects* on pupil attainment. Accompanying suggestions for further reading include a cautionary paper by Blease (1983) on necessary conditions for the successful communication of teacher expectations, a brief account of Green's (1982) empirical study of differential behaviour by teachers towards children of non-white ethnic origin, and a report by Short (1983) of teachers' racial stereotyping in respect of the intelligence, attainment and behaviour of boys and girls of West Indian origin.

Reading 12
UNDERACHIEVEMENT: SOME DIFFERING PERSPECTIVES
L. Cohen and L. Manion[1]

INTRODUCTION

During the late 1960s and early 1970s, several studies of academic achievement in different ethnic groups predicted that given equal conditions immigrant pupils would do as well as their English classmates. Others, however, pointed to the underachievement of black children, particularly pupils of West Indian origin.

Little (1975) for example, concluded that underpriveleged white pupils performed at a higher level than children of West Indian origin and suggested that the needs of these latter pupils should be given the highest priority. Yule *et al.*'s (1975) large-scale survey also showed the extent to which children of West Indian origin born in Britain were performing below the average scores of an indigenous sample of pupils. Information on West Indian underachievement also comes in the interim report of the so-called Rampton Committee (1981). This survey of school leavers in six English towns where the majority of West Indians live showed how badly black children fared in 'O', 'A' and C.S.E. examinations compared to white and to children of Asian origin. In all C.S.E. and O level exams only 3 per cent of pupils of West Indian origin obtained five or more grades. The comparative figures for children of Asian origin were 18 per cent and for other school leavers 16 per cent. The Rampton Committee interim report further revealed that only 1 per cent of West Indians went on to full time degree courses compared with 5 per cent of Asians and 4 per cent of other leavers.

Our task in this chapter is to examine some psychological and sociological explanations of underachievement (in particular, West Indian underachievement) in multicultural classrooms. Specifically, we look at research to do with:

(1) Black children's intellectual ability.
(2) Teachers' attitudes towards these children.
(3) The over-representation of certain black pupils in schools for the educationally subnormal.
(4) The home circumstances of black pupils.

[1] In Cohen, L. and Manion, L. (1983) *Multicultural Classrooms*, Croom Helm, London; pp. 53–76.

RACE AND INTELLIGENCE

In 1969 Arthur Jensen (1969), an American psychologist, publ
which he proposed that the differences in intelligence test scores
populations in Great Britain and the USA are caused 80 per
factors (called the *heritability estimate*) and 20 per cent by environ   ... ιactors
(*the environmental estimate*). Jensen went on to show that blacks in the USA
score, on average, 15 points lower on I.Q. tests than whites. Since the heritability
estimate for whites is 80 per cent, Jensen argued, it follows that 80 per cent of the
15 I.Q. points difference between blacks and whites is caused by genetic factors.
It should come as no surprise that Jensen's assertions have generated considerable and continuing debate! One of the most readable rebuttals of Jensen's
arguments has been made by Hebb (1979)

A critique of Jensen's theory of the relationship of race and I.Q.

Just suppose that all baby boys are kept in barrels from birth and fed through
bung-holes until they are mature. If their I.Q.s are then tested and compared
with the I.Q.s of girls who have been brought up normally, it will most
probably be found that the girls' I.Q.s are considerably higher than the boys'.

Since all the boys have been reared in identical environments any differences in their I.Q.s can be attributed to *genetic factors*. Are we then able to say
that boys are less intelligent than girls and therefore that because the
differences among the boys' I.Q.s are largely created by genetic factors, the
differences between boys and girls are also attributable to genetics? Certainly
not! In the first place we cannot compare the part played by heredity in
determining intelligence unless both boys and girls have been brought up in
identical environments. Secondly, our comparison of boys' and girls' I.Q.
scores will not tell us about the nature of intelligence as a whole.

Now apply this analogy, says Hebb, to the debate about race and I.Q. How
can we compare the effects of genetics in determining blacks' and whites'
I.Q.s unless we can be sure that they have been reared in identical environments?

Jensen claims that because he has compared *middle-class* blacks with
middle-class whites, and *working-class* blacks with *working-class* whites, he has
successfully controlled for the environment! How sufficient is such a crude
control and is it of the right kind? (Adapted from Hebb, 1979).

In choosing to avoid the fruitless debate on how much of the difference in
intelligence is due to genes or environment, we follow Ryan (1972) who argues

the idea of genetically-determined potential ability 'involves the notion of ability that is characteristic of an individual *prior to any interaction* with the environment and thus independent of any social or specific educational influences'. Clearly, however, potential ability is necessarily expressed in actual behaviour. As Ryan observes, the notion of potential ability both as something abstracted from all interactions with the environment and at the same time as something measurable in a person's behaviour simply does not make sense'. Nevertheless, we need to examine the proposals of those who assert that the difference between 'black' and 'white' intelligence is biological in origin rather than due to social constraints on achievement or differences in motivation. We need also to identify the counter-arguments that have been raised in response to these assertions.

Jensen (1969) proposes that there are two different types of learning ability which he identifies as Level I and Level II. These two levels correspond roughly to rote learning and conceptual learning, respectively. While Level I is distributed *similarly* in different populations, Jensen asserts, Level II is distributed *differently*. Children with white faces according to Jensen have the monopoly of Level II ability. That is to say, blacks are good at rote learning alone; whites are good at both rote and conceptual learning. Both British and American studies, however, have shown that when groups of black and white children are given the opportunity to learn fairly complex concepts from scratch the different racial groups achieve similarly.

Jensen's ideas in America, and those of his counterpart Eysenck (1971) in Britain, have provoked acrimonious debate. Eysenck asserts, for example, that blacks in America are inherently stupid since it was the more stupid Africans who allowed themselves to be caught and enslaved. Moreover this black stupidity has been genetically transmitted. Imagine, comments Bagley (1975), blacks are responsible for their own slavery! What humanity, what scientific insight, what profound genius has inspired such an observation.

Jensen's most recent publication (1980) is directed at those of his numerous critics who decry the bias in the design of mental tests which favours the performance of white middle-class children:

> If we take bias to mean that the same test for blacks and whites is actually measuring different things, then it is impossible to show that such bias exists. In other words, the differences between blacks and whites in whatever the tests measure are genuine.

Jensen's critics respond to this assertion as follows:

> The fact that differences exist between black and white pupils requires serious

study by educationalists because it brings to light certain disadvantages among some groups with respect to basic cognitive skills on which the very process of education depends. Such differences, however, prove nothing about their supposedly genetic origins.

Bynner (1980) summarizes the basic objections to Jensen's thesis as follows. First, there is the biological argument. Jensen defines intelligence in two distinct ways which he then proceeds to equate. The first is biological: the capacity to adapt behaviour. The second is psychological: the capacity for abstract reasoning and problem-solving, involving the use of language and symbols.

The biological argument can be used to distinguish between species in terms of their intelligence: thus chimpanzees are more intelligent than rabbits. Clearly, these differences in intelligence have a genetic origin. But to go on from this to say that differences within a species with regard to problem-solving and abstract reasoning must have a genetic base is far more difficult to justify. Language, that distinctive feature of humans that sets them apart from any other species, is a remarkably complex skill that is mastered with relative ease by virtually every member of the species. The application of this skill in the development of those activities with which mental tests are concerned need not have any genetic origins at all.

Second, Jensen's case depends upon amassing evidence for 'isolating' from mental-test performances what amounts to a quality of pure reasoning, 'g'. This quality is thought to reside in people independently of any environmental influences to which they are subjected and to correlate only with physical, that is genetically-determined, attributes. Bynner is critical of Jensen's out-of-date research methods and his attempts to isolate 'g'. Jensen ignores more recent techniques, says Bynner (1980), enabling the researcher to test *any* model of the structure of a set of abilities.

Finally, given that differences in test scores between races exist, there are two equally plausible theories to account for them: the *hereditary* and *environmental* with a range of positions between them. In the absence of total experimental control over human mating, reproduction and development, there is no entirely satisfactory test that can adjudicate between them. Jensen believes in the importance of an inherited component in intellectual capacity. He directs his energies to determining the boundaries it sets on intellectual growth and bases his educational prescriptions on the use of tests to select individuals for appropriate educational environments. In contrast, a psychologist like Hunt, believing in the modifiability of human potential in response to the environment from conception onwards, devotes his research to isolating those features in the environment that restrict intellectual growth and devizes educational experiences that will enhance it. Ultimately, says Bynner, it comes down to a distinction between the pessimists and the optimists about human potential. Contrast Bynner's critique with that of Leon Kamin (1975). In his book, *The Science and Politics of I.Q.* Kamin argues that intelligence testing has been fostered by people committed to a particular view of society, a view that includes the belief that those on the bottom are genetically inferior victims of their own immutable defects. In consequence, intelligence testing has served as an instrument of oppression. 'There are few more soothing messages', Kamin asserts,

> than those historically delivered by I.Q. testers. The poor, the foreign-born and racial minorities were shown to be stupid. They were shown to have been born that way. The underprivileged today are demonstrated to be ineducable, a message as soothing to the public purse as to the public conscience.

In this part of the chapter we have tried to show a range of views that psychologists and sociologists hold with respect to intelligence and race. We end with some observations that are particularly appropriate for teachers to consider.

In his book, *The Myth of The Deprived Child*, Ginsburg (1972) argues that by the very nature of their construction, standardized I.Q. tests seek to *maximize differences* between subjects. But those very differences, Ginsburg says, may obscure certain factors that many children share in their intelligent behaviour and which they possess at much more equal levels than intelligence test scores imply. He suggests that we should concentrate instead on *cognitive universals*, that is the achievement of important cognitive stages in intellectual growth which the vast majority of children, black or white, have in common at similar ages.

TEACHER ATTITUDES AND PUPIL UNDERACHIEVEMENT

One sentence in particular in the Rampton Committee's interim report raised many eyebrows especially among teachers: 'A profession of half a million must reflect the attitudes of society at large and contain some with racist views . . .'. Thankfully, the Report goes on, racist teachers are in a minority; it is *unintentional racism*, says Rampton, that is a major concern in the teaching profession, and it cites the following example. Teachers see West Indian pupils as problems or, at best, deserving sympathy. They expect that these children are unlikely to do well academically although it is commonly believed that they can excel in sport, drama and art. And teacher expectations, the Rampton Committee warns, frequently turn into self-fulfilling prohecies.

Little and Willey's (1981) extensive survey of provision for multi-ethnic education in England and Wales comes to somewhat similar conclusions about teacher attitudes as those expressed by Rampton:

> Many authorities and schools emphasize [the need to convince] teachers that they should consider the implications of a multi-ethnic society for their teaching.
>
> [. . .] the first priority is to persuade teachers that relevant curriculum development is necessary.
>
> [. . .] we need to help teachers develop positive attitudes towards cultures other than their own and to develop realistic expectations towards children's academic performance.
>
> [. . .] the major difficulty is intransigent attitudes from unawareness to outright prejudice.

These undisguised criticisms of teachers come at a time of economic cutbacks in education and widespread redundancies in the profession; a time when morale is low and the feeling among teachers is that the public at large is all too ready to criticize their efforts without due regard to the difficulties they have to contend with.

One can understand and, indeed, have some sympathy with the teacher quoted in the Rampton Report as saying, 'We've had mixed ability; we've gone Community; and now it's bloody multi-cultural.' Sympathy notwithstanding, our task is to examine what Rampton calls *unintentional racism* among teachers as it relates to the underachievement of black pupils.

Let us begin with perhaps the best example of unintentional racism that we have come across as it relates to children of West Indian origin. In 1978 the report of a study undertaken by the Local Community Relations Council of the London Borough of Redbridge confirmed the underachievement of black pupils that earlier studies had identified from the late 1960s onwards. Part of the comment of the Chairman of Redbridge Education Committee on that report went as follows:

> In general terms, and I mean this in the nicest possible way, the West Indian children are more interested in the creative activities, in sports [. . .] Do you want a hard-working, high-achieving young man or woman, or do you want to develop their present happy approach and make things up in due course?

The Chairman's words exactly illustrate the negative stereotypes of the West Indians which the Report suggest are associated with their underachievement! Recall that in our discussion of *stereotyping* we drew upon a definition of Bruner *et al.*'s (1956) to the effect that stereotyping involves grouping people, objects and events around us into classes and responding to them in terms of their class membership rather than their uniqueness. Tajfel *et al.* (1964), for example, has shown how individuals tend to characterize racial and ethnic groups on the basis of beliefs about the attributes of members of those groups rather than on a more objective appraisal of the characteristics and behaviour of individual members.

Applying the idea of stereotyping and categorizing to classrooms, there is evidence that teachers may have in mind stereotypes of the *sort-of-children-who-do-well-at-school*. Two studies (Nash, 1973; Blease, 1978) employing repertory grid techniques have shown how *ability* and *achievement* in classroom settings are closely associated with an affectual dimension of teacher behaviour; put simply, whether or not teachers like the children in question.

What of teachers in multicultural classrooms? Tomlinson's (1981) research demonstrates the results of stereotyping and ethnic categorization in a group of teachers in the Handsworth district of Brimingham:

> There were distinct differences in the ways heads and teachers viewed West Indian and Asian children in their schools [. . .] On the whole, Asian families were felt to be supportive of schools, keen on education, and their children were viewed as likely to persevere in acquiring some kind of school or work qualifications.
>
> By contrast, children of West Indian origin and their parents were viewed as more problematic. Pupils were considered to be 'less keen on education', 'lacked ability to concentrate', and were more likely to need remedial teaching [. . .] The learning problems of children of West Indian origin were thought to be more acute than white or Asian children [. . .] The behaviour of pupils of West Indian origin was also viewed as a serious problem. At primary school level the children were thought to be more 'boisterous, disruptive and aggressive', than white or Asian children, and by secondary level the defiance and hostility of some pupils was felt to seriously disrupt the normal school processes. (Adapted from Tomlinson, 1981).

Both Rex and Tomlinson (1979) study of teachers' perceptions of Asian and West Indian children and Brittan's (1976) large-scale survey of teacher attitudes towards children of immigrant groups suggest that school staff may tend to operate within a framework of stereotypes which are reinforced rather than negated by the responses of the pupils themselves.

On the other hand, as Giles (1977) discovered in his study of West Indian boys and girls in London schools, teachers may deliberately ignore questions of race and ethnicity and by insisting on treating all children alike deny the existence of real differences and difficulties arising in multicultural classrooms.

'What then is to be done?' readers may well ask. We suggest the following.

Making accurate and up-to-date information readily available about children from different ethnic backgrounds offers teachers opportunities to examine assumptions about race and ethnicity as they affect their teaching in multicultural classrooms. Such information also enables teachers to understand *where* and *how* the educational process is affected by the existence of real and/or significant ethnic or social class characteristics among pupils born in Britain from ethnic-minority backgrounds. Accurate and up-to-date information about ethnic-minority groups, we suggest, should be an integral part of initial and in-service teacher education programmes irrespective of the multicultural composition of the classrooms in which teachers are placed.

We turn now to the question of *overt racism* among teachers. What do we know of its incidence and effects in multicultural classrooms? Let us start with a concrete example of overt racism. Jeffcoate recounts an incident that occurred in a school where he was responsible for a small group of West Indian children:

I was teaching [. . .] a group of West Indian children in a secondary school one morning. The room I used has a glass door which meant that anyone passing had a clear view of whoever was inside. On this occasion a senior member of staff passed, paused and looked in. He opened the door, grinned at me and said in a voice loud enough for all to hear, 'Excuse me, is this Dudley Zoo?' (Adapted from Jeffcoate, 1979)

Like Jeffcoate we can see no place in teaching for anyone guilty of this kind of professional misconduct. Hopefully, incidents such as this are rare. Recall however that in defining racism we suggested that it manifested itself in the inferior or unequal treatment accorded to certain groups of people. Applying this criterion to classrooms we might ask whether it has been demonstrated that prejudiced teachers do, in fact, treat black pupils in an unequal (i.e. inferior) way? The answer is *yes*, although systematic, observational evidence is hard to come by. Such evidence, however, has been provided by a study of 1814 children and their teachers in four middle schools. The 28 male and 42 female teachers were all white British nationals. The pupil sample consisted of 940 white, 449 Asian and 425 West Indian children between the ages of eight and thirteen.

Teacher-pupil interaction data were collected by means of the well-known Flanders' ten-category classification of verbal communication. The Flanders' schedule is a relatively simple categorization of the teacher's professional behaviour in the classroom and pupils' reactions to it. From the interactional analysis Green (1982) the researcher, calculated the amount of time each teacher engaged in interaction with the class as a whole and with individual boys and girls of European, Asian and West Indian origin. Furthermore, he calculated the amount of time in which each of his 70 teachers was engaged in using different types of interaction as revealed by the Flanders' schedule.

From the data it was possible to deduce the emphasis given to various categories of interaction with various ethnic groups by each class teacher. Over 3000 observations of teacher–pupil interactions were recorded *in each classroom*. Green then invited the 70 participating teachers to complete an attitude inventory in which a 25-item prejudice scale had been 'buried'. The prejudice scale was scored and 24 teachers were identified, 12 of whom were highly-prejudiced and 12 of whom scored lowest on prejudice. Only then did the researcher return to examine the teacher–pupil interaction data, asking, 'Do highly-prejudiced teachers behave differently towards black pupils when compared with teachers who score low on prejudice?' Some of Green's results are summarized here:

Differences in the behaviour of ethnically highly tolerant and ethnically highly intolerant teachers

(1) Highly intolerant teachers gave significantly less time to *accepting the feelings* of children of West Indian origin.

(2) Highly intolerant teachers gave only *minimal praise* to children of West Indian origin.

(3) Highly intolerant teachers gave significantly *less attention to the ideas* contributed by children of West Indian origin.

(4) Highly intolerant teachers used *direct teaching of individual* children significantly less with pupils of West Indian origin.

(5) Highly intolerant teachers gave significantly more *authoritative directions* to children of West Indian origin.

(6) Highly intolerant teachers gave significantly less time to children of West Indian origin to *initiate contribution to class discussions*.

Green's study usefully maps out broad areas of differential treatment towards certain ethnic-minority pupils. What is now required by way of complementing his quantitative approach is qualitative data on teacher–pupil interactions in multicultural classrooms, in particular the interpretations that each party places on the on-going dialogue or, as Green has shown, the lack of it in the case of certain ethnic-minority pupils and their teachers.

EDUCATIONAL SUBNORMALITY: A STUDY IN DECISION MAKING

In a recent study of the ways in which professional people make decisions placing children in the category mild educational subnormality (E.S.N.–M.), Tomlinson

(1981) explores the accounts and explanations given by heads of referring schools, educational psychologists, medical officers and special school head-teachers. She concludes that their judgements and decisions are constituted by *their own beliefs about 'what is' an E.S.N.—M. child* rather than on any agreed objective criteria. The extensive interviews undertaken by Tomlinson reveal that the criteria upon which professionals come to their decisions are 'complex, sometimes unformulated and unclarified, based upon qualities within the child and his family other than educational qualities, and closely connected to the vested interests of the professionals although overlain by an ideology of humanitarianism'.

Tomlinson identifies 10 possible accounts of 'understandings' to which professionals have recourse in describing and explaining what they consider an E.S.N.–M. child to be.

Thus, a *functional* account might contain the observation that 'the child cannot communicate adequately'. Similarly, a *statistical* account can be illustrated by the statement, 'the child has a low I.Q'. The remainder of Tomlinson's 10 categories are as follows: *behavioural* ('child is disruptive'); *organic* ('child has innate incapacity'); *psychological* ('child is emotionally disturbed'); *social* ('family is disorganized'); *school* ('child rejects school'); *statutory* ('child may be certified as in need of special education'); *intuitive* ('child has something wrong with him'); and *tautological* ('child is in need of special education treatment').

Using these 10 broad generalizations, Tomlinson then goes on to classify the frequencies of the various 'explanations' of educational subnormality gathered in her interviews with headteachers, psychologists and medical officers. The variety of beliefs about what an E.S.N.–M. child 'is' is well demonstrated in the strikingly different profiles shown in Figures 12.1, 12.2, 12.3 and 12.4.

Having shown that professionals referring and assessing children as E.S.N.–M. act upon criteria that are unformulated, unclarified and largely non-educational, Tomlinson then asks the more fundamental question as to the purpose that a subnormality categorization serves in complex industrialized societies such as Britain.

She proposes the following sociological explanation of the increasing numbers of E.S.N. – M. children who over the past 30 years or so have been excluded from 'normal' education:

Professionals such as psychologists, medical officers and headteachers have socially-constructed a category of people who are denied a 'normal' education and instead, receive a stigmatised 'special' or non-education but who are subsequently employed as part of the lowest strata of a productive work-force. In effect, professionals legitimate the reproduction of a part of the lower social

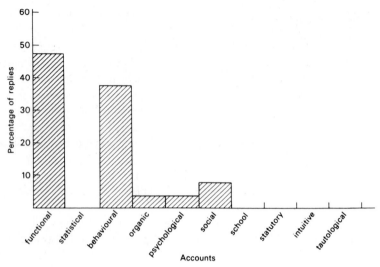

Figure 12.1   Referring heads' accounts of ESN–M children

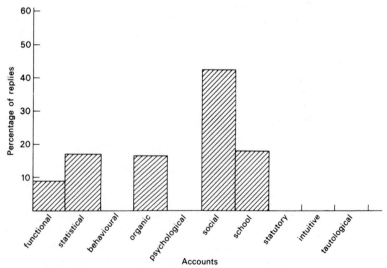

Figure 12.2   Doctors' accounts of ESN–M children

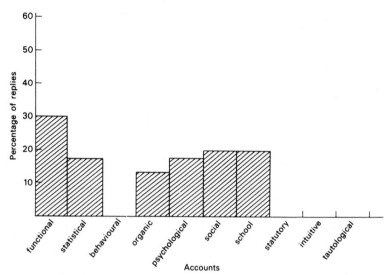

Figure 12.3   Educational psychologists' accounts of E.S.N.–M. children

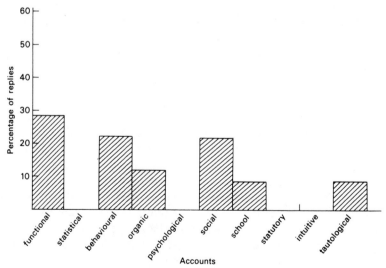

Figure 12.4   Special schools heads' accounts of E.S.N.–M. children

class, the category E.S.N. being a form of social control for a potentially troublesome section of the population [. . .] a major social function of the category of mild educational subnormality and the 'special' education for those in this category – may be to permit the relatively smooth development of the 'normal' education system. From a structural point of view [. . .] the special education system can be regarded as institutionalising the exclusion of a section of the population from chances of social mobility, from the acquisition of cultural and economic capital and as a mechanism for ensuring their placement in the lowest social class (Tomlinson, 1981)

EDUCATIONAL SUBNORMALITY AND PUPILS OF WEST INDIAN ORIGIN

The issue of educational subnormality in respect of black pupils is almost solely concerned with children of West Indian origin. The disproportionate number of pupils of West Indian origin who were being assessed as educationally subnormal and despatched to special schools began to concern the West Indian community in the mid 1960s. The 'overplacement' of this ethnic minority group in E.S.N. schools is documented in the statistics shown in Table 12.1

What do the figures in Table 12.1 show? Taking 1972 as our example, they reveal that 4.9 per cent of all children in E.S.N. schools were of West Indian origin whereas they constituted 1.1 per cent of the total school population. In effect, there were four times as many of these children in special schools as there 'ought' to have been. Chief Education Officers' explanations of this state of affairs in response to a D.E.S. inquiry in 1973 mentioned difficulties with discipline, dialect and teachers' assessments as factors in the over-representation of children of West Indian origin.

An alternative explanation of West Indian children's disproportionate presence in E.S.N. schools is given by Coard in a document entitled *How the West Indian is Made Educationally Subnormal in the British Schools System.* Coard (1971) a West Indian, and for some time a teacher in E.S.N. schools, argues that the organization and the curriculum activities of E.S.N. schools are geared to pupils of below normal academic ability and that West Indian pupils who are misclassified and assigned to such schools are not encouraged to perform to the best of their ability. Misclassification, he says, arises out of differences in culture and social class and low expectations of West Indian pupils on the part of their teachers. The very process of being assessed for possible placement in a special school, Coard asserts, makes the black pupil 'feel deeply that racial discrimination and rejection have been practised towards him by the authorities'. Once there, his refusal to cooperate and take part in the school's programme of

Table 12.1 (a) Total number of children in maintained primary and secondary schools and total number of children in E.S.N. schools/classes; (b) Total numbers of children of West Indian origin in maintained primary and secondary schools and total number placed in E.S.N. schools/classes

(a)

Year	Column 1 'Normal' school	Column 2 E.S.N. school/classes	Column 2 as a percentage of Column 1
1968	8 190 745	49 818	.59
1969	8 391 756	49 931	.59
1970	8 597 451	51 768	.60
1971	8 800 843	52 843	.60
1972	9 032 999	60 045	.66
1974	9 560 060	53 353	.55
1975	9 617 474	52 744	.54
1976	9 669 000	53 772	.55

(b)

1968	89 988	—	—
1969	106 126	—	—
1970	109 963	2551	2.3
1971	107 136	2896	2.7
1972	101 898	2972	2.9

Source: Adapted from Tomlinson (1981).

activities not only makes him appear retarded, but in the course of time, results in him becoming retarded through lack of mental activity.

THE HOME CIRCUMSTANCES OF BLACK PUPILS

Large-scale longitudinal studies show a close association between the material circumstances of the home and the intellectual ability and academic achievement of the child, none perhaps more clearly than the report of the National Child Development Study (Davie *et al.*) entitled *From Birth To Seven* (1972). In that account, bar graphs are used to illustrate differences in I.Q., arithmetic and reading achievement that are associated with variations in social class background, home circumstances and geographical location.

Consistently throughout the analyses in the National Child Development Study, *social class* (identified by *occupational status*) is shown to be the variable most strongly associated with children's intellectual ability and academic attainment. It comes as no surprise to learn that offspring of professionals, employers and managers do best at school, and that chidren from semi-skilled and unskilled manual backgrounds do worst. Occupational status is widely used as an index of social class in educational research despite scope for argument about the crudity of such a measure. We use it here to find out whether members of black ethnic-minority groups are distributed across socioeconomic categories in similar fashion to the general population of Britain. Any marked dissimilarity in distribution, we suggest, may help illuminate the central theme of the present [Reading] – the underachievement of certain black pupil groups.

Table 12.2 shows the percentage socioeconomic distribution of economically-active males and females in Great Britain. It reveals significant differences between ethnic-minority groups and indigenous whites. In particular, West Indians and Pakistanis are under-represented in higher socioeconomic groups and West Indians and Asians generally are over-represented in lower socio-economic categories, a trend that persists throughout the years under consideration. *Social class*, that is to say *occupational status*, is not of course a single factor; it is best viewed as an amalgam of factors that operate in different ways. Broadly speaking we can say that in comparison with members of lower socioeconomic groups, people in higher socioeconomic categories

> [. . .] enjoy better health; live longer; live in superior homes with more amenities; have more money to spend; work shorter hours; receive different and longer education and are educationally more successful [. . .] to mention only a few examples (Reid, 1981)

The statistics in Table 12.2 show that black ethnic-minority groups are relatively disadvantaged as a result of their social class distribution. Using data from the Home Office Research Study No. 68 (1981) and the Runnymede Trust/Radical Statistics Research Group (1980) let us now look briefly at one aspect of socioeconomic circumstances as it bears upon the underachievement of certain black pupils. We deal with *housing*.

Housing

On any measure of housing quality (age of fabric, location, amenities such as bath, plumbed hot water, inside W.C., etc.) the dwellings occupied by black immigrants coming to Britain after the Second World War were substantially worse than those of the general 'white' population. Quality of housing is, of course, related to the position a person occupies in society. Because black ethnic-minority groups were (and still are) disproportionately located in 'lower' socioeconomic categories, their overall representation in poor quality housing can, in part, be accounted for. But this is not the whole story, as we shall see.

Table 12.2   Percentage socioeconomic distribution of economically-active males and females in 1966, 1971 and 1977

| Socioeconomic grouping | | *Country of birth* | | | |
		West Indies	India	Pakistan	Great Britain
Professionals,	1966	1.8	15.1	6.0	11.6
employers and	1971	1.9	13.4	7.2	13.7
managers	1977	2.5	14.5	8.7	16.1
Semi-skilled	1966	53.1	32.2	64.3	30.5
and unskilled	1971	47.1	37.7	60.7	28.3
manual workers	1977	43.3	36.6	53.2	25.3

Source: Adapted from Home Office Research Study No. 68.

Since the Second World War there has been a general rise in housing standards in Britain, though it is not easy to ascertain the extent to which black immigrants have fully shared in these improvements or have 'caught up' with the rest of the population. Black groups tend to be concentrated in certain large cities in major industrial areas. Within these cities, they tend to be concentrated in particular boroughs or even particular wards. Using Office of Population Censuses and Surveys measures of overcrowding (1.5 persons per room) we can see from the statistics in Figures 12.5, 12.6 and 12.7 that there appears to be an increasing degree of convergence between the conditions enjoyed by black groups and the general population at large. Many, however, would judge one person per room per household as indicative of overcrowding. If the official measure of overcrowding (1.5 persons per room) were to be redefined downwards, says the 1981 Home Office Research Study report, then the relevant figures would appear as follows:

Living at more than one person per room

General population	= 3 per cent of households
West Indians	= 12 per cent of households
and Asians	= 24 per cent of households.

Briefly let us look at the picture (Field *et al.*, 1981) in one Inner London Borough and the disadvantageous home circumstances experienced by its West Indian residents. Research showed that only 4 per cent of the main breadwinners in West Indian families had non-manual jobs compared with 20 per cent of the indigeneous population. Fifty per cent of the West Indian families lived in overcrowded conditions, 43 per cent did not have sole use of the kitchen, bathroom, toilet or plumbed hot water. (The comparative figures for the

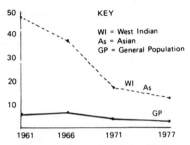

Figure 12.5   Percentage of households in shared dwellings

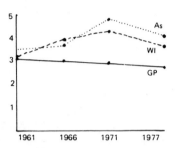

Figure 12.6   Average household size

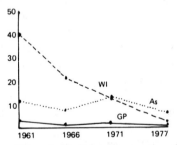

Figure 12.7   Percentage of households living at more than 1.5 persons per room

Source: Adapted from the Home Office Research Study, No. 68.

indigeneous population were 20 per cent and 16 per cent respectively.)

There is, too, the difficult problem of identifying racial discrimination in respect of housing whether practised by those selling properties, or financing their purchase, or allocating council dwellings or approving improvement-grant applications to owner-occupiers. Despite the fact that *direct* discrimination in housing became an offence under the Race Relations Act (1968) and *indirect* discrimination was deemed unlawful by the Race Relations Act (1976), there is evidence of the operation of a so-called *colour-tax* causing black groups difficulty in obtaining finance for house purchase, a result of which is that they pay more when they do obtain it. In addition, there is evidence that black groups pay more for rented unfurnished accommodation and that they are less successful than whites in obtaining improvement grants in respect of the properties they occupy.

Black ethnic minority groups, as Deakin (1977/8) observes, still face difficult housing problems, a result 'not so much [. . .] of overt discrimination as of a subtle and complex sifting process, which race relations legislation has not so far proved effective in combating'.

From our discussion so far we may conclude that black ethnic-minority groups in general are over-represented in lower socio-economic categories, in bad housing conditions and, though space precludes discussion of the evidence, they are also over-represented both in lower-paid uncongenial employment and in unemployment statistics. These are crucial facts to be borne in mind in connection with the discussion of the home circumstances and achievement of black pupils.

Recall that at the beginning of this section we referred to the ongoing research of the National Children's Bureau, a cohort study of some 16 000 children (now young adults) that began in 1958. As part of that large-scale study, achievement data to do with first- and second-generation immigrants were extracted, analyzed and reported in several publications. Two important conclusions have been drawn from these data:

> Firstly, immigrants tend to have relatively poor attainment overall, but *when children of similar financial and other material circumstances are compared most immigrant groups do as well as non-immigrants,* [our emphasis] the main exception to this being West Indians.
>
> Secondly, the poor school performance is generally only found among first-generation immigrants, not second-generation immigrants, and to some extent is relatively short-term and language specific. (Pilling, 1980).

REFERENCES

Bagley, C. (1975) On the Intellectual Equality of Races, in G.K. Verma and C. Bagley (eds), *Race and Education Across Cultures*, Heinemann Educational Books Ltd, London
Blease, D. (1978) Teachers perceptions of slow-learning children: an ethnographic study, *Research Intelligence*, Vol. 4, No. 1, pp 39–42
Brittan, E.M. (1976) Multi-racial education 2: teacher opinion on aspects of school life. Part 2: pupils and teachers, *Educational Research*, Vol. 18, pp 182–91
Bruner, J., Goodnow, J. and Austin, G. (1956) *A Study of Thinking*, John Wiley, New York
Bynner, J. (1980) Black and white arguments, *Guardian*, 18 March

Coard, B. (1971) *How the West Indian Child is Made Educationally Subnormal in the British School: The Scandal of the Black Child in Schools in Britain*, New Beacon Books, London

Davie, R., Butler, W. and Goldstein, H. (1972) *From Birth to Seven*, N.F.E.R., Slough

Deakin, N. (1977/8) Housing and ethnic minorities – an overview, *New Community*, Vol. 6, No. 182, pp 4–7

Eysenck, H. (1971) *Race, Intelligence and Education*, Temple Smith, London

Field, S., Mair, G, Rees, T. and Stevens, P. (1981) *Ethnic Minorities in Britain: A Study of Trends in Their Position since 1961*, HMSO, London

Giles, R. (1977) *The West Indian Experience in British Schools*, Heinemann, London

Ginsburg, H. (1972) *The Myth of the Deprived Child*, Prentice Hall, New Jersey

Green, P.A. (1982) Teachers' Influence on the Self Concept of Ethnic Minority Pupils, Unpublished Ph.D. Thesis, Univeristy of Durham.

Hebb, D.O. quoted in Hardy, M. and Heyes, S. (1979) *Beginning Psychology*, Weidenfeld and Nicolson, London

Home Office Research Study No. 68 (1981) HMSO, London

Jeffcoate, A. (1979) *Positive Image: Towards a Multicultural Curriculum*, Chamleon, London

Jensen, A.R. (1969) How much can we boost, I.Q. and scholastic achievement?, *Harvard Educational Review*, Vol. 39, pp 1–123

Jensen, A.R. (1980) *Bias in Mental Testing*, Methuen, London

Kamin, L. (1975) *The Science and Politics of I.Q.*, John Wiley, New York

Little, A. (1975) Performance of children from ethnic minority backgrounds in primary schools, *Oxford Review of Education*, Vol. 1, No. 2, pp 117–35

Little, A. and Willey, R. (1981) *Multi-ethnic Education: The Way Forward*, Schools Council Pamphlet 18, Schools Council, London

Nash, R. (1973) *Classrooms Observed*, Routledge and Kegan Paul, London

Pilling, D. (1980) *The Attainment of Immigrant Children: A Review of Research*, Highlight No. 40, National Children's Bureau, London

The Rampton Committee Report (1981) *West Indian Children in Our Schools: Interim Report*, HMSO, London

Redbridge Community Relations Council and Black Peoples Progressive Association (1978) *Cause For Concern: West Indian Pupils in Redbridge*, Redbridge C.R.C., London

Reid, I. (1981) *Social Class Differences in Britain*, 2nd ed, Grant McIntyre Ltd, London

Rex, J. and Tomlinson, S. (1979) *Colonial Immigrants in a British City: A Class Analysis*, Routledge and Kegan Paul, London

The Runnymede Trust/Radical Statistics Research Group (1980) *Britain's Black Population*

Ryan, J. (1972) I.Q. – The Illusion of Objectivity, in K. Richardson and D. Spears (eds) *Race, Culture and Intelligence*, Penguin Books, Harmondsworth

Tajfel, H., Skeikh, A. and Gardner, R. (1964) Content of stereotypes and the inference of similarity between members of stereotyped groups, *Acta Psychologica*, Vol. 22, pp 191–201

Tomlinson, S. (1981) Multi-racial schooling: parents' and teachers' views, *Education 3—13*, Vol. 9, No. 1, pp 16–21

Yule, W., Berger, M., Rutter, M. and Yule, B. (1975) Children of West Indian immigrants II: intellectual performance and reading attainment, *Journal of Child Psychology and Psychiatry and Allied Disciplines*, Vol. 16, pp 1–17

TOPICS FOR DISCUSSION

1. Discuss the critique of Jensen's theory of the relationship of race and I.Q. (p 243).
2. Discuss the assertion that *unintentional racism* should be of major concern to the teaching profession.
3. What part do *home circumstances* play in the underachievement of certain ethnic minority pupils?

SUGGESTIONS FOR FURTHER READING

1. Craft, M. (1984) *Education and Cultural Pluralism*, Falmer Press, London. P. Figueroa, 'Minority Pupil Progress' (pp 117–41) is a critical review of the methodology, findings and policy implications of studies reporting the 'underachievement' of minority pupils.
2. Driver, G. (1980) *Beyond Underachievement*, Commission For Racial Equality, London. Reports a study of the 16+ examination results of five multi-ethnic secondary schools for the period 1975–78, and concludes that, in general, pupils of West Indian origin did *better* than their English peers; in some instances West Indian pupils overtook English pupils during their time in secondary school; on average, West Indian girls did better than West Indian boys.
3. Taylor, M. (1981) *Caught Between: A Review of Research into the Education of Pupils of West Indian Origin*, N.F.E.R., Windsor. See pp 113–22 for a detailed critique of the methodology and the conclusions of G. Driver (1980) *Beyond Underachievement*, Commission For Racial Equality, London

Reading 13
THE POWER OF TEACHER EXPECTATIONS
J. Twitchin and C. Demuth[1]

In November 1980, the H.M.I.s brought out a report on the I.L.E.A., the largest authority in the country. It was based on five years of inspections and discussion about the facts that nearly a quarter of all pupils leave London schools with no graded exam result at all (compared with 13.8 per cent nationally) and that only 4.9 per cent of pupils leave with five or more higher grade 'O' levels or C.S.E. (compared with 9.1 per cent nationally). 'These schools frequently blame their pupils' background for the poor results', said the report. 'This is largely unjustifiable. The fault lies in low teacher expectation'. Such under-expectation

---

[1] In Twitchin, J. and Demuth, C. (1981) *Multicultural Education: Views from the Classroom*, B.B.C. London, pp 153–60

has been found by the H.M.I.s in other national surveys of both primary and secondary education.

We thought it might be useful to have a brief reminder of what is known in general about how far a teacher's view of his or her pupils, and particularly, expectations of their success, has a powerful influence on their progress and performance in school. According to many experts, these researches have important relevance for teachers of ethnically mixed classes. However, we leave the reader to decide exactly what this relevance is. We have met some teachers who apparently have particularly high expectations of ethnic minority pupils. We have met others who say they find it difficult to avoid discriminating between minority groups, based on an assumption that some bring a stronger 'culture of learning' to the school than others. There are certainly very many teachers who are concerned that minority pupils are often perceived (usually by their colleagues!) as too intellectually or culturally disadvantaged, or as deprived and burdened with too many personal and social problems, to succeed well in school. These questions are seen to be a serious concern to teachers in the film *School Report* and brought out again in *Teacher, Examine Thyself!*

There is no doubt that many parents of British Caribbean children feel that pupils are encouraged to achieve in the West Indies, whereas they are still expected to underachieve by many teachers in Britain. We asked Maggie Ing of London University's Institute of Education, to give us a brief summary of the classic research on the effects of expectations. The question her summary raises, in the context of multicultural education, is this: Are minority children failing to make the most of their abilities in our schools, not just because of the language difficulties and cultural differences our schools have yet properly to come to terms with, but because many teachers underrate their potential on the basis of stereotypical thinking – whether consciously or not?

'SMART AND DUMB'

Most teachers have heard of R. Rosenthal and L. Jacobson's (1968) classic research, but it is not so generally known that the authors first tested out their hunch four years earlier in a small-scale study of psychology students training rats to learn their way through a maze. Eight students were told that their animals had been specially bred to learn quickly; six were told that their rats were from a slow-learning strain. In fact, the animals were randomly drawn from the same strain and no great variation in their speed of learning would be expected. The 'smart' rats, however, learned better and the students reported that they enjoyed working with them. The 'dumb' rats were slower and disliked by their trainers. It is possible that the students did not record their animals' progress with perfect accuracy (which in itself would be significant if we transpose the findings to teachers with children) but it is highly likely that the differences in handling the animals, frequently and gently for the 'bright' ones, rarely and brusquely for the 'dim' ones, had an influence on the rats' performance.

If expectation can affect the performance of creatures who can be hardly influenced by the subtler social and cultural messages inherent in the way they are handled, we might expect it to be even more true of people. Too much has perhaps been made of the original experiment, where teachers were falsely informed at the beginning of the school year that some children would bloom academically. There were increased I.Q. scores for the bloomers, but this was only in the first two grades and there are several interpretations of the results. However, Rosenthal (1973) subsequently collected data from 242 studies in all sorts of situations where the Pygmalion effect might operate. Eighty-four studies showed the predicted results, where by the rules of statistical significance only 12 (about five per cent) would have turned out by chance alone.

TEACHERS' IMPRESSIONS

These data indicate that, at least some of the time, the expectations of those in control of situations affect the outcomes. They do not tell us how expectations are expressed in action and just what goes on between the persons involved. A few studies to date have explored the details of contacts in the classroom and Ray C. Rist's (1970) paper is one of the most sensitive and saddening.

A single group of children, half of them black, just starting their kindergarten year in a North American urban school, were observed closely twice a week for the first year and a half, and their progress followed up for a further year. By reputation their teachers were both experienced and competent; in interviews they were seen to be committed and without prejudice.

As early as the eighth day in the kindergarten of schooling, the children had been assigned to one of the three tables, according to the teachers' assessment of them as 'bright', 'average' or 'below average'. Two and a half years later, these labels were still firmly stuck.

The kindergarten teacher's first impressions had decided the children's fate. Intelligence tests of young children are notoriously poor predictors, but the teacher had not referred to even this attempt at objective classification. The teacher, Rist found, like so many others had in fact formed impressionistic opinions from social information – on who was on welfare; on who was from a single-parent family; on an initial interview with the mother; on any experience she had of children from the same families; and on whatever she gathered of the child's abilities after eight days in school. Tables 1, 2 and 3 in fact turned out to represent a clear stratification of social class, with Table 1 children neatly dressed, clean and better off, and Table 3 children scruffy and shabby (and, as it happens, darker-skinned).

LIFE ON TABLE 3

Once allotted to Table 3, the children had very different experiences from their class-mates. The teacher talked less to them and they talked less to her. On the Friday after Halloween, for example, she announced that she would allow time for *all* the children to come to the front of the class and tell their experiences. In fact, she then called on only six children, five from Table 1 and one from Table 2. On another day in May, Rist noted that for a whole hour, she made no communication at all with Tables 2 and 3 save two commands to 'sit down'.

Although the blackboard extended along a wall parallel to all three tables, the teacher tended to use the part of the board nearest to Table 1, even occasionally reprimanding Table 3 children who stood up to see it better. Her assessment towards the end of the first year was,

> Those at Table 1 gave consistently the most responses throughout the year and seemed most interested and aware of what was going on in the classroom.
>
> It seems to me that some of the children at Table 2 and most all the children at Table 3 at times seem to have no idea of what is going on in the classroom and were off in another world all by themselves. It just appears that some can do it and some cannot. I don't think that it is the teaching that affects those that cannot do it, but some are just basically low achievers.

Rist's findings however, were that the children on Table 3 were trying to learn; cut off from much direct contact with the teacher, they sometimes tried to learn from each other, or from listening to what the teacher was saying in her dialogues with the more favoured pupils. But when the frustrations were too great, many of them switched off.

When the children moved up to the First Grade, they were allotted to the new table groupings according to their performance on 'readiness materials' at the end of the kindergarten year. No child from Tables 2 or 3 was promoted to the 'fast learners'. The same process, with additional information from reading tests, was repeated when they progressed to the Second Grade. All three groups were now using different reading schemes and each child had to complete one book before tackling the next in the series. As they were not allowed individual reading time to finish a book on their own and move ahead, a child designated as 'slow' would of course always remain 'slow'.

The Second Grade teacher was found to be using more controlling and fewer supportive contacts with the slow learners. This Rist saw as a reflection of the more disruptive behaviour of children with two years' experience of neglect and low expectations by their teachers.

The I.Q. scores for these children, taken at the end of the kindergarten year, had showed no statistically significant difference among the children at each table. The Table 1 scores were slightly higher, but the highest individual score was from a Table 2 child and several Table 2 and 3 children scored higher than some from Table 1.

Whatever the basis for the initial stratification of the children, it was not their academic potential. Nor could it be ascribed to any racial antagonism by the teachers towards the Table 3 pupils – for the teachers in this study were themselves all black. However, in interviews with the teachers, Rist found that they had a picture of the 'Ideal pupil' which reflected their own cultural values and experiences.

IDEAL PUPILS

What this perception of the ideal pupil can mean is that a child from a comfortable middle-class background, speaking standard English and relating easily to adults, is all too easily perceived as a potentially 'successful' pupil. Those who fit the ideal least closely may be perceived as unable to learn or, in extreme cases, as unteachable. When we add factors of race to the social indicators operating against some children, the effect of teacher expectations is likely to be magnified.

It is not a matter of being overtly racist; it seems to be more a matter of checking whether we have an 'ideal pupil' cast in our own image, and as a result perhaps unconsciously categorize children who are 'different' as less educable and treat them in subtly different ways.

Not much research has actually been done on the sensitive question of how far teachers' stereotypes of the abilities of different ethnic groups affects children's progress, but the few studies available do confirm that the stereotypes exist.

Rubovits and Maehr (1973) set up experimental lessons with 66 student teachers, each of whom had four pupils, two black and two white. One white and one black child in each group were randomly labelled 'gifted', setting expectations to which the student teachers' responses were studied. The particular responses observed were: teacher's attention to pupil statements, encouragement of pupil statements, elaboration, ignoring, praise and criticism. The pupils in fact initiated contact with the teacher about equally, but the teachers clearly favoured the 'gifted' white pupils, followed by the 'non-gifted' whites, then the 'non-gifted' blacks and, last, the 'gifted' blacks. If this finding is at all representative of what goes on in schools, it is profoundly alarming. It demonstrated a racial stereotyping so strong that ability is a positive quality in some teachers' eyes *only* if it is shown by a white pupil; an able black pupil is likely to have even more negative teacher contact than a slow one.

The 'teachers' in the experiment were students, but in previous interview they had all expressed entirely 'liberal' beliefs.

EXPECTATIONS INTO ACTION

There are at least four ways in which a teacher can communicate a good or bad opinion of a child's potential. First, by a range of non-verbal as well as verbal cues, she can create a warm or cold *climate*. Smiling, nodding, looking into the eyes, leaning towards or away from the child, tone of voice, can all convey as much as words of approval or disapproval. Second, the 'ideal' students tend to get more *feedback* about what they are doing. In one study quoted by Rosenthal, researchers observed how teachers behaved towards the pupils they (the teachers) had named as high or low achievers; only 3 per cent of the high achievers' responses were ignored, but 15 per cent of the low achievers'. Whether they are right or wrong, the 'good' pupils get more information, which obviously makes it easier for them to learn. Third, it appears that teachers tend to give *more, and more demanding, material* to their 'good' students. Victor Beez (1968), working with teachers of preschool children in the Headstart programme, told half of them that they could expect exceptionally good progress from their children and the other half that they could expect very little. Observers, who were not told the teachers' expectation, noted the subsequent interactions. The teachers who thought they had 'bright' children attempted to teach them far more, and the children actually learned far more, than the group of whom poor performance was expected. Closely linked to this is the fourth factor of *output*. Teachers tend to give favoured pupils more chance to respond; they are asked more questions, given more time to reply, and more guidance.

CLASSROOM INTERACTION

What happens in classrooms is not just a matter of communication between teacher and pupils, but also between pupils. Very early, children pick up how the teacher views them and their classmates and the effects of expectation spread. Rist details the ways in which the kindergarten children responded to one another. The Table 1 children soon felt safe in ridiculing those at Tables 2 and 3. When Tony (Table 3) was asked a question and didn't know the answer, Gregory and Ann (Table 1) called out 'He don't know. He's scared,' and 'It's sixteen, stupid'. Jim (Table 1) was heard saying over and over to Tom (Table 3): 'I smarter than you. I smarter than you.' When the observer asked Lilly (Table 3) what she was drawing, she replied 'A parachute', but Gregory (Table 1) interrupted, 'She can't draw nothin'.

Table 1 children tended to be given responsible jobs and quickly imitated the teacher's more disciplinary approach to the Table 3 group. 'Girl, leave that piano alone', Pamela ordered, when the teacher was out of the room. Then, in time, it was noticed that the children at Tables 2 and 3 turned on one another the same kind of cruelty that they had themselves experienced.

The research evidence is that the hidden assumptions within the classroom, and the subtle or gross differences in the way that the teacher treats different pupils will readily be perceived by the whole class and are likely to be incorporated into the pupils' attitudes towards themselves and others.

STRATEGIES FOR CHANGE

How can we avoid creating or reinforcing poor expectations of some of our pupils? Every teacher must start with his own perceptions and attitudes. As the science teacher confirms in the film *School Report*, well-meaning teachers tend to deny that they or their colleagues or, sometimes, their pupils, do have stereotyped expectations of different groups, yet half-an-hour of staffroom conversation will often reveal quite blatant categorization. Among remarks heard from kindly, concerned primary school teachers: 'The black kids are boisterous and can't settle'; 'The Asians work hard but show no initiative'; 'You can't expect much creative work – they're mainly Irish'.

Honest reflection on our own half-buried assumption may be revealing. Better still, feedback about our own *behaviour* in the classroom makes it more difficult to imagine that we do one thing, yet behave in a quite different way. A videotape recording of a classroom session, or a sound recording, or a colleague acting as observer and making notes may be needed to help us become conscious of which children are attended to and which are ignored.

Some points to consider in such observation:

Who is asked questions?
Who is not?
How long do you wait for an answer?
When a child initiates communication, do you: Ignore it? Acknowledge it? Expand it? Ask for more information?
Do you ever try to give more difficult tasks to your 'slow' learners?

What do you do if one child speaks contemptuously of another?
Ignore it (and so tacitly agree)? Or reprimand him?
How do you check that your pupils have understood instructions?
Which children do you consider fast, average and slow learners?
On what grounds do you make those distinctions?
How would you list the characteristics of your 'ideal pupil'?
How closely does that list relate to your rating of pupils' ability?
Which children tend to be nearest you most of the time? Why?
Which children do you like best? (Honestly!) Are you fair to the others?

POSITIVE EXPECTATIONS

No one can avoid forming expectations of others, and a lot of social interaction is eased by our knowing roughly what to expect. Teachers have a duty to provide their pupils with *appropriate* work, which involves some judgement of what they can do. But the research shows that damage to some pupils seems to come from *poorly-based* judgements (the state of a child's clothes is not an adequate indicator of his mental capacity; nor his accent), *made too soon* and *inflexibly* held. If we can be slow to label a child, insist on gathering more evidence, be prepared for him or her to surprise us and give him or her plenty of chance to show what he or she can do, the negative effects of expectation might be much reduced.

For every reported instance of failure following upon a teacher's low expectations of pupils there are positive results from those whom the teacher expected to do well. Table 1 children with a measured ability lower than some of their Table 2 and 3 classmates prospered in school. This effect would obviously not be unlimited, but we have got nowhere near expecting *all* our pupils to learn and giving them all the attention, input, feedback and opportunity to make it possible. The positive power of teacher expectations has still to be harnessed.

REFERENCES

Beez, W.V. (1968) Influence of biased psychological reports on teacher behaviour and pupil performance. *Proceedings of the 76th annual convention of the American Psychological Association*, No. 3, pp 655–66

Rist, R.C. (1970) Student social class and teacher expectations: the self-fulfilling prophecy in ghetto education, *Harvard Educational Review*, Vol. 40, No. 3, (August)

Rosenthal, R. (1973) The Pygmalion effect lives, *Psychology Today*, Vol. 7, No. 7, pp 56–63

Rosenthal, R. and Jacobson, L. (1968) *Pygmalion in the Classroom*, Holt, Rinehart and Winston, New York

Rubovits, P.C. and Maehr, M.L. (1973) Pygmalion black and white, *Journal of Personality and Social Psychology*, Vol. 25, No. 2, pp 210–18

TOPICS FOR DISCUSSION

1. From your *own experience* as a pupil at school, identify the impact of a teacher's expectations on your performance, perseverance, or choice of subject(s).
2. What is the significance of the statement in the Rist (1970) investigation, that: 'The I.Q. scores for these children taken at the end of the kindergarten year had shown no statistically significant difference among the children at each table (p 265)
3. What, in your view, is the most disturbing aspect of the findings of the Rubovits and Maehr (1973) experiment?

SUGGESTIONS FOR FURTHER READING

1. Blease, D. (1983) Teacher expectations and the self-fulfilling prophesy, *Educational Studies*, Vol. 9, No. 2, pp 123–9. The article discusses the mechanism of the self-fulfilling prophecy in relation to the concepts of feedback, pupil self-expectancy and the wider educational environment. Five necessary conditions for the successful communication of teachers' expectations are identified.
2. Cohen, L. and Manion, L. (1983) *Multicultural Classrooms: Perspectives For Teachers*, Croom Helm, London. A study by Green[2] is described (pp 62–3), which shows how prejudiced teachers behave differently towards non-white children in British schools, particularly towards pupils of West Indian origin.
3. Short, G. (1983) Rampton revisited: a study of racial stereotypes in the primary school, *Durham and Newcastle Research Review*, Vol. 10, No. 51, pp 81–6. This describes an experiment in which 65 teachers, three of whom were Asian and the rest white, in 11 London schools scored pupils on a checklist of characteristics commonly used to describe children. The study reports the extent of the teachers' less favourable ratings of West Indian boys and girls in respect of intelligence, attainment, motivation and behaviour.

---

[2] Green, P. (1982) 'Teachers' influence on the self-concept of ethnic minority pupils'. Unpublished Ph.D. Thesis, University of Durham.

SECTION 6

PARENTS AND THE COMMUNITY

INTRODUCTION

If the views of indigenous parents about education are influenced by their own socioeconomic backgrounds and levels of education, then, according to Tomlinson (1984) it follows that the views of ethnic minority parents depend upon their colonial and cultural backgrounds and the high aspirations that are nurtured in their countries or origin. Reading 14 is an account of minority parents' views of education in contemporary Britain. In summary, whatever the social class of minority parents, they exhibit high 'middle-class' expectations of the British education system and show enthusiasm both for schools and for British education. Reading 14 is supplemented by an extract from Stone (1981) who voices criticism of the British education system that has led some black parents to set up *supplementary schools*. A paper from the Council of British Pakistanis (1984) reports the views of some Muslim parents about the school curriculum and a review by Bhachu (1985) contains interesting case study material on the educational aspirations of a number of Sikh families.

Reading 15 by Nixon (1985) summarizes several reported attempts to draw schools and communities closer together through P.T.A. links and 'open' school policies. The emotive issue of *'freedom of information'* is touched upon; so too, the relationship between schools and their local police forces. The latter part of the article describes supplementary school provision for pupils of Asian origin in the Coventry area.

Suggestions for further study include references to the Swann Report Appendices (1985) dealing with the educational needs of children of Chinese, Cypriot, Italian, Ukranian and Vietnamese origin; to a selection of readings by Cheetham *et al.* (1982) concerned with poverty, ill health, housing, etc., in ethnic minority settings, and to Thomas *et al.* (1984) whose Schools Council 'Lifestyles' Pack provides the means of greater appreciation of the cultural differences and similarities of several British families of various national and religious origins.

Reading 14
MINORITY PARENTS' VIEWS OF EDUCATION
S. Tomlinson[1]

The dream of a good education for their children has always had a particular significance for black people. White colonists fed generations of Asians, Africans and West Indians the myth that the reason they were being economically exploited was not because of race or colour but because they were backward, undeveloped and uneducated. The old colonialist equation of 'education equals power' explains why so many black parents passionately wanted for their children the education they never had. (Organization of Asian and African Women, 1979)

If relations between schools and minority homes are to be improved, educationalists will need to understand more clearly the views and expectations that minority parents hold about education, and why those views are often held so strongly. There is to date, however, limited research evidence which might help such an understanding along. While, in general, the way most indigenous parents view education depends a good deal on their own levels of education and socioeconomic background, minority parents' views are also influenced by their colonial and cultural backgrounds and the high expectations of education often nurtured in their country of origin; by their own levels of knowledge about an unfamiliar education system; and by their experience of schools and teachers in Britain. This means that minority parents' views and expectations will be different to those of indigenous parents. In particular, although most minority parents in Britain are, in crude socioeconomic terms, 'working class', their views and expectations have always approximated more to those of the 'middle class', but without the detailed knowledge of the education system and its intricacies that middle-class parents in Britain usually possess.

Despite different colonial and cultural backgrounds and despite disappointments engendered by their encounters with the education system, both research and opinion suggest that most minority parents are anxious for their children to do well in education and to acquire skills and qualifications which will enable them to find employment or go on to further education or training.

This Reading examines the expectations and views of education that minor-

[1] In Tomlinson, S. (1984) *Home and School in Multicultural Britain*, Batsford Academic, London, pp. 51–67

ity parents hold and discusses some of the contradictions inherent in these expectations.

VIEWS AND EXPECTATIONS

There is currently much scope for conflict of opinion concerning minority parents' views and expectations of schools and education. This stems from the paucity of actual research in which the parents have been asked about their views. As so often in the area of race and ethnic relations, different opinions and speculations are offered as hard evidence. In general, research suggests that whatever the class position, educational levels and colonial backgrounds of migrant parents, they mostly share high expectations about education, and they view schools as places where their children's life chances should be enhanced. Many migrant parents working in low-paid jobs have felt that their efforts might be justified if their children could acquire a more favourable position in society than *they* were able to achieve. This is not a situation specific to Britain. Rex pointed out in 1971 that an open education system may be the one means whereby occupational and status mobility is made possible for migrants in any country, and education has always been regarded by migrants from colonial countries as a way into the established social order of their 'mother' country (Rex, 1971).

There has been considerable stereotyping on the part of educationalists concerning supposed differences between Caribbean and Asian parent's views of education. Asian parents are considered to be more interested in their children's education and more supportive of schools. In fact, there is little direct evidence to support this claim. What is noticeable is that more educational researchers, particularly those of Asian origin themselves (Dosanjh, 1969; Bhatti, 1978; Ghuman 1980a; 1980b) have stressed the positive interest and characteristics of Asian families; while (mainly white) researchers attempting to explain poor West Indian school performance, have often stressed supposedly negative family characteristics. Also, more research has been carried out inquiring into the career aspirations of Asian school-leavers than of other minority groups, and this research has tended to stress Asian parents' support for their children staying on in education. Foner did record, in her comparative study of Jamaicans in London and Jamaica (Foner, 1979), that the Jamaican migrants to London did not accord the same status to education in London as they did in Jamaica (in London they were more concerned about racial discrimination!), but they still regarded it as very important. Rex and Tomlinson found in their Birmingham research that West Indian parents displayed an interest in education equal to that of Asian parents, and were actually rather more likely to have visited their children's schools (Rex and Tomlinson 1979).

What may be an important difference between Caribbean and Asian parents is that from the early 1960s Caribbean parents' expectations have centred around the view that schools would be able to offer their children 'equality of opportunity' and that this would be reflected in examination passes. Anxiety and frustration has resulted from the inability of schools to satisfy these expectations. The 'underachievement' of pupils of West Indian origin and the variety of explanations offered to account for underachievement is probably the most-documented characteristic concerning ethnic minority pupils in Britain (see Taylor, 1981; Reeves and Chevannes, 1981).

Asian parents, also expecting 'equal' opportunities to be offered to their children, have been more satisfied with schools, which from the early 1960s did take their children's learning problems seriously (particularly those connected with language) and have been able to help a number of Asian children to achieve examination passes and qualifications (Tomlinson, 1983). Asian parents' anxieties and frustrations have centred more around the expectations that schools would also accommodate to cultural diversity. A West Indian father encapsulated this difference thus:

> West Indians have a different philosophy to Asians – we look on education as creditation, exam passes which we didn't have – when our kids don't pass – the world falls apart. Asians are more concerned with religion and things like that.[2]

The Redbridge parents studying the education of West Indian pupils in the Borough also pointed out that the disappointment of their expectations has been felt more acutely by West Indian parents than by other ethnic groups:

> Many West Indian adults are understandably bitter at their rejection by the 'mother' country and this may be conveyed to the youth – such parental bitterness may not be matched by other immigrant groups whose emotional links with Britain were not as deep. (Redbridge study, 1978, p. 12)

This is not to say that West Indian parents are not concerned with cultural differences and an acceptance of their children as respected, black young citizens. The Redbridge parents considered that the poor school achievement of West Indian children could be traced to the effects on black children's identity of living in a hostile white society, and they wanted changes in the school curriculum and in teachers' attitudes. But, by and large, pressures to change the curriculum in a 'multicultural' direction have not come from West Indian parents. Maureen

---

[2] West Indian parents at a meeting of Northern School parents, February 1983

Stone, a black academic, has argued that because they are mainly concerned with achievement, West Indian parents want a traditional, basic curriculum and do not want multicultural innovation designed to enhance their children's sense of cultural identity. Although she herself has not carried out any systematic research asking parents, her views are supported in other work. Rex and Tomlinson (1979), for example, found that few of the West Indian parents they interviewed favoured the idea that 'black studies' be taught in schools, although they did support local community organizations who offered courses in Afro-Caribbean history. The debate, however, is not an 'either–or' one; the desire for equality of opportunity on the part of West Indian parents does include the wish that their children be respected, understood, and accepted in schools much more than hitherto, and this demands changes from schools in a 'multicultural' direction. Taylor, concluding her review of literature on the education of pupils of West Indian origin, wrote that the majority of West Indian parents

> [. . .] believe that ultimately education is the most reliable means available whereby their group as a whole, through their children, can receive recognition and status on an equal footing with others in society. (Taylor, 1981, p. 43)

This can only be achieved if schools now genuinely begin to make changes in a 'multicultural' direction.

Asian parents also share expectations that their children will be offered equal opportunity to succeed, and view education as a major means of upward social mobility for them. Indeed, it is relatively commonplace to hear teachers complaining that Asian parents have 'unrealistically' high aspirations for their children. However, Vellims, in an analysis of university entrance statistics recently demonstrated that 'South Asians are proving more successful in penetrating the higher levels of the British education system than their white working-class peers' (Vellims, 1982, p. 212). Aspirations on the part of Asians may be as realistic as those of any other group of parents.

High expectations were noted in one of the earliest studies of Asian parental attitudes to education in Britain (Dosanjh, 1969). Dosanjh compared Sikh and Muslim Punjabi parents in Derby and Nottingham, and found that although the Nottingham parents were better educated and working in more skilled occupations than the Derby parents, both groups shared a very strong desire for upward social mobility for their children, and education was seen as the key to this. The parents did not know much about school organization, methods, or curriculum at that time, but they did complain about 'too much play, too little homework, and lack of discipline in schools'.

There has been a variety of research studies subsequently pointing to the support and encouragement Asian parents offer to their children, particularly encouraging them to stay on for further education and training. For example, Gupta (1977) studied a sample of English and Pakistani school-leavers, and concluded that Asian parents 'did exert a clear-cut influence over their children's educational and subsequent occupational choice'. Bhatti (1978) studying young Pakistanis, supported the claim that Asian parents expect to exert much influence on their children, and he regretted the lack of home–school contacts whereby parents could make their views known to schools. Fowler *et al.* (1977) also noted Asian parental encouragement for their children to acquire school qualifications, but noted a 'readiness on the part of Asian parents to accept school definitions of what the best interests of their children were' (p. 69).

Asian parental enthusiasm for school, and desire to see their children acquire credentials, has been matched by expectations that schools would also accommodate to different cultural traditions and arrangements in the Asian communities, and much of the continuing anxiety about schools on the part of Asian parents has derived from the persistent reluctance of schools genuinely to recognize and accept cultural diversity. Major sources of anxiety for Asian parents are mother-tongue and religious teaching, crucial aspects of cultural identity; dress and food, crucial cultural symbols; and single-sex education, P.E. and swimming for girls, crucial areas in relation to the place of women in Asian cultures. While schools serving Asian communities do not need to be told that these are important issues for the communities, research by Noor and Khalsa (1978), Ghuman (1980b), Ghuman and Gallop (1981), and Tanna (1981) has confirmed that these remain central and important areas where Asian parents' expectations that schools will make changes and accommodations remain unsatisfied. Home–school conflicts and misunderstandings are therefore likely to occur.

Chinese parents, according to Wang, have never made their expectations particularly clear to schools, but like other Asian communities, their anxieties have centred more round schools' attempts to assimilate their children, rather than respect their cultural separateness. Chinese parents have not pressed for examination success, although those children who have shown exceptional ability have not lacked home encouragement (Wang, 1982). Overall, minority parents' expectations of schools and education centre round the very important notions that schools should offer 'equality of opportunity', and should be able to help their children acquire skills and credentials, to accept cultural difference and diversity as legitimate processes, and to respect all the children equally. However, as further discussions will show, it is not surprising that schools have had problems in satisfying these expectations.

SATISFACTIONS AND DISSATISFACTIONS

Despite the anxieties expressed by both Caribbean and Asian parents about education, in the few studies that have actually sought the views of parents, most have indicated an overall satisfaction with their children's education (Dosanjh, 1969; Rex and Tomlinson 1979; Norburn and Wight 1980, Tanna 1981). The researchers have suggested that this finding might be explicable in terms of the colonial educational background of the parents, which meant they lacked knowledge about the school system, and the failure of schools to explain their practices adequately. As Tanna commented of the 10 Gujerati Muslim families she interviewed in Lancaster: 'parental lack of understanding is perhaps most clearly indicated by their inadequate knowledge of what exactly their children were learning and how they were taught' (Tanna, 1981, p. 36). Minority parents have always had to rely more on schools and teachers to inform them about school processes. Indigenous parents, although they may have left school at the minimum leaving age, at least have the advantage of having been through the school system, and have some working knowledge of its intricacies. In the absence of adequate information, many parents perforce may have to be 'satisfied'. There is some evidence that minority parents have been reluctant to admit their lack of knowledge to schools, and some of the supplementary schools now provide information about state education and counsel parents.

To illustrate minority parental views of education, their satisfactions, dissatisfactions and confusions due to lack of knowledge, several research studies are summarized below. They are: firstly, a study in Handsworth, Birmingham, which compared the views of West Indian, Asian (mainly Indian) and 'white British' parents (this study had been reported in Rex and Tomlinson 1979; and Tomlinson 1980; 1981); secondly, a series of small-scale studies undertaken by Ghuman; and thirdly, parental interviews recorded for a study of multi-ethnic schools currently in progress.[3]

THE HANDSWORTH STUDY

As part of a research study enquiring into the housing, employment and education of 395 West Indian, 263 Indian, 42 Pakistani and 400 white British heads of households in Handsworth, those parents who had children at school were asked their views on education. The minority parents had all been educated

---

[3] This study is being jointly undertaken by the Policy Studies Institute, London, and the University of Lancaster. A report is due in 1984. The study, directed by Mr David Smith and Dr Sally Tomlinson, is following the progress of all pupils through 20 multi-ethnic schools in Britain. Parents are also being interviewed.

overseas and had limited knowledge about how schools worked, particularly the mysteries of curriculum and examinations, but they demonstrated an eagerness for their children to take advantage of educational opportunities which they had never had. There was little evidence of parental apathy in this study. Most parents were intensely interested in their children's education, even if they had not had much contact with schools. Indeed, there was reluctance on the part of some (mainly Asian) parents to 'interfere' with what was felt to be the school's expertise; 80 per cent of West Indian, 70 per cent of Asian and 88 per cent of British parents had paid a recent visit to their child's school, although many of these visits were on parents' evening or open day – which may not be the best times to establish much contact with teachers. West Indian and Asian parents were more likely to be working longer hours and doing shift work than British parents in the area, making it more difficult for them to visit schools. The British parents' views of schools were, as might be expected, influenced by their own limited schooling, and they were less willing than the minority parents to accept what teachers told them about school and their children's progress. The West Indian and Asian parents demonstrated a greater reliance on teachers' opinions, and on what they were told by teachers about schools and the process of education.

Table 14.1 below, illustrates reasons the parents gave for satisfaction and dissatisfaction with their children's schooling; 440 parents said they were satisfied, as against 105, who were, occasionally quite vociferously, dissatisfied.

If children get good reports, appear to be doing well and have 'good teachers', all groups of parents view school with some satisfaction. However, the minority parents did perhaps place more faith in the phrase 'doing well' and on the comments of teachers. There is the possibility that teachers can give good reports, and encourage basic literacy and the use of English language at school, without necessarily keeping to a 'standard' similar to that of non-multiracial schools, or producing the 'results' the parents hope for. There was some confusion, particularly amongst Asian parents, about the difference between 'O' level and C.S.E., and the appropriate age to begin studying for these courses; and there was insufficient appreciation of the fact that a two-year 'A' level course was the normal route to higher education and professional jobs. More British than minority parents expressed satisfaction because of 'good teachers', and it was interesting to see what parents meant by this. All groups had in mind teachers who got down to the business of teaching literacy and numeracy at primary level, and subjects leading to examination at secondary level. The minority parents preferred teachers who were strict and 'pushed' the children, but who were also kind. When referring to discipline, both West Indian and Asian parents defined it as a firm controlled environment where it was possible to get on with the business

Table 14.1 Parental satisfaction and dissatisfaction with school

Satisfied because:	West Indian %	Asian %	British %
Children doing well/good reports	77	56	64
Good teachers	11	11	22
Regular schooling	5	16	6
Happy at school	4	8	—
Not held back by coloured children	—	—	4
Other	3	9	4
	100%	100%	100%
Dissatisfied because:			
Held back by coloured children	4	14	48
Teachers no good	16	19	4
Low standard of education	22	14	19
Poor teaching methods	22	11	15
Poor discipline	4	18	7
No encouragement for slow learners	16	3	—
Didn't get school of choice	4	4	—
Other	12	17	7
	100%	100%	100%

of learning rather than punishment. Minority parents also wanted teachers who were non-racist. They were well aware that schools reflect the wider society and that teachers can carry racist attitudes into the classroom. One West Indian mother said that she had been told her children were 'not fit to clean Enoch Powell's shoes'.

A minority of all groups of parents were dissatisfied with their children's education and viewed schools with some dismay. The British parents particularly were worried that their children were 'held back by coloured children', although there has never been evidence to support this view. Interestingly, a few West Indian and Asian parents took this view as well. Some members from all the groups were critical of what they saw as a low standard of education, compared to other schools they knew of, and also criticized teaching methods, curriculum content and discipline.

The West Indian and Asian parents were aware that their children would be at a disadvantage in education if they did not acquire fluency in the English language; but only a quarter of the Asian parents and three West Indian parents thought their children had had difficulty with language on starting school. Asian parents were aware that special language help was available for their children, either at a centre or at school; but West Indian parents who spoke Creole in the home used it as any regular linguistic system, and did not see such use of dialect as impeding their children's progress at school. They expected schools to teach and improve on standard English. A quarter of Asian parents reported sending their children to a mosque or temple school for instruction in mother tongue and religion, and felt quite strongly that this was important to keep their children in contact with their own culture. On the other hand, West Indian parents were ambivalent about the idea of promoting a West Indian or 'black' culture. Only a few reported sending their children to the black holiday school run locally by a group of black community workers. They viewed the introduction of 'black studies' or cultural programmes in schools with some suspicion. Some parents were influenced by their own educational background which had stressed European history and achievements, and wanted their children to 'learn about Britain'. Others though that time spent away from 'ordinary' subjects and acquiring the credentials to succeed in British society was time lost. As one parent put it, 'there ain't no "O" level in black studies yet'.

In the Handsworth study, an analysis of parental 'satisfaction' by school, showed that at two of the secondary schools in particular minority parents were more likely to express satisfaction, while at two other schools more dissatisfaction was expressed. Thus, some schools do appear to be able to meet the expectations of minority parents more easily than others.

THREE STUDIES OF ASIAN PARENTS

Ghuman, who has consistently deplored the stereotyped use of the term 'Asian' and the level of ignorance in schools about Asian cultures and communities, has undertaken several small-scale research studies of different Asian communities which are extremely valuable for teachers wishing to inform themselves.

In an article on Bhattra Sikhs in Cardiff (Ghuman, 1980a) he describes interviews with 20 Bhattra male heads of households, 12 of whom were skilled workers or shopkeepers, six unskilled or unemployed. The interviews were designed to draw out views on marriage, family, education, and the 'British way of life'. Of the three major Sikh groups in Britain – Jats, Ramgharias and Bhattras – the Bhattras are, according to Ghuman, the least-known group, and in the Punjab are considered a low-status group. The men he interviewed were aged between 25 and 65, had been in England for more than 15 years, but still had a poor command ōf English. From the interviews, Ghuman concluded that the Bhattra Sikhs as a community appeared to be more tightly knit and traditional in their outlook than other groups. He speculated that the Bhattras may want to adhere to their religious and social way of life to compensate for their low status, but he also noted that their perceptions of their white neighbours were very negative. The whites were perceived as morally lax and there was no desire to mix with them. The group's view of the education system was also very negative.

> The community, being ultra-conservative, actually feels its identity and way of life threatened by the schools. The Bhattras feel so unfamiliar with the British education system that the parents do not in any way participate in the education process. (Ghuman, 1980a, p. 314)

Bhattra children leave school at the minimum leaving age, do not go into the sixth form, and do not participate in extra-curricular activity. However, the Cardiff schools the children attended had taken no interest in Bhattra history, language or religion and had made no attempt to explain an unfamiliar education system; and there had been no effort on the part of schools to allay fears about 'anglicization' and the threat to the Bhattra way of life. Bhattra Sikh parents thus represented an extreme position, of dissatisfaction with (Welsh) education, lack of knowledge, and non-communication with schools. The views of the Bhattras, as Ghuman points out, contrast sharply with those of other Asian groups who mostly, despite some dissatisfaction, view education in a positive light and as a means to occupational and social improvement.

In a study of 40 Jat Sikh Punjabi families living in London, Nottingham, Derby, Leicester and Bradford, Ghuman solicited the views of 30 fathers and 10 mothers on school curriculum, uniform, discipline, teaching methods, coeducation, prejudice, the employment of Punjabi teachers and English schooling in general (1980b). Thirteen of the parents were graduates but 10 had had no education; while they had mostly held non-manual or skilled jobs abroad, in Britain only nine were employed in professional or non-manual jobs. Overall, Ghuman found that these parents expressed satisfaction with English schooling, valued education for its own sake, and expressed faith in teachers and their professionalism – although the middle-class families had more anxieties about academic achievements. There were, however, some important reservations: while corporal punishment was deplored, discipline in schools was considered to be lax, homework was insufficient, and there was criticism of coeducation. Over half the sample wanted single-sex schooling. As one father said, 'There should be a choice open to parents. In a democracy it should be possible to choose'. The parents wanted their children to be taught Punjabi and have some knowledge of cultural traditions, but felt that this was the job of the community. Less than half wanted 'mother-tongue' taught in schools – they felt that the Gurdwara school on Sunday should teach the language.

The parents exhibited considerable ignorance about what actually went on in school; 58 per cent had no views on the curriculum or could not discuss it in any meaningful way. Lack of knowledge meant that some parents were driven to rely on hearsay and opinion – not a good basis for genuine understanding. As one father (a bus driver) remarked:

> I can't say much on this topic as I am not knowledgeable about these issues. However, in my opinion there is no 'routine' work, and as a consequence children cannot add up. Some teachers pass time and do not teach children whole-heartedly. (Ghuman 1980b, p. 125)

The parents in this sample felt that the employment of more Punjabi teachers in schools would help their children 'build up positive self-concepts of themselves through identification', and would help to teach Punjabi language and culture; but they also held white teachers in high esteem and valued the contribution teachers made towards making school a pleasant place for their children.

The third study undertaken by Ghuman involved 30 Bengali families in Cardiff, 11 Hindu Bengalis from India, and 19 Muslim Bengalis from Bangladesh (Ghuman and Gallop 1981). The level of education, command of English, occupational position, and housing circumstances of the Hindu parents were superior to those of the Muslim parents, although on average all the parents had been in Wales for 15 years. The Hindu migrants came from professional families in areas well provided with secondary education, they themselves had professional qualifications and spoke good English. They had, in turn, high aspirations for their own children, and expectations that they would do well in education. The Muslim Bengalis, coming from areas where educational facilities were poor had a much lower level of schooling, felt they had had little parental help with their own schooling and, even with the best intentions, could not provide much support for their own children. One father said, 'as I spend all night in the restaurant, I sleep all day and the child is at school; I don't have enough time to spend with my child'.

Another parent indicated that lack of knowledge about education in Britain inhibited him from even trying to help his children:

> Because we do not know exactly what or how they teach in schools here we cannot help our children at home. Even if we want to coach them at home we don't know how. Most of the mothers don't know English so cannot help the children with their studies.

Muslim parents tended to express more dissatisfaction with schools, particularly over religious and mother-tongue teaching, dress, food and coeducation. They felt that their Islamic way of life was threatened if schools would not relax rules and change regulations. One or two parents had considered sending their daughters back to Bangladesh rather than allow them to 'wear skirts and be educated with boys.' The parents appreciated the difficulties involved in teaching Bengali in schools (it is interesting to note that the schools their children attended taught Welsh, so that the children were tri-lingual – in English, Welsh and Bangali!) and in teaching Islam as well as Christianity. They made their own community arrangements, but they still expressed a desire for schools to do more. The Hindu parents were less likely to object to coeducation than the Muslims.

Both Hindu and Muslim parents expressed overall satisfaction with their children's education, mainly centred on the positive attitudes and professionalism of the teachers. They felt the teachers were 'dedicated' and racial tensions and discrimination were absent. Muslim parents exhibited less knowledge and active interest in their children's education than Hindu parents, but Hindu parents felt overwhelmingly that the influence of the home was more important than that of the school.

Northern School

As part of a longitudinal study of children attending 20 multi-ethnic schools in four areas of England, one school was visited during a series of interviews which the school had arranged with minority parents. The school, with 70 per cent minority pupils – mainly of Asian origin – was remarkable in that staff were painstakingly beginning to explore in practice what the rhetoric of 'multicultural education' and 'home–school links with minority parents' really might mean. As part of a programme of curriculum development and community cooperation, meetings had been arranged with different ethnic groups. The head wrote in 1982:

It is anticipated that members of staff will meet with representatives [. . .] of the Moslem, Sikh, and West Indian communities. Interpreters will be present and social and other workers will help to bring as many people as possible. Parents will be asked what *they* expect from the school and what role *they* see the school as playing [. . .] we should know what our parents consider a good education.

The meetings, advertised by letters taken home by pupils, were in fact attended by only small numbers of parents. Nine Sikh fathers and a Sikh social worker attended the meeting for Sikh parents; 10 fathers, three mothers and a local Imam attended the Muslim parents evenings; and five West Indian parents and a West Indian youth worker attended the meeting for West Indian parents. The parents informed the staff that several of their friends who would have liked to attend were on shift work. An interpreter was required for the meetings of the Muslim and Sikh parents.

The issues raised at these meetings illustrated vividly the overwhelming concern of the Asian parents with cultural issues (concern with examination passes taking second-place in the discussions), while West Indian parents were more concerned with education as a credentialling process. None of the parents demonstrated much knowledge as to what the school actually taught, or about assessment and examinations.

To open the discussion the head invited parents to express their views of the education offered in the school and to talk about any anxieties they might have. The Muslim and Sikh parents immediately raised issues concerning the education of girls (particularly P.E., swimming and clothing), religion, mother-tongue teaching and food, and the possibility of the L.E.A. opening a single-sex school. One father said: 'What we want for our daughters is a basic Islamic training – they must cover themselves modestly – we are worried that our girls get much Western influence.' He produced a set of cuttings from the *Daily Telegraph* reporting arrangements made by Bradford L.E.A. to accommodate Muslim and other ethnic minority community practices and asked why similar arrangements could not be made in his L.E.A. The head had to explain the constraints placed on her by the L.E.A., and in the subsequent discussion the parents agreed that there was a need for compromise; they were willing to compromise over particular issues if they could see the school making similar compromises: one parent pointed out that in response to school complaints, 'we have cut down on the time our children spend at the mosque schools'. The Asian parents were in favour of mother-tongue teaching in schools, but not in place of other lessons (they pointed out that their children mainly spoke three languages anyway); would prefer their children not to take part in extra-curricular activities, including sport, that took place after school; and were critical of school discipline, which they felt did not encourage children to respect adults. One parent complained that 'the state is taking away the rights of parents', and feared that this would 'encourage communism, which we do not want here'.

The Asian parents did not spontaneously raise issues concerning curriculum or examinations. When the head mentioned the phrase 'equality of opportunity' one father remarked that there was no equality in England, but it transpired that he was referring to immigration laws concerning the entry of fiancées into Britain. They agreed that passing exams and possibly going into further or higher education was a good thing, although one Sikh father said 'with all the unemployment we ask ourselves whether it is worth them staying on to study'.

The West Indian parents focused their discussion on the aims of education, and the ways of overcoming failure. They regarded education as a 'good' which their children ought to take advantage of. As one mother remarked: 'I send them to school to be better than me; the education is free, it's up to them to take advantage of it.' Another mother said she encouraged her children because if they returned to the West Indies they would find a job easily – 'English education is highly regarded there'.

While the head expressed concern at the low achievement of West Indian pupils in public examinations and stressed how much the school wanted to improve this situation, the parents were worried that the school could not teach them successfully – but opinion was divided as to why this happened. Poor discipline was held to be a factor, although in fact the school is a remarkably friendly and well-disciplined place. One father said, 'you make too many allowances, I send my kids to school to be taught in a disciplined way'. But while agreeing that discipline was stricter in the West Indies, the parents said they did not necessarily support the use of corporal punishment. They felt it was important to make this point as they were aware that West Indian parents were often stereotyped as 'all' wanting corporal punishment. The parents felt that in the West Indies there was more individual contact between parents and teachers, and teachers had high expectations. They said parents asked the advice of teachers more, and there was more private tuition offered if a child was failing in a particular subject. They did not feel that dialect interfered with their children's learning, although one father thought West Indian children had more problems 'expressing themselves on paper'. They did not think their children had identity problems, and were not in favour of any curriculum change from 'ordinary subjects'. While the West Indian parents appeared more conversant with subjects taught in secondary schools than Asian parents, they were not too clear about the nature of examinations. One father did not realize that 'O' levels were marked by examiners external to the school, and they complained that because they did not understand the teaching methods, they were unable to help their children. Overall, the parents were agreed that because of the worsening employment situation, it was *more* important that their children passed examinations.

A MISMATCH OF EXPECTATIONS

Research into parental views and expectations of school indicates that, overall, minority parents regard English education as potentially good, and that it should allow for the possibility of passing examinations that will enhance employment prospects or allow chances for further and higher education. West Indian parents expect schools to teach their children in a disciplined and orderly manner and find it hard to understand why teachers find this a difficult task. Asian parents expect that more of their cultural traditions will be incorporated into school practices, and that schools will take more seriously the issues which concern them as parents. The parents in Northern School showed that they at least are willing to make compromises and have positive suggestions to offer.

However, there are considerable problems involved in satisfying these parental expectations. As indicated earlier, teachers' views of minority parents and pupils make it unlikely that they can actually meet parental expectations unless changes take place. There has certainly been, and may still be, a mismatch between parental expectations and what schools and teachers feel they can actually offer minority parents. The basis for this mismatch, however, may ultimately be the existing structures and functions of the education system and its cultural content. Minority parents' satisfaction with the education system – it's there for them to take advantage of', as one West Indian mother put it – rests on the post-war liberal ideology that equality of opportunity, or at least equal chances to be unequal, would prevail. But the ending of the tripartite system and moves to comprehensivization have not increased the possibility of equality of opportunity for large numbers of children. The chances of pupils of manual working-class parents being selected and prepared for an academically-orientated education which allows access to higher education have not improved (Halsey *et al.*, 1980) and inner-city comprehensive schools, which are the schools attended by most minority pupils, do not generally offer a high-status, academic curriculum. It should, perhaps, be noted that the arrival of minority parents did enhance equality of opportunity for many white working class parents, who were able to move to more desirable jobs and areas. The schools attended by minority children are thus likely to contain the residual white 'disadvantaged', and to be geared to lower-level academic work. For teachers to be able to offer 'equal opportunities' with even white surburban comprehensives is difficult. Many inner-city schools are now beginning to realize that they incorporate all levels of ability as far as minority pupils are concerned, and that it is a mistake to regard all the children as 'disadvantaged', but they do not necessarily have the resources or skills to develop these abilities. There are thus likely to be confusions and difficulties in explaining all this to minority parents.

The parents, as research indicates, have always depended more on schools and teachers to explain school processes, and have been handicapped by their lack of knowledge about schools – particularly about curriculum and examinations. But again, it has never been part of the English educational system to explain too clearly to parents why promises of 'equality' were not realizable in practice.

In the late 1960s, [. . .] a debate began as to whether minority parents and pupils had 'unrealistic' expectations and aspirations regarding education and careers. We now know that minority parents are no more unrealistic than white parents in expecting schools to prepare their children for access to jobs or training, and are perhaps *more* realistic in recognizing the additional problem of discrimination which their children face. In the current employment situation, minority parents, as the Northern School Sikh father demonstrated, may be as realistic as many other parents in beginning to question the 'point of education'. Overall, though, the present structure of education, with its 'stop–go' policies of comprehensivization and selection, and the limitations on resources, make it unlikely that the equal opportunities minority parents expect will be realized.

The expectations regarding cultural diversity, and the ability of schools to satisfy these expectations, is another area where misunderstandings may be perpetuated. The multicultural education movement is currently focusing on the curriculum as a target for reform. Changed curriculum practices are expected to ensure both that cultural groups will have an enhanced 'cultural identity' and that white pupils will be taught in less ethnocentric ways. Minority parents have some difficulty in understanding this, and there is little evidence of demand for a changed curriculum in terms of basic subjects, from the parents. The areas where Asian parents would like to see changes – in the education of girls, mother-tongue teaching, religious education, and the negative demand for less participation in extra-curricular activities – are those which teachers may find most difficulty in accepting. The cultural content of the English education system is based on particular beliefs and values which may be distinctly at odds with some Asian cultural beliefs and values. This is not to deny the importance of curriculum change, particularly to decrease ethnocentricism and to combat racist beliefs exhibited by the majority society; but it is important to note that the issue of compulsory swimming lessons for girls may be more important to Muslim parents than multi-ethnic mathematics or anti-racist teaching. The mismatch between schools' and parents' understandings of 'cultural diversity' may continue to be a source of confusion.

SUMMARY

This Reading has attempted to show that whatever the social class of minority parents they exhibit high, 'middle-class', expectations of the education system, and show enthusiasm for schools and for English education. These expectations are linked to their own colonial educational backgrounds. Minority parents depend more on teachers to explain school processes, and expect schools to be places where both equal opportunity and cultural diversity can be offered. There may be considerable scope for misunderstanding as there is a mismatch between parental expectations and what schools can actually offer.

REFERENCES

Bhatti, F.M. (1978) Young Pakistanis in Britain. Educational needs and problems, *New Community*, Vol. 6, No. 3

Dosanjh, J.S. (1969) Punjabi immigrant children – the social and educational problems in adjustment, *Education Paper No. 10*, University of Nottingham, Nottingham

Foner, N. (1979) *Jamaica Farewell*, Routledge and Kegan Paul, London

Fowler, R., Littlewood, B. and Madigan, R. (1977) Immigrant school-leavers and the search for work, *Sociology*, Vol. 11, No. 1

Ghuman, P.A.S. (1980a) Punjabi parents and English education, *Educational Research*, Vol. 22, No. 2, pp 121–30

Ghuman, P.A.S. (1980b) Bhattra Sikhs in Cardiff. Family and kinship organization, *New Community*, Vol. 8, No. 3, pp 309–16

Ghuman, P.A.S. and Gallop, R. (1981) Educational attitudes of Bengali families in Cardiff, *Journal of Multicultural and Multilingual Development*, Vol. 2, No. 2

Gupta, P. (1977) Educational and vocational aspirations of Asian immigrants and English school-leavers, *British Journal of Sociology*, Vol. 28, No. 2, pp. 185–98

Halsey, A.H., Heath, A.F. and Ridge, J.M. (1980) *Origins and Destinations – Family, Class and Education in Modern Britain*, Clarendon Press, Oxford

Noor, S.N. and Khalsa, S.S. (1978) *Educational Needs of Asian Children in the Context of Multiracial Education in Wolverhampton. A Survey of Parents' Views and Attidues*, Indian Workers' Association, Wolverhampton

Norburn, V. and Wight, J. (1980) Parents, children and prejudice, *New Community*, Vol. 8, No. 3

Organisation of Asian and African Women (1979) Black education, *Forward*

Redbridge Study (1978) *Cause For Concern, West Indian Pupils in Redbridge*, Redbridge and Black Parents' Progressive Association, Community Relations Council

Reeves, F. and Chevannes, M. (1981) The underachievement of Rampton, *Multiracial Education*, Vol. 10, No. 1, pp 35–42

Rex, J. (1971) *Race Relations in Sociological Theory*, Weidenfeld and Nicolson, London

Rex, J. and Tomlinson, S. (1979) *Colonial Immigrants in a British City – A Class Analysis*, Routledge and Kegan Paul, London

Tanna, K. (1981) Gujerati Muslim Parents in Lancaster – their Views on Education, Unpublished Independent Study for B.A. degree, University of Lancaster

Taylor, M.J. (1981) *Caught Between – A Review of Research into the Education of Pupils of West Indian Origin*, National Foundation For Educational Research, Slough

Tomlinson, S. (1980) Ethnic Minority Parents and Education, in M. Craft, J. Raynor, and L. Cohen (eds) *Linking Home and School* (3rd edn), Harper & Row, London 9, No. 1, pp 3–13

Tomlinson, S. (1981) Multiracial schooling – Parents' and teachers' views, *Education*, Vol. 9, No. 1, pp. 3–13

Tomlinson, S. (1983) The educational performance of children of Asian origin, *New Community*, Vol. 10, No. 3, pp 381–92

Vellims, S. (1982) South Asian students in British universities – a statistical note, *New Community*, Vol. 10, No. 2, pp 206, 212

Wang, B. (1982) Chinese Children in Britain. Unpublished paper from Conference on Multi-ethnic Education, College of St Peter and St Paul, Cheltenham

TOPICS FOR DISCUSSION

1. In what ways are the expectations of ethnic minority parents shown to relate to their own colonial educational backgrounds?
2. Discuss the differences in the levels of parents' dissatisfaction reported in the Handsworth study (p 281).
3. What particular difficulties might teachers anticipate as a result of a *mismatch of expectations* (p 288) on the part of some ethnic minority parents? How might such difficulties be minimized?

SUGGESTIONS FOR FURTHER READING

1. Council of British Pakistanis (1984) Voices from the other side, *Multicultural Teaching*, Vol. 2, No. 2, pp 8–9. A report on the views of Pakistani parents about the school curriculum and the ways in which anti-racist teaching can result in stereotyping the Pakistani minority and the Muslim religion.
2. Stone, M. (1981) *The Education of the Black Child in Britain: The Myth of Multiracial Education*, Fontana, London. Criticism of the education system by some black parents, teachers and community workers has led to supplementary schools being set up to give additional schooling as a way of enhancing children's life chances in terms of employment and social mobility. In Chapter 4, the author discusses the programmes in four supplementary schools in London.
3. Bhachu, P. (1985) Multicultural education; particular views, *New Community*, Vol. 12, pp9–21. Reviewing the literature on multicultural education the author concludes that little or no attention has been paid to the needs and expectations of ethnic minority parents, nor has there been a great deal of understanding of the social organization and values of the very communities that are the intended beneficiaries. The article contains interesting case study material on the aspirations and expectations of Sikh families in particular.

Reading 15
PARENTS AND THE COMMUNITY
J. Nixon[1]

In 1977 the Taylor Report stated: 'It is the individual parent who is in law responsible for securing the child's education and whose support in this task is vital. There should therefore be at the individual level also a partnership between home and school' (D.E.S., 1977). Since the publication of that report, the idea of a 'partnership between home and school' has been the subject of political debate,

[1] In, Nixon, J. (1985) *A Teacher's Guide to Multicultural Education*, Basil Blackwell, London, pp. 113–32

legislative action and professional concern. In each of these spheres discussion has centred on three main issues: the constitution of the governing body of the school, the right of choice for parents about which school to send their child, and their right of access to information held by the school on that child. Each of these issues has been sharpened by the frequently expressed sense of alienation felt by working-class and black parents in relation to the British school system. This Reading looks at some of the ways in which schools might begin to redefine their role within the community so as to bridge what, according to the Rampton Report, has become a 'wide gulf in trust and understanding' (D.E.S., 1981).

LEGISLATION IS NOT ENOUGH

Hard on the heels of the Taylor Report, the Conservative Party 1979 Election Manifesto promised to give parents greater influence over education by granting them the right of choice between schools. Referring to its proposal as 'our parents' charter', the Conservative Party resolved to 'place a clear duty on government and local authorities to take account of parents' wishes when allocating children to schools'. Accordingly, on coming to power it proposed an Education Bill which was passed by Parliament a year later.

The Education Act 1980 does not in fact give parents the right of choice between schools. Instead, it grants them the right 'to express a preference [. . .] and to give reasons for this preference'. Even this minimal right is whittled away by the right of the local education authority (L.E.A.) to ignore the preference stated 'if compliance with the preference would prejudice the provision of efficient education or the efficient use of resources'. Although L.E.A.s are, under the terms of the Act, obliged to set up appeals procedures against admission decisions, the legal rights of parents as defined in the act fall far short of those promised in 'our parents' charter' of the previous year.

In tracing this history I am not trying to score a party political point, but to stress that legislation is not enough. The weakness of legislation in this area becomes even more apparent if we turn to the question of school government. According to the Education Act 1980, school governing bodies must now include a parent or parents elected by the whole parent body. For those who would wish to see a greater representation of black and working-class parents on school governing bodies, this ruling poses a number of problems. These were articulated clearly in a recent interview with Ambrozine Neil of the Association for Educational Advance:

> I think that part of the law has literally no significance. I'll tell you why. There are two reasons.

First, headmasters and headmistresses are tin gods. And they are extremely intelligent people. They know what they want and they are able to assess which parents will 'fit in' and which parents will cause trouble for them. They inform the parents they want to be governors. They tell them it is a good idea to stand for election. When these elections happen at the P.T.A.s, the people at the P.T.A.s get the idea which parent the head wants to see elected.

The other reason is that every parent cares first of all about their own child or children. To stand for election as a parent governor, you have to have a child at the school. If something is wrong at the school parent-governors will want to speak up for all children. But this might mean going against the head and maybe teacher representatives on the governors. Because they must worry about their own child, they are sometimes afraid of the possibility of a backlash against their own child in the school. This makes it a difficult position to be in. (Neil, 1982)

Some readers may find this hard to swallow. Yet the points Ambrozine Neil makes are fundamental to any attempt to forge closer links between the school and the community. For she reminds us that the notion of a 'parent body' is a misleading metaphor. Parents share in the divisions between the social classes and ethnic groups from which they derive. Communities are in the main fractured and deeply fissured by social inequality. The idea of election by the whole parent body is, therefore, erroneous. Black and working-class families are likely to fall foul of this romanticized view of a unified community. A ruling is required whereby the place of such parents on governing bodies is guaranteed in those schools that serve their needs.

This was, presumably, the point being made by the Rampton Report when it suggested that 'one way in which West Indian parents can be actively involved in shaping the school's overall policies, including its curriculum, is through appointment to school governing bodies' (D.E.S., 1981). Unfortunately, however, the actual recommendation made by Rampton on this point is somewhat ambiguous or, at least, open to interpretation, since it simply charges L.E.A.s with the responsibility for ensuring that 'ethnic minority interests are fully taken into account' in the appointment of school governors.

There is no stipulation here, it should be noted, concerning the composition of the governing body. Nevertheless, the spirit, if not the letter, of Rampton is, I think, clear: the governing bodies of multiracial schools should include members of minority ethnic groups.

Given that in most areas this must remain a very distant goal, a number of practical suggestions made by the Afro-Caribbean Education Resource Project in its comments on the Rampton Report are particularly helpful. These include the recommendation that 'schools should devize ways of ensuring that parents know each other before electing the parent governors' and 'should actively encourage parent governors to meet with parents, to report on their work and to discuss matters of concern with parents' (Afro-Caribbean Education Resource Project, undated). The school might also encourage closer liaison and consultation betwean parents and the community representatives on the governing body. Indeed, Ambrozine Neil's reservations concerning the power of parent governors to effect change within the school would suggest that the role of the community representatives is crucial in any effective representation of minority groups. Procedures such as these, if implemented, would go some way towards compensating for the inadequacies of existing legislation and thereby creating a more democratic system of school government.

If teachers rely solely upon the 1980 Education Act to create community links for them, then schools will become increasingly isolated and will continue to alienate many of the parents and pupils they purport to serve. Legislation, it must be repeated, is not enough. Indeed, it barely begins to address the urgent question of how to share decision-making power and create a curriculum that might reflect more truthfully the concerns and needs felt by minority groups. It is to innovative and socially committed teachers that we must look for an articulate response to this question.

THE OPEN SCHOOL

Teachers, in short, must learn to listen. This is not easy for any group of professionals, but for those whose authority is far too often vested in their capacity to talk at length on a variety of subjects it is an extremely difficult task. The willingness of teachers to expose themselves to face-to-face interaction with parents and to give them open access to school records pertaining to the achievement and progress of individual pupils is crucial in this respect. The mark of extended professionalism must be seen as a willingness to move beyond the limits of one's own expertise and to identify with the problems and dilemmas of the parents and pupils for whose benefit the school exists. In making this movement many teachers may feel out of their depth. They may even feel incompetent. Unless they are willing to put themselves at risk in this way, however, there can be little hope of placing the school at the service of the whole community.

Face-to-face contact

Ironically, the very mechanisms by which schools try to involve parents may serve to increase their sense of alienation. Here, for example, is a black parent talking about the importance of parental involvement in schools:

> Concerning Parent Teacher Groups and meetings – it depends on what the group is like. Some groups actually discuss the children and their problems. Other groups tend to concentrate on raising funds to buy curtains and nonsense like that. But I think it's important to discuss the children and how they're getting on because that's the whole point of it. And therefore if your school is one where you're discussing your children's future, then I think it's fine, but otherwise it's a waste of time. (A.F.F.O.R., 1982).

This parent is very clear about what it is she wants from her involvement with the school. She wants to be able to talk with her child's teachers about the education of her child. She is also, however, very clear about what she does not require from the school. She is not looking to the school as a means of extending her social life and mentions the cosiness of certain parent–teacher groups as being a barrier to the development of genuine dialogue between parents and teachers. Equally, she might have mentioned the strained formality of many parents' evenings, with their lack of privacy or of any opportunity for sustained consultation. Or she might have pointed to the difficulty parents sometimes have in making contact, not with the head of year or head of house, nor with the head of department or even the head of school, but with those teachers who actually teach their children. The bureaucracy of the school – however caring and well intentioned are those who operate it – can act as a block to important face-to-face exchanges between parents and teachers.

The first step towards creating a more open school must, therefore, be a thorough review of the procedures governing parental and community access. Rather than adding to these procedures, or instituting new ones, it might be more effective to begin stripping away the old ones. The procedures relating to the employment of non-certified teachers and to the involvement of parents and ancillary workers in the classroom are a case in point. In the present economic climate there is justifiable resistance, by those who take the view that unemployed teachers should have priority when work is being handed out or discussed, to any attempt at challenging existing practice in this area. There is, nevertheless, a need for a much wider definition of who can be involved in the teaching role, so that, for example, many of the community language speakers already concerned with the school – school keepers, nursery nurses, dinner persons, parents, governors – can also be involved in the academic and pastoral curricula. Opening up the teaching role in this way is, of course, also a way of opening up the possibility of a much broader-based public resistance to central and local government policies that lead to teacher unemployment. Parents working alongside teachers are much more likely to see the inanity of teacher unemployment. A second step is to ensure that the school is always welcoming, that there is always at least one interview room for use by staff and parents, and that if parents are to be kept waiting they should be told why and how long they might be expected to wait. These points may sound obvious, but in the majority of cases they are overlooked: schools are not geared to informal or 'crisis' visits by parents, and teachers lower in status than a pastoral or year head are likely to be faced with the embarrassing situation of having to conduct an interview with parents in the corridor. The parents understandably feel affronted. The real fault, however, lies in the funding priorities of those who control the purse strings. Teachers, even in the most sympathetic L.E.A.s, have been harassed by school amalgamations and closures and by threats of redeployment and redundancy. This makes it extremely difficult for them to extend their professional role in any way. Central and local government must take the lead if schools are to serve the community.

Thirdly, schools should think carefully about the venue and timing of meetings between parents and teachers. More often than not the school will be the most convenient place for parents and teachers to meet. In certain instances, however, the physical location of various activities (e.g. pastoral work and information sessions) could be shifted to, say, a local community centre or church hall. An ideal site for discussions between parents and teachers is the home. Given the present pressure on teachers, the idea of extending the pastoral role from school to home in this way remains utopian. Nevertheless, among some groups of highly committed teachers home visiting is an important aspect of the pastoral support offered by the school. The appointment of community liaison coordinators, although important in itself, cannot compensate for the lack of dialogue between parents and teachers. Indeed, if an appointment of this kind is seen as a substitute for such dialogue, rather than as a means of facilitating it, it will only serve to erect yet another bureaucratic barrier to effective face-to-face contact.

Freedom of information

If the debate about education in and for a multicultural society is to be broadened to include a wider range of parental opinion, it is essential that parents have access, not only to the teachers of these children, but also to any information held by the school on these children. This is an emotive issue and one to which teachers frequently respond by appealing to the notion of professional privilege. Teachers, it is claimed, need to pass on to one another frankly and without fear of recrimination, important information about their pupils and can only do so provided that record cards remain closed to both parents and pupils. In contrast to this claim a growing number of parents, pupils and teachers take the view that access to such records should be open. The report of a conference organized jointly by Haringey Black Pressure Group on Education and Haringey National Association for Multiracial Education states this position unequivocally: 'school record cards should be open and schools should publicize the fact that records/ reports are open to the parents at any time' (Black Pressure Group on Education, 1984).

This recommendation had in fact been made equally strongly seven years earlier in a 'note of extension' to the Taylor Report. Seven members of the committee added their names to this 'note of extension' which suggested 'that it is not enough that individual parent's access to information should be expressed as a 'reasonable expectation'. It should be a right'. They went on to specify the parent's right of access to 'records kept in a permanent form in the school' as an instance of the general right of all parents to have access to any information concerning the education of their children (D.E.S., 1977). Not surprisingly, since this argument was not even included in the main body of the Taylor Report, the Education Act of 1980 made no mention of any such right. Section 8 of the Act, which deals with the question of information from schools to parents, is couched in terms of the responsibilities of L.E.A.s, rather than the rights of parents, and is limited in its terms of reference to information concerning admission arrangements.

The Rampton Report, in its recommendations on this issue, offers no radical alternative to the perspective adopted in the legislation of the previous year. Welcoming the provisions in the Act requiring L.E.A.s to publish annually detailed information about their schools, it simply recommends that this information should be 'easily understood by parents, particularly those from ethnic minority groups, and by the wider community' (D.E.S., 1981). While stressing the importance of regular, accurate and detailed school reports and of active parent–teacher associations, it does not affirm parental right of access to information contained in school records. According to the report it is the school that should decide what information is given to the parents and not the parents themselves. Among many individual black parents and black parent pressure groups this remains a major weakness of the Rampton Report and a rallying point for future action.

If the notion of 'a partnership between home and school' as couched in the Taylor Report is to be anything other than empty rhetoric, schools must give parents all the means necessary to play their part in the education of their children. These means, as we have seen, include access to serious educational discussion with the teachers concerned and, as I am now suggesting, access to all information upon which teachers make their judgements and formulate their expectations of individual pupils. Without this access education will remain a purely 'professional' concern from which very many parents will continue to feel alienated. Clearly, in recognizing the right of parents to consult their children's files, the school will need to assume responsibility for deciding exactly what kinds of information should be recorded. An assessment of the pupil's achievement in each subject area, together with evidence to support this assessment, should form the basis of the record. In the case of information concerning serious breaches of discipline a statement by the pupil should be included if that pupil so wishes.

Unless accompanied by a genuine desire among all teachers to create closer links between home and school, granting parents access to pupil files will accomplish very little. Teachers need to work on many fronts if they are to help produce a more open system of schooling. The following checklist of questions produced by Brent L.E.A. serves as a useful summary of issues that schools might consider in attempting to involve parents more fully in the education of their children:

(1) Is the use of jargon in letters to parents avoided?
(2) Are letters written in languages which are the most appropriate to parents?
(3) Is the strategy of parents' evening suited to the parents or do the parents have to fit into 'the system'?
(4) Is the strategy of parents' evening really designed to cater for one hundred per cent attendance by parents?
(5) Is non-attendance of parents at formal parents' evening interpreted as lack of interest in the child's education?
(6) Is the suitability of the strategy in operation ever questioned and are other strategies considered?
(7) Are parents only seen when problems occur?
(8) Are teachers encouraged to meet parents in routine non-problem situations?
(9) Is this achieved by home visiting or by holding routine clinics in school?
(10) Are teachers aware of parents with particular expertise and knowledge who may be able to contribute to the resources of the school?
(11) Are suitably qualified parents utilized in any way as a non-teaching resource? (Brent London Borough, 1983).

THE SCHOOL WITH THE COMMUNITY

These questions remind us, by implication, that parents are a wide, disparate group and that there is always a danger of the parental links forged by the school extending only to a small coterie. This rather obvious point is overlooked in the recent government Green Paper, *Parental Influence at School* (D.E.S., 1984), in which school accountability is discussed only in terms of ensuring a majority of parents on governing bodies. Any such legislative initative as that recommended in the Green Paper would in fact barely begin to address the problem of how schools might communicate across the boundaries of class, race and culture. For the popular mandate of the parent governor is often extremely limited. If the school is to address the needs of all the families it serves, it must reach out to the disparate community of which each family is a part.

Legislation on its own, to return to the main theme of this Reading, is not likely to give parents any real power to influence school decision-making. For parents to want to win and exercise such power, schools have to demonstrate that education is important. Schools can best do this by reaching out to parents on issues that concern the local community. The school thus becomes an outward-looking institution – a campaigning institution even – which draws up its agenda of concerns and its programme of action as much from dialogue with the community as from its own professional preoccupations. Teachers in such a school achieve professional identity, not through working *for* the community, but by working in partnership *with* it.

At a time when teachers are frequently accused of encroaching upon the territory of the social worker and the therapist, the idea of the school working with the community is an important means of redefining the role of the teacher as primarily an educational one. For what brings schools and communities into genuine partnership is a shared commitment to education. It is those schools that set themselves apart from the concerns of the local community that are most likely to define their relationship to it in terms of some kind of compensation for social and psychological disadvantage. In working alongside parents and community organizations on issues which concern them, teachers can only serve to reaffirm the central importance of education in the lives of all their pupils.

The following account by a primary school teacher of the Fulham 'Save Our Baths Campaign' shows how just such an issue can be brought into school and taken out again as part of a community campaign while still providing a valuable educational experience:

> The Fulham Baths issue occurred in our locality and was of great importance to the children. The Council decided to close the Baths, which included swimming pool, laundry and slipper baths, claiming that the structure was dangerous. Opponents claimed that this was an excuse, a small expenditure would make the baths safe, and that the site was earmarked for development. Immediate savings and lucrative development prospects in the future were claimed as the real reason for closure. There was a big campaign in which many children took part when they realized that their leisure time and school

swimming was at risk. We discussed the issue at school, basing it on evidence from local newspapers and the broadsheet produced by the S.O.B. (Save Our Baths) Campaign. We did some role play in which pensioners and children took on a cost cutting councillor. We spent an art lesson making Save Our Baths posters, and a language lesson writing open letters to the Council arguing the case for saving the baths. We discussed how these could usefully be used and decided to take them down to the baths for the workers to use. They were displayed outside the building when the baths were eventually occupied by local people [. . .] .

One wonders how many opportunities of this kind are being missed by teachers, when so much is happening in many towns and cities which affects the lives of local communities. For example, the closure of factories. A factory closure may not touch the immediate lives of children in the same way as a swimming pool, though it may be ultimately more devastating if their parents work there, and will certainly affect the community as a whole. Should not young people learn to understand the forces at work around them? (Issues in Race and Education, 1982)

Another teacher tells how, by organizing a meeting for parents and other members of the local community about the implications of the Nationality Act, she inadvertently provided an ideal opportunity for serious discussion between parents and teachers on educational matters:

After the talk, there were several questions, based on individual anxieties and people sat around waiting for a chance to discuss their own particular case with the speaker from the Law Centre. While they were waiting many of the parents began to question closely the teachers who had come along about the books on the shelves in the library, about the way in which we taught their children, and about the progress of their own children and particular areas of concern. That wasn't what they had come to talk about, but maybe that's why the talk about their children was much more relaxed and open than any of us teachers present could remember from previous open evenings, and other formal occasions set up for the purpose of discussing 'educational matters'. Another positive factor may have been that the teachers present at the meeting, simply by being there, were openly demonstrating concern for the effects of our immigration and nationality laws on black families – showing solidarity.

These two cases stand as examples of how parental demands and community issues can and should be translated into good practice at both the classroom and school level. Clearly, the relevance of particular issues will vary from community to community. In one area it may be the threat of a school closure that will focus community action; in another it may be the continuing underachievement of a particular group of pupils. The important point is that teachers should respond promptly to the concerns of the community and should work alongside parents and community organizations in alleviating the causes of those concerns. There are, nevertheless, two important issues of general concern which are consistently overlooked by schools and ignored by L.E.A.s in their policy documents and deliberations. Both these issues strike to the heart of the deep social divisions within British society and urgently require a joint response by the school and those sections of society that suffer as a result of those divisions.

Police, schools and the community

The relationship between a school and the local police force is one of the most critical topics to have emerged in the 1980s. Yet very few schools have a clearly formulated policy to cover the various aspects of this relationship and even less have a policy which results from joint discussions between the police, the school and the community. The result of this unwillingness to confront the issue can be as disastrous as that recorded in the following account taken from evidence given to the Scarman Inquiry and cited by Kathryn Riley:

> M, a black former pupil, revisits the school to keep an appointment with a member of staff. A senior teacher, who is new to the school and therefore unaware that he is talking to a former pupil, calls the police because, as he puts it later, the boy did not show 'due deference'. When the police arrived, M was in the school tuck shop in the company of the member of staff with whom he had the appointment. He was pulled out of the shop and pinned to the ground by several policemen. At one point there were thirteen policemen in the school playground. This all took place in front of young impressionable pupils waiting to buy goods from the tuck shop. (Riley, 1982)

This incident occurred in Brixton in February 1981, a month before what Lord Scarman was later to refer to as 'the Brixton disorders'.

It is not enough to suggest, as Scarman does, that greater police involvement in schools – through participation in discussion groups, classes on the police, and road safety activities – will resolve the problem and to express the 'hope that teachers and parents will welcome and encourage this' (Scarman, 1982). Black pupils and their parents do not need the Policy Studies Institute, whose report, *Police and People in London*, is undoubtedly the most detailed and extensive study to date of contemporary British policing, to inform them that 'the level of racial prejudice in the Force is cause for concern' (Policy Studies Institute, 1983).

They know it from their own experience. It is highly unlikely, therefore, that attempts to increase police involvement in schools will be welcomed by the black community, unless these attempts are accompanied by a frank recognition of racism within the police force, together with serious and widespread discussion concerning the implications of that racism and the need for greater community control of the police.

This point is acknowledged by the Policy Studies Institute, which in the recommendations to its report stresses the need for 'explicit discussion and thinking about the ethnic dimension in policing', and, in particular, the 'need to expose police officers to the views and attitudes of people outside the Force, especially members of ethnic minority groups'. At the school level such discussion might usefully include a consideration of the following questions:

(1)   Under what circumstances should the police be called into the school?
(2)   What steps should be taken to ensure that, if and when the police are called in, their presence causes the least possible disturbance?
(3)   What are the responsibilities of the school with regard to any pupil taken into police custody?
(4)   Ought the police ever to be invited to participate in classroom activities? If so, what procedures should be adopted to ensure that this is an educative and informative experience?

Open discussion of these issues by the police, the school and the community is not, of course, a guarantee of progress. It is, however, a necessary condition. Without a willingness to enter into genuine dialogue with teachers, parents and members of the local community, the police force cannot hope to participate in any useful way in the life of the school.

The questions raised above are sensitive ones and require careful handling. Teachers, whether they like it or not, are themselves agents of social control and cannot afford to enter the debate in a spirit of self-righteousness. Equally, though, the police cannot afford to adopt a defensive position. The warning given by Paul Boateng is as relevant to local discussions concerning the role of the police in schools as it is to the national debate on police accountability:

> We must not conduct this debate on the basis that those who call for reform of our existing institutions are somehow subversive. It seems that anyone who calls for radical changes in the institutions and methods of policing is labelled 'anti-police' and regarded as someone who desires to let loose elements whose main aim is to bring about the end of law and order and civilized behaviour as we know it. This is a dangerous myth [. . .] we all have a common interest in maintaining the position in which our institutions are capable of changing and altering and adapting to a society that is very different from the one which

existed when they were instituted. We have to recognize that the debate must be couched in these terms, and not in the terms of polarization that it sometimes is. (Boateng, 1984)

School and after

A second important issue requiring urgent action by school and community relates to the kinds of support that should be offered to pupils after they have left school. Teachers can hardly claim to be *in loco parentis* unless they take seriously their continuing responsibility for young people whom they have taught. This is particularly so in an age of widespread unemployment when many of the pupils we teach are destined for the dole queue. Even those who gain employment may benefit from a continuing relationship with the school they attended and those who taught them.

In making this point I am not underestimating the importance of a fully structured careers education programme running throughout the school and supported by a full-time trained careers teacher. On the contrary, such a programme is essential and should be an integral part of every pupil's social and pastoral curriculum. While no pupil should be educated for unemployment, all pupils should be informed about the reality of unemployment in contemporary society and about their rights as unemployed persons. This much is spelled out clearly in the recommendations of the Rampton Report (D.E.S., 1981), and is now being implemented, with varying degrees of success, by schools up and down the country. The kinds of questions that schools might consider when developing a careers programme have been usefully summed up in a checklist produced by the I.L.E.A.:

Is the advice of teachers – both subject specialists and those concerned with the pastoral care of pupils – linked to the broad careers support within the school to provide effective help and guidance for the individual pupil?

Does the school offer careers counselling facilities which are effective in meeting the needs of pupils from all ethnic groups?

What does the school do to counter any stereotyping of pupils on racial or cultural grounds which may adversely affect their choice of careers?

Does the school help pupils to understand the potential opportunities of a wider range of occupations than those open to their parents or grandparents, who first settled in this country?

Does the school have a strategy for meeting the career needs of pupils who enter school from overseas in the later years of secondary school?

Does the school observe and monitor the experience of pupils from all ethnic groups when they transfer from school to further or higher education, training, work or unemployment? (I.L.E.A., 1981)

That last question points to an area of serious neglect within contemporary schooling. Teachers in fact know very little about what happens to those they have taught. Monitoring the experience of school-leavers would enable teachers to perceive recurring patterns and locate the special needs of particular groups. For example, the Rampton Report suggested that entry to apprenticeship schemes was, in the main, limited to those with close family connections and that young people of West Indian origin were, therefore, often unfairly excluded from such training programmes (D.E.S., 1981). If this is still the case, then teachers need to be aware of it. They also need to know whether the effects of this discrimination are limited to those of West Indian origin or whether, as seems likely, it also operates against other groups of migrant workers and their families. By collecting information of this kind schools could begin to act more effectively on behalf of their former pupils, by offering them some kind of consultancy service on matters relating to education and employment and by initiating discussions with local employers and institutions of further and higher education concerning the needs of the community and how these might best be met. The school's relationship to the school-leaver should be one of ongoing commitment.

SUPPLEMENTARY SCHOOLS

In looking at the ways in which schools might begin to redefine their role within the community, teachers can learn a great deal from the development of supplementary education over the last 10 years. Supplementary schools, or Saturday schools as they are sometimes called, are, like the Sunday school movement of the last century, a direct response to the failure of the state to provide adequately for the educational needs of particular groups of children. Precisely because they point so accurately to weaknesses in the existing school system, supplementary schools should be assisted financially by L.E.A.s and viewed as equal partners by those working in mainstream schools.

The West Indian supplementary school movement has been well documented by Maureen Stone (1981), who has highlighted its very real achievements in providing large numbers of black British children with a means of improving their academic work. Less well documented are those supplementary schools that provide instruction in the religion of a particular religious group or offer to children of minority group lessons in their mother tongue. These groups include Europeans (Italians, Poles, Cypriots and Spanish) and Asians (Bengali, Hindu and Urdu speakers). Very often, particularly among the Asian communities in Britain, one supplementary school will include religious and cultural subjects in its curriculum as well as language tuition.

J.S. Nagra, in his survey of Asian supplementary schools in Coventry, defines the aims of these schools as follows:

(1)   To enable the children to communicate with their parents and other persons of their own community;

(2)   To give the children a clear sense of identity;

(3)   To assist them to understand and hence participate more fully in their particular social and cultural environment;

(4)   To pass on religion and culture. (Nagra, 1981/2)

Given that there are nine such schools in Coventry, catering for 1500 young people, and organized entirely by the communities themselves, there can be no doubting the genuine need for supplementary education of this kind.

The Islamic Studies School in Coventry serves as a useful example of Asian supplementary schooling. Run by the Hillfields Gujerati Muslim Society, this school was opened in 1976 and runs weekday and evening classes for 50 students between the ages of five and fourteen. Although the main aim of the school is religious education it also offers tuition in Urdu. Boys and girls are taught separately by teachers who give their service voluntarily. The West Indian supplementary school curriculum tends to be broader (see Table 15.1) and aims at building upon the structure of subjects offered within the mainstream school. While the emphasis is on the acquisition of 'basic' skills, the timetable leaves room for a varied curriculum input and gives most pupils the opportunity of working with those younger and older than themselves during at least some of the sessions. A timetable in fact gives little impression of the diversity of experience available within supplementary education schemes. There are, as Maureen Stone has pointed out, 'many outings and activities associated with the Saturday schools which make them part of the family's life' and help create an atmosphere that is 'relaxed, informal and friendly' (Stone, 1981).

Such schools are justifiably proud of their independence from a state education system which many black parents and teachers see as having failed their pupils. It is not surprising, therefore, that successful supplementary schools, having developed as self-help groups, are wary of risking their autonomy by receiving financial backing from official sources. In seeking to support supplementary schools, L.E.A.s and individual mainstream schools should realize that the strength of the supplementary school movement lies in its independence.

Table 15.1   Timetable for the Paddington Supplementary Education Scheme 1981–82

		6.45–7.30 p.m.	7.50–8.30 p.m.
Monday	Junior	Mathematics	Mathematics
	Senior	Mathematics	Mathematics
Tuesday	Mixed	Physics	Physics
Wednesday	Junior	Basic Maths	Basic English
	Senior	Chemistry	Chemistry
Thursday	Mixed	Introductory Zoology	Introductory Botany and Rural Science

N.B. During the weeknight sessions assembly is held between 6.30 and 6.45 p.m. and breaktime between 7.30 and 7.50 pm

		10.15–11.00 a.m.	11.00–11.35 a.m.	12.15–1.00 p.m.
Saturday	Junior	Basic Maths	Written English	Introductory Science
	Senior	Oral English	Written English	Mathematics

N.B. On the Saturday assembly is held between 10.00 and 10.15 a.m. and refreshments and games between 11.35 and 12.15 p.m.

Source: Cleveland, 1983

By showing a willingness to learn from this independent tradition, those involved in mainstream education might eventually learn how to work alongside it in a spirit of equal partnership. There is certainly a great deal to be learnt from the aims and practices of supplementary schools, in terms of parental involvement, curriculum content and teaching methods, and pupil–teacher relationships. A respect for, and understanding of, these achievements is a prerequisite of effective dialogue between mainstream and supplementary education.

At the heart of the supplementary school movement is a desire to equip young people with what Richard Johnson (1979), in a rather different context, has referred to as 'really useful knowledge'. This phrase – central to the aims of radical education in the first half of the nineteenth century – expressed the conviction 'that real knowledge served practical ends, ends, that is, for the knower' (Johnson, 1979). It was a way, on the one hand, of distancing working-class education from immediate instrumentalist aims and, on the other, of distinguishing it from merely recreational pursuits. Similarly, the recent development of supplementary schooling among minority ethnic groups is a demand for fully comprehensive education; education, that is, that is both widely available and extensive in content. Such an education should equip young people, not only with the skills necessary to cope within the world of work, but also with the necessary self-determination and sense of human agency to participate actively in every aspect of adult life.

Where it is an oppressed group that is acquiring this 'really useful knowledge', education necessarily becomes a political activity. Ultimately, therefore, teachers have to decide whose side they are on. The notion of 'community', as I have stressed throughout this chapter, can be a misleading one if it is taken to imply a lack of deep social divisions. A community which is devoid of social justice is no community at all. As a first step towards bridging the accountability gap, schools must acknowledge, in their practices and policies, that there can be no neutrality in the struggle against racism. 'If we are not for oppression', Barbara Rogers reminds us, 'then we must fight against it, with solidarity between the oppressed and those who wish to abandon the corruption of being the oppressor (Rogers, 1980). The relationship between schools, parents and community should be based upon precisely that principle.

To sum up. This Reading has argued that teachers cannot afford to rely upon legislative reorganization of the school governing body as a means of creating closer links between school and community. Such reorganization places undue emphasis on the power of parent governors, many of whom are unrepresentative of the community as a whole. If schools genuinely seek to forge closer relationships with the community, they must ensure that all parents have access to individual teachers and to any information pertaining to their children that is held in school files. They must also find ways of acting with the community on issues of immediate concern to parents and pupils. Some of these concerns – such as the undue proportion of black youths stopped on the street by the police and the impact of rising unemployment on black and working-class families – have barely begun to work their way onto the agenda of the mainstream school. It is to supplementary schools, therefore, that teachers need to look for a new model of partnership between school and community. In doing so they will have to call to account their own practice and that of the institutions in which they work.

REFERENCES

A.F.F.O.R. (1982) *Talking Chalk: Black Pupils, Parents and Teachers Speak about Education,* A.F.F.O.R., Lozells, Birmingham

Afro-Caribbean Education Resource Project (undated). *Links Between Schools and Community: Comments on the Rampton Report,* Kennington Lane, London

Black Pressure Group on Education (1984) Report on the Conference entitled 'Racism in Schools: Ways Forward for Haringey' held at Haringey Teachers' Centre, 10 March 1984. West Green Community Centre, Tottenham, London

Boateng, P. (1984) The police, the community and accountability, in J. Benyon (ed.) *Scarman and After*, Pergamon Press, Oxford

Brent London Borough (1983) *Education For a Multicultural Democracy, 2*, Education Committee

Cleveland, R. (1983) A Study of the Relationship between some Afro-Caribbean Supplementary schools and the State system. Unpublished study. B.Ed. (Hons.) degree, Middlesex Polytechnic

Conservative Party (1979) The Conservative Manifesto 1979, in *The Times Guide to the House of Commons*, Times Books, London

D.E.S. (1984) *Parental Influence at School* (Green Paper), HMSO, London

I.L.E.A. (1981) *Education in a Multi-ethnic Society: an Aide-memoire for the Inspectorate*, County Hall, London

Issues in Race and Education (1982) *Parents Teachers Communities. No. 37*, Carelton Gardens, Brecknock Road, London

Johnson, R. (1979) Really Useful Knowledge. Radical Education and Working Class Culture, in J. Clarke, C. Critcher and R. Johnson (eds) *Working Class Culture: Studies in History and Theory*, Hutchinson, London

Nagra, J.S. (1981/2) Asian supplementary schools: a case study of Coventry, *New Community*, Vol. 8, No. 3, pp 431–6

Neil, A. (1982) In loco parentis, in Issues in Race and Education (No. 37) *Parents Teachers Communities* pp. 6–7 (Autumn), Carelton Gardens, Brecknock Road, London

Policy Studies Institute (1983) *Police and People in London*.
  (1) 'A Survey of Londoners', D.J. Smith
  (2) 'A Group of Young Black People', S. Small
  (3) 'A Survey of Police Officers', D.J. Smith
  (4) 'The Police in Action', D.J. Smith and J. Gray

The Rampton Report (1981) *West Indian Children in Our Schools. Interim report on the committee of inquiry into the education of children from ethnic minority groups*, HMSO, London

Riley, K. (1982) Policing the police, teaching the teachers: Scarman, Rampton and MPs read the riot lessons, *Multiracial Education*, Vol. 10, No. 2, pp 3–10

Rogers, B. (1980) *Race: No Peace Without Justice*, World Council of Churches, Geneva

Scarman (1982) *The Brixton Disorders 10–12 April 1981* (The Scarman Report), (first published by HMSO, 1981), Penguin, Harmondsworth

Stone, M. (1981) *The Education of the Black Child in Britain: the Myth of Multiracial Education*, Fontana, London

The Taylor Report (1977). *A New Partnership for Our Schools*, HMSO, London

TOPICS FOR DISCUSSION

1. What problems of parental representation on school governing bodies are said to arise from the wording of the 1980 Education Act?

2. Discuss the *openness* and *availability* of information held on pupils in school record files.

3. What can teachers learn about school/community partnership from the philosophy and practice of supplementary schools?

SUGGESTIONS FOR FURTHER READING

1. Thomas, K. *et al.* (1984) *The School's Council 'Lifestyles' Pack*, Schools Council and Nottingham University School of Education, London. The 'Lifestyles' pack is intended to offer a means of opening up a more effective and sensitive appreciation of the cultural differences and similarities to be found in comparing family backgrounds and lifestyles. The basic pack takes the form of a 'kit' which can be used with one of several British families of different national and religious origins (Chinese, English, Hindu, Italian, Jamaican, Moslem, Sikh).

2. Cheetham, J. *et al.* (1982) *Social and Community Work in a Multiracial Society*, Open University Press, Milton Keynes. A selection of readings dealing with broad policy issues as well as topics of everyday concern for social and community workers with ethnic minority groups (ill-health, poverty, inferior jobs, housing).

3. For accounts of ethnic minority groups in Britain whose origins are other than the Indian subcontinent, Africa or the West Indies, see: HMSO (1985) *Education For All: The Report of The Committee of Inquiry into the Education of Children From Ethnic Minority Groups*, (The Swann Report), HMSO, London. Particular attention should be paid to: 'The Educational Needs of Children of Chinese Origin' (pp 653–70); 'The Educational Needs of Children of Cypriot Origin' (pp 671–92); 'The Educational Needs of Children of Italian Origin' (pp 695–707); 'The Educational Needs of Children of Ukranian Origin' (pp 711–16); 'The Educational Needs of Vietnamese Children' (pp 719–29).

INDEX